"OFFERS TASTY, HEALTHFUL EATING . . . a perfect companion to a doctor's advice to lower cholesterol. It combines the knowledge of an experienced nutritionist with the talent of a skilled chef."

—David S. Sobel, M.D., Regional Director of Patient Education and Health Promotion, Kaiser Permanente Medical Care Program

"Ranks first for the committed." —*New York Post*

"Recipes are creative and quite flavorful."

—*Houston Chronicle*

"A RESPONSIBLE, WELL-RESEARCHED COLLECTION . . . good-tasting, easy-to-prepare food for busy Americans."

—*Quincy Patriot Ledger*

HARRIET ROTH is a practicing nutritionist who holds a B.S. degree from Carnegie Mellon University. A former student of Simone Beck and Roger Vergé, she taught French and Italian cookery for eighteen years until her appointment as Director of the Pritikin Longevity Center Cooking School. She now runs a private dietary consulting service in Los Angeles, California, where she lives with her husband. Author of the bestselling cookbooks *Deliciously Low* and *Deliciously Simple* (both available in Plume editions), Mrs. Roth frequently consults with chefs around the world who share her dedication to good health and good eating in the gourmet tradition.

"A GOOD SELECTION OF RECIPES for all three meals and snacks and good ideas about lowering the saturated fat in old favorites."   —*Chattanooga Times*

"These days low-cholesterol cookbooks are coming out of the woodwork. . . . Roth's book makes more sense than most."   —*Washington Times*

"The quick and easy recipes avoid the deprivation of most medical and health diets. Readers are astonished at the enormous variety she offers."   —*Vineland Egg Harbor News*

"A good addition to a growing category."   —*Library Journal*

Other books by Harriet Roth

Deliciously Low
Deliciously Simple
Harriet Roth's Guide to Low-Cholesterol Dining Out

Harriet Roth's Cholesterol Control Cookbook

A PLUME BOOK

Plume
Published by the Penguin Group
Penguin Books USA Inc., 375 Hudson Street,
New York, New York 10014, U.S.A.
Penguin Books Ltd, 27 Wrights Lane,
London W8 5TZ, England
Penguin Books Australia Ltd, Ringwood,
Victoria, Australia
Penguin Books Canada Ltd, 2801 John Street,
Markham, Ontario, Canada L3R 1B4
Penguin Books (N.Z.) Ltd, 182–190 Wairau Road,
Auckland 10, New Zealand

Penguin Books Ltd, Registered Offices:
Harmondsworth, Middlesex, England

Published by Plume, an imprint of New American Library, a division of Penguin Books USA Inc. Previously published in an NAL Books edition.

First Plume Printing, May, 1991
10 9 8 7 6 5 4 3 2 1

LIBRARY OF CONGRESS CATALOGING-IN-PUBLICATION DATA
Roth, Harriet.
[Cholesterol-control cookbook]
Harriet Roth's cholesterol-control cookbook.
p. cm
ISBN 0-453-00662-0
ISBN 0-452-26612-2 (pbk.)
1. Low-cholesterol diet—Recipies. I. Title. II. Title:
Cholesterol-control cookbook.
RM237.75.R67   1989
641.5′6311—dc19   89-3011
                                                    CIP

Designed by Julian Hamer
Photography by Dan Kozan
Food stylist: Diane Elander
Prop stylist: Randi Barritt

Printed in the United States of America

*This book is dedicated to the memory of Irene Pink
whose words and wisdom have left their mark
on my books as well as on those of countless others.
Her judgment and sensitivity will be missed by all
who had the privilege to know and love her.*

Acknowledgments

As a health professional and food person, I have spent the past ten years on an odyssey, sharing my thoughts about how what you buy, cook, and eat strongly determine the state of your health. It has been a most rewarding period in my life.

However, it is because of the incredible support system, both personal and professional, that all of my hopes have become a reality. Not many authors can claim that their publishers are also their friends, but I can. Thank you, Bob Diforio and Elaine Koster. Thanks also to Maryann Palumbo, Lisa Berkowitz, Judy Courtade, and Pat Doyle of NAL. Your encouragement and enthusiasm have indeed helped me to realize my "impossible dream."

Blank pages and ideas only become a book with a team effort. My special thanks to Molly Allen, my outstanding editor. She has been indispensable in the writing and the completion of this book. Ronny Johnson's dependable judgment as line and copy editor was as always impeccable and is greatly appreciated. Julian Hamer, who designed my other books, has once again designed a wonderful book for me, and Mary Siegel has created a handsome cover. Thank you both.

Many other people made valuable contributions to this book whether by lending an ear, their mostly eager palates, or by making suggestions or testing recipes. I could never have done this without them. Sharon Berryhill's constant assistance through months of writing and rewriting made meeting deadlines with a smile possible. Nanette Nathanson's help was always just a phone call away. My thanks also go to Randi Barritt, Dari Birnel, Frances Cook, Diane Elander, Dr. John Farquhar, Michelle Harrison, Michael Jacobson, Ph.D., Judi Kaufmann, Helen Kolatch, Dan Kozan, Joyce Lapin, Sally Mackey, Marge Perlow, Harriet Root, Ed and Penny Saltsburg, Janet Schnoll, Eva and Jerry Silver, Dr. David Sobel, Dr. Irvin Sobel, and Edith Wahl.

My thanks also to Bridgett Elliot, R.D., and Computrition, Inc., Chatsworth, California, for providing the nutritional information that provides the data base for the recipes in this book.

Thanks too to Sally, my daughter, and Larry, my son, my devoted supporters.

As happens in so many instances, I have saved the best for last— my husband Harold. His presence, everlasting patience, and love have been the source of the positive energy I have needed to sustain me in both my professional and personal life.

—HR

Foreword

by John W. Farquhar, M.D.
Author of *The American Way of Life*
Need Not Be Hazardous to Your Health

In her two previous books, *Deliciously Low* and *Deliciously Simple*, Harriet Roth brought out many recipes for healthy living.

In this new and expanded book, she has once again shown that she has the ability to meet the practical needs of the American people by creating an even more useful guide to healthy eating. Now, as never before, such advice is needed, given the new scientific evidence for the benefits of keeping blood cholesterol levels down. She has included a concise review of this evidence, a discussion of all risk factors for heart attack, advice on healthy cholesterol levels, and tips on what medications may be needed (with a physician's help) to work in concert with diet. She correctly points out that at least six months of working with (and enjoying) new patterns of healthy eating are needed before medications are added, and that the vast majority of those with high blood cholesterol levels can be taken care of completely by changes in eating habits. The main benefits of her book come from the specific two-week diet plan for cholesterol lowering and from the menus and easy-to-prepare recipes. One more thing, let the American public be forewarned: All the food tastes good. Harriet Roth has the number for our taste buds, while she lowers our cholesterol numbers.

Contents

Introduction:
On a Personal Note

I can hardly believe that ten years have already passed since my husband developed a coronary problem and we made a conscious choice to eliminate damaging overly fatted, high-cholesterol foods from our lives. It was a wise decision although naturally it would have been better if we had reached it years before my husband's problem occurred. However, it is important to realize that it is never too late to adopt good food habits—whether this decision is used as prevention or cure.

Back in 1978, I was a person who "thought food." I had a deep appreciation of and devotion to fine foods, and I prided myself on being a gourmet cook. I guess I was one of those people who "lived to eat." Although I was a nutrition professional, when I taught others how to cook I used butter, egg yolks, heavy cream, and animal protein with a generous hand. In fact, one of my instructors had told me when I once questioned the use of all these high-cholesterol ingredients: "Harriet, if the ingredients are fresh and natural, you don't have to worry about the cholesterol."

But in my house we *did* have serious cause for worry, for while I was cooking all those fatty, high-cholesterol foods with abandon, I was helping to build up a problem that affected my family directly.

My husband loved my cooking, and, oh, how I enjoyed preparing all his favorite foods. Suddenly and unexpectedly the endless banquet came to a halt—he had a serious coronary condition and dangerously high levels of cholesterol. What were we to do?

The doctors all suggested medication and, ultimately, bypass surgery. However, bypass surgery is not a cure, only a temporary aid. Nor are drugs alone a solution, for without a change in lifestyle, plaque buildup in vein grafts and arteries can continue. None of the professionals who saw my husband emphasized the importance of a shift to low-fat, low-cholesterol eating. There was no *nutritional* guidance.

1

In spite of my involvement with gourmet delights, my background in nutrition plus my common sense told me that somehow diet had to be important. I began to read everything I could get my hands on, and I was particularly influenced by the philosophy of Nathan Pritikin with his emphasis on a low-fat, low-cholesterol diet. (I subsequently became director of the Pritikin Longevity Center Cooking School.)

I began to make some changes in our eating habits. I started with the foods I bought at the market and the way I prepared them in the kitchen. I loved my husband dearly and I wanted him to savor the food I prepared—but more important, I wanted to share the rest of my life with him, and I wanted him to be well enough to enjoy the tennis, the exercise, the professional life, the travel, all the many happy times that made up our life together. I knew there had to be a way to enjoy meals without a cost to health. I was determined to find a way to make low-cholesterol, low-fat dishes taste good so that mealtimes would be a pleasure, not a sentence or punishment.

I stopped teaching classes in classic French and Italian cuisine, and started modifying my recipes and creating exciting new ones. I must admit that in the beginning it wasn't easy to eat in the new style without feeling deprived. It took a while, but everyone in my family adjusted. Today, those traditional recipes, with their cloying sauces, high in fat and cholesterol, seem heavy and not at all appealing to the palate.

From the beginning I had decided I would not cook separate dishes for my husband—we would all eat together as a family and enjoy the same foods and, subsequently, the same good health. For my children and me, it would be prevention; for my husband, it would be an urgently needed cure. We had to forget the bread slathered with butter, margarine, or mayonnaise, the frequent large servings of animal protein, the rich sauces, and the cakes, cookies, and desserts, all filled with saturated fat and cholesterol.

At the time, our two children were teenagers. In the beginning, they would open the refrigerator and complain, "There's nothing to eat, Mom!" What they meant was, "There's no junk food to eat." Our pantry was soon filled with nourishing whole-grain cereals and breads, fruits, vegetables, salads, nonfat yogurt and milk, muffins, and other healthful foods and snacks. I reversed the traditional ratio of large servings of protein and limited complex carbohydrates, serving instead small portions of animal protein and large servings of vegetables, salads, and grains.

And it wasn't just family dining that changed. Company meals, too, reflected our new way of life. These days I'm delighted to find that friends look forward to a dinner invitation to our home. They say the food I serve them tastes great, and I'm always told how wonderful they feel afterwards—no sensation of being uncomfortably overstuffed and no guilt because their dinner was damaging to their health. I love it when they say, "This is delicious; is it a recipe from one of your books?"

While, years ago, reliable information was not available about the dangers of cholesterol and saturated fat in food, today we have so much documentation and good information that it would be sheer folly not to listen to what the experts say and follow their advice.

I continue to do just that, and today we are a family who *eats to live*, while still enjoying the pleasures of delightful, healthful meals—perhaps enjoying them even more because we now know that the foods we eat are helping us to lead healthier and more productive lives.

In the following pages I will explain just what cholesterol is, where it is found, how saturated fat dangerously affects your cholesterol level, and how to avoid these risks and hazards. For those who need to take immediate action, I offer a two-week diet plan that will reduce cholesterol levels and take off pounds. To help with everyday meal planning, I have provided delicious, complete menus with flavorful recipes to tempt your palate—recipes and menus that will *not only lower but also maintain low levels* of cholesterol.

By following my suggestions you will enjoy the rewards of "preventive nutrition" and in addition, reduce any existing problems of atherosclerosis and heart disease. Research shows that by reducing the harmful ingredients in your diet you not only may be staving off future problems, but actually may be reversing present damage by decreasing the plaque that has already accumulated in your arteries.

While routine exercise, not smoking, and stress management are all important factors in avoiding heart disease, meals low in saturated fat and cholesterol and high in fiber provide the key that opens the door to good health.

Of course, in advanced cases medication may also be indicated, but *in no instance* is a sensible diet not absolutely necessary. Admittedly it does take a little more effort to change your lifestyle than to "pop a pill"—but with a change in diet the only side effects will be a healthier, more vital you.

I started out trying to help someone I love. Then I began to do nutritional counseling to help others. I am now reaching out to a larger audience.

Like you, I love good food, but more importantly, I know how what you eat daily can affect your health now and in the future—and in the battle against heart disease, a low-fat, low-cholesterol diet is a major weapon.

PART I

The
Cholesterol-Control
Story

• 1 •

Learning About Cholesterol and Saturated Fat

In 1978, when my husband first learned he had a coronary problem, cholesterol was only casually linked to heart trouble, although its role as a culprit was recognized by many cardiologists. Now, however, cholesterol is a household word, and we are constantly bombarded in the media with information about the connection between high cholesterol levels and heart disease, the nation's number-one killer. Cholesterol is a topic of conversation everywhere, among people in all walks of life.

This concern is also reflected by food manufacturers who proudly proclaim on labels, in newspapers, and on television that their products have no cholesterol or are low in cholesterol. These companies spend millions of dollars to develop low-cholesterol, low-fat crackers, cookies, cakes, ice creams, mayonnaise and salad dressings, cheeses, and sour cream.

The menus of many restaurants offer low-cholesterol selections, and some fast-food chains feature salads or salad bars, fish, and skinless cuts of chicken, or use polyunsaturated vegetable oils instead of saturated animal fats and/or palm or coconut oil for frying. (Even so, the fat and sodium content of these foods is, in most cases, still too high.) A number of caterers give customers the option of selecting low-cholesterol low-saturated-fat foods for their parties. And pediatricians are now testing cholesterol levels in children, particularly in families where there is a history of heart disease.

Fortunately, while the facts about cholesterol have not changed substantially in the last few years, people's attitudes about addressing this problem have changed. There is an increased awareness that what you eat has a definite role in staving off the heart attacks and strokes associated with blocked coronary arteries.

Yet, even knowing this for those of us who want to be healthy,

7

creating a healthful style of eating is not easy. This is what I want to help you achieve. This book will not only provide you with the necessary facts so that you can understand the dangers of high blood cholesterol levels, it will also supply you with menus, recipes, a special diet, and many tips so that you can effectively lower and control your cholesterol. Each chapter in this book is a link in a lifestyle plan.

What Is Cholesterol and Where Do We Get It?

In combatting the problem of too much cholesterol it helps to know a little about what it is. Cholesterol per se is not bad—in fact, it is essential to life. A fatty, waxlike material, cholesterol forms protective sheaths around the nerves, helps make hormones and vitamin D, and combines with the bile acids that aid in the digestion of fat. Everyone needs cholesterol in correct amounts for good health, but too much cholesterol encourages the development of heart and blood vessel disease.

Our bodies obtain cholesterol in two ways: from the liver, which manufactures it, and from the food we eat. The liver synthesizes enough cholesterol for our body needs—about 75 percent of the cholesterol in the average person's body; any we get from food is extra. The body can dispose of some of the extra cholesterol, but not all. Cholesterol is circulated through the body in the bloodstream. As cholesterol levels in the blood rise, excess cholesterol is deposited in the lining of the arteries, eventually narrowing them and impeding the blood flow. To avoid this, we need to be careful about the amount of cholesterol we eat. Moreover, there are some people whose bodies tend to produce excessive amounts of cholesterol. These people in particular must limit the amount of cholesterol they get from food.

The average American consumes about 400 to 500 milligrams of cholesterol daily, a range that is in excess of the 100 to 300 milligrams *or less* that is generally advocated. The American Heart Association suggests an allowance of 100 milligrams of cholesterol for every 1000 calories you consume (not to exceed 300 milligrams). I believe that limiting dietary cholesterol to about 100 milligrams per day, regardless of the number of calories consumed, is the safest rule for a low-cholesterol lifestyle.

To many people, a "low-cholesterol diet" suggests simply avoiding egg yolks and organ meats. Although these foods *are* extremely high in cholesterol, it would be a gross oversimplification to assume that you can solve the cholesterol problem merely by eliminating them. Unfortunately, not only are there many other foods laden with cholesterol (*all are foods from animal sources*) to worry about, but you must also be wary of any foods containing saturated fats because the liver creates additional cholesterol from these fats. Foods high in saturated fats are not merely those from animal sources, such as meat, poultry (especially the skin), cheeses, whole milk, butter, and ice cream. Some vegetable oils (particularly coconut and palm oils), cocoa butter (found in chocolate), and hydrogenated fats (particularly those made from coconut or palm oil) also contain high levels of saturated fat which can raise cholesterol to a dangerous degree. Thus, to be effective, a low-cholesterol diet must cut down on or eliminate all of these foods.

The following chart will help alert you to some of the worst sources of cholesterol and saturated fat. (For cholesterol, saturated fat, and calorie counts of commonly used foods, see pages 351–81.)

PRIME SOURCES OF SATURATED FAT AND CHOLESTEROL

FOOD	PORTION SIZE	SATURATED FAT (GRAMS)	CHOLESTEROL (MILLIGRAMS)
Cheeses			
American	1 oz.	5.6	27
Blue	1 oz.	5.3	21
Cheddar	1 oz.	6.0	30
Creamed cottage cheese (4%)	1 cup	6.4	34
Cream cheese	1 oz.	6.2	31
Mozzarella (whole milk)	1 oz.	3.7	22
Muenster	1 oz.	5.4	27
Ricotta (whole milk)	1 cup	20.4	124
Swiss	1 oz.	5	26
Dairy Products			
Butter	1 tbsp.	7.1	31

PRIME SOURCES OF SATURATED FAT AND CHOLESTEROL

FOOD	PORTION SIZE	SATURATED FAT (GRAMS)	CHOLESTEROL (MILLIGRAMS)
Dairy Products (cont.)			
Cream (sweet) coffee	1 tbsp.	1.8*	10
Cream, heavy whipping	1 tbsp.	3.5	21
Sour cream	1 tbsp.	1.6	5
Coffee whitener (liquid, frozen; contains coconut or palm kernel oil)	1 tbsp.	1.4*	0
Coffee whitener (powdered; contains coconut or palm kernel oil)	1 tbsp.	1.8*	0
Whole milk (fluid)	1 cup	5.1	33
Canned condensed milk	1 cup	16.8	104
Canned evaporated whole milk	1 cup	11.6	74
Chocolate milk (regular)	1 cup	5.3	31
Eggnog	1 cup	11.3	149
Milkshake, vanilla	10 oz.	5.3	33
Ice cream (16% fat)	1 cup	14.7	88
Soft-serve frozen custard	1 cup	13.5	153
Yogurt, plain, whole milk	1 cup	4.8	29
Eggs, raw	1 whole	1.7	213
Eggs, cooked in butter	1 whole	3.2	221
Salad Dressings			
Blue cheese	1 tbsp.	1.5	3
French	1 tbsp.	1.4	0
Thousand island	1 tbsp.	1.0	4
Tartar sauce	1 tbsp.	1.2	4
Mayonnaise	1 tbsp.	1.7	10

* While these figures may not seem so high, remember that coffee drinkers will use a lot of cream or whitener during the day. Using powdered nonfat milk will eliminate the problem.

PRIME SOURCES OF SATURATED FAT AND CHOLESTEROL

FOOD	PORTION SIZE	SATURATED FAT (GRAMS)	CHOLESTEROL (MILLIGRAMS)
Cakes and Pies			
Devil's food cake with frosting	1 piece 2" × 2"	3.5	37
Chocolate chip cookies	4 small	3.5	37
Pound cake	1 slice	5.9	21
Plain sheet cake with frosting	1 slice 2" × 2"	4.6	70
Carrot cake with cream cheese frosting	1 slice	4.1	74
Cheesecake	1 piece	4.9	170
Danish pastry	1 pastry	3.6	49
Croissant	1 croissant	3.5	13
Doughnut	1 doughnut	5.2	21
Creme pie	1 slice	15.0	8
Custard pie	1 slice	5.6	169
Lemon meringue pie	1 slice	4.3	143
Pecan pie	1 slice	4.7	95
Pumpkin pie	1 slice	6.4	109
Meats			
Ground beef, broiled	3 oz.	6.9	76
Rib roast	3 oz.	11.7	72
Rack of lamb	3 oz.	12.1	77
Sirloin steak	6 oz.	12.8	154
Pork loin chops (pan fried)	3.1 oz.	9.8	92
Veal rib roast	3 oz.	6.0	109
Liver, fried	3 oz.	2.5	410
Bacon	3 med. slices	3.3	16
Braunsweiger	2 slices	6.2	89
Bologna (10 slices to a pound)	2 slices	6.1	31
Frankfurters	1 frankfurter	4.8	23
Salami	2 slices	4.6	37

PRIME SOURCES OF SATURATED FAT AND CHOLESTEROL

FOOD	PORTION SIZE	SATURATED FAT (GRAMS)	CHOLESTEROL (MILLIGRAMS)
Organ Meats			
Beef brain	3½ oz. cooked	7.3	2054
Beef heart	3½ oz. cooked	5.7	274
Beef kidney	3½ oz. cooked	12.0	387
Beef liver (fried)	3½ oz. cooked	10.6	410
Sweetbread (calf)	3½ oz. cooked	3.2	466
Beef tongue, smoked	3½ oz. cooked	28.8	210
Chicken liver	3½ oz. cooked	1.4	631
Poultry			
Chicken breast, fried with skin, batter-dipped	4.9 oz.	4.9	119
Roasted duck, meat only	3½ oz.	4.7	84
Miscellaneous			
Chicken à la king	1 cup	12.9	221
Quiche Lorraine	1 slice	23.2	285
Macaroni and cheese	1 cup	9.8	44
French toast	1 slice	1.6	112
Waffles	1 7-inch	4.0	102
Pancakes	3 4-inch	1.5	48
Egg noodles	1 cup cooked	0.5	50
Cream of mushroom soup	1 cup	5.1	20
Cheese sauce	1 cup	9.3	53
Hollandaise sauce	1 cup	11.6	52
White sauce	1 cup	9.1	32
Fudge	1 oz.	2.1	0
Dark chocolate candy	1 oz.	5.9	6
Bitter baking chocolate	1 oz.	9.0	0
Baked custard	1 cup	6.8	278
Canned pudding, chocolate or vanilla	5-oz. can	9.5	1
Fudge sauce	2 tbsp.	3.1	0
Au gratin potatoes	1 cup	11.6	56

PRIME SOURCES OF SATURATED FAT AND CHOLESTEROL

FOOD	PORTION SIZE	SATURATED FAT (GRAMS)	CHOLESTEROL (MILLIGRAMS)
Potato salad with mayonnaise	1 cup	3.6	170
Mashed potatoes with butter	1 cup	7.2	29
Cheese soufflé	¾ cup	16.0	132
Spinach soufflé	1 cup	7.1	184
Saltines	4 crackers	2.0	4

USDA Nutritive Values of Foods, Home and Garden Bulletin #72, Revised 1981; and *Bowes and Church's Food Values of Portions Commonly Used* (Fourteenth Edition, Pennington and Church).

Your Cholesterol Level and What It Means

The first step in cholesterol control is to find out what your own cholesterol picture is by having your cholesterol level tested. The amount of cholesterol in the body is measured by determining the amount of cholesterol in the blood—referred to as the serum cholesterol level. Both the National Institutes of Health and the American Heart Association recommend that you have your serum cholesterol level checked at least every five years after the age of twenty, or at least every three years if there is a history of heart disease in your family. You should take nothing by mouth except water for at least 12 hours prior to testing. To ensure the accuracy of test results, your physician should seek a laboratory that participates in a suitable standardization program. Because cholesterol levels can fluctuate considerably from day to day depending upon what you have eaten, it is also suggested that more than one cholesterol measurement be obtained and then the averaged values used as your baseline.

The Total Cholesterol (TC) Count

When you have a routine cholesterol test at the doctor's office, the reading you are given is referred to as your total cholesterol. Optimally, your total cholesterol reading should be well under 200 milligrams per deciliter of blood (200 mg/dl). Dr. Basil M. Rifkind of the National Heart, Lung and Blood Institute has said that "there is no safe level of blood cholesterol above 175 milligrams. . . . It might be necessary to get down to 150 milligrams." Certainly it is clear that the further below 200 it is, the better for you.

If your cholesterol level is under 200, you probably need not be concerned. However, if it is between 200 and 239, you are borderline, or at moderate to high risk. If your cholesterol is above 240, then you are at high risk and should take corrective measures immediately.

WHAT IS YOUR RISK FACTOR?

AGE	MODERATE RISK	HIGH RISK
20 to 29	200 to 220 mg/dl	Greater than 220 mg/dl
30 to 39	220 to 240 mg/dl	Greater than 240 mg/dl
40 and over	240 to 260 mg/dl	Greater than 260 mg/dl

Chart based on the 1985 National Institutes of Health Consensus Conference on Cholesterol.

The Kinds of Cholesterol—"Good" and "Bad"

If your total cholesterol reading is 200 or over, you need to get further information. There are different types of cholesterol and it can be important to know what your specific cholesterol makeup is.

Because cholesterol is a sterol and not soluble in water, the body combines it and other fats with protein to form complexes known as lipoproteins so it can be carried in the bloodstream. For our purposes, there are two lipoproteins that are of concern—high-density lipoproteins and low-density lipoproteins. The high-density lipoproteins, or HDLs, are often called "the good cholesterol" because they carry cholesterol away from the body tissues and return it to the liver for recycling. The function of the low-density lipoproteins, or LDLs, is to carry cholesterol to the cells where it is deposited. However, if they transport more than the cells can use, the excess collects, forming plaque which builds up within the arteries, producing a condition known as atherosclerosis, the precursor to heart attacks and strokes. Thus, LDLs are often called "the bad cholesterol."

Since your total cholesterol count does not tell you whether your cholesterol is the "good" or the "bad" kind, you also need to know what your level of HDLs is and the ratio of HDL to total cholesterol, known as the heart-risk ratio. Dr. William Castelli, medical director of the pioneering Framingham Study on Heart Disease, has suggested that to survive in America you should know three numbers: your total cholesterol, your HDL ratio, and your Social Security number. Unfortunately, most of us know only the third one.

I would add another number to this—your LDL number. We still have a great deal to learn about HDL's role in preventing heart disease; however, according to a recent article in *Archives of Internal Medicine* (vol. 148:36, January 1988) "there is substantial evidence that lowering total cholesterol and LDL cholesterol levels will reduce the incidence of coronary heart disease."

To determine your HDL and LDL numbers you should have another blood test taken. Ask for a written copy of your blood chemistry, not just a verbal report over the phone.

The High-Density Lipoprotein (HDL) Count

Because higher levels of HDLs may promote healthier arteries, the higher your HDLs, the lower your risk of developing heart disease. Recent studies suggest that HDL cholesterol even has the ability to remove plaque previously deposited on artery walls, thereby reversing atherosclerosis.

The National Heart, Lung and Blood Institute recommends an HDL count above 35. In general, HDLs are found to be higher in

---

HOW TO RAISE YOUR LEVEL OF HDL— THE GOOD CHOLESTEROL

1. Limit your consumption of foods that are high in saturated fat and cholesterol.

2. Engage in regular aerobic exercise.

3. Stop smoking.

4. Eat more fish (at least two to three times a week). Select coldwater fatty fish because they have high levels of Omega-3 fatty acids (see page 21).

5. Use extra-virgin olive oil and/or canola (both monounsaturated) in limited amounts as fats of choice (see page 25).

6. Lose weight if you are overweight. Maintaining a healthy body weight is essential to keeping total cholesterol down, thereby raising HDLs and lowering LDLs.

thin people, nonsmokers, people who exercise regularly, and those who drink moderate amounts of alcohol (about one drink per day). They are also higher in premenopausal women; for this reason some doctors recommend administering and monitoring *low* levels of estrogen in menopausal and postmenopausal women with high cholesterol counts.

The Low-Density Lipoprotein (LDL) Count

Most of the cholesterol in blood serum is found in the LDLs. Since the low-density lipoproteins deposit cholesterol on the artery walls, the higher the level of LDLs in the blood, the greater your risk of heart disease. The National Heart, Lung and Blood Institute recommends an LDL count under 130. A count over 160 is considered to put you at serious extra risk.

The Heart-Risk Ratio

Ideal cholesterol test results would show:
1. a total cholesterol count of under 200 milligrams
2. an LDL count that is as low as possible (under 130)
3. an HDL count that is as high as possible (35 or over)

In addition, the test results also carry a determination of the heart-risk ratio, the ratio of HDL to total cholesterol, which is obtained by dividing the TC count by the HDL count. The target or ideal number for this ratio is 4.5 or under. For example, if your TC is 180 and your HDL is 40, your heart-risk ratio would be 4.5.

$$180 \div 40 = 4.5$$

Although some experts believe that even if your total cholesterol is higher than 200 a high HDL level may result in an acceptable

---

THE HAPPY HEART FORMULA

lower levels of total cholesterol and lower LDLs

+

higher levels of HDLs

= a lower risk of coronary heart disease

heart-risk ratio, I believe that you should still try to reduce the total cholesterol count to under 200.

The Triglyceride Count

In addition to the three cholesterol measurements, your blood chemistry tests should also measure the triglyceride count. Triglycerides are blood fats that transport energy to the cells of the body. There is increasing evidence that connects triglycerides with atherosclerosis. The optimal average triglyceride levels for men are about 140–150 mg/dl; for women, about 100–120 mg/dl. When these levels are elevated, they become risk factors, particularly in people with heart disease or diabetes or who are obese. They are, however, certainly not as critical as elevated total cholesterol or LDL levels.

A study at the National Institutes of Health has indicated that for every 1 percent decrease in blood cholesterol there is a 2 percent decrease in the chance of coronary artery disease.

The Next Step—Cholesterol Control

If your cholesterol readings show that you are at risk, you will need to reduce your cholesterol level and then work to keep it under control by making some changes in your diet. If you are not at risk, you will still need to watch your cholesterol intake so that you can maintain your safety margin. If you can maintain an acceptable level of cholesterol steadily over the years, you are not likely to develop atherosclerosis.

How Dietary Fat Contributes to Cholesterol

That the foods we eat can have a major role in increasing or decreasing cholesterol levels is an established fact. Five years ago, however, health professionals only emphasized the importance of avoiding foods high in cholesterol. Today we know that other elements come into play as well, and one of the most important is the amount and kinds of fat we eat. There are three kinds of fat in our food: saturated fat, polyunsaturated fat, and monounsaturated fat. Since they all—

particularly saturated fat—can have a direct bearing on high cholesterol levels, it pays to know something about them.

At present, 40 percent of the calories in the diet of the average
American comes from fat. Although many experts feel that this figure
should be lowered to 30 percent, I believe that ideally it should be
a safer 15 to 20 percent. Others, like Pritikin followers, insist on no
more than 10 percent, but for many people this restriction is too rigid.
In my nutrition counseling practice, I have found that an allowance
of 15 to 20 percent makes it easy for people to be satisfied and stay
with a healthful eating program—and after all, that's what cholesterol
control is all about. (A guide to reducing your total dietary fat is
included in the Appendix.)

But whether it's 10 percent or 30 percent, not more than 7 percent
of your total daily calories should come from saturated fats, for saturated fats can cause problems by raising the level of the "bad" low-
density lipoproteins.

Saturated Fats—The Dangerous Culprit

All saturated fats raise cholesterol. Saturated fats, which are generally solid at room temperature, are found primarily in foods of
animal origin such as whole milk dairy products (butter, cream, milk,
sour cream, ice cream, cheese), all kinds of meats, lard, and chicken
and beef fat. In addition, they are found in coconut and coconut oil,
palm oil, palm kernel oil, cocoa butter, and any vegetable oils that
have been hydrogenated, including margarine made from these oils.
When any oils are hydrogenated (particularly palm and coconut oils),
they are altered and become more saturated than they were to begin
with, and are thus more likely to raise cholesterol levels.

The Hidden Saturated Fat in Commercial Foods

It is important to remember that hydrogenated oils (especially those
made from palm or coconut oil) are used in many processed foods,
bakery goods, popcorn oils, and nondairy creamers because they are
cheaper and have a long shelf-life. For this reason, it is essential to
read labels carefully to detect any hidden enemies. Be aware of the
fine print and read between the lines. Buy only those products that
list the type of fat they contain. A good nutrition label should include
the grams and kind of fat in each portion.

A well-known cracker company has recently brought out a salt-
reduced version of an all-time favorite—only 35 milligrams of salt in
three wafers. That's good news. The label says that it's made from
100 percent vegetable shortening—but on closer inspection that veg-

etable oil turns out to be "partially hydrogenated soybean and palm oils." So that's bad news because soybean oil becomes more saturated when hydrogenated and palm oil is a highly saturated fat to begin with.

Many consumers will just pay attention to the "100% vegetable shortening" on the label. To them this means cholesterol-free—but the fine print tells a different story.

If the ingredient list on any product states "Contains one or more of the following: hydrogenated soybean, corn, palm, and/or coconut oil," *do not buy it*. Whether it is a bottle of oil, a package of margarine, a nondairy creamer, or a snack or cracker, switch brands. The manufacturer uses hydrogenated oil or tropical oils such as palm or coconut oil because it gives the product a longer shelf-life and/or is cheaper— but it's not good for you.

Saturated fats can also be "hidden" simply because people do not realize that a number of seemingly innocent foods contain them. A prime offender is commercial snack food which is often a source not only of "quick calories" but also of cholesterol boosters. The following label is from a "healthy" fruit and nut mix:

NATURAL FOOD— NUTRITIOUS AND DELICIOUS FRUIT AND NUT MIX

NO PRESERVATIVES	INGREDIENTS: PEANUTS,[1] RAISINS, GOLDEN
NO ADDITIVES	RAISINS,[3] DRIED DATES (ROLLED IN OAT FLOUR,
NO ARTIFICIAL FLAVORING	CASHEWS,[1] ALMONDS, CHIP COCONUT,[2]
NO ARTIFICIAL COLORING	PINEAPPLE,[3] PAPAYA,[3] BRAZILS,[1] COCONUT
	OIL,[2] SALT,[4] SULFUR DIOXIDE.[3]

1. First of all, except for the almonds, the nuts in this mixture are high in saturated fat.
2. Coconut chips and coconut oil are both high in saturated fat.
3. Despite the "no preservatives" claim, sulfur dioxide has been added to the golden raisins, pineapple, and papaya to preserve color. Many people are allergic to sulfites like sulfur dioxide and it has caused a fatal reaction in some individuals. Presently it must be listed on the label, if used at all.
4. Although the label says no additives, the product contains salt, one of the most common additives used in foods.

This label has sinned by omission as well as commission. Not only does it make false claims about additives and preservatives, but it does not list the kinds of fat, the number of grams of fat, or the total calories in one serving. In this case, if you didn't read between the lines, you bought a high cholesterol level—not a nutritious snack!

Mandatory comprehensive nutrition labels on all processed foods could extend millions of lives by giving consumers the necessary information to make intelligent choices. In the meantime, you have to be on guard.

Polyunsaturated Fats

The good news about polyunsaturated fats is that they lower LDL cholesterol. Since the body does not manufacture these fats, they can

NUTS AND SEEDS FROM GOOD TO BAD				
PORTION: 1 OUNCE	CALORIES	SATURATED FAT (GRAMS)	TOTAL FAT (GRAMS)	POLYUNSATURATED FAT (GRAMS)
Chestnuts (European, peeled)	163	0.06	0.35	0.14
Ginkgo nuts	99	0.1	0.57	0.2
Soybeans	129	0.9	6.8	3.6
Black walnuts	172	1.03	16.07	10.6
Pumpkin & squash seeds	127	1.04	5.5	2.5
Filberts or hazelnuts	179	1.3	17.7	1.7
Peanut butter (½ oz. or 1 tablespoon)	95	1.3	8.1	2.4
Almonds	167	1.4	14.8	3.1
Sunflower seeds	165	1.4	14.1	9.3
Pecans	190	1.5	19.2	4.7
English walnuts	182	1.5	17.5	11.1
Pistachios	164	1.7	13.7	2.07
Peanuts	161	1.9	13.9	4.4
Sesame seeds	161	1.9	13.6	5.9
Hickory nuts	187	1.9	18.2	6.2
Pine nuts (pignolia)	146	2.2	14.4	6.06
Cashews	163	2.6	13.1	2.2
Macadamia nuts	199	3.1	20.9	0.36
Brazil nuts	186	4.6	18.8	6.8
Coconut	187	16.2	18.3	0.2

Adapted from USDA, Composition of Foods: Nut and Seed Products, Agriculture Handbook Number 8–12, Revised, 1984.

only be obtained from the food you eat. Good sources are most nuts and seeds (however, they also contain saturated fats—see the chart opposite), soybeans, corn, and most vegetable oils, such as safflower, soy, corn, sunflower, and sesame oils (see chart on page 25).

Unlike saturated fats, polyunsaturated fats are liquid or soft whether they are kept at room temperature or under refrigeration. The softer the fat, the more polyunsaturates it contains (for example, soft margarine contains more polyunsaturates than does stick margarine and is therefore a better choice *in moderation.*

While polyunsaturated fats can be beneficial, even here don't go overboard. You must limit them as well if you are to stay within the recommended daily amounts for total fat. Too much of any fat has been linked to cancer and definitely produces weight gain.

The Omega-3s in Seafood

Omega-3 fatty acids, which are found in fish and shellfish, have received a good bit of attention recently. Some research indicates that they may be useful in lowering blood triglycerides and cholesterol levels and may actually help prevent atherosclerosis and clotting, lowering the risk of heart attacks and strokes. Because of the special benefits associated with these particular polyunsaturated fats, it's a good idea to eat fish two to three times a week. Select those that live in deep, cold water, for they are particularly high in Omega-3s. Among them are salmon, Atlantic herring, albacore and bluefin tuna, sablefish, sturgeon, Atlantic mackerel, and lake trout. (Don't forget easily available salmon and tuna canned in water.)

A *word of caution:* Because of the current interest in Omega-3s, many people have begun to take fish oil capsules. This is not advisable because the long-term safety of these supplements has not been determined and they are still considered experimental. What we do know is that fish oil supplements add calories and fat. My advice is to skip the capsules and take the safer and healthier route by adding fish to your meals.

The following chart will help you see at a glance the total fat, Omega-3 fatty acids, and cholesterol of a selection of fish and shellfish. Interestingly, the fact that saturated fat has been targeted as a culprit has led to some revised thinking about shellfish, most of which were once considered totally off-limits because of their high cholesterol content. Today, however, because they are known to be very low in saturated fat, most shellfish are allowed on a low-cholesterol diet *in limited portions,* provided no cream, butter, or cheese is used in their preparation.

THE TOTAL FAT, OMEGA-3S, AND CHOLESTEROL IN COMMONLY USED SEAFOOD

Fish

PORTION: ABOUT 3 OZ. RAW	TOTAL FAT (GRAMS)	OMEGA-3 FATTY ACIDS (GRAMS)	CHOLESTEROL (MILLIGRAMS)
Mackerel, Atlantic	11.81	2.5	60
Herring, Atlantic	7.68	1.6	51
Rainbow trout	2.85	1.6	45
Tuna, bluefin	4.17	1.6	32
Sablefish	13.00	1.5	42
Sturgeon	3.43	1.5	NA
Salmon, sockeye	7.27	1.3	53
Sardines, Atlantic (24 gm, about 2 sardines with bones, oil drained)	5.91	1.2	3.4

Avoid fish that is fried or processed with salt.

Shellfish

PORTION: ABOUT 3 OZ. RAW	TOTAL FAT (GRAMS)	OMEGA-3 FATTY ACIDS (GRAMS)	CHOLESTEROL (MILLIGRAMS)
Mollusks			
Abalone	0.64	0.04	72
Clams	0.83	0.12	29
Mussels, blue	1.90	0.37	24
Oysters, eastern	2.08	0.40	46
Scallops	0.64	0.17	28
Squid	1.18	0.30	198
Crustaceans			
Crab, Alaska King	0.51	0.40	35
Crab, blue	0.92	0.40	66
Crab, Dungeness	0.83	0.40	50
Crayfish	0.90	0.15	118

Shellfish (cont.)

PORTION: ABOUT 3 OZ. RAW	TOTAL FAT (GRAMS)	OMEGA-3 FATTY ACIDS (GRAMS)	CHOLESTEROL (MILLIGRAMS)
Lobster, northern	0.76	0.07	81
Shrimp	1.47	0.40	130

Seafood lovers may rejoice—all shellfish are low in fat! Jacob Exler, Ph.D., the principal author for the USDA's new handbook on fish, reports that only 0.05 to 2 percent of all shellfish is fat, and much of that is Omega-3 fatty acids. However, some shellfish are high in cholesterol; particularly crayfish, squid, and shrimp. Frequently these shellfish are also fried, adding fat calorie as well as saturated fat if the oil used for frying contains palm or coconut oil.

Adapted from: USDA Handbook 8–15; and Composition of Foods: Finfish and Shellfish Products, Principal Investigator, Jacob Exler.

Monounsaturated Fats

Because monounsaturated fats may raise the HDL level, they may offer an effective way to decrease your total heart-risk ratio (the ratio of HDLs to total cholesterol). The best source of monounsaturated fat is olive oil, a discovery triggered by the observation that people in the Mediterranean area, who use olive oil in their cooking almost exclusively, have a lower incidence of cardiac disease. Other good sources of this kind of fat are canola oil, olives, almonds, and avocados. Here, too, however, you could overdose if you aren't careful: The amount of monounsaturated fat must also be limited, both to stay within the daily recommended fat allowance and to monitor calories.

How to Choose Fat Wisely

The chart on page 25 compares the fatty acid and cholesterol content of commonly used fats and oils. Notice the difference in the saturated fat content, even in polyunsaturated and monounsaturated vegetable oils. In my recipes, I have recommended using canola (Puritan) oil, cold-pressed safflower oil, and sunflower oil because of their low saturated fat content, and extra-virgin olive oil because of its high monounsaturated fat content and wonderful flavor. Regardless of your choice, limit the amount of any fat that you use.

How to Calculate the Percentage of Total Fat in the Recipes in this Book

The diet plan and all the menus and recipes in this book focus on helping you lower your saturated fat and total fat intake as well as your cholesterol intake. Since your goal is to derive no more than 15 to 20 percent of your *daily total calories* from all fat, use the following formula to calculate the *percentage of fat calories* in each serving of any recipe in this book.

Multiply the number of grams of fat listed in each serving by 9 (since there are about 9 calories in each gram of fat). Divide this number by the total number of calories per serving. The resulting figure is the percentage of fat calories per serving.

EXAMPLE: *Mini Turkey Loaves with Piquant Salsa* (page 194)

Grams of *fat* per serving: 4.7×9 calories $= 42 \div 210$ (total calories) $= 20$ percent of total calories from fat

Grams of *saturated fat* per serving: 0.97×9 calories $= 8.73 \div 210 = 4$ percent of total calories from saturated fat

Remember that no more than 7 percent of your total daily calories should come from saturated fat. (The Appendix table on pages 351–81 will help you determine at a glance just what kind of fat a given food or commercial product contains.) The recipes in this book list the grams of total fat as well as saturated fat per serving.

How Dietary Fiber Affects Cholesterol

Foods that contain large amounts of soluble fiber offer another way to help control cholesterol. A few years ago, if I had told you that eating fresh fruit, vegetables, and grains would help lower your risk of heart disease, you would probably have thought I was a health food faddist. Today, however, because of reliable research by experts like Dr. James W. Anderson, Professor of Medicine and Clinical Nutrition at the University of Kentucky Medical Center, and others, we know that some of these foods do indeed help lower cholesterol as well as stabilize blood sugar.

Dietary fiber is that portion of fruits, vegetables, and grains that your body does not break down during digestion. This fiber falls into

THE FATTY ACID CONTENT OF COMMONLY USED FATS AND OILS

PORTION: 1 TABLESPOON	CHOLESTEROL (MG/TBSP)	PERCENT SATURATED	PERCENT MONO- UNSATURATED	PERCENT POLY- UNSATURATED
Canola (Puritan) (made from rape seed)	0	6	62	32
Hazelnut oil	0	7	*	*
Walnut oil	0	9	*	*
Safflower oil	0	10	13	77
Sunflower oil	0	11	20	69
Corn oil	0	13	20	62
Olive oil	0	14	77	9
Soybean oil	0	15	24	61
Sesame seed oil	0	15	40	40
Avocado oil	0	15–20	*	*
Peanut oil	0	18	49	33
Margarine	0	19	49	32
Hydrogenated vegetable short- ening (Crisco)	0	27	44	28
Cottonseed oil	0	27	19	54
Chicken fat	11	31	47	22
Lard	12	41	47	12
Palm oil	0	49	37	9
Beef fat	14	52	44	4
Cocoa butter	0	61	*	*
Butter	33	66	30	4
Palm kernel oil	0	81	11	2
Coconut oil	0	87	6	2

References: Canola, vegetable shortening data on file, Proctor & Gamble. All others from *Composition of Foods* by Reeves & Weihrauch and USDA Handbook 8–4.
* Data not available.

two categories: insoluble and soluble. Insoluble fiber (cellulose, hemi-cellulose, and lignin), which does not dissolve in water, is found in the plant walls of all vegetables, fruits, and whole grains. Soluble fiber (pectins and gums), which is soluble in water, is found in large amounts in oat bran and oatmeal and the husks of psyllium seeds* and also in barley, legumes (dried peas, beans, and lentils), apples, pears, figs, corn, peas, and the pulp of citrus fruits.

Insoluble fiber helps principally to expedite the passage of foods through the gastrointestinal tract. It also helps prevent constipation. *Soluble fiber*, with its gel-like pectins and gums, helps to lower serum cholesterol by as much as 10 percent by trapping the bile acids needed to make cholesterol and carrying them to the large intestine where they can no longer be absorbed and are subsequently excreted. Moreover, as a "bonus," when you increase your intake of fiber, which is filling, you generally decrease your intake of other foods, some of which undoubtedly would contain saturated fat and cholesterol. A chart showing the dietary fiber content of many common foods is included in the Appendix.

> Fiber is the dieter's best ally because it is not calorically dense. High-fiber foods are low in saturated fat and contain no cholesterol. They are also high in vitamins, minerals, and complex carbohydrates. They slow down digestion and take up room, making you feel fuller. High-fiber foods also require more chewing, so that your body has more time to get the message from the brain (if you listen!) that you've had enough to eat.

How Much Fiber Do We Need?

We should try to consume 30 to 35 grams of dietary fiber (both soluble and insoluble) daily. Ironically, the American diet at the turn of the century was in some ways more healthful than it is today because high-fiber unprocessed foods were a more integral part of the diet. Unfortunately, it is estimated that the average American today consumes only 10 to 15 grams of total fiber a day. Our "Western diet," which relies heavily on processed and highly refined foods and is lacking in fiber, has been linked to atherosclerosis and to a variety of other health problems as well, among them diabetes, colon cancer, and diverticulitis.

* Sold under the brand names Metamucil, Konsyl, Fiber-all, Modane Bulk, etc.

Good sources of dietary fiber (both soluble and insoluble) include:

- Whole grain bread (not white bread)
- Whole fruits, including *pulp* and skin when possible (not just the juice)
- Potatoes and other vegetables, with edible skins or stems
- Whole grain, high-fiber cereals, and whole grain pastas
- Brown rice, barley, bulgur wheat and buckwheat
- Corn tortillas, whole wheat pita, and whole grain crackers
- Fresh vegetable salads (not just lettuce)
- Dried fruits (more fiber, but also more calories)
- Dried peas, beans, and lentils
- Air-popped popcorn

Because soluble fiber is so important in combatting cholesterol, a large portion of the fiber you consume each day should be soluble.

If you haven't already been eating a high-fiber diet, it may take a few weeks for your body to adjust. Initially some people have complained of gas, but this problem usually levels off quickly. You generally need not worry about getting too much fiber—the very bulk

---

GOOD SOURCES OF SOLUBLE FIBER

To maintain a diet that is *high enough in soluble fiber to lower cholesterol*, you should eat daily:

- One serving of oat bran (⅓ cup uncooked) and two Oat Bran Muffins (page 106)
- At least two to three servings of whole fruits (unwaxed apples, pears with skin, or orange or grapefruit with pulp)
- At least one serving of legumes: dried or canned peas, beans, or lentils (include these in soups, salads, or casseroles)
- 1 heaping teaspoon of psyllium in 8 ounces of liquid

of the food will keep you from overeating. Nor should you be concerned about an abnormal loss of vitamins and minerals on a high-fiber diet resulting when food moves quickly through the digestive tract, because the increased intake of vitamins and minerals in whole grains, fruits, and vegetables means additional nutrients that will more than take care of any losses.

◆ 2 ◆

Preventing the Hazards of High Cholesterol

Today we know that the only cause of coronary artery disease is atherosclerosis—the accumulation of plaque along the inner walls of an artery that transports blood from the heart to the organs and tissues of the body. This plaque is composed of cholesterol, fat, fibrous tissue, and in the late stages, some calcium. When it accumulates, the artery thickens and becomes narrowed, blocking the normal flow of blood to the heart. This restriction may cause damage to the heart, and, ultimately, a heart attack or stroke. So it's clear that having a high cholesterol level puts you at serious risk of coronary problems, circulatory disorders, strokes, and intermittent claudication (a severe blockage of the blood vessels in the legs that produces pain on walking). However, while high cholesterol levels are the major factor in causing atherosclerosis (and the risks are greater for men than for women), there are other causes as well, as the list that follows shows.

Risk factors that contribute to atherosclerosis and heart disease include:

- ◆ Elevated blood cholesterol (over 200 mg/dl)
- ◆ High blood pressure
- ◆ Smoking
- ◆ Diabetes
- ◆ Obesity (being more than 30 percent overweight)
- ◆ Inactivity or sedentary lifestyle
- ◆ Stress

29

- Elevated blood triglycerides (over 120 for women and over 150 for men)
- High LDL levels: 130 or above (see page 16)
- Low HDL levels: 35 or under (see page 15)
- Having a parent or sibling who suffered a heart attack or died suddenly of heart disease before the age of 65
- Being a male

If your total cholesterol is under 200 milligrams as an adult, you are at relatively low risk from cholesterol-related heart disease. If it is above 240 milligrams, you are at high risk. Indeed, your risk is almost double the risk of someone with a count of 200 or under.

Today, *more than half of all American adults have cholesterol levels over 200, and one out of every four Americans has a cholesterol level that puts him at serious risk* (see page 14). In plain numbers, that means that there are 60 million people in the United States who are at risk because their counts exceed 200; these are people who should actively be taking steps to lower their cholesterol levels.

Under the most recent guidelines issued in 1987 by the National Cholesterol Education Program, it is recommended that all Americans follow a prudent diet plan (no more than 300 mg. of cholesterol and 10 percent of calories from saturated fat daily). It is further suggested that doctors treat all those patients with serum cholesterol counts in excess of 200, first by using a special diet for six months and then, if diet therapy alone is not sufficient, ultimately with drugs and diet. *It is now recognized that making nutritional changes is the first and most important weapon in combatting elevated serum cholesterol levels.*

Indeed, among health experts, the focus has shifted from emphasizing nutritional deficiencies to the role nutrition can play in *preventing* disease. That we are now entering the age of prevention is reflected in the U.S. government's 1990 Health Goals, which include:

1. Lowering serum cholesterol in the adult population to below 200 mg/dl.

2. Identifying recommended foods that are low in fat and sodium and high in fiber, as well as warning people about foods that are high in calories and sugar.

3. Labeling all packaged foods with calorie counts and nutrition information so that consumers can make more intelligent choices.

In the United States today the typical diet is about two-thirds foods of animal origin and one-third plant foods. Years ago, Frances Moore Lappe, in her book *Diet for a Small Planet*, encouraged us to eat lower on the food chain (i.e., more plant foods)—and she was right. By reversing the ratio and returning to a diet in which two thirds of calories are derived from plant foods (that is, complex carbohydrates like whole grains, cereals, vegetables, and fruits) and the remainder a balance between protein and fat (I recommend a maximum of 15 to 20 percent fat), we could help erase heart disease as the nation's number-one killer.

Changing our eating habits in order to reduce serum cholesterol and the risk of heart attacks "is no longer hypothesis or theory but very sound science," according to Dr. DeWitt Goodman, chairman of the panel that drafted the National Cholesterol Education Program's new cholesterol guidelines.

Heredity and What You Can Do to Help Your Children

Heredity plays an important role in determining which of us will develop atherosclerosis. The diet I am suggesting to avoid heart disease (low-fat, high-fiber) may also help prevent obesity and, very likely, certain major adult-onset cancers such as breast and colorectal cancer. As I mentioned earlier, your genes also have something to do with how you handle cholesterol. Some people seem to be "cholesterol-sensitive"; that is, their cholesterol level is raised much more readily by eating foods high in cholesterol and saturated fats. Obviously, we cannot change our genes, at least not at this point in medical history. However, we now know that what we eat and how we live are of enormous importance in determining our cholesterol levels.

Studies have shown that children with high cholesterol will probably grow up to be adults with cholesterol problems and therefore have a greater chance of developing heart disease unless we change their food and exercise patterns. About 30 percent of American children already have cholesterol levels that many experts consider abnormally high. In the last two decades, obesity in American children between the ages of five and eleven has increased by 54 percent,

A low-saturated-fat, low-cholesterol diet will:

♦ Prevent new lesions and plaque from forming in the arteries

♦ Stabilize old lesions

♦ Eventually contribute to the reversal of existing lesions or plaque

according to federal nutrition surveys. This is attributed to an increase in sedentary activities like TV watching, a reduction in exercise programs in schools, and a higher consumption of convenience foods and high-fat fast foods.

As parents, we are constantly concerned about our children's education, morality, and general development. What about their food habits and long-term health? Are the consequences of frequent fast-food restaurant meals, frozen dinners high in cholesterol and fat, and snacks of hot dogs, hamburgers, cheese-laden pizzas, ice cream, cookies, and candy worth the time saved in the kitchen? Is that convenience worth the ultimate increased risk of heart disease?

Our children inherit our health histories as well as our other features. If a tendency toward high cholesterol levels is present in your family, you can address this problem early on. Have your pediatrician check your child's cholesterol level, particularly if there is a history of heart disease in your family.

As early as 1984, the National Institutes of Health Consensus Conference on Cholesterol recommended a prudent diet lower in fat and higher in complex carbohydrates for *all Americans over the age of two*. This is a true public health approach. You can start to control your children's nutritional environment by limiting and moderating their cholesterol and fat intake, both by setting a good example and by preparing healthful meals.

Remember, it is not the occasional indulgence that raises cholesterol levels. It is the foods you buy, keep on hand, cook, and have available for your family *on a daily basis* that determine the state of their health. The best way to live longer is to start eating right.

Are You Sabotaging Yourself?

If it seems frightening that there can be a genetic predisposition to heart attacks or that they can even be predicted, the good news is that they can also be prevented. According to *Preventive Medicine* (12:868, 1983), fibrous plaques first appear in the coronary arteries between the ages of fifteen and twenty. There is no such thing as a "sudden heart attack"; it has been in the works for years. Unfortunately, too many people have just not made the effort to head it off.

Make sure you aren't in that group by answering these questions honestly.

♦ Are you someone who eats everything you feel like eating, someone who "lives to eat"?

♦ Do you refer to yourself as a meat-and-potatoes person? Do you include animal protein at every meal and avoid whole grains, salads, fresh vegetables and fruits as much as possible?

♦ Do you think of bread'n'butter as one word?

♦ Do you never miss a chance to have a rich dessert?

♦ Are your pantry shelves filled with processed and refined foods?

♦ Do you seldom read the labels on foods to check what they contain?

♦ When you eat fast foods, are they fat-laden hamburgers, hot dogs, French fries, malts, tacos, and cheesy pizzas?

♦ Do you feel that a low-cholesterol diet just means avoiding egg yolks and red meat?

♦ Are you a couch potato? If you get the urge to exercise, do you just relax until the feeling passes over?

♦ Do you count on the fact that if you ever develop a coronary problem there will be a drug or some other medical miracle to rescue you?

If you answer *yes* to all or most of these questions, it is probably time to make some changes.

What You Can Do to Help Yourself

Step One: Have at least two blood tests taken. Average the results to determine your average total cholesterol. (The results may vary due to lab error or biological variation; cholesterol is like blood pressure—it changes from day to day.) If the final average is 200 or over, have a fasting blood test taken (i.e., nothing other than water for at least 12 hours prior to testing) in order to determine what your HDL, LDL, and triglyceride levels are.

Step Two: If your cholesterol is at a safe level and you want to maintain it, follow the guidelines for a low-cholesterol lifestyle in Chapter 5. If you find you have a cholesterol problem:

1. Switch to a diet low in saturated fat and cholesterol and high in soluble fiber. Follow my two-week diet plan described in Chapter 4.
2. Try to reach and maintain your optimum weight— the diet plan is designed to help you lose weight as well as lower your cholesterol.
3. Engage in regular aerobic exercise—20 minutes a day four times a week or build to walking 3 miles in 45 minutes.

Step Three: If after six months of diet therapy you still have a problem and your physician recommends it, drug therapy may be necessary.

The Down Side of Drugs

We tend to think that no matter what happens to us, we can probably find some medication that will take care of everything. Unfortunately, this just isn't so. Although there have been many remarkable advances in drug therapy, the fact is that there are short- and long-term side effects with all medications. The National Cholesterol Education Program panel recommends that "a minimum of six months of intensive dietary therapy and counseling should usually be carried out before drug therapy" and further, that any drug therapy should be *added* to diet therapy, not substituted for it. Drs. Michael Brown and Joseph Goldstein, whose Nobel Prize-winning research led to the development of the cholesterol-lowering drug Lovastatin, still caution that the drug should never be considered an alternative to a healthful diet but rather an adjunct to it.

The chart on page 35 lists the most effective drugs commonly used to lower cholesterol; it also shows possible side effects and lists the precautions that must be taken in some conditions.

Obviously, there are situations in which drug therapy is absolutely necessary, but if you can avoid resorting to drugs by changing your lifestyle, that is a more satisfactory route to take. It's a far more economical one, too; the bill for some of these drugs may run as high as $1000 a year. It is also important to realize that when you stop

CHOLESTEROL-LOWERING DRUGS

	REDUCED HEART ATTACK RISK PROVEN?	EVIDENCE FOR LONG-TERM SAFETY	EASY TO TAKE?	DECREASE IN LDL ("BAD") CHOLESTEROL	SIDE EFFECTS*	SPECIAL PRECAUTIONS
Cholestyramine (Questran) Colestipol (Colestid)	Yes	Considerable	No	15–30%	Gastrointestinal (G-I) disturbances (constipation, flatulence, stomach upset)	May interfere with absorption of other drugs. May increase blood triglyceride levels.
Nicotinic acid† (Nicamin, Nico-400, Nicobid, Nicocap, Nicolar, SK-Niacin, Wampocap)	Yes	Considerable	No	15–30%	Flushing; itching; rashes; blurred vision; infrequent upper G-I disturbances (heartburn, stomach upset)	Not recommended for individuals with peptic ulcer, liver disease, gouty arthritis, significant heart rhythm disturbances, or diabetes. Liver function and blood glucose and uric acid levels should be monitored.
Lovastatin (Mevacor)	No	Limited	Yes	25–45%	Infrequent G-I disturbances and/or painful muscle inflammation	Patients should be monitored for changes in liver function and for cataracts.
Gemfibrozil (Lopid)	Yes	Moderate	Yes	5–15%	Infrequent G-I disturbances	Increases risk of gallstones; strengthens effect of oral blood-thinning drugs; occasional blood and liver changes.
Probucol (Lorelco)	No	Limited	Yes	10–15%	Infrequent G-I disturbances (less than 5% of patients)	Reduces HDL ("good") cholesterol. Not recommended for some patients at risk for heart rhythm disturbances.

* May diminish over time.
† Sold over the counter.

Source: National Cholesterol Education Program, *Report of the Expert Panel on Detection, Evaluation, and Treatment of High Blood Cholesterol in Adults,* 1987.

taking any cholesterol-lowering drug, your cholesterol level will rise again.

What About Niacin?

Recently, niacin (nicotinic acid, see chart page 35) has been touted as a wonder-worker for lowering cholesterol. However, even niacin, a B-complex vitamin (B₃) that is needed by the body *in limited amounts*, becomes a drug when prescribed in megadoses to lower cholesterol. In many people, niacin may produce uncomfortable side effects such as flushing, itching, rashes, and blurred vision. It should not be used by people who have had ulcers, gout or high uric acid levels, liver malfunction, or diabetes. Although niacin is sold over the counter, you should consult your physician before taking it in any doses over 1 gram per day. And, remember, as with *any* cholesterol-lowering drug, *when you stop taking niacin your cholesterol level will rise again*.

How This Book Will Help You

I know that it is possible to prepare easy, appealing low-cholesterol meals that are neither spartan nor "dietetic" because I've done it for my family and I have shown others how to do it both in my consulting practice and in my previous books, *Deliciously Low* and *Deliciously Simple*.

This book will help you lower and control your cholesterol—*and learn to help yourself*—by changing the way you eat.

It has over 250 low-cholesterol dishes and over 100 menus to keep you on course. The recipes include many of the culinary tricks I have found that cut the amounts of cholesterol and saturated fat.

It provides a guide to selecting low-cholesterol products for your pantry and alerts you to the cholesterol and saturated fat content of many foods.

It presents a special two-week diet that is designed to substantially lower your cholesterol if you need to take immediate action and at the same time lower your weight.

Regardless of your cholesterol level or your age, by following the suggestions in this book, you can start today to lower your cholesterol and keep it under control. *Remember: It is never too late to start to reduce your risk of heart disease—and the sooner you begin, the better.* Cholesterol control is up to you.

Many of the people referred to me by physicians were initially told that they would need drug therapy. Yet in reviewing my files I have had only two patients whose cholesterol levels were not lowered to safe enough limits within six to twelve weeks of *diet therapy alone* to make drug therapy unnecessary.

PART II

◆

Adopting the Cholesterol-Control Lifestyle

◆

• 3 •

Stocking the Low-Cholesterol Kitchen

Adopting a low-cholesterol lifestyle doesn't mean that you have to forgo all your favorite foods forever, but it does mean that you have to exercise good judgment in your daily food selections.

It's important to always have the most healthful foods close at hand. If you don't—and you make do with unhealthy foods just because they're there on the shelf—all your best intentions of eating properly to lower your cholesterol will come to naught.

To help you make low-cholesterol cooking a reality in your home, I have listed the healthful foods you should have on hand or choose in your menu planning and the unhealthful high-cholesterol, high-fat foods you should avoid. If you are diabetic, hypertensive, or concerned about weight control, you will also want to avoid foods with added sweeteners or high sodium content. To make your shopping easier, I have included a section on deciphering labels.

Staples for a Low-Cholesterol Lifestyle

In the Refrigerator

Nonfat or skim milk—Use with whole grain cereals, in cooking and baking, or just to drink.

Nonfat plain or fruit yogurt—Use in salad dressings, cooking, or as a food itself.

Tofu—Use in limited amounts in stir-frys, salad dressings, or as a food.

Part-skim ricotta cheese—Use sparingly as a spread on bread or in limited amounts in cooking.

1%-fat cottage cheese—Use in limited amounts.

Part-skim mozzarella cheese—Use in limited amounts in cooking.

Low-calorie Italian or vinaigrette salad dressings—The calorie count should be *no more than 10 calories per tablespoon.* Check the sodium content, because often in lowering calories, excess salt is added for flavor.

Weight Watchers reduced-calorie no-cholesterol mayonnaise—Use sparingly as it does contain fat calories.

Extra-virgin olive oil—It is expensive, but a little goes a long way. Olive oil is believed to raise your HDLs.

Cold-pressed safflower oil, sunflower oil, or canola (Puritan) oil—Cold-pressed means that no chemicals have been used to extract the oil. Canola oil, made from rapeseed, has the lowest amount of saturated fat of any oil and the best fatty acid ratio. Since you use so little at a time, keep refrigerated.

Extra-large eggs—Since you will be using only the whites, they're a better buy.

Egg substitute (low-fat, cholesterol-free)—Egg Beaters.

Chopped or crushed garlic—a readily available seasoning for many foods, available in jars.

Sugar-free preserves—a good substitute spread for butter or margarine.

Corn tortillas—Do not use flour tortillas; generally they contain lard, a highly saturated fat.

Fruits—Use seasonal fresh fruit preferably, particularly apples, pears, oranges, and grapefruit because they are higher in the soluble fiber that lowers cholesterol. If fresh is not available, use frozen unsweetened fruit and fruit juice concentrate, canned fruit without sugar added, or dried fruit. Have lemons on hand as a seasoning or for salads.

Vegetables—Whenever possible, use fresh seasonal vegetables; their flavor is preferable. However, for convenience, frozen (without sauces) are acceptable. Salad greens, green and red peppers, carrots, tomatoes, broccoli, cauliflower, and cucumbers are particularly good because they are high in insoluble fiber, which aids digestion. Prepare by steaming or microwaving.

In the Pantry

Choose whole grain, unrefined carbohydrates such as whole grain breads, cereals, and pastas, as well as legumes, potatoes, and corn. They are all low in fat but high in vitamins, minerals, and fiber.

Canned goods that have added fat or meat or high sodium levels should be avoided. Use only those that contain no preservatives, MSG, or sugar. Select salt-reduced products if salt-free are not available. Rinse salted canned products to remove added salt.

Nonstick cooking spray (*without fluorocarbons*)—Use in cooking pan instead of butter or oil.

Butter Buds or Molly McButter—May be used to season vegetables or popcorn.

Dried split peas, beans, and lentils—high in soluble fiber.

Brown rice, wild rice, barley, bulgur, pilaf mix, and other whole grains—high in insoluble fiber. (If brown rice is kept a long time, store it in the refrigerator to keep it from becoming rancid.)

Pasta—whole grain or those made with semolina and no egg yolks.

Oat bran—a great source of soluble fiber. Use as a hot cereal or in baking and cooking whenever possible.

Oatmeal, steel-cut oats, oat bran cereal (such as New Morning Oatios, Kolln's Oat Bran Crunch, Health Valley Oat Bran Flakes, Health Valley Fiber 7 Flakes, Health Valley Oat Bran O's, New Morning Super Bran)—all cereals high in soluble fiber.

Shredded wheat and bran—a salt-free sugar-free whole-grain cereal high in insoluble fiber.

Potatoes and onions

Canned Goods

Salmon (pink or red)—high in Omega-3 fatty acid that lowers cholesterol.

Albacore tuna in water—contains Omega-3 fatty acid that lowers cholesterol.

Unsweetened fruit in natural juice.

Whole-kernel corn (preferably sodium-reduced)—high in soluble fiber.

Kidney, pinto, and garbanzo beans—high in soluble fiber.

Black-eyed peas—high in soluble fiber.

Sodium-reduced chicken broth, defatted.

Sodium-reduced or salt-free tomato paste, tomato sauce, diced tomatoes, and Italian plum tomatoes.

Sodium-reduced or salt-free marinara sauce (no meat added).

Vegetarian split-pea soup or lentil soup—high in soluble fiber.

Sodium-reduced vegetable juice

Seasonings

Balsamic, red or white wine, and brown rice vinegars

Sodium-reduced soy sauce

Dijon mustard

Worcestershire sauce (use in limited amounts)

Salt-free vegetable seasonings

Fresh garlic

Garlic and onion powders (not salts)

Italian herb blend

Crushed red pepper flakes

Dried thyme, dill, bay leaves and any other of your favorite herbs and spices

Black peppercorns (in mill for fresh grinding)

Dehydrated onion, garlic, shallot, and vegetable flakes

Hungarian paprika (once opened, it should be stored in the refrigerator)

Nutmeg (preferably whole, to be used with a grater)

Ground cinnamon

Pure vanilla extract

Dairy Products

Nonfat evaporated milk—also called evaporated skim milk. Use for cooking or baking.

Nonfat powdered milk—also called dried skim milk. Use as a lightener in coffee instead of most nondairy creamers that may be high in tropical oils and/or saturated fat.

Snacks

Brown rice crackers, Finn-Crisp, whole wheat matzo wafers, Melba toast, bagel chips, Wasa bread, Unseasoned Rye Krisp, or other crackers that are whole grain with no fat aded are good for snacking.

Popcorn—low-calorie, high soluble fiber. Make in an air popper or microwave. Make sure it has no added oil, butter, or salt.

In the Freezer

The freezer offers an "emergency shelf" of items that can help you put together healthful meals without having to make a trip to the store. While fresh fruits and vegetables in season have wonderful flavor and are certainly preferable to frozen, foods properly frozen and stored still have good flavor, food value, and convenience.

Frozen vegetables—particularly corn, peas, and mixed beans, which are high in soluble fiber and can be added to salads as well as served as vegetables. Avoid any vegetables frozen in butter or other sauces.

Frozen pasta and vegetable mix—Use as salad, hot pasta (add sauce), or stir-fry.

Natural fruit juice bars—an acceptable, non-nutritive, no-cholesterol snack.

Frozen unsweetened fruit juice concentrates—apple, pear, grape, pineapple, or orange (to be used in cooking, not as juice).

Unsweetened frozen fruit.

Freshly grated Reggiano Parmesan cheese—Use sparingly as a seasoning.

Nonfat frozen yogurt—an acceptable occasional dessert.

Almonds or hazelnuts (filberts)—limited use in baking or sometimes as a garnish. They do contain fat, although the fat is principally polyunsaturated.

Whole wheat flour—Because the germ has not been removed, it will become rancid if stored a long time at room temperature.

Whole grain breads—preferably those without added fat and sugar, such as Pritikin breads and Pritikin English muffins. (I suggest freezer storage since no preservatives are added.)

Oat Bran Muffins (recipe, page 106)—Prepare a double recipe and store in freezer for future use.

Skinned chicken breast fillets or turkey breast slices (4 or 5 ounces raw*)—a ready convenience for quick cooking.

Ground turkey breast (skin and fat removed)

The Great Cholesterol Battle: Foods to Enjoy, Foods to Avoid

ENJOY	AVOID

Meats

If you eat meat occasionally after you have lowered your cholesterol to a safe level, make sure it's not more than once a month. Limit all servings to no more than 4 or 5 ounces raw (3 or 4 ounces cooked), with all visible fat removed. Try to use the leanest cuts; buy Grade "Good" or "Select"—both have less fat.

Beef—round or tenderloin	Most beef, pork, veal, lamb, and other meats such as cold cuts, sausage, bacon, spare ribs, frankfurters, and canned meats
Lamb—leg	
Pork—tenderloin	
Veal—round, cutlet, or loin chop	All organ meats (heart, liver, kidney, brains, sweetbreads)

Poultry

Limit all servings to no more than 4 or 5 ounces raw* (3 or 4 ounces cooked) and remove all skin and visible fat.

Chicken, turkey	Duck, goose, squab, quail
Cornish hen	All giblets and poultry skin

Fish

Limit all servings to no more than 4 or 5 ounces raw* (3 or 4 ounces cooked).

All fresh or frozen fish	Shrimp, crayfish, and squid
Fresh oysters, mussels, clams, and scallops	
Canned fish in water, mustard, or tomato sauce (no oil)— particularly good are salmon, albacore tuna, and mackerel	

* 4 ounces raw if on the two-week diet.

The Great Cholesterol Battle (cont.)

ENJOY	AVOID

Eggs and Dairy Products

Egg whites, low-fat, cholesterol-free egg substitutes (Egg Beaters)

Nonfat (skim) milk, nonfat evaporated milk, nonfat dried milk

Nonfat plain or fruit yogurt

Part-skim mozzarella cheese and grated Parmesan cheese, in limited amounts

Part-skim ricotta cheese

1% fat cottage cheese

AVOID:

Egg yolks

All whole milk and whole-milk dairy products (yogurt, evaporated milk, half and half, heavy cream, sour cream)

All powdered and liquid nondairy creamers, especially those containing coconut, palm, or palm kernel oil

Whole-milk cheeses or cheeses that have more than 5 grams of fat per ounce

Fruits

All fresh fruits

Any unsweetened frozen fruit

Any unsweetened canned fruit in natural juice

Frozen unsweetened fruit juice concentrate

AVOID:

Coconut, avocado, olives

Vegetables

Any fresh vegetable

Frozen vegetables

AVOID:

Prepared vegetables that have butter, cream, or cheese sauces added or are fried

Vegetables frozen in butter or sauces

Grains and Grain Products

Whole wheat flour

Brown rice, wild rice, pilaf mix, or any other whole grain rice

Bulgur wheat, barley, quinoa

Oat bran

AVOID:

White flour

White rice

Refined cereals with sugar, coconut or palm oil added

Granola or muesli cereals with coconut, coconut oil, or palm oil added

The Great Cholesterol Battle (cont.)

ENJOY	AVOID
Whole grain cereals without sugar added, such as Shredded Wheat and Bran, oatmeal, oat bran flakes, Ralston, Roman Meal	Breads made from refined flours
	Breads made with egg yolk or whole eggs, butter, hydrogenated fat, palm or coconut oil: egg bread, egg bagel, pastries, croissants, doughnuts, biscuits; commercial muffins, waffles, and pancakes, flour tortilla with added fat
Whole grain breads without sugar added, such as whole wheat, rye, pumpernickel, sourdough; whole wheat pita; corn tortillas; water bagels, Pritikin English muffins	
Homemade muffins, pancakes, waffles and cornbread	Buttered popcorn or popcorn with palm or coconut oil added
Air-popped popcorn, salt-free whole wheat pretzels without shortening added	High-fat crackers like cheese or butter crackers; any crackers made with any tropical oil (coconut oil, palm oil) or hydrogenated fat
Rye or whole wheat melba toast, rye crackers, flatbread, matzo crackers, whole wheat bread sticks, brown rice crackers	

Pasta

Whole wheat, soba, or any pasta made from whole-grain or semolina flour	Fettuccine, or any pasta made with whole eggs
Suggested sauces: marinara (no meat added) fresh tomato and basil, primavera, red clam	Prepared pastas with cream or cheese sauces

Beans and Legumes

All dried and canned beans, lentils, etc.

Nuts and Seeds

Chestnuts	Cashews, macadamia nuts, pine nuts, Brazil nuts, and pistachios
(Almonds, black walnuts, and hazelnuts in limited amounts)	Pumpkin, sunflower, and sesame seeds (used only in very limited amounts)

The Great Cholesterol Battle (cont.)

ENJOY	AVOID

Fats and Oils

Vegetable oils like Canola (Puritan), cold-pressed safflower oil, sunflower oil, and extra-virgin olive oil, all in limited amounts

Diet soft margarine (in limited amounts)

Tropical oils such as coconut oil, palm oil, palm kernel oil, cocoa butter (watch for especially in bakery products, commercially fried foods, processed foods, and candy)

Hydrogenated vegetable oils and shortening, butter, lard, stick margarine, peanut and cottonseed oil, meat drippings

Salad Dressings

Low-calorie (about 10 calories per tablespoon or less), preferably oil-free, or those made with reduced oil, nonfat yogurt, or buttermilk

"No oil" dry salad dressing mixes that require only the addition of vinegar and water

Weight Watchers reduced-calorie no-cholesterol mayonnaise

Any salad dressing made from whole eggs (Caesar), cheese, cream, or mayonnaise combinations

Mayonnaise

Soups and Broths

Homemade or canned vegetarian split-pea or lentil, minestrone, bean, barley, or vegetable soups, or red (tomato-based) fish chowders, or broths (with fat removed)

Cream soups and meat-based soups

Desserts and Snacks

Nonfat frozen yogurt, frozen natural fruit juice bars (no coconut), fruit sorbets or ices

Fresh fruit

Unsweetened frozen fruit

Homemade cakes or cookies, custards or puddings made with

Ice cream (especially chocolate with cocoa butter or eggs added)

Tofutti

Whipped cream

Commercial cakes, cookies, ice cream mixes, pies, custards, puddings or Jell-O

The Great Cholesterol Battle (cont.)

ENJOY	AVOID
skim milk, egg whites, and safflower, sunflower, or canola oil	Homemade cakes or cookies with butter and/or eggs
Baked salt-free corn chips	Any fried chips or snacks
	Granola bars

Beverages

Mineral water	Coffee, tea, whole milk, cream
Water-processed decaffeinated coffee or tea or herb tea	Limit alcoholic beverages to 2 servings per week (1 serving = 1 ounce liquor, 8 ounces beer, or 6 ounces wine)
Hot cereal beverages (Postum)	
Fruit juices without added sugar (in limited amounts—has calories and provides no fiber)	Alcoholic beverages with coconut, cream liqueurs, or heavy cream (pina colada)
Sodium-reduced vegetable juice	
Water—6 to 8 8-ounce glasses of water per day	

Red Alert in Shopping: Read the Fine Print and Read Between the Lines

Consumers today are far more aware than they were just a few years ago that the foods they buy may contain various things they don't want. It's not at all unusual these days to see shoppers reading the labels before they put products in their market baskets. An FDA survey revealed that most of the Americans who do read labels do so principally to avoid or limit saturated fat, sodium, cholesterol, sugar, and additives. Labels must be read carefully—as I pointed out earlier, often the necessary information can only be found in fine print, and sometimes not at all. Where possible, you can refuse to buy those foods without adequate nutrition information.

Cholesterol: At present, cholesterol is a buzzword with consumers, "No Cholesterol" claims abound, even on products that couldn't contain it anyway. For example, I have seen "Contains No Cholesterol" claims on packages of frozen vegetables. Of course they don't contain any—no vegetable contains cholesterol! In the same fashion the "100 percent vegetable oil" in stick margarine is often labeled "Cholesterol Free"—what else could it be? However, this product may also contain hydrogenated, highly saturated palm or coconut oils which can *raise* cholesterol.

A recent FDA proposal would standardize cholesterol labeling as follows:

Cholesterol-Free = less than 2 milligrams per serving.
Low Cholesterol = less than 20 milligrams per serving.
Cholesterol Reduced = the product's recipe is changed so that it contains at least 75 percent less cholesterol.
Less or Lower Cholesterol = cholesterol reduced, but by less than 75 percent.

If the food processor chooses to use one of these labels, he is also required to provide complete nutrition labeling, including the amount of cholesterol and/or saturated and unsaturated fat.

Fat: A nutrition label must list the grams of fat in a serving *but is not required to list the number of grams of saturated or polyunsaturated fat*, so that if you are trying to limit saturated fat, you must read between the lines. Look for foods containing polyunsaturated fats such as safflower, sunflower, soy, corn, or canola oils, or mono-unsaturated fats such as olive oil. *Avoid tropical oils like coconut, palm, or palm kernel oils which,* like animal fats such as butter, lard, or chicken fat, *are highly saturated.* Since you are trying to limit your saturated fat, *beware of labels that read: "Contains 1 or more of the following: safflower or hydrogenated palm, soy, or cottonseed oil."* Watch that *or* after safflower! This labeling allows the food processor to choose fat by price or shelf-life instead of your good health, and coconut, palm, and palm kernel oil are among the cheapest and most stable fats available.

Calories: Don't be fooled by a label that says "light" or "lite." These foods may only be lighter in color, texture, or taste, not lower in fat or calories. For example, light olive oil refers to color, not calories.

Low-Calorie foods means only that there are fewer than 40 calories per serving and less than 0.4 calorie per gram. The product still may contain too much fat. Check the grams of fat per serving. In salad dressings, it is better to choose one that has no more than 1 gram of fat per serving, or preferably, one that is oil-free.

"Reduced-Calorie" foods such as salad dressings must have at least one-third fewer calories than the regular preparation, and there must be a nutritional comparison of products, such as the labels on some reduced-calorie mayonnaise or light-style sour cream.

"Sugar-Free" or "sugarless," according to the FDA, just means that no table sugar is added. But there may be other types of sugar, such as fructose, corn syrup, honey, glucose, or sorbitol, that are adding calories.

Meat Grading: Grading terms on meat labels can be misleading. "Extra-Lean," "Gourmet Lean," "Leanest," or "Super-Trim" mean only what your neighborhood butcher or market intends them to mean. There is no government regulation for labeling meat once it gets to the market. According to the U.S. Department of Agriculture, the only official labeling is "Prime," "Choice," or "Good" ("Select"), based on the age and amount of fat and marbling of meat, and it is only *optional* for meat sellers to use this government grading. If you do select beef, choose grade *Good* or *Select*—it has the least fat.

Sodium: An adequate range per day for sodium intake is 1600 to 3000 milligrams, depending on the state of your health.

There are now new mandatory FDA labeling standards for the amount of sodium in your packaged products.

Sodium-Free = less than 5 milligrams per serving.
Very Low Sodium = 35 milligrams or less per serving.
Low Sodium = 145 milligrams or less per serving.
Unsalted = processed without added salt.

The FDA also requires that products list sodium amounts in milligrams per serving and include the sodium content of high-sodium additives such as baking soda and MSG. However, sodium often lies in hiding; there are at least seventy additives containing sodium that can be found in foods, and not all of them contain "sodium" in their name. The table on page 351 will help alert you to the hidden sodium in foods that are consumed daily.

In the recipes in this book, I have not called for added salt except as an optional ingredient (usually in soups). You must make the decision in using salt, following the advice of your physician if you have cardiac disease, high blood pressure, kidney disease, or problems with fluid retention. You can replace salt with salt-free vegetable seasoning or your favorite spices and herbs.

• 4 •

Lose Pounds While You Lower Your Cholesterol: A Two-for-One Diet for Immediate Action

Nothing catches the popular fancy more than an easy solution to a tough problem—and generally nothing is farther from reality. People who need to lose weight are happy to find a diet that promises they can become sylphlike simply by eliminating a few foods. And many people who have to lower their cholesterol like to think they will be home free if they just cut out eggs, whipped cream, steaks, and butter. Alas, it isn't so.

Where cholesterol is concerned, the truth of the matter is that you have to make major changes in the foods you eat and those changes have to be permanent—it's really a lifestyle change, with the emphasis on *life*.

For those of you who want to lower your cholesterol level, I have put together a special diet plan. The diet is based on years of experience with clients who have been referred to me by their physicians in order to correct cholesterol levels without resorting to drugs. In many instances, excess weight has contributed to their problems, so a low-calorie diet has been in order initially as well as one that is low in cholesterol and saturated fat and high in complex carbohydrates and fiber. Thus, this diet will give you two benefits for the price of one: It will help you lose up to three pounds a week and lose them safely—and it will bring down your cholesterol.

The diet has the added advantage that it does not demand that you be preoccupied with food or how to prepare it. It does not call for exotic or expensive foods. The meals are nutritious and simple and can be prepared without difficulty. Many of them can also be easily ordered in restaurants—for let's face it, most of us have some meals out, if not for pleasure, simply out of necessity.

Obviously, when I consult privately with clients I can take into consideration different individual requirements and food preferences. However, the more generalized basic diet in this book should give you good results quickly and safely. It allows no more than 100 milligrams of cholesterol a day and only about 1000 calories daily for women and 1200 calories for men. (The suggested calories for women are lower because women tend to lose weight less readily than do men, and also because women can generally operate on fewer calories due to their size.)

The diet may seem restrictive, but remember that it produces results because it imposes limits. I have found that clients prefer a diet plan that is simple, with meals that do not require too much effort to prepare. And I have had constant positive feedback: The people who have gone on my diet regimen say they are never hungry and have never felt better or more energetic. Once your cholesterol has been brought down to a safe level, you can progress to a much more varied maintenance diet *while still limiting your cholesterol to no more than 100 milligrams per day*.

The people who have come to me for consultation generally stay on their individualized diets for a minimum of six weeks, or until their desired goals of lowered cholesterol and/or weight are reached. Once they have reached their goals, they are given low-cholesterol lifestyle menus like the ones in Chapter 5. Of course, my clients have been referred to me because their cholesterol levels are dangerously high. You may simply want to bring your cholesterol (and weight) down a bit to fall within the safe range. The diet in this book is less drastic, designed to be practiced for only two weeks at a time, followed by a week on your choice of the menus in Chapter 5. If you find after that that you still have a way to go, return to the diet for another two weeks. Repeat this rotation until you have reached a cholesterol level that is under 200 and are at your optimal weight.

Once you have your cholesterol and weight under control, you can maintain both by following the ongoing cholesterol lifestyle plan in Chapter 5. You will be consuming more calories than on the diet, but you won't be overdosing on foods that will raise your cholesterol.

Remember, the two-week diet is designed to be a quick way to lower cholesterol and lose weight, and is meant to be followed for only two weeks at a time. The menus and recipes in the lifestyle plan are suggested for a way of eating that will keep your cholesterol low and excess pounds off for the rest of your life.

Caution: Although this diet is nutritionally sound and conforms to the recommended dietary allowances, I do not suggest *unsupervised* weight loss if you are taking medication for diabetes, hypertension,

or cardiac problems or if you are pregnant. Before you try any re-
stricted diet, you must *first consult your physician*. If he or she
approves, then you are ready to start to take control of your health.

WHAT THIS DIET OFFERS YOU

1. Reduced amounts of cholesterol and saturated fat
2. Increased amounts of complex carbohydrates and fiber, particularly cholesterol-reducing soluble fiber
3. No empty calories
4. A nutritionally sound plan

Directions for
Following the Two-Week Diet

1. The diet prescribes complete menus and recipes for two weeks.
   Follow the diet plan exactly as directed and *never skip meals
   or snacks*. When you miss a meal, you place unnecessary strain
   on your body and also run the risk of eating larger portions at
   the next meal.

2. Exercise portion control—don't exceed the amounts listed.

3. Eat *all* the foods listed.

4. Make sure you always get adequate oat bran daily—1⅓ cups oat
   bran cereal (⅓ cup uncooked) plus 2 Oat Bran Muffins.

5. Take a heaping teaspoon of psyllium in an 8-ounce glass of water
   each day before breakfast.

6. Drink six to eight 8-ounce glasses of water a day (particularly
   since you are taking psyllium), including one full glass before
   each meal and snack.

7. Take a multivitamin, multimineral supplement every day after
   breakfast.

8. Include at least 30 to 45 minutes of walking, swimming, or
   bicycling for a minimum of four days a week. (If walking, try to
   build up to three miles in 45 minutes.) *Physical activity is a
   very important factor in both weight and cholesterol reduction*

and control. Exercise throws your metabolism into high gear while it *dampens* your appetite.

9. Do not drink alcoholic beverages. Alcohol is off-limits because it produces dehydration and adds calories that have no nutritive value. (When you go to the everyday "lifestyle" menus, try to limit your intake for the same reasons.)

Crucial Components That Make the Diet Work

Limited Protein: The maximum amount of animal protein allowed daily is about 4 to 5 ounces of raw (which translates into 3 to 4 ounces cooked). Two days a week are basically vegetarian days—one strictly vegetarian and one allowing minuscule amounts (1 to 1½ ounces) of animal protein.

Oat Bran: Because oat bran, a soluble fiber, has been found to be especially effective in lowering cholesterol, it is included in the diet every day. For optimal results, you need to eat about ⅔ cup (or 2 ounces) of oat bran daily in some form. The basic diet calls for cooked oat bran cereal for breakfast with two oat bran muffins daily as snacks. If you do not like cooked cereal or don't want to take the time to make it, the note on breakfasts, page 59, will give you some alternative suggestions.

*Psyllium:** For an additional quick and easy source of lots of soluble fiber to lower cholesterol, I prescribe as part of the diet a heaping teaspoon of unsweetened psyllium in an 8-ounce glass of water each day, preferably before breakfast or with it, followed by several additional glasses of water throughout the day. The active ingredient in psyllium is the plant fiber which is derived from the husks of psyllium seeds. According to a study by Dr. James W. Anderson at the University of Kentucky College of Medicine, it may lower cholesterol by increasing the excretion of bile acids, digestive substances that are made from cholesterol. Normally, bile acids are reabsorbed from the intestines, but if they are excreted instead, the body then takes cholesterol from the blood to make a new supply, thus lowering cholesterol levels. Unlike potent cholesterol-reducing drugs, psyllium generally has no undesirable side effects if taken as prescribed above

* See footnote, page 26, for brand names.

with lots of water. And, as an added bonus, psyllium is a bulking agent so it helps in weight reduction and aids regularity.

Adequate Water: On the diet drink one glass of water *before* each meal and snack, with *a total of six to eight 8-ounce glasses of water every day*, particularly when you are using psyllium. Drinking a glass of water before each meal helps you feel a bit full before you start to eat. (Coffee, tea, or soft drinks don't count.) The more water you drink, the less fluid your body retains. Adequate water prevents fluid retention, gives a feeling of satiety, and aids regularity.

Whole Fresh Fruit: The diet calls for lots of unpeeled pears and apples and whole oranges and grapefruit with the pulp because of the fiber they supply. Never select juice if the whole fruit is available. In addition to valuable fiber the fruit gives you fewer calories. For example, one small apple contains only 60 calories plus fiber, while 8 ounces of apple juice contain 118 calories and no fiber.

Vitamins: While on the diet, since the calories are limited, you must take a multivitamin, multimineral supplement once a day *after* breakfast to ensure that your individual vitamin and mineral requirements are met. Make certain that these supplements contain no sugar, sodium, or added preservatives.

A SCALE FOR PORTION CONTROL

Having a food scale in your kitchen will help ensure that you are getting the right amount of food in your diet.

What You Will Need for the Two-Week Diet

To help make it easy for you to follow the diet plan, I have prepared a shopping list for each of the two weeks so that with only one shopping trip a week you can be sure you will have everything on hand that you will need. But to ensure that you "stay on the straight and narrow," it might help to rid your pantry of any high-fat, high-cholesterol foods (see the list of foods to avoid in Chapter 3).

Before shopping, you should read the entire diet to get a feeling for what you will be doing. In some cases there are choices to be made. When you shop, follow the guidelines for stocking the low-cholesterol kitchen in Chapter 3.

In general, in my menus and recipes, I prefer to use fresh fruits and vegetables. However, I know that convenience is part of staying on a diet even for just two weeks, and for that reason, I have also suggested frozen fruits and vegetables and sodium-reduced canned soups and beans. If time permits, you can prepare your own beans and soup and freeze the leftovers for future use. If you use canned beans, rinse them with cold water first to remove as much added salt as possible.

Further Advice
About How to Proceed

When You Eat Matters, Too

As in other areas of life, timing is everything when you are dieting. It is important to have meals at regular times: ideally, breakfast between 7 and 9, lunch between 12 and 2, and dinner early, between 6 and 7.

Of course, this isn't always possible. Dinner time is the most common problem. If you find it is necessary to eat your evening meal later than 7:00, then switch lunch and dinner menus on the diet and eat the larger meal at noon, so that you can work it off. For people who are working, this is often more convenient—the business lunch, which can undermine a diet plan, can then become the day's dinner, leaving the evening meal a light one.

Try not to eat after dinner. Although the diet contains optional evening snacks, it is best if you can avoid eating anything after dinner. Try drinking salt-free bottled water or seltzer with a wedge of lime, lemon, or orange instead. If a snack is absolutely necessary, limit yourself to the air-popped popcorn (without fat or salt), a natural sugar-free fruit juice bar, or dry cold oat bran cereal the diet provides. Although a snack at night is more a psychological need than a nutritional necessity, if you feel the urge it is better to indulge it wisely than to give in to a midnight raid on the refrigerator.

Switching Meals

Just as you will sometimes want to switch lunch and dinner menus, feel free to exchange the mid-morning and mid-afternoon snacks.

But whatever you do, *do not skip any meals or snacks*; it is important to eat all the foods listed each day for optimal results.

A Word About Breakfast

The diet plan breakfast is simple and unvaried. It calls for fresh fruit rather than fruit juice because of the fiber content, and includes oat bran every day. Since oat bran is such a good source of the soluble fiber that helps lower cholesterol, you should try to consume the equivalent of ⅔ cup uncooked oat bran daily. You can meet this goal by eating two oat bran muffins (page 106) a day plus 1⅓ cups of hot cooked oat bran cereal.

Some Alternative Breakfasts

If you find cooked oat bran cereal not to your liking, try:

Plain Oatmeal: Substitute oatmeal made by combining ⅓ cup of uncooked rolled oats with 2 tablespoons of oat bran prepared according to package directions. (Although oatmeal contains oat bran, the bran isn't concentrated enough to give you your quota by itself.)

Oat Bran Muffins: Substitute two additional Oat Bran Muffins for the hot cooked oat bran cereal, but remember, if you do this you will add about 100 calories to your diet.

A Quick Breakfast Beverage: If you simply don't have time to prepare cooked cereal, try the Oat Bran Quickie Breakfast Beverage or Quick Breakfast in a Bowl (page 109).

Coffee and Tea

Go slow on coffee—percolated coffee has been associated with elevated cholesterol. If you drink coffee or tea for breakfast, choose a water-processed decaffeinated coffee, herbal tea, or roasted cereal beverage (such as Postum). If you use a lightener in your coffee, tea, or beverage, use powdered or liquid nonfat milk. *Avoid nondairy creamers*—they are too high in fat and sugar and generally contain saturated fat.

Eating Out

If you are eating out, order fruit and cooked oatmeal, but try to eat the oatmeal without milk since nonfat milk is not available in most restaurants.

Before You Begin . . .

You will notice that I suggest that you start your diet on Saturday. This is deliberate since weekends are often conducive to "falling off the wagon"—a time when you consume too many high-calorie foods or simply eat too much. By starting on Saturday, you head this problem off at the pass.

I have deliberately put salads first on many of the menus because, like a glass of water taken before you eat, they help fill you up so that you do not feel deprived of food.

One final word of advice: Don't "weigh yourself down" by getting on the scale every day. Instead, weigh yourself when you start the diet and not again until the end of the first week. For a more accurate reading, always weigh yourself at the same time of day, with the same mode of dress or undress.

A FACT OF LIFE

We tend to gain only an average of one pound a year after the age of twenty-five; after fifty our metabolism slows down even more, so we need fewer calories. For this reason, the nutritional quality of each bite is more important than ever. We cannot afford wasted calories.

The Two-Week Diet for Cholesterol and Weight Reduction

Recipes for dishes in the daily menus begin on page 81.

When a salad is called for, be sure to eat it first—not with or after the meal. Salads help fill you up so that you are satisfied with the more reduced portions on the diet.

Remember to include psyllium every day as a part of your two-week diet: 1 heaping teaspoon of unsweetened psyllium dissolved in an 8-ounce glass of water.

WEEK ONE DIET

Week 1, Day 1—Saturday   ABOUT 1000 CALORIES

BASIC BREAKFAST
½ grapefruit or 1 small orange
1⅓ cups cooked oat bran (⅓ cup uncooked oat bran)*
½ cup nonfat milk

MID-MORNING SNACK
½ *small* apple or pear, unpeeled
1 Oat Bran Muffin (page 106)

LUNCH
3 cups mixed vegetable salad: 1 tablespoon Marinated Kidney Beans (page 81) or plain kidney beans *and* a combination of your choice of the following: broccoli, red cabbage, zucchini, cauliflower, mushrooms, radishes, cucumber, green or red pepper, spinach, romaine and/or other leafy lettuces, and a few onions if you like, mixed with 2 tablespoons low-calorie oil-free Italian dressing, lemon juice, balsamic vinegar, *or* salsa
2 Finn-Crisp crackers or 1 unseasoned Rye-Krisp

---

* For alternative suggestions, see page 59.

MID-AFTERNOON SNACK

1 cup plain nonfat yogurt (mixed with 1 teaspoon sugar-free jam or 2 tablespoons fresh or frozen berries, if desired) *or* 1 cup nonfat milk

1 Oat Bran Muffin (page 106)

DINNER

2 cups mixed green salad topped with 1 shredded carrot, mixed with 1 tablespoon low-calorie oil-free Italian dressing, or lemon juice, *or* balsamic vinegar

3 ounces broiled or poached salmon (4 ounces raw) brushed with 1 teaspoon mustard and ¼ teaspoon chopped garlic (*or* 3 ounces canned drained salmon)

1½ cups combined fresh or frozen broccoli, cauliflower, and zucchini

P.M. SNACK (OPTIONAL)

1½ cups air-popped popcorn (no salt or fat added)*, *or* ¼ cup dry cold oat bran cereal with ¼ cup nonfat milk

Expansion to 1200 Calories for Men:

♦ *Breakfast:* Add 1 slice whole wheat, rye, or oatmeal toast (*or* ½ Pritikin English muffin) with 1 teaspoon sugar-free jam

♦ *Mid-morning snack:* Eat 1 whole *small* apple or pear instead of ½

♦ *Dinner:* Add 1 slice whole grain bread

NOTE: Be sure you have eaten two Oat Bran Muffins.

---

* Season with salt-free vegetable seasoning if you like.

Week 1, Day 2—Sunday

ABOUT 1000 CALORIES

BREAKFAST
 See Day 1

MID-MORNING SNACK
 See Day 1

LUNCH
 1½ ounces drained and flaked, canned albacore tuna in water mixed with 2 cups mixed vegetable salad (see Day 1 lunch for vegetable suggestions), mixed with 2 tablespoons low-calorie oil-free Italian dressing, lemon juice, *or* balsamic vinegar
 ½ 6-inch whole wheat pita bread

NOTE: You can make this into a sandwich if you wish.

MID-AFTERNOON SNACK
 See Day 1

DINNER
 1 cooked fresh artichoke, *or* 8 slim asparagus spears, with a lemon wedge and 1 tablespoon low-calorie oil-free Italian dressing
 1½ cups cooked egg-free linguini with Light Tomato-Mushroom Sauce (page 82)
 1 cup sliced zucchini, steamed
 ¼ small cantaloupe

P.M. SNACK (OPTIONAL)
 See Day 1

Expansion to 1200 Calories for Men:

 ♦ *Breakfast:* Add 1 slice whole wheat, rye, or oatmeal toast (*or* ½ Pritikin English muffin) with 1 teaspoon sugar-free jam
 ♦ *Mid-morning snack:* Eat 1 whole *small* apple or pear instead of ½
 ♦ *Dinner:* Increase pasta to 2 cups

Week 1, Day 3—Monday

ABOUT 1000 CALORIES

BREAKFAST
See Day 1

MID-MORNING SNACK
See Day 1

LUNCH
Antipasto Salad (page 83)
2 Finn-Crisp crackers or 1 unseasoned Rye-Krisp
1 6-ounce can chilled sodium-reduced vegetable juice with lemon

MID-AFTERNOON SNACK
See Day 1

DINNER
½ cup Vegetarian Lentil Soup (page 84) or canned vegetarian lentil soup
2 cups mixed spinach, watercress, and mushroom salad with 2 tablespoons oil-free Italian dressing
½ baked potato topped with 1 tablespoon plain nonfat yogurt and chopped green onion
1 cup fresh or frozen French-cut green beans, with water chestnuts if desired
1 Baked Stuffed Tomato (page 83)
½ cup sliced banana and berries

P.M. SNACK (OPTIONAL)
See Day 1

Expansion to 1200 Calories for Men:

♦ *Breakfast:* Add 1 slice whole wheat, oatmeal, or rye toast (*or* ½ Pritikin English muffin) with 1 teaspoon sugar-free jam
♦ *Lunch:* Eat 1 whole *small* apple or pear instead of ½
♦ *Dinner:* Increase to 1 whole baked potato *or* 1 cup lentil soup

Week 1, Day 4—Tuesday

BREAKFAST
  See Day 1

MID-MORNING SNACK
  See Day 1

LUNCH
  3 cups mixed vegetable salad with 1 tablespoon Marinated Kidney Beans
    (page 81, see Day 1 lunch for vegetable suggestions), mixed with 2
    tablespoons oil-free Italian dressing
  2 Finn-Crisp crackers or 1 unseasoned Rye-Krisp
  ½ small apple or pear, unpeeled

MID-AFTERNOON SNACK
  See Day 1

DINNER
  2 cups watercress and romaine, topped with 2 orange slices
  1 tablespoon yogurt combined with 1 tablespoon low-calorie oil-free Italian
    dressing
  3 ounces broiled (4 ounces raw) fillet of sole (or any lean white fish),
    brushed with 1 teaspoon mustard and 1 tablespoon lemon juice
  1 cup steamed broccoli, cauliflower, and/or carrots
  ½ ear corn (save the other half for lunch salad Wednesday)
  ½ cup fresh fruit salad

P.M. SNACK (OPTIONAL)
  See Day 1

Expansion to 1200 Calories for Men:

  ♦ *Breakfast:* Add 1 slice whole wheat, rye, or oatmeal toast (*or* ½ Pritikin
    English muffin) with 1 teaspoon sugar-free jam
  ♦ *Lunch:* Add 1 cup homemade or canned Vegetarian Lentil Soup (page
    84)
  ♦ *Dinner:* Add 1 slice whole grain bread

Week 1, Day 5—Wednesday

ABOUT 1000 CALORIES

BREAKFAST
See Day 1

MID-MORNING SNACK
See Day 1

LUNCH
2 cups Marinated Broccoli, Corn, Artichoke Heart, and Red Pepper (page 85) or 3 cups mixed vegetable salad (see Day 1 lunch for vegetable suggestions)
2 Finn-Crisp crackers or 1 unseasoned Rye-Krisp
1 6-ounce can sodium-reduced vegetable juice
¼ cantaloupe

MID-AFTERNOON SNACK
See Day 1

DINNER
1 cup Spicy Tomato Soup (page 85)
Seafood Salad Vinaigrette (page 86)
½ 6-inch toasted whole wheat pita bread
1 sliced kiwi with 2 tablespoons berries

P.M. SNACK (OPTIONAL)
See Day 1

Expansion to 1200 Calories for Men:

- ♦ *Breakfast:* Add 1 slice whole wheat, rye, or oatmeal toast (*or* ½ Pritikin English muffin) with 1 teaspoon sugar-free jam
- ♦ *Lunch:* Add 1 cup homemade or canned Vegetarian Lentil Soup (page 84)
- ♦ *Dinner:* Increase pita bread to 1 whole

Week 1, Day 6—Thursday
(Vegetarian Day)

ABOUT 1000 CALORIES

BREAKFAST
  See Day 1

MID-MORNING SNACK
  See Day 1

LUNCH
  ½ cup homemade or canned Vegetarian Lentil Soup (page 84)
  3 cups mixed vegetable salad (see Day 1 lunch for vegetable suggestions),
    mixed with 2 tablespoons low-calorie oil-free Italian dressing
  2 Finn-Crisp crackers or 1 unseasoned Rye-Krisp

MID-AFTERNOON SNACK
  See Day 1

DINNER
  Caesar Salad (page 88)
  2 cups Quick Vegetable Lo Mein (page 87)
  3 cantaloupe slices with ¼ cup berries

P.M. SNACK (OPTIONAL)
  See Day 1

Expansion to 1200 Calories for Men:

  ◆ *Breakfast:* Add 1 slice whole wheat, rye, or oatmeal toast (*or* ½ Pritikin
    English muffin) with 1 teaspoon sugar-free jam
  ◆ *Lunch:* Eat 1 whole *small* apple or pear instead of ½
  ◆ *Dinner:* Add 1 slice whole grain bread

Week 1, Day 7—Friday

BREAKFAST
See Day 1

MID-MORNING SNACK
See Day 1

LUNCH
½ Tuna-Apple Salad Sandwich on whole grain bread (page 89)
Crudités: 2 carrot sticks, 2 green pepper sticks, 2 broccoli or cauliflower
  flowerets, 3 cucumber sticks, 3 radishes
1 6-ounce can sodium-reduced vegetable juice

MID-AFTERNOON SNACK
See Day 1

DINNER
1½ cups Artichoke, Mushroom, and Pepper Salad with Yogurt Dressing
  (page 89)
2 ounces sliced roast turkey breast *or* 2 ounces grilled turkey breast with
  salsa
1 cup steamed spinach with lemon juice
1 cup steamed yellow crookneck squash
½ cup mixed fresh fruit (use any fruits left over from week)

P.M. SNACK (OPTIONAL)
See Day 1

Expansion to 1200 Calories for Men:

♦ *Breakfast:* Add 1 slice whole wheat, rye, or oatmeal toast (*or* ½ Pritikin
  English muffin) with 1 teaspoon sugar-free jam, *or* 1 Oat Bran Muffin
  (page 106)
♦ *Lunch:* Add another slice of whole grain bread to the sandwich
♦ *Dinner:* Add ½ baked potato with mustard or green onion

WEEK TWO DIET

One week down and another to go. If you've cheated just a bit, don't give yourself a hard time. Remember, the occasional urge to indulge won't wreck your long-term efforts for a low-cholesterol life-style and weight control. Treat it as a temporary diversion and don't feel you are doomed to overeat forever.

Week 2, Day 1—Saturday   ABOUT 1000 CALORIES

BREAKFAST
½ grapefruit or 1 small orange
1⅓ cups cooked oat bran (⅓ cup uncooked oat bran)*
½ cup nonfat milk

MID-MORNING SNACK
2 small carrots
1 Oat Bran Muffin (page 106)

LUNCH
½ water or oat bran bagel (no egg) scooped out and filled with 2 tablespoons each chopped tomato and green onion and 1 tablespoon shredded part-skim mozzarella cheese, lightly broiled
12 *assorted* crudités (3 each): broccoli flowerets, green pepper sticks, cucumber sticks, radishes or raw vegetables of your choice
1 6-ounce can chilled sodium-reduced vegetable juice with lemon

MID-AFTERNOON SNACK
½ *small* apple or pear, unpeeled
1 Oat Bran Muffin (page 106)

DINNER
½ cup Vegetarian Split Pea Soup (page 90) or canned vegetarian split pea soup
2 cups mixed greens with red onion rings and pepper strips, with 2 tablespoons low-calorie oil-free Italian dressing
Pasta Primavera (page 91)
10 seedless grapes

* For alternative suggestions, see page 59.

P.M. SNACK (OPTIONAL)

1½ cups air-popped popcorn (no salt or fat added)* *or* ¼ cup dry cold oat bran cereal with ¼ cup nonfat milk

Expansion to 1200 Calories for Men:

- *Breakfast:* Add 1 slice whole wheat, rye, or oatmeal toast (*or* ½ Pritikin English muffin) with 1 teaspoon sugar-free jam
- *Dinner:* Increase to 1 cup split pea soup

NOTE: Be sure you have eaten two Oat Bran Muffins.

* Season with salt-free vegetable seasoning or pepper if you like.

Eating lunch in a restaurant? Try to choose one with a salad bar and refer to the salad suggestions in the menu for Week 1, Day 1 so that you will know what to select.

Week 2, Day 2—Sunday

BREAKFAST
   See Day 1

MID-MORNING SNACK
   See Day 1

LUNCH
   1 cup Tomato Bouillon (page 92)
   1 Quesadilla (page 92)
   12 *assorted* crudités (3 each): snow peas, red pepper strips, broccoli flowerets, cucumber sticks
   ¼ cantaloupe

MID-AFTERNOON SNACK
   1 cup plain nonfat yogurt (mixed with 1 teaspoon sugar-free jam or 2 tablespoons fresh or frozen berries, if desired) *or* 1 cup nonfat milk
   1 Oat Bran Muffin (page 106)

DINNER
   2 cups mixed greens with shredded red cabbage, mixed with 2 tablespoons low-calorie oil-free Italian dressing
   3 ounces broiled tuna or salmon brushed with balsamic vinegar (*or* 3½ ounces canned albacore tuna in water or salmon, drained)
   1 cup cooked spinach
   2 small steamed new potatoes
   ½ cup berries

NOTE: Broil 7 ounces of fish at dinner and save 2 ounces (⅓) for lunch salad on Monday.

P.M. SNACK (OPTIONAL)
   1 natural fruit juice bar, 1½ cups air-popped popcorn (no salt or fat added), *or* ¼ cup cold oat bran cereal and ¼ cup nonfat milk

Expansion to 1200 Calories for Men:

   ♦ *Breakfast:* Add 1 slice whole wheat, rye, or oatmeal toast (*or* ½ Pritikin English muffin) with 1 teaspoon sugar-free jam
   ♦ *Lunch:* Use 2 corn tortillas instead of 1 in the Quesadilla (see page 92)
   ♦ *Dinner:* Add 1 slice whole grain bread and increase berries to 1 cup

Week 2, Day 3—Monday
ABOUT 1000 CALORIES

BREAKFAST
See Day 1

MID-MORNING SNACK
See Day 1

LUNCH
1 6-ounce can chilled sodium-reduced vegetable juice with lemon
Tuna or Salmon Niçoise Salad (page 93)
1 unseasoned Rye-Krisp cracker

MID-AFTERNOON SNACK
See Day 1

DINNER
½ cup Vegetarian Split Pea Soup (page 90) or canned vegetarian split pea soup
3 ounces baked sweet potato
1 cup steamed broccoli
Vegetable Kebab: 3 chunks each squashes, cherry tomatoes, and mushrooms brushed with low-calorie oil-free Italian dressing and broiled
½ cup fresh fruit salad with 1 teaspoon plain nonfat yogurt

P.M. SNACK (OPTIONAL)
See Day 1

Expansion to 1200 Calories for Men:

♦ *Breakfast:* Add 1 slice whole wheat, rye, or oatmeal toast (*or* ½ Pritikin English muffin) with 1 teaspoon sugar-free jam
♦ *Dinner:* Increase to 1 cup split pea soup and 1 cup fresh fruit salad

Week 2, Day 4—Tuesday

ABOUT 1000 CALORIES

BREAKFAST
See Day 1

MID-MORNING SNACK
½ *small* apple or pear, unpeeled
1 Oat Bran Muffin (page 106)

LUNCH
3 cups mixed vegetable salad with 1 tablespoon Marinated Kidney Beans
(page 81, *and* a combination of your choice of the following: broccoli,
red cabbage, zucchini, cauliflower, celery, carrot, mushrooms, radishes,
cucumber, green or red pepper, spinach, romaine and/or other leafy
vegetables, and a few onion slices if you like, mixed with 2 tablespoons
low-calorie oil-free Italian dressing, salsa, lemon juice, *or* balsamic
vinegar)
2 Finn-Crisp crackers or 1 unseasoned Rye-Krisp

MID-AFTERNOON SNACK
See Day 2

DINNER
Parsley and Tomato Salad with Basil Vinaigrette (page 94)
7 ounces boneless chicken breast broiled and glazed with ½ teaspoon
Dijon mustard and 1 teaspoon apple juice concentrate (defrost breast
in refrigerator the night before)
½ cup fresh or frozen French-cut green beans
1 cup crookneck squash
1 sliced kiwi with 1 tablespoon berry puree

NOTE: Save one third of chicken breast for Thursday lunch.

P.M. SNACK (OPTIONAL)
See Day 2

Expansion to 1200 Calories for Men:

♦ *Breakfast:* Add 1 slice whole wheat, rye, or oatmeal toast (*or* ½ Pritikin
English muffin) with 1 teaspoon sugar-free jam
♦ *Lunch:* Add ½ cup Vegetarian Split Pea Soup (page 90)
♦ *Dinner:* Add 1 slice whole grain bread

Week 2, Day 5—Wednesday ABOUT 1000 CALORIES

BREAKFAST
See Day 1

MID-MORNING SNACK
See Day 1

LUNCH
6 ounces sodium-reduced vegetable juice
Vegetarian Chop Suey Salad Sandwich in pita bread (page 96)

MID-AFTERNOON SNACK
See Day 1

DINNER
½ cup Vegetarian Split Pea Soup (page 90)
Ceviche Salad (page 95)
½ 6-inch pita bread, toasted
½ papaya with lime

P.M. SNACK (OPTIONAL)
See Day 1

Expansion to 1200 Calories for Men:

- *Breakfast:* Add 1 slice whole wheat, rye, or oatmeal toast (*or* ½ Pritikin English muffin) with 1 teaspoon sugar-free jam
- *Mid-afternoon snack:* Increase apple to 1 whole *small* apple
- *Dinner:* Increase pita bread to 1 whole pita bread

Avoid fast foods. They are generally high in cholesterol-producing saturated fat, cholesterol, and fluid-retaining sodium.

Week 2, Day 6—Thursday

ABOUT 1000 CALORIES

BREAKFAST
See Day 1

MID-MORNING SNACK
See Day 1

LUNCH
½ papaya with Curried Chicken Salad (page 97)
1 unseasoned Rye-Krisp cracker
12 assorted crudités (3 each): snow peas, red pepper strips, broccoli flowerets, radishes

MID-AFTERNOON SNACK
See Day 2

DINNER
2 cups mixed greens with 1 tablespoon Marinated Kidney Beans (page 81) and 4 quarters artichoke hearts
1½ cups spaghetti squash or 1 cup cooked pasta, mixed with ⅔ cup salt-free marinara sauce or Light Tomato Mushroom Sauce from Week 1 (page 82)
½ cup each steamed broccoli, eggplant, and carrot
½ cup fresh fruit salad with 1 teaspoon balsamic vinegar and ⅛ teaspoon vanilla

P.M. SNACK (OPTIONAL)
See Day 2

Expansion to 1200 Calories for Men:

- *Breakfast:* Add 1 slice whole wheat, rye, or oatmeal toast (*or* ½ Pritikin English muffin) with 1 teaspoon sugar-free jam
- *Dinner:* Increase to 2½ cups spaghetti squash or 1½ cups pasta with 1 cup sauce; increase to 1 cup fresh fruit salad

Week 2, Day 7—Friday

BREAKFAST
   See Day 1

MID-MORNING SNACK
   1 cup nonfat plain yogurt or nonfat milk
   1 Oat Bran Muffin (page 106)

LUNCH
   1 6-ounce can reduced-sodium vegetable juice
   1 cup defrosted Pasta Salad Orientale from Week 1 (or cold cooked spaghetti squash or pasta from night before) mixed with ½ cup each: julienne carrots, zucchini, and red pepper, mixed with 2 tablespoons low-calorie oil-free Italian dressing

MID-AFTERNOON SNACK
   See Day 1

DINNER
   Broiled eggplant and bell pepper strips on lettuce with basil vinaigrette (dressing from Tuesday dinner, page 73)
   3 ounces broiled (4 ounces raw) scallops brushed with balsamic vinegar
   Mixture of chopped artichoke and tomato with basil
   2 small steamed summer squash with grated carrot
   ½ cup fresh fruit salad

P.M. SNACK (OPTIONAL)
   See Day 1

Expansion to 1200 Calories for Men:

   ♦ *Breakfast:* Add 1 slice whole wheat, rye, or oatmeal toast (*or* ½ Pritikin English muffin) with 1 teaspoon sugar-free jam
   ♦ *Lunch:* Increase pasta to 1½ cups
   ♦ *Dinner:* Increase to 4 squash and add ½ baked potato with chives

Shopping Lists
for the Two-Week Diet

Week 1

Before shopping, read the entire diet. Don't be put off by the length of the shopping list for Week 1. You will only have to go to the market once a week, and many of the foods are to be used both in Week 1 and Week 2. Some may be ingredients that you already have in your pantry.

You will notice that these lists specify if perishables like seafood should be frozen. If you prefer not to use frozen items or do not wish to wait for them to thaw, you can simply buy the items on the day you plan to cook them.

1 jar multivitamin, multimineral supplement (100 tablets)
21-ounce jar unflavored psyllium (see page 26 for brand names)

1 quart nonfat milk
8 8-ounce containers nonfat plain yogurt, or (if you do not eat yogurt) 1 additional quart nonfat milk
1 dozen eggs (for Weeks 1 and 2)
2 ounces freshly grated Parmesan cheese (for Weeks 1 and 2)

2 pounds oat bran (for Weeks 1 and 2)
1 package cold oat bran cereal (oat bran flakes, Crunch, or Oatios (for Weeks 1 and 2)
1 package Finn-Crisp crackers or unseasoned Rye-Krisp (for Weeks 1 and 2)
1 package Pritikin (or Pritikin-style) whole wheat bread (for Weeks 1 and 2)
1 package 6-inch whole wheat pita bread (for Weeks 1 and 2)

4 grapefruit, or 8 small oranges
8 small apples or pears
1 small cantaloupe
1 banana
1 pint seasonal berries, or 1 16-ounce package frozen unsweetened berries
2 lemons

2 limes
1 kiwi

4 ounces salmon fillet, or 1 3½-ounce can salmon
4 ounces fillet of sole or any lean whitefish (freeze for Tuesday)
3 ounces canned or fresh bay shrimp, crab, or lobster (if fresh, freeze for Wednesday), or 1 3½-ounce can albacore tuna in water
3 ounces cooked sliced turkey breast, or 1 4-ounce slice of raw turkey fillet (freeze for Friday)
1 3½-ounce can albacore tuna in water

1 fresh artichoke, or 8 slim asparagus spears
2 bunches (about 3 pounds) broccoli
1 small head (about 1 pound) cauliflower
1 bunch carrots
1 bunch celery (for Weeks 1 and 2)
1 head each: romaine, red lettuce, and butter lettuce or any other variety you want
1 small head radicchio
1 bunch watercress
½ small head red cabbage, or 1 package shredded red cabbage (for Weeks 1 and 2)
5 small zucchini
3 crookneck squash
2 ears fresh or frozen corn (or 1 can or package frozen corn)
1 pound fresh green beans, or 1 16-ounce package frozen French-cut green beans with water chestnuts
1 bunch radishes
1 small green pepper
1 small red pepper
1 cucumber
8 ounces fresh mushrooms
2 16-ounce packages washed fresh spinach
1 medium tomato
10 fresh Italian plum tomatoes, 2 8-ounce cans salt-free tomato sauce, or 1 16-ounce jar salt-free tomato sauce
1 small red onion
1 small yellow onion or 2 shallots
1 6-ounce baking potato
1 bunch green onions
Garlic or 1 jar chopped garlic (for Weeks 1 and 2)

1 16-ounce package frozen broccoli, cauliflower, and carrots (for Monday lunch, if not using fresh)

1 16-ounce package frozen broccoli, corn, and red peppers (for Wednesday lunch, if not using fresh)

1 16-ounce package frozen Pasta Salad Orientale, or 2 ounces egg-free linguini (if using fresh vegetables for Thursday dinner's Vegetable Lo Mein)

1 jar sugar-free jam (optional)

1 bottle sodium-reduced soy sauce (for Weeks 1 and 2)

6 6-ounce cans sodium-reduced vegetable juice

1 can sodium-reduced chicken broth (Pritikin if available)

1 jar salt-free salsa (as spicy as you like), or 1 carton fresh salsa (for Weeks 1 and 2)

1 15-ounce can quartered artichoke hearts

1 14-ounce can kidney beans, or 1 cup (6 ounces) dried (for Weeks 1 and 2)

1 bottle low-calorie oil-free Italian or herb salad dressing (for Weeks 1 and 2)

1 bottle balsamic vinegar

1 16-ounce jar popcorn for optional snacks (for Weeks 1 and 2)

2 cans vegetarian lentil soup, or for homemade soup, add 1 16-ounce package lentils, 1 onion, and 1 28-ounce can crushed Italian plum tomatoes in puree

Week 2

Before shopping, check the list for any leftover ingredients from Week 1 so that you do not purchase unnecessary items.

1 quart nonfat milk

4 8-ounce containers nonfat plain yogurt, or 1 additional quart nonfat milk

4 ounces shredded part-skim mozzarella cheese

1 package 6-inch corn tortillas

1 water or oat bran bagel (no egg)

1 8-ounce package pasta (penne)

4 grapefruit, or 8 small oranges

4 small apples or pears

1 banana

1 pint seasonal berries, or 1 16-ounce package frozen unsweetened berries

2 lemons

2 limes

2 kiwis

1 cantaloupe

1 papaya
1 bunch seedless grapes (16)

7 ounces tuna or salmon fillet, or 2 3½-ounce cans albacore tuna in water
   or salmon
7 ounces skinned, boned chicken breast
8 ounces bay scallops (divide and freeze for Wednesday and Friday)

2 bunches broccoli (about 3 pounds)
1 head each: romaine, red lettuce, butter lettuce, radicchio, or any variety
   you want
1 large bunch fresh parsley
1 bunch fresh basil
1 small spaghetti squash
2 bunches radishes
3 bunches carrots
1 green pepper
1 red pepper
1 pint cherry tomatoes
1 tomato
4 ounces fresh mushrooms
2 Japanese eggplant or ½ pound eggplant
1 cucumber
1 16-ounce package washed fresh spinach
¼ pound green beans, or 1 10-ounce package frozen French-cut green
   beans
4 crookneck squash
3 zucchini
2 summer squash
1 3-ounce sweet potato
2 small new potatoes
12 snow peas

1 16-ounce package frozen broccoli, corn, and red peppers (if not using
   fresh)
1 16-ounce package frozen broccoli, zucchini, and red peppers (if not using
   fresh)
1 15-ounce can quartered artichoke hearts in water
1 can sodium-reduced chicken broth
1 can vegetarian split pea soup, or for homemade, add 1 onion and 16
   ounces green or yellow split peas

Recipes for the Diet

All recipes are for 1 serving unless otherwise indicated.

Week 1, Saturday

Marinated Kidney Beans ⓠ

Yield: 1½ cups (1 tablespoon = 1 serving)

1½ cups cooked kidney beans *or* 1 15½-ounce can kidney beans, rinsed and drained

¼ cup low-calorie oil-free Italian dressing

½ teaspoon dried Italian herb blend, basil or oregano crushed

1 tablespoon red wine, balsamic, or tarragon vinegar (optional)

1 tablespoon chopped red onion (optional)

1. Combine the beans with the dressing, herbs, and vinegar (if desired) and mix well.

2. Place in a covered dish and allow to marinate in the refrigerator. These beans will keep for up to 2 weeks in the refrigerator, so that they may be used in both Week 1 and Week 2.

Per serving: 0 mg cholesterol, 0.01 gm saturated fat, 0.1 gm total fat, 0.3 gm fiber, 17 mg sodium, 12 calories

---

RECIPE SYMBOLS

ⓠ indicates recipe may be prepared in 30 minutes or less.

Ⓜ indicates recipe may be prepared in a microwave oven.

Week 1, Sunday

Light Tomato-Mushrooom Sauce Ⓠ

Yield: 3 cups sauce (1 serving = about 1 cup)

Use 1 cup sauce over 1½ cups cooked pasta and sprinkle with 1 teaspoon grated Parmesan cheese. Freeze the rest to use in Week 2 if desired.

Before freezing, remove ¼ cup sauce (without mushrooms) and refrigerate to use in Week 1 Wednesday's soup.

1 shallot *or* ¼ small onion, minced
1 clove garlic, minced
3 tablespoons dry white wine or defatted chicken broth
1 cup thinly sliced fresh mushrooms
8 fresh Italian plum tomatoes, diced, *or* 2 8-ounce cans salt-free tomato sauce

¼ teaspoon Italian herb blend
Few grains crushed red pepper flakes
4 leaves fresh basil, chopped, *or* 1 teaspoon dried basil, chopped

1. In a small nonstick saucepan, sauté the onion, garlic, and wine or broth for 2 minutes. Add the mushrooms and sauté 2 minutes.

2. Add the tomatoes, herb blend, pepper flakes, and basil, combine well, and cook 5 minutes.

NOTE: If you don't want to make your own sauce, substitute about 2 cups of salt-free canned marinara sauce, and add sautéed mushrooms and herbs as directed above.

Per serving: 0 mg cholesterol, 0.09 gm saturated fat, 0.8 gm total fat, 2.8 gm fiber, 26 mg sodium, 75 calories

Week 1, Monday

Antipasto Salad ⓠ

1¾ ounces canned albacore tuna in water, drained and flaked (save the other half can for Friday lunch)

1 cup mixed fresh broccoli, cauliflower, and carrots, steamed, *or* 1 cup frozen mixed broccoli, cauliflower, and carrots, thawed, drained on paper towels

1 tablespoon Marinated Kidney Beans (page 81)

2 tablespoons low-calorie oil-free Italian dressing

1 cup shredded romaine

1. Mix the tuna, vegetables, and beans with the dressing until combined. Chill at least 30 minutes.

2. Add the romaine and toss, and serve in pita bread.

Per serving: 21 mg cholesterol, 0.39 gm saturated fat, 1.7 gm total fat, 3.2 gm fiber, 409 mg sodium, 142 calories

Baked Stuffed Tomato ⓠ

1 medium tomato

¼ cup chopped broccoli, steamed or microwaved until crisp

2 tablespoons soft breadcrumbs

½ teaspoon Italian herb blend

½ teaspoon grated Parmesan cheese

1. Cut tomato in half; scoop out pulp.

2. Combine pulp, broccoli, breadcrumbs, and herbs.

3. Fill each tomato half with the broccoli mixture and sprinkle with Parmesan cheese.

4. Bake in a preheated 400° oven for 5 minutes.

Per serving: 1 mg cholesterol, 0.29 gm saturated fat, 1 gm total fat, 1.6 gm fiber, 79 mg sodium, 65 calories

Vegetarian Lentil Soup

Yield: about 6 cups (½ cup = 1 serving)

This quick and easy soup may be prepared ahead and frozen in ½- or 1-cup portions.

1 onion, finely chopped
2 stalks celery with leaves, finely chopped
3 carrots, finely chopped
2 garlic cloves, minced
2 teaspoons extra-virgin olive oil
1 teaspoon dried thyme, crushed
1 teaspoon Italian herb blend, crushed
½ teaspoon crushed red pepper flakes

1 bay leaf
8 ounces lentils, washed and drained
5 cups hot water
1 cup crushed Italian plum tomatoes in puree
1 cup fresh sliced mushrooms

1. Add the onion, celery, carrots, and garlic to the oil in a 6-quart saucepan. Sauté about 5 minutes.
2. Add the thyme, herb blend, pepper, bay leaf, and lentils and stir to combine.
3. Add the hot water, tomatoes and mushrooms, bring to a boil, reduce to simmer, and cook for 1 hour.
4. Taste and adjust seasonings.

NOTE: If you find your time is limited, a good canned vegetarian lentil soup may be substituted—but don't forget to check the sodium content; high sodium contributes to fluid retention while you are trying to lose pounds.

Per serving: 0 mg cholesterol, 0.12 gm saturated fat, 0.8 gm total fat, 2.2 gm fiber, 35 mg sodium, 66 calories

Week 1, Wednesday

Marinated Broccoli, Corn, Artichoke Heart, and Red Pepper ⓠ

2 cups fresh chopped broccoli and corn, steamed until crisp *or* 2 cups frozen broccoli, corn, and red peppers, thawed, drained on paper towels
4 thin slices red pepper (unless frozen combination is used)

4 quarters canned artichoke heart, rinsed and drained
2 tablespoons low-calorie oil-free Italian dressing
¼ teaspoon Dijon mustard

1. Combine the steamed vegetables with red peppers and artichoke heart.
2. Add salad dressing and toss to combine.
3. Chill 15 minutes before serving.

Per serving: 0 mg cholesterol, 0.07 gm saturated fat, 0.5 gm total fat, 6.5 gm fiber, 330 mg sodium, 84 calories

Spicy Cold Tomato Soup ⓠ

Yield: Serves 1 (¾ cup = 1 serving)

¼ cup nonfat plain yogurt
1 teaspoon lime juice
½ teaspoon curry powder
¼ teaspoon ground cumin
¼ teaspoon spicy salt-free vegetable seasoning
Freshly ground pepper
2 drops Tabasco

¼ cup crushed tomatoes in juice or puree, *or* reserved Light Tomato-Mushroom Sauce (do not add mushrooms) from Sunday (page 82)
¼ cup canned sodium-reduced vegetable juice

Nonfat yogurt for garnish (optional)

1. Whisk the yogurt in a mixing bowl until smooth.
2. Add the remaining ingredients, blend thoroughly, and chill in freezer for 20 minutes.

3. Taste and adjust seasonings before serving.

To Serve: Spoon into a chilled cup or bowl and garnish with a dollop of nonfat yogurt if desired.

Per serving: 0 mg cholesterol, 0.03 gm saturated fat, 0.1 gm total fat, 0.2 gm fiber, 37 mg sodium, 16 calories

Seafood Salad Vinaigrette ⓠ

This salad may be prepared without the dressing hours in advance and chilled until serving time.

2 cups mixed torn greens (romaine, red lettuce, spinach, or butter lettuce)
3 ounces precooked or canned bay shrimp, lobster, and/or crab, *or* 3½ ounces canned albacore tuna in water
½ cup sliced fresh mushrooms
4 quarters canned artichoke heart, rinsed and drained

¼ green pepper, sliced
1 carrot, sliced
½ cup diced cucumber
1 Italian plum tomato
1 slice red onion (optional)
2 tablespoons low-calorie oil-free Italian dressing, lemon juice, *or* balsamic vinegar

1. Place all ingredients except the dressing in a salad bowl and toss lightly.
2. Add dressing and toss lightly again before serving.

Variation: 3 tablespoons salsa may be substituted for the Italian dressing.

Per serving: 91 mg cholesterol, 0.29 gm saturated fat, 1.9 gm total fat, 5 gm fiber, 935 mg sodium, 200 calories

Week 1, Thursday

Quick Vegetable Lo Mein ⓠ

Serves: 1

As my life gets busier, I'm always looking for easier answers to my cooking that are still healthy. Frozen vegetables are often more nutritious than old or out-of-season produce from the market, and, of course, they are time-savers, so I use them in this recipe. However, if you prefer to use fresh produce, combine 2 ounces linguini or cappellini, cooked and drained, with 2 cups of a mixture of raw sliced asparagus, green beans, broccoli, carrots, water chestnuts, bean sprouts, green pepper, and/or bok choy that have been stir-fried and substitute the combination for the frozen pasta-vegetable mixture. Either way, this recipe fulfills all the nutritional requirements and is delicious—in fact, so delicious that you must watch your portions and stick to the recipe.

½ 16-ounce package frozen Pasta Salad Orientale (pasta, broccoli, Chinese pea pods, water chestnuts, and red bell peppers—save ½ in freezer for Week 2 Friday lunch)

1 cup frozen French-cut green beans and water chestnuts *or* fresh green beans cut into julienne strips

1 teaspoon cold-pressed safflower oil

1 large clove garlic, minced, or ½ teaspoon chopped garlic

1 tablespoon sodium-reduced soy sauce

1 green onion, sliced

1. Place the frozen pasta salad and beans in a colander and defrost under cold running water for 1 to 2 minutes. Drain thoroughly.
2. Heat the oil in a nonstick skillet. Add the garlic and stir-fry for ½ minute.
3. Add the pasta and vegetable mixture and stir-fry for 2 minutes.
4. Add the soy sauce and stir-fry one minute.
5. Sprinkle with green onion and serve immediately.

Per serving: 0 mg cholesterol, 0.53 gm saturated fat, 5.2 gm total fat, 5.9 gm fiber, 512 mg sodium, 214 calories

Caesar Salad ⓠ

1 egg white
2 tablespoons low-calorie oil-free
  Italian dressing
⅛ teaspoon minced garlic
½ teaspoon Worcestershire sauce
2 teaspoons fresh lemon juice
1 teaspoon grated Parmesan
  cheese

2 cups torn chilled romaine leaves
1 cup radicchio or shredded red
  cabbage

1. Place the egg white in a 1-cup glass measure and cook in microwave on high for 25 seconds (or cook whole egg in shell in boiling water for 2 minutes and use only white).

2. Add dressing, garlic, Worcestershire sauce, lemon juice, and cheese. Beat with a fork to blend.

3. Put the romaine in a bowl, drizzle with dressing, and toss lightly to coat the greens. Serve immediately.

Per serving: 1 mg cholesterol, 0.35 gm saturated fat, 0.8 gm total fat, 0.8 gm fiber, 378 mg sodium, 61 calories

Week 1, Friday

Tuna-Apple Salad Sandwich ⓠ

1¾ ounces canned albacore tuna in
  water, drained and flaked
1 tablespoon nonfat plain yogurt
½ small unpeeled apple, diced

1 slice whole wheat or rye bread
½ cup shredded romaine

1. Combine the tuna, yogurt, and apple.
2. Spread on the bread, top with the shredded romaine, cut in half, and
close sandwich.

Per serving: 19 mg cholesterol, 0.45 gm saturated fat, 2 gm total fat, 3.9 gm fiber,
301 mg sodium, 156 calories

Artichoke, Mushroom, and
Pepper Salad
with Yogurt Dressing ⓠ

4 quarters canned artichoke heart,
  halved
4 fresh mushrooms, sliced
2 tablespoons diced green pepper
2 tablespoons diced red pepper
2 tablespoons nonfat plain yogurt
1 tablespoon low-calorie oil-free
  Italian dressing
1 teaspoon Worcestershire sauce

⅛ teaspoon dried tarragon *or*
  ½ teaspoon fresh tarragon
Drop of Tabasco
¼ teaspoon Dijon mustard
Red leaf lettuce

1 red onion, sliced and separated
  in rings, for garnish

1. Combine the artichoke hearts, mushrooms, and peppers in a bowl.
2. *To make the yogurt dressing*, mix the yogurt, Italian dressing, Worcestershire, tarragon, Tabasco, and mustard.
3. Add dressing to vegetables, mix well, and serve on lettuce garnished
with red onion rings.

Per serving: 1 mg cholesterol, 0.11 gm saturated fat, 0.6 gm total fat, 1.2 gm fiber,
233 mg sodium, 66 calories

Week 2, Saturday

Vegetarian Split Pea Soup

Yield: 14 to 15 cups (½ cup = 1 serving)

Make your own and freeze in 1-cup portions, or buy canned vegetarian split pea soup. (*Check the sodium content.*)

1 large onion, finely chopped

2 garlic cloves, minced

3 stalks celery with leaves, finely chopped

6 carrots, finely chopped

2 teaspoons extra-virgin olive oil or canola oil

1½ teaspoons dried thyme, crushed

2 teaspoons salt-free vegetable seasoning

½ teaspoon crushed red pepper flakes

2 bay leaves

16 ounces green and/or yellow split peas, washed and drained

2 quarts hot water

Freshly grated nutmeg (optional)

Freshly ground pepper (optional)

1. In a 4-quart saucepan, sauté the onion, garlic, celery, and carrots in oil for 5 minutes, stirring constantly.

2. Add the thyme, seasoning, and pepper flakes and sauté 5 minutes.

3. Add the bay leaves, split peas, and hot water, bring to a boil, reduce to simmer, and cook 2 hours.

4. Remove the bay leaves. (If you desire, the soup may be pureed at this point.)

5. Add freshly grated nutmeg and/or freshly ground pepper to taste if you like.

Per serving: 0 mg cholesterol, 0.08 gm saturated fat, 0.6 gm total fat, 1.3 gm fiber, 11 mg sodium, 65 calories

Penne Primavera ⓠ

1½ cups hot cooked penne or any
  other egg-free pasta
½ cup each hot steamed broccoli,
  zucchini, and red pepper
½ cup salt-free marinara sauce
  mixed with ⅛ teaspoon chopped
  garlic

1 teaspoon grated Parmesan
  cheese (optional)

1. Combine the hot cooked pasta with the hot vegetables.
2. Sprinkle with sauce and toss lightly to coat.
3. Serve topped with Parmesan cheese, if desired.

Per serving: 0 mg cholesterol, 0.17 gm saturated fat, 1.2 gm total fat, 3.7 gm fiber,
43 mg sodium, 257 calories

Week 2, Sunday

Tomato Bouillon ⓠ

⅓ cup sodium-reduced vegetable juice

⅔ cup sodium-reduced chicken broth (spoon off fat)

1–2 teaspoons lemon juice

1. Combine juice and broth; bring to a boil.
2. Season with lemon juice and serve.

Per serving: 0 mg cholesterol, 0.28 gm saturated fat, 1 gm total fat, 0.3 gm fiber, 183 mg sodium, 41 calories

Quesadilla ⓠ

1 6-inch corn tortilla
3 tablespoons chopped tomato
1 green onion, sliced

1–2 tablespoons salsa
1½ tablespoons shredded part-skim mozzarella cheese

1. Heat the tortilla briefly on a nonstick skillet.
2. Sprinkle with the tomato, onion, and salsa and top with the shredded cheese. Heat in the nonstick skillet until the cheese is melted.
3. Fold in half and serve.

NOTE: *For men on the diet:* After sprinkling with cheese, top with another tortilla and heat quesadilla on both sides. Cut in half before serving.

Per serving: 12 mg cholesterol, 2.28 gm saturated fat, 4.6 gm total fat, 1 gm fiber, 155 mg sodium, 133 calories

Week 2, Monday

Tuna or
Salmon Niçoise Salad Ⓠ

3 cups torn salad greens
½ 3½-ounce can tuna or salmon
(or flaked fish left over from
Sunday dinner)
1 tablespoon Marinated Kidney
Beans (from Week 1, page 81)
½ cup raw broccoli and red
peppers
2 cherry tomatoes, halved

1 tablespoon capers, rinsed
(optional)
3 snow peas
Balsamic or red wine vinegar,
lemon juice, or low-calorie oil-
free Italian dressing

1 slice red onion for garnish
(optional)

1. Place the greens in a bowl. Add the fish, beans, broccoli and peppers, tomatoes, capers, and snow peas.

2. Sprinkle with vinegar, toss lightly, and serve, garnished with the red onion slice if you like.

Per serving: 18 mg cholesterol, 0.38 gm saturated fat, 1.7 gm total fat, 4.3 gm fiber, 442 mg sodium, 123 calories

Week 2, Tuesday

Parsley and Tomato Salad with Basil Vinaigrette ℚ

This oftimes overlooked salad green is not just a garnish—it is high in Vitamin A and flavor and low in calories. It is also a natural diuretic. If you substitute sun-dried tomatoes for cherry tomatoes, let them stand in salad dressing for at least 30 minutes before serving.

2 cups parsley sprigs (stems removed)
4 red or yellow cherry tomatoes, halved, *or* 1 tablespoon sun-dried tomatoes, sliced
⅓ cup low-calorie oil-free Italian dressing

1–2 tablespoons lemon juice
8–10 fresh basil leaves
1 large clove garlic, minced
1 tablespoon grated Parmesan cheese
Freshly ground pepper

1. Wash and thoroughly dry the parsley. Toss with the tomatoes.
2. *To make the basil vinaigrette*, combine the Italian dressing, lemon juice, basil, garlic, cheese, and pepper in a blender or food processor mini-mixer and process until pureed.
3. Pour half of dressing* over parsley; toss to blend.

Per serving: 1 mg cholesterol, 0.17 gm saturated fat, 0.8 gm total fat, 1.9 gm fiber, 335 mg sodium, 84 calories

* Save half dressing to serve Friday on the eggplant and bell pepper salad.

Week 2, Wednesday

Ceviche Salad

4 ounces *defrosted* bay scallops (or sea scallops, quartered) *or* firm-fleshed fish (sea bass, halibut, or tuna) cut into 1-inch cubes
2 cups boiling water
Juice of ½ lemon or lime
Juice of ½ orange
2 tablespoons diced red onion

½ clove garlic, minced
4 strips red pepper
4 strips green pepper
4 quarters canned artichoke hearts
2 cherry tomatoes, quartered
3 tablespoons salsa
Butter lettuce and radicchio leaves

1. Place the scallops or fish in a strainer and pour the boiling water over them. Drain.

2. In a bowl, sprinkle the juices over the fish. Combine with the remaining ingredients and toss lightly to blend.

3. Marinate 20 minutes at room temperature, stir, and chill, covered, in the refrigerator for at least 20 minutes.

To Serve: Line a soup bowl with butter lettuce and radicchio and spoon the ceviche onto the greens.

Per serving: 37 mg cholesterol, 0.13 gm saturated fat, 1.1 gm total fat, 1 gm fiber, 201 mg sodium, 153 calories

Vegetarian Chop Suey
Salad Sandwich ℚ

A total of 1½ cups of any raw vegetable mixture that you favor may be substituted for those listed there.

¼ cup chopped fresh broccoli
¼ cup chopped cucumber
¼ cup chopped carrots
¼ cup sliced radishes
¼ cup sliced red or green pepper
1 sliced green onion

3 cherry tomatoes, quartered
¼ cup nonfat plain yogurt
1 teaspoon dried dill *or* 1 table-
    spoon chopped fresh dill
½ 6-inch whole wheat pita bread

1. Mix the vegetables with the yogurt and dill until well combined.
2. Stuff into the pita pocket and serve.

Per serving: 1 mg cholesterol, 0.19 gm saturated fat, 1.2 gm total fat, 4.4 gm fiber, 75 mg sodium, 132 calories

Week 2, Thursday

Curried Chicken Salad ©

1 tablespoon nonfat plain yogurt
1 teaspoon frozen unsweetened
 apple juice concentrate or
 sweet pickle relish
¼ teaspoon salt-free vegetable
 seasoning
¼ teaspoon curry powder

2 ounces shredded chicken (from
 Tuesday dinner)
2 tablespoons chopped celery
2 tablespoons chopped red pepper
½ papaya, seeded

1. Combine the yogurt, apple juice concentrate or relish, seasoning, and curry powder.
2. Add the chicken, celery, and red pepper; stir with a fork to blend.
3. Spoon into the papaya half and chill until serving time.

Per serving: 48 mg cholesterol, 0.67 gm saturated fat, 2.4 gm total fat, 1.6 gm fiber, 72 mg sodium, 166 calories

Maintaining a Low-Cholesterol Lifestyle

Now that you have been on the diet plan for two weeks, the time has come to take a break and move on to the greater variety of the low-cholesterol lifestyle plan presented in the next chapters. (Of course, you may want to go back to the diet if your cholesterol and/or weight haven't reached the levels you want; stay on the menu maintenance plan for a week, then return to the diet. Remember, you should not be on the diet for more than two weeks at a time.)

The menus and recipes in the lifestyle plan will help you stay on track; by following them you can be sure of keeping your cholesterol consumption around 100 milligrams a day. You should still eat oat bran or oatmeal with 2 tablespoons of oat bran for breakfast five days a week and take psyllium daily. Be sure to include two oat bran muffins or a variation (pages 106–108) in your daily diet so that you will still get enough soluble fiber to maintain the right cholesterol levels.

• 5 •

Menus and Recipes for Low-Cholesterol Meals: An Ongoing Lifestyle Plan

If your total cholesterol reading is under 200, you can't just sit back and rest on your laurels. As we have seen, to be assured of keeping a healthy cholesterol level, you must adopt a whole new approach to eating in which you limit your cholesterol and saturated fat in a conscientious and consistent way—"preventive nutrition," if you will.

The easy-to-prepare, flavor-filled meals that follow are meant to serve as a model for this new way of eating. They are high in complex carbohydrates and fiber and low in cholesterol and fat, and are based on the following recommended total daily calorie distribution:

65–70% Complex Carbohydrates ▷

◁15–20% Fat*

◁15% Protein

They allow you to eat varied and appealing meals and still limit your cholesterol to no more than 100 milligrams a day.

This new approach to eating will mean a change not only in your eating habits but also in your shopping and cooking habits—a whole new lifestyle. But it will be worth the effort. When you adopt this lifestyle plan, not only will you reduce your risk of heart disease, stroke, and even certain kinds of cancer (breast, colon, prostate, and pancreas), but you will find that after following it only a few weeks you'll feel terrific and have more energy.

---

* No more than 7% of total calories from saturated fat.

How the Menus Work

The menus are organized by category: breakfast, lunch or supper (light meals), and dinner (main meals). You simply combine your choice of breakfast, lunch, and dinner menus to make up your daily meals, following the requirements in the guidelines. In the beginning you may find it easier to use the two-week diet plan as a base, substituting recipes from Chapters 5–7 as you choose.

No recipes are included for some of the dishes in the menus because they are basic recipes easily found in many cookbooks. It is important that these generic dishes be prepared with low-cholesterol and low-saturated-fat ingredients. On the other hand, many recipes are included in the book that are not called for in the menus. These are meant to be substituted in the menus as you choose. In addition, any of the recipes in my two previous books, *Deliciously Low* and *Deliciously Simple*, can also be used. After you have followed the menus and recipes for a while, you will find it easy to create your own low-cholesterol menus and recipes.

Easy-to-Follow Guidelines for a Low-Cholesterol Lifestyle

Daily Do's

1. *Limit all animal protein*. Do not eat more than a total of 4 ounces of cooked (5 ounces of raw) meat or fish a day (that's about the size of a deck of cards). This can be eaten at either lunch or dinner, but not both. Select lean meat; although it has as much cholesterol as fatty meat, it is a bit lower in saturated fat.

   TIP: One way to cut down on animal protein is to use it as an accent or seasoning in stir-fried dishes, casseroles, or salads of vegetables and/or grains. Often just a small amount (1 to 1½ ounces) is enough to make an otherwise vegetarian dish acceptable to the most ardent meat lover.

2. Keep in mind that only 15 to 20 percent of your total daily calories should come from fat and no more than 7 percent of your total daily calories should come from saturated fat.

3. Include some source of *soluble fiber*—plain oat bran cereal (⅓ cup dry cereal, cooked), 2 oat bran muffins, and three servings from any of the following: barley, dried peas, lentils, or beans, corn, peas, apples, pears, or citrus fruit.

4. Include as sources of *insoluble fiber* at least two servings each of whole fresh fruits, vegetables, salads, and whole grains such as bulgur wheat, brown rice, whole-grain breads (wheat, rye, pumpernickel), corn or whole wheat tortillas, or whole-grain cereals.

5. *Before breakfast*, take 1 heaping teaspoon of psyllium in 8 ounces of water, and drink six additional glasses of water throughout the day. Current research indicates that this natural soluble fiber helps to lower total cholesterol as much as 10 percent.

Weekly Do's:

1. *Serve fish 2 to 3 times a week*. Include some coldwater fatty fishes like salmon, albacore tuna, mackerel, or trout because these fish contain high levels of desirable Omega-3 fatty acids.

2. *At least two days a week have all vegetarian or mostly vegetarian meals*.
   TIP: This doesn't mean just rice and bean sprouts—how about a pasta dinner with a tomato or primavera sauce, a vegetable salad, whole grain bread, and fresh fruit for dessert?

3. Be alert when shopping; *read all labels carefully* and check the guidelines for healthful ingredients in Chapter 3.

4. Try to *include garlic and onions* in your recipes; they contain allicin, a chemical that may inhibit blood clotting. Like olive oil, these are commonly used ingredients in Greek and Italian dishes, and may account for the lower incidence of cardiovascular disease among Mediterranean people.

Avoid:

1. *Egg yolks* (one egg yolk contains 275 milligrams of cholesterol). Use egg whites instead.

2. *All whole-milk dairy products*. Use nonfat (skim) or at most 1 percent fat products. Select cheeses that are made at least par-

tially from nonfat milk, such as part-skim ricotta or part-skim mozzarella, and use them only very sparingly.

3. *Butter, stick margarine, lard, and chicken fat.* When choosing fats, select vegetable oils like canola, cold-pressed safflower oil, or sunflower, olive, or corn oil.

4. *Coconut and palm oils, chocolate, and hydrogenated fats, or any foods that contain them.*

5. *Fried food.* Broil, bake, poach, steam, or grill instead, and use a nonstick frying pan or nonstick spray when cooking instead of butter or oil.

A Note on Salt and Sugar

The average American is addicted to salt. It is an acquired taste, and with all the emphasis on lowering the sodium in our diets, many people are gradually weaning themselves away from unnecessary salt by not adding salt in cooking, not using salt shakers on cooked foods, and by judiciously reading product labels to determine the sodium content.

In my recipes I recommend using many sodium-reduced or low-sodium products and generally add no salt in cooking.

If you are hypertensive, have cardiac or kidney problems, or are just prone to fluid retention, keep your sodium consumption to a moderate amount (about 1600 to 3000 milligrams per day).

Remember, too, that although we all know sugar has only "empty calories," excessive amounts may also raise triglyceride levels, which can contribute to cardiac disease. Here, again, I use limited amounts of sugar in all my recipes, if I use it at all.

RECIPE SYMBOLS

Ⓠ indicates recipe may be prepared in 30 minutes or less.

Ⓜ indicates recipe may be prepared in a microwave oven.

Breakfast and Brunch

You owe it to yourself to take a few minutes to enjoy a heart-healthy breakfast—one that's high in cholesterol-lowering soluble fiber. The two Basic Breakfasts in this section include high-fiber fruit (grapefruit or orange) and oat bran cereal or muffins to give you the advantage you need to keep your cholesterol low. The other breakfast menus will give you some variety as well as the proper nutrition.

Because brunches can be deadly, I have suggested some ways you can be good to yourself without being denying. The average brunch as found in restaurants (and those served in homes too) are often terribly high in fat, cholesterol, and calories. Consider eggs Benedict (599 milligrams of cholesterol, 10.7 grams of saturated fat, and about 1040 calories), cheese omelettes with fried potatoes (924 milligrams of cholesterol, 20.1 grams of saturated fat, and about 850 calories), corned beef hash with poached eggs (706 milligrams of cholesterol, 11.8 grams of saturated fat, and about 600 calories). Request some bacon, sausage, or ham on the side and you add on 200-plus calories and loads of sodium, to say nothing of more artery-clogging fat and cholesterol. This doesn't include the fat-laden muffins, croissants, pastries, or rolls with butter—never mind the dessert! It really adds up. To help avoid these problems, I have created some taste-tempting brunch menus and recipes for you, your family, and your friends.

Recipes

Breakfast:

Hot Oat Bran Cereal
Basic Oat Bran Muffins with 13 variations
Oat Bran Quickie Breakfast Beverage
High-Fiber Granola
Triple Oat Porridge with Raisins
Buckwheat Blueberry Pancakes
Oatmeal Pancakes with Orange Slices
Sourdough French Toast
Oat Bran Waffles

Brunch:

Scrambled Eggs with Zucchini, Red Onion, and Red Pepper
No-Cholesterol Frittata
No-Yolk Spinach and Mushroom Omelette
Assorted Vegetable Platter with Dill Sauce
Salmon Hash
Pasta and Vegetable Casserole
Cheese Bread Soufflé
Bristol Farms Chicken and Rice Jardinière
Breakfast Burritos

Breakfasts

BASIC BREAKFAST I
Half Grapefruit (with all the fiber)
♦Hot Oat Bran Cereal♦
Nonfat Milk or Nonfat Yogurt

Hot Oat Bran Cereal Ⓠ Ⓜ

Serves: 1

Oat bran cereal is the best low-cholesterol breakfast you can have. Because oat bran is high in soluble fiber it not only lowers your cholesterol level, but also helps you maintain the desired level once you have reached it.

1 cup cold water or nonfat milk
⅓ cup oat bran
Nonfat milk or yogurt

¼ teaspoon brown sugar, or 1 teaspoon sugar-free apple butter (optional)

1. Place the cold water or milk and oat bran in a heavy saucepan; mix well.
2. Bring to a boil over high heat, stirring occasionally.
3. Reduce heat to low and cook 1 to 2 minutes or until desired consistency is reached.

To Serve: Serve with nonfat milk or yogurt. Sweeten with brown sugar or sugar-free apple butter if you like.

To Microwave: Combine the cold water and cereal in a microwave-proof cereal bowl. Cook on high for 2 to 2½ minutes. Stir and serve.

Per serving: 0 mg cholesterol, 0 gm saturated fat, 2.8 gm total fat, 7.3 gm fiber, 3 mg sodium, 111 calories

BASIC BREAKFAST II

Orange Wedges
◆Basic Oat Bran Muffins◆
Nonfat Milk or Nonfat Yogurt

Basic Oat Bran Muffins Ⓠ

Yield: 12 muffins (1 muffin = 1 serving)

Because oat bran is high in soluble fiber that lowers cholesterol, you should eat two Oat Bran Muffins (or any of the variations *each day* in addition to other foods high in soluble fiber. If you are really on the run, two Basic Oat Bran Muffins may also be substituted for hot oat bran cereal at breakfast, giving you a total of four Oat Bran Muffins that day.

2½ cups oat bran*
½ cup whole wheat flour
1½–2 teaspoons ground cinnamon
1 tablespoon baking powder
3 tablespoons brown sugar
3 extra-large egg whites, slightly beaten
1¼ cups nonfat milk or nonfat evaporated milk

⅓ cup frozen unsweetened apple juice concentrate
1 tablespoon canola or cold-pressed safflower oil
2 teaspoons pure vanilla extract
½ cup dark raisins, chopped dates, chopped figs, or dried tart red cherries (optional)

1. Preheat the oven to 425° and coat muffin tins with nonstick cooking spray or line with paper baking cups.
2. Combine the dry ingredients in a mixing bowl and blend with a fork.
3. Beat the remaining liquid ingredients except fruit in a separate bowl with a fork.
4. Add the liquid ingredients to the dry and stir with a spoon until flour disappears. (Optional dried fruit may be added now.)
5. Fill the muffin tins, place in the preheated oven and lower the temperature to 400°.

---

* Sometimes oat bran that is purchased in health food stores is slightly coarser than the oat bran purchased in a box in your local grocery store (such as Mother's or Quaker's). It will give you a slightly more textured product. I don't find this objectionable; however, if you do, the oat bran can be milled in your blender or food processor before measuring so that you get a finer-textured product.

6. Bake 17 to 20 minutes or until lightly browned. Cool slightly before removing from tins.

Suggestion: Since I recommend that you eat two muffins a day, make a double recipe and freeze some for future use. These muffins will also keep fresh in the refrigerator for three to four days. I feel they taste a little better if they are heated briefly in a toaster oven or microwave before serving.

Per serving: 1 mg cholesterol, 0.15 gm saturated fat, 2.9 gm total fat, 4.7 gm fiber, 107 mg sodium, 126 calories

Variations:

For Banana Bran Muffins:
Substitute two very ripe bananas (⅔ cup mashed) for the frozen apple juice concentrate and add 1 teaspoon banana extract.

For Spicy Apple Bran Muffins:
Substitute ⅔ cup sugar-free applesauce for the frozen apple juice concentrate. Add 1 cored chopped apple to the liquid ingredients, and 1½ teaspoons cinnamon, ½ teaspoon ground nutmeg, and 2 tablespoons chopped almonds to the dry ingredients.

For Blueberry Bran Muffins:
Add 1 cup frozen (not defrosted) or fresh blueberries after liquid and dry ingredients are combined.

For Banana-Blueberry Bran Muffins:
Add 1 cup frozen or fresh blueberries to the Banana Bran Muffin mixture.

For Pear Bran Muffins:
Substitute 1 small ripe pear, peeled and mashed, for the frozen apple juice concentrate in the recipe and add 1 cored chopped pear.

For Cranberry Bran Muffins:
Add 1 cup chopped raw cranberries mixed with 3 tablespoons frozen apple juice concentrate to liquid ingredients.

For Boysenberry or Raspberry Bran Muffins:
Add 1 cup berries after the liquid and dry ingredients are combined.

For Jelly Bran Muffins:
Fill each muffin cup ⅓ full with batter, add 1 teaspoon sugar-free jam on top of the batter, and top with the remaining batter.

For Honey Double-Bran Muffins:
Add 1 cup shredded whole bran to the dry ingredients and substitute ¼ cup honey for 3 tablespoons sugar.

For Streusel-Topped Oatmeal Bran Muffins:
Substitute 1 cup rolled oats for 1 cup oat bran and soak in the 1¼ cups milk called for in the recipe for 10 minutes. Combine with the other liquid ingredients before adding to dry ingredients. To make streusel topping: Chop ¼ cup rolled oats, ¼ cup pecans, 2 tablespoons oat bran, and 2 tablespoons brown sugar in the food processor and sprinkle on top of the muffins before baking.

For Pineapple Bran Muffins:
Substitute 1 5½-ounce can unsweetened crushed pineapple with its juice for the ⅓ cup frozen apple juice concentrate.

For Upside-Down Prune Bran Muffins:
In the bottom of each muffin well, place 1 stewed, drained, and pitted prune. Cover with batter and bake as directed.

For Wild Rice Bran Muffins:
Substitute 1 cup cold cooked wild rice for 1 cup of the oat bran and omit the sugar, cinnamon, and vanilla. Because these are not sweet, they are delicious served as a dinner roll.

One of my clients who chooses not to make and eat two Oat Bran Muffins each day compensates for this by doubling his serving of hot oat bran cereal in the morning. To some this may seem an enormous amount, but it works for him.

Oat Bran Quickie Breakfast Beverage ℚ

Serves: 1

Perhaps you are one of those people who doesn't start your day by sitting down to breakfast, enjoying your food and relaxing. Some hurried (or harried) people who don't have the time or inclination to bake muffins, cook hot cereal, or even serve cold cereals may be interested in preparing this breakfast beverage, which contains as much soluble fiber as a serving of Hot Oat Bran Cereal (page 105) or two Basic Oat Bran Muffins (page 106). It also makes a great afternoon pick-me-up.

1 cup *cold* nonfat milk, or ⅓ cup
    nonfat dry milk plus 1 cup cold
    water
⅓ cup oat bran
½ large *ripe* banana, sliced

1 teaspoon pure vanilla or almond
    extract
Dash of ground cinnamon or
    freshly ground nutmeg

1. Blend all the ingredients except the cinnamon or nutmeg together in a blender for 6 seconds or until foamy.

2. Pour into a glass and sprinkle with cinnamon or nutmeg and serve immediately.

Variation: 1 small ripe sliced peach, nectarine, or pear, ½ cup fresh or frozen strawberries, or ¼ ripe sliced papaya may be substituted for the banana. You may also add ¼ cup nonfat yogurt to the recipe.

Per serving: 5 mg cholesterol, 0.45 gm saturated fat, 3.6 gm total fat, 10.4 gm fiber, 131 mg sodium, 294 calories

For Quick Breakfast in a Bowl: Serve ½ cup cold Oat Bran Crunch, Kellogg's Heartwise, Quaker Oat Squares, or General Mills Benefit flakes sprinkled with 2 tablespoons of oat bran, banana slices, and nonfat milk.

Papaya with Fresh Lime
♦High-Fiber Granola♦
with Sliced Banana and Nonfat Milk

High-Fiber Granola

Yield: 4 cups (½ cup = 1 serving)

Here's another quick breakfast that requires no cooking. Unlike most commercial granolas, which have coconut and/or coconut and palm oil added, (high in *saturated fat*), this granola recipe is high in fiber, particularly soluble fiber, with *no added fat*.

2 cups rolled oats
1 cup 7-grain cereal
½–⅔ cup apple juice or papaya juice, no sugar added
1 red apple with skin, cored and grated
1 cup cold oat bran cereal, no sugar added (use Oat Bran Flakes, Oatios or Oat Crunch)
¼ cup oat bran

⅓ cup nonfat powdered milk
¼ cup frozen unsweetened apple juice concentrate mixed with 1 tablespoon vanilla extract
2 tablespoons ground cinnamon
1 teaspoon freshly ground nutmeg
½ cup dark seeded Monukka raisins
1 split vanilla bean

1. Place the oats and 7-grain cereal in a bowl; mix. Add apple juice and apple; mix with a fork.
2. Add the dry cereal, oat bran, powdered milk, apple juice concentrate, cinnamon, and nutmeg. Mix thoroughly with a fork.
3. Place on a nonstick baking sheet (15½″ × 10″) and bake in a preheated 350° oven for 30 minutes or until lightly browned. Mix halfway through baking time.
4. Add the raisins; cool, and store in a tightly sealed jar to which you have added a split vanilla bean for flavor.
To Serve: Serve as a cold cereal topped with nonfat milk and sliced bananas. In winter you may decide to use warm milk instead of cold.

Variation: Use blueberries or sliced fresh peaches, strawberries, mango, or other fruit instead of banana.

NOTE: Any of the cold oat bran cereals recommended in Chapter 3, page 43, may be substituted for High-Fiber Granola:

Per serving: 1 mg cholesterol, 0.55 gm saturated fat, 2.2 gm total fat, 4.2 gm fiber, 112 mg sodium, 208 calories

Sliced Bananas and Blueberries
with Nonfat Yogurt
♦Triple Oat Porridge with Raisins♦

Triple Oat Porridge with Raisins ⓠ

Serves: 4 (1 cup = 1 serving)

By starting to cook your cereal in cold water and milk you get a creamier consistency.

2½ cups cold water
½ cup nonfat milk
1 cup rolled oats

½ cup oat bran
¼ cup steel-cut oats
¼ cup dark raisins

1. Put the cold water and milk into a saucepan. Add all the cereals and raisins and mix thoroughly.
2. Place over medium heat, stirring occasionally, until the mixture starts to boil. Reduce to a simmer, cover, and cook for 12 to 15 minutes.

To Serve: Serve hot with cold nonfat milk.

Per serving: 1 mg cholesterol, 0.34 gm saturated fat, 2.7 gm total fat, 4.8 gm fiber, 19 mg sodium, 177 calories

Orange Wedges
◆Buckwheat Blueberry Pancakes◆
with
Fresh Blueberries and Yogurt

Buckwheat Blueberry Pancakes ⓠ

Yield: 12 3-inch pancakes (3 pancakes=1 serving)

These light and luscious pancakes are well worth the time and effort it takes to beat the egg whites.

½ cup buckwheat flour
¼ cup unbleached white flour or
  whole wheat flour
¾ cup oat bran
2 teaspoons baking powder
2 tablespoons frozen unsweetened
  apple juice concentrate
2 extra-large egg whites, slightly
  beaten
1 cup nonfat plain yogurt
¼ cup nonfat milk

2 extra-large egg whites, beaten
  until stiff
1 cup fresh or frozen blueberries

¼ cup nonfat plain yogurt mixed
  with ½ teaspoon pure vanilla
  extract and 1 cup fresh blueberries, for garnish

1. Mix the flours, oat bran, and baking powder, in a bowl.
2. Blend the fruit juice concentrate, 2 slightly beaten egg whites, yogurt, and milk.
3. Add the yogurt mixture to the flour mixture and blend with a fork.
4. Fold the stiffly beaten egg whites and the blueberries into the mixture.
5. Immediately cook on a hot nonstick griddle or skillet coated with non-stick spray, using ¼ cup batter for each pancake.

To Serve: Place the hot pancakes on warm plates and garnish with a dollop of yogurt and fresh blueberries.

NOTE: Leftover batter does not give fluffy pancakes because of beaten egg whites that are used.

Per serving: 1 mg cholesterol, 0.14 gm saturated fat, 2.1 gm total fat, 5.5 gm fiber, 261 mg sodium, 185 calories

Baked Apple with Nonfat Milk
♦Oatmeal Pancakes with Orange Slices♦
Sugar-free Boysenberry Syrup or Preserves

Oatmeal Pancakes with Orange Slices ⓠ

Yield: 15 3-inch pancakes (3 pancakes = 1 serving)

These pancakes are a low-cholesterol quadruple header—the 1%-fat buttermilk and egg whites (no yolks) keep cholesterol intake down, and the rolled oats and oat bran help to reduce serum cholesterol levels. Best of all, they taste delicious.

1 cup rolled oats
1¾ cups buttermilk, strained, or nonfat evaporated milk
2 tablespoons frozen unsweetened apple juice concentrate
¾ cup unbleached white or whole wheat flour
2 tablespoons oat bran

1 teaspoon baking powder
½ teaspoon baking soda
½ teaspoon cinnamon
2 extra-large egg whites, slightly beaten

1 orange, sliced, for garnish

1. Combine the rolled oats, buttermilk, and apple juice concentrate and let stand for 5 minutes.
2. Mix together the flour, oat bran, baking powder, baking soda, and cinnamon and stir into the oat mixture.
3. Add the egg whites, mix with a spoon, and let rest 10 minutes. If batter is too thick, thin with a little more buttermilk.
4. Cook on a hot nonstick griddle or skillet coated with butter-flavored nonstick spray, using ¼ cup batter for each pancake.

To Serve: Place the hot pancakes on warm plates, garnish each plate with an orange slice, and serve with boysenberry syrup or preserves.

NOTE: Leftover batter may be refrigerated and used the next day.

Per serving: 3 mg cholesterol, 0.7 gm saturated fat, 2.2 gm total fat, 1.9 gm fiber, 258 mg sodium, 188 calories

Cantaloupe Wedges
◆Sourdough French Toast◆
with
Sugar-free Applesauce

Sourdough French Toast Ⓠ

Yield: 16 half pieces (4 halves = 1 serving)

In a restaurant, French toast usually means *egg bread*, dipped in an *egg batter* and *deep-fried in oil* (that usually contains palm or coconut oil that is highly saturated) or *fried in butter*. At home, instead of the usual bread, I use either sourdough or whole wheat bread (sometimes raisin bread), and the batter has no whole eggs, oil, or sugar added. I then grill the French toast in a nonstick pan—with tasty results!

4 extra-large egg whites
1 cup nonfat milk, nonfat evaporated milk, or fresh orange juice
3 tablespoons unsweetened frozen
   apple or pineapple juice
   concentrate

2 teaspoons pure vanilla extract
8 ¾-inch slices sourdough or whole
   wheat bread, halved

1. In a shallow pan, beat all ingredients except the bread with a fork.
2. Soak both sides of the bread in the mixture.
3. Heat a nonstick skillet coated with nonstick spray over medium-high heat; add four slices of the bread. Reduce to medium heat and brown both sides. Repeat this process.
4. Remove the toast to a heated serving dish and serve with applesauce.

Variation: Instead of applesauce, serve with fresh berries.

Per serving: 4 mg cholesterol, 0.34 gm saturated fat, 1.6 gm total fat, 4.2 gm fiber, 344 mg sodium, 182 calories

Sliced Fresh Fruit with Yogurt
♦Oat Bran Waffles♦
with
Sugar-free Boysenberry Syrup

Oat Bran Waffles ⓠ

Yield: 8 waffles (½ waffle = 1 serving)

This is a delicious way to incorporate more oat bran (soluble fiber) into your daily diet as a breakfast or brunch dish or a snack. The oat bran gives the waffles a crispy texture. It is one of my family's favorites.

1¼ cups oat bran
¾ cup unbleached white flour or
whole wheat flour
1½ teaspoons baking powder
½ teaspoon baking soda
4 extra-large egg whites, slightly
beaten, or 2 extra-large egg
whites plus ¼ cup egg substitute

2 cups nonfat evaporated milk
1½ tablespoons canola oil
2 tablespoons frozen unsweetened
apple juice concentrate
(optional)

1. Coat a waffle iron with butter-flavored nonstick spray and preheat.
2. Combine the oat bran, flour, baking powder, and baking soda in a mixing bowl.
3. Combine the eggs, milk, and oil and add to the dry ingredients. Blend thoroughly.
4. Pour about 1 cup waffle mixture into the preheated waffle iron, close lid, and bake according to manufacturer's directions, or until steaming stops. Repeat until all batter is used.

To Serve: Place on a warm plate and serve with sugar-free boysenberry syrup.

Variation: Instead of boysenberry syrup, serve with sugar-free pancake syrup and/or fresh fruit with yogurt.

To Freeze for Future Use: Place single browned waffle squares in an airtight plastic bag and freeze. To use, remove from plastic bag and heat in toaster oven or toaster.

Per serving: 3 mg cholesterol, 0.24 gm saturated fat, 4.1 gm total fat, 3.7 gm fiber, 212 mg sodium, 174 calories

Brunches

Stewed Prunes and Apricots with Lime Wedges
♦Scrambled Eggs with Zucchini, Red Onion, and Red Pepper♦
Sliced Tomatoes, Green Onions, and Carrot Sticks
Toasted Whole Wheat or Water Bagels with
Part-Skim Ricotta Cheese with Chives

Scrambled Eggs with Zucchini, Red Onion, and Red Pepper ⓠ

Serves: 8

If you are going to eat an egg occasionally, this dish is relatively low in cholesterol. One serving has less cholesterol than a 4-ounce serving of chicken! Of course, you can eliminate the yolks and cholesterol entirely by using only egg whites.

½ tablespoon extra-virgin olive oil
1 medium red onion, thinly sliced and separated
2 large garlic cloves, minced
2 small zucchini, thinly sliced
½ red pepper, seeded and cut into ¼-inch strips

2 whole eggs
8 extra-large egg whites
Freshly ground black pepper
2 teaspoons salt-free vegetable seasoning
2 tablespoons shredded part-skim mozzarella cheese

1. Place the oil in a nonstick skillet; add the onion and garlic and stir-fry 3 to 5 minutes.
2. Add the zucchini and red pepper and sauté for 3 minutes.
3. Place the eggs and egg whites in a large bowl, add the pepper and vegetable seasoning, and beat thoroughly with a whisk until foamy. Add the sautéed vegetable mixture and mozzarella cheese and blend well.
4. Heat a nonstick skillet and pour in the egg mixture. Cook over medium heat, lifting the cooked portion as it sets.
5. Serve immediately, while hot.

Per serving: 50 mg cholesterol, 0.77 gm saturated fat, 2.9 gm total fat, 0.4 gm fiber, 75 mg sodium, 63 calories

Assorted Melon Slices
◆No-Cholesterol Frittata◆
Broccoli Crown Vinaigrette (page 299)
Toasted High-Fiber Whole Grain Onion Bread (page 329)
Blueberry Bran Muffins (page 107) with Sugar-free Jam

No-Cholesterol Frittata ⓠ

Serves: 6 (1 slice = 1 serving)

This frittata contains no egg yolks, yet its taste does not suffer. One serving of a traditional eight-egg frittata contains about 360 milligrams of cholesterol. One serving of *this* frittata has *no* cholesterol.

1 large onion, peeled, halved, and thinly sliced
1 large clove garlic, chopped
2 teaspoons extra-virgin olive oil
8 mushrooms, cleaned and sliced
1 small zucchini, thinly sliced
2 green onions, thinly sliced
6 slim asparagus spears, cut into 1-inch pieces (set tips aside for garnish)

1 8-ounce carton egg substitute
8 extra-large egg whites
1 Italian plum tomato, diced
¼ teaspoon white pepper
4 teaspoons thinly shredded Parmesan cheese

Cherry tomatoes and asparagus tips, for garnish

1. Sauté the onions and garlic with oil in a nonstick skillet for about 5 minutes or until wilted and *lightly* browned.
2. Add the mushrooms, zucchini, green onions, and asparagus and sauté 3 minutes.
3. Beat the egg substitute and egg whites with a whisk or fork until well blended. Add the tomato, white pepper, 2 teaspoons of the cheese, and the sautéed vegetables. Blend well.
4. Pour the egg mixture into a hot nonstick skillet that has been coated with nonstick spray and arrange the asparagus tips in spokelike fashion on top.
5. Cook over medium heat until bottom is lightly browned.
6. Sprinkle with the remaining 2 teaspoons cheese and place under a preheated broiler until the top is golden brown and the mixture is set.
7. Loosen the bottom and slide onto a warm serving plate.

To Serve: Cut into six pie-shaped pieces and surround with cherry tomatoes.

Per serving: 0 mg cholesterol, 0.52 gm saturated fat, 3.1 gm total fat, 0.8 gm fiber, 142 mg sodium, 96 calories

Assorted Melon Chunks with Grapes
♦No-Yolk Spinach and Mushroom Omelette♦
Wild Rice Bran Muffins (page 108)

No-Yolk Spinach
and Mushroom Omelette ℚ

Serves: 1

In this omelette, I combine egg substitute with egg whites. The egg whites give it a much better flavor than egg substitute alone.

3 mushrooms, cleaned and sliced
1 clove garlic, minced
1 teaspoon extra-virgin olive oil
2 cups fresh spinach leaves, washed and drained, stems removed
1 teaspoon lemon juice

½ cup egg substitute, or 3 extra-large egg whites
2 extra-large egg whites
⅛ teaspoon white pepper
⅛ teaspoon salt, optional

1 green onion, sliced, for garnish

1. Sauté the mushrooms and garlic in olive oil in an 8-inch nonstick skillet for 2 to 3 minutes. Add the spinach and lemon juice and sauté until the spinach is wilted. Remove mixture from pan and keep warm.
2. Beat the egg substitute, egg whites, and pepper with a fork until foamy.
3. Add egg mixture to a heated nonstick skillet that has been coated with butter-flavored nonstick spray.
4. When the egg mixture becomes firm around the edges, lift and push the solid portion toward the center of the pan, allowing the uncooked portion to flow to the edge of the pan and set.
5. When slightly brown on the bottom, turn the egg over to just dry.
6. Flip the egg onto a warm plate, place the drained spinach and mushroom mixture on one half, and fold over the other half.
To Serve: Sprinkle with green onion and serve immediately.

Per serving: 1 mg cholesterol, 1.53 gm saturated fat, 9.1 gm total fat, 4.9 gm fiber, 429 mg sodium, 226 calories

Mixed Fresh Berries
Poached Salmon with Lemon Wedge
♦Assorted Vegetable Platter with Dill Sauce♦
Whole Wheat or Water Bagels with Part-Skim Ricotta Cheese
Assorted Oat Bran Muffins (page 107) with Sugar-free Jam

Assorted Vegetable Platter with Dill Sauce ⓠ

Serves: 4

For a change, it's nice to have your serving of fish for brunch. Of course, this means your food choices for the remaining meals that day should exclude any animal protein: Select from soups, salads, vegetables, whole grains, or pastas in the Mix and Match section or a vegetarian dish from this section.

12 fresh or frozen asparagus spears, steamed
8 radishes
1 10-ounce package frozen baby corn, steamed, or 1 16-ounce can baby corn, drained
4 green onions
2 large beefsteak tomatoes, sliced
1 red onion, very thinly sliced

½ cup very fresh part-skim ricotta cheese
1 small Kirby pickling cucumber, finely chopped
1 teaspoon dried fines herbes
1 teaspoon red wine vinegar
⅛ teaspoon white pepper
2 tablespoons chopped fresh dill, or 2 teaspoons dried dill and 2 tablespoons chopped fresh parsley

Dill Sauce:
½ cup nonfat plain yogurt

3 sprigs fresh dill for garnish

1. Place bundles of asparagus in spokelike fashion in center of 12- to 14-inch platter. Leave room in the center for a bowl of sauce.
2. Fill spaces between spokes with radishes, corn, and green onions.
3. Arrange the tomatoes and onions around perimeter of the platter.
4. *To make the dill sauce:* Process all the ingredients but the dill sprigs in a food processor or blender.
5. Pour the sauce into a footed bowl, garnish with sprigs of fresh dill, and place the bowl in the center of the platter.

Per serving: 10 mg cholesterol, 1.61 gm saturated fat, 3 gm total fat, 3.5 gm fiber, 77 mg sodium, 154 calories

Sliced Fresh Pineapple with Blueberries
◆Salmon Hash◆
Sliced Tomato   Steamed Broccoli
Pumpernickel Bread
Assorted Oat Bran Muffins (page 107) with Sugar-free Jam

Salmon Hash

Serves: 4 to 6

This delicious dish will allow you to reap the health benefits of Omega-3 fatty acids in the salmon.

1 small onion, chopped
1 small green pepper, seeded and chopped
1 small red pepper, seeded and chopped, or 2 ounces canned chopped pimiento, drained
2 teaspoons canola or cold-pressed safflower oil
4 cups diced cooked potato or left-over baked potato
Freshly ground pepper
8 ounces poached fresh salmon, drained (save liquid) and flaked, or 1 7½-ounce can red salmon, drained (save juice), skin and bones removed, and flaked
1 tablespoon fresh lemon juice
⅔ cup defatted sodium-reduced chicken or vegetable broth combined with drained salmon liquid to equal 1 cup
2 teaspoons grated Parmesan cheese mixed with ½ cup dry breadcrumbs

Chopped fresh dill or parsley for garnish

1. Sauté the onion and peppers in oil in a nonstick skillet until limp.
2. Add the potatoes, sprinkle with pepper, and heat briefly.
3. Sprinkle the flaked salmon with lemon juice, add to the potato mixture with the salmon juice and broth, and mix lightly with a fork.
4. Coat a 10-inch glass pie plate with butter-flavored nonstick spray and heat in 400° oven for 3 minutes.
5. Spoon the salmon mixture into the heated pie plate. Sprinkle with the breadcrumb mixture and bake in the upper third of a preheated 400° oven for 20 to 25 minutes or until browned.
6. Sprinkle with fresh dill before serving.

Variation: Poach 4 extra-large egg whites and place them on top of the hash before sprinkling with dill.

Per serving: 31 mg cholesterol, 0.96 gm saturated fat, 5.6 gm total fat, 1.2 gm fiber, 156 mg sodium, 295 calories

Melon Wedges with Fresh Strawberries
♦Pasta and Vegetable Casserole♦
Four-Leaf Salad with Black-Eyed Peas
Whole Grain Toast

Pasta and Vegetable Casserole

Serves: 8

1 shallot, minced
2 large cloves garlic, minced
½ red pepper, seeded and diced
½ green pepper, seeded and diced
1 small zucchini, thinly sliced
1 tablespoon extra-virgin olive oil
½ pound fresh mushrooms, cleaned and sliced
½ pound eggplant, diced
2 small zucchini, diced
½ cup sliced green onion
5 extra-large egg whites, lightly beaten
1 cup 1%-fat cottage cheese, blended in food processor until smooth

1 12-ounce can nonfat evaporated milk
½ cup nonfat milk
Freshly ground pepper
2 teaspoons salt-free vegetable seasoning
8 ounces whole wheat linguini, cooked *al dente**
1 tablespoon grated Parmesan cheese

2 Italian plum tomatoes, diced, and 2 green onions, sliced, for garnish

1. Sauté the shallot, garlic, peppers, and zucchini slices in oil in a nonstick skillet for 2 to 3 minutes. Remove zucchini slices.

2. Add the mushrooms and sauté 3 minutes. Add the eggplant, diced zucchini, and green onion and sauté 3 minutes.

3. Combine the egg whites, cottage cheese, milk, pepper, and vegetable seasoning. Mix until smooth.

4. Add the sauce and the cooked pasta to the vegetable mixture. Blend thoroughly.

5. Spoon the mixture into a 3-quart rectangular casserole coated with nonstick spray. Arrange a line of zucchini slices down the center of the casserole and sprinkle with Parmesan cheese. Bake in a preheated 350° oven for 40 to 45 minutes.

To Serve: Sprinkle with tomatoes and green onions as garnish.

Per serving: 3 mg cholesterol, 0.65 gm saturated fat, 3.9 gm total fat, 3.6 gm fiber, 113 mg sodium, 220 calories

* Whole wheat linguini must be slightly undercooked because it will continue cooking in the casserole when baking in the oven.

◆Cheese Bread Soufflé◆
Marinated Three-Bean Salad
Assorted Oat Bran Muffins (page 107)
Poached Pears with Strawberry Sauce (page 316)

Cheese Bread Soufflé

Serves: 6

6 slices day-old whole wheat or
    sourdough bread
4 leeks, white part only, washed
    and sliced
2 teaspoons extra-virgin olive oil
5 extra-large egg whites
2 cups nonfat milk
1 teaspoon Worcestershire sauce
¼ teaspoon ground white pepper
2 teaspoons salt-free vegetable
    seasoning

1 teaspoon dried thyme, crushed,
    or 1 tablespoon fresh thyme,
    chopped
½ teaspoon garlic powder
3 ounces shredded part-skim moz-
    zarella cheese
1 cup 1%-fat cottage cheese,
    blended in food processor until
    smooth
1 tablespoon Parmesan cheese
    (optional)

1. Cut the bread into 1-inch cubes and place in a 2-quart rectangular baking dish sprayed with butter-flavored nonstick spray.

2. In a nonstick skillet, sauté the leeks 3 to 5 minutes or until wilted in olive oil.

3. Beat the egg whites with a whisk until foamy. Add the milk, Worcestershire sauce, pepper, seasoning, thyme, and garlic powder and combine.

4. Add the cheeses and leeks to the egg white mixture; blend well with a fork.

5. Pour the mixture over the bread and let stand 20 minutes. If desired, sprinkle with Parmesan cheese.

6. Bake in a preheated 325° oven for 35 to 40 minutes.

Per serving: 16 mg cholesterol, 2.4 gm saturated fat, 5.1 gm total fat, 2.5 gm fiber,
300 mg sodium, 195 calories

♦Bristol Farms Chicken and Rice Jardinière♦
Sliced Tomato and Cucumbers with Nonfat Plain Yogurt
Whole Wheat Baguette
Assorted Sliced Fruits

Bristol Farms Chicken and Rice Jardinière

Serves: 10 (1 cup = 1 serving)

This warm salad entrée provides a flavorful change for brunch. Linda Hammerschmidt, Executive Chef of the Catering Service at Bristol Farms Market in Pasadena has been kind enough to share this healthful recipe.

1¼ cups defatted chicken broth
1 shallot, minced
1 tablespoon dried rosemary, crushed
½ teaspoon dried thyme, crushed
½ cup chopped fresh Italian parsley
2 pounds skinless, boneless, defatted chicken breast, cut into 1-inch cubes
½ cup dry white wine or vermouth
1 cup slivered carrots
½ pound yellow squash, cut ¼-inch slices

1 cup green onion, sliced diagonally
1½ cups washed brown rice or converted white rice, cooked in 3 cups defatted chicken broth until tender, and kept warm
½ cup washed wild rice, cooked in about 2 cups defatted chicken broth until tender, and drained
⅔ cup fresh lemon juice or to taste
2 teaspoons Hungarian paprika

Chopped fresh Italian parsley for garnish

1. Place the chicken broth, shallot, rosemary, thyme, and parsley in a nonstick skillet, bring to a boil, and reduce by half.
2. Add the chicken cubes and sauté until transparent. Remove the chicken and juices and keep warm.
3. Add the wine to the skillet and deglaze. Add the carrots, squash, and green onion. Stir-fry 3 minutes or until barely tender.
4. Combine the warm rice, chicken with juices, and vegetables. Add the lemon juice and paprika; toss to blend. Taste and adjust seasonings. Serve warm.

To Serve: Mound on a platter and sprinkle with parsley.

Per serving: 57 mg cholesterol, 1.89 gm saturated fat, 6.7 gm total fat, 1.5 gm fiber, 61 mg sodium, 308 calories

Papaya with Fresh Raspberries
♦Breakfast Burritos♦
Cafe con Leche

Breakfast Burritos ℚ

Yield: 2 burritos (1 burrito = 1 serving)

Instead of huevos rancheros for breakfast or brunch, how about a breakfast burrito? Its beans are high in cholesterol-lowering soluble fiber and it contains *no* saturated fat or cholesterol.

2 corn tortillas
⅔ cup canned *vegetarian* refried beans, or cooked pinto and/or red beans (page 129) mashed with 1 teaspoon canola oil
1 tablespoon chopped red onion
¼ cup chopped fresh Italian plum tomatoes

¼ cup Fresh Salsa (page 183) or salt-free canned salsa

2 tablespoons plain nonfat yogurt and 1 tablespoon chopped fresh cilantro, for garnish

1. Microwave the tortillas between two sheets of slightly dampened white paper towels on high for about 15 seconds.
2. Mix the beans with the onion and tomatoes. Divide the mixture between the two tortillas.
3. Fold each tortilla to enclose filling. Place on a microwave-safe serving dish and spoon salsa over each burrito.
4. Microwave on high for about 15 seconds.
To Serve: Top each burrito with yogurt and sprinkle with chopped cilantro.

Per serving: 0 mg cholesterol, 0.33 gm saturated fat, 3.8 gm total fat, 2.9 gm fiber, 69 mg sodium, 187 calories

---

One of my clients chose this for a vegetarian dinner. He started with a salad, then had burritos with fresh broccoli, and fruit for dessert. By the way, he lowered his cholesterol from 239 to 166 in just six weeks—a 30 percent reduction!

Lunch or Supper

The menus for lunch and supper can be used interchangeably since both are meals that require less preparation time than the main meal and tend to be rather simple—generally some combination of soup, salad, sandwich, or casserole.

Remember, if you choose to eat animal protein for lunch or supper, select a pasta dish or vegetarian entrée for your main meal—or at the very most, a dish that uses only a minimal amount of fish, poultry, or meat—an Oriental stir-fry recipe, for example, or a casserole in which animal protein is used just as a flavoring ingredient.

I have included basic directions for preparing dried peas, beans, lentils and grains since they are frequently used in many of the dishes.

Recipes

Some Basics:
Chicken Broth in the Microwave
Basic directions for preparing dried peas, beans, and lentils
Basic directions for preparing grains

Soups:
Old-Fashioned Bean Soup
Hearty Eight-Bean Soup
Daal (Indian Yellow Split Pea Soup)
Mother's Potato, Leek, and Carrot Soup
Country-Fresh Vegetable Soup
Hot Cabbage Borscht

Sandwiches:
Tuna Melt
Open-Faced Eggplant and Mozzarella Sandwiches
Stuffed French Toast
Salmon Burgers
Healthy Burgers
Spicy Pita Roll
Pesto, Cheese, and Tomato Sandwich
Chopped Vegetable Spread

Salads:
Michelle's Chinese Tuna Salad
Pasta and Vegetable Salad with Fresh Salsa
Turkey Chef's Salad with Green Goddess Dressing (2 recipes)
Pasta Salad with Seafood
Warm New Potato and Green Bean Salad
Layered Luncheon Salad
Marinated Mixed Vegetable Salad
Fresh Vegetable Salad with Japanese Noodles
Italian Bean and Tuna Salad

Casseroles and One-Dish Meals:
Pastel de Calabacitas (Zucchini Pie) with Salsa
Beef Skillet Supper
Spinach Frittata
Chili Beans
Black Bean Chili

Some Basics

Making Chicken Broth

Chicken broth is essential for low-cholesterol cooking. Not only is it the basis for many soups and sauces, but it is an essential cooking liquid in a great variety of dishes, can be used instead of fat in sautéeing and stir-frying, and is also used as a seasoning.

In the recipes in this book, when I call for chicken broth, I mean either defatted, sodium-reduced homemade broth or defatted canned broth. Canned sodium-reduced chicken broth is more costly than the regular. I would like to think that this is because the food processor has to use better quality ingredients to develop flavor in salt-free broth than in salted. To defat canned broth, chill first and then spoon the globules off the top.

Making your own broth is really not a chore, especially if you prepare it in a microwave oven. You can make it with chicken parts, and freeze the meat for future sandwiches, salads, or casserole dishes. Or you can buy chicken wings, necks, and backs to use as the basis of your stock. Collect leftover bones and scraps in your freezer and add them to the stockpot as well.

It is extremely important to defat your homemade broth before using or storing. The easiest way is to chill the broth in the refrigerator or freezer: the fat will rise to the top and solidify and then can easily be removed with a spoon. If you need to use the broth right away, you can either pour the fat off with a special pitcher called a "gravy strain" or pour the broth through a large paper coffee filter.

The basic recipe for microwave (with instructions for stove top preparation) appears on the next page.

Chicken Broth
in the Microwave Ⓜ

Yield: about 8 cups (1 cup = 1 serving)

3-pound chicken (remove giblets), cut into 8 pieces, fat removed, or 3 pounds halved chicken breasts
1 medium onion, coarsely chopped
2 stalks celery with leaves, coarsely chopped
2 carrots, coarsely chopped, or 4 whole green onions

1 whole leek, washed and sliced
1 parsnip, quartered
Bouquet garni (parsley, bay leaf, fresh dill, peppercorns, and thyme)
1 cup cold water
7 additional cups cold water
Kosher salt (optional)*
White pepper to taste

1. Place the first eight ingredients in a large 5-quart microwave casserole, cover, and cook on high for 5 minutes.

2. Stir, add the 7 cups cold water, cover, and continue cooking on high for 40 minutes. Stir once during cooking.

3. Remove chicken, cool slightly; skin, bone, and refrigerate or freeze the meat for future use.

4. Strain, chill, and defat the broth. It can be stored in the refrigerator for several days (no more than 3), or frozen for future use.

Variation: To make Chicken in the Pot, skin the chicken but leave the bones in. Return the chicken and vegetables to the strained and defatted broth and add a bit of salt and white pepper and cooked rice.

To Freeze Broth: Divide it among several small airtight containers (1 cup is a useful size), leaving an inch of head space for expansion, and cover tightly.

On the Stove: Place chicken and 8 cups cold water in a 5-quart saucepan. Bring to a boil; remove scum. Add remaining ingredients and simmer for 2 hours, partially covered. Proceed as in steps 3 and 4 above.

Per serving: 0 mg cholesterol, 0 gm saturated fat, 0 gm total fat, 0 gm fiber, 5 mg sodium, 34 calories

* Remember, each teaspoon of salt contains about 2000 milligrams of sodium.

Basic Directions for
Preparing Dried Peas, Beans, and Lentils

Rich in protein, iron, complex carbohydrates, and other nutrients, dried beans were one of the earliest foods to be cultivated. You can cut way down on the preparation time if you use a microwave.

In the Microwave:

To Soak:

1. Place 1 to 2 cups beans in 2-quart casserole with 2 cups water.
2. Cover tightly with microwave plastic wrap and cook on high for 15 minutes. Remove from oven.
3. Let stand 5 minutes, uncover, and add 2 cups *hot* water.
4. Recover and let stand 1 hour. Drain.

To Cook:

1. Place presoaked beans in a microwave casserole.
2. Add 4 cups water, cover tightly with 2 sheets microwave plastic wrap, and microwave on high for about 35 minutes.
3. Let stand 20 minutes before using.

NOTE: Navy beans and white beans require 40 minutes of cooking time and 30 minutes of standing time.

On the Stove:

To Soak:

1. Rinse beans in cold water thoroughly and drain. (Small lima beans, lentils, or split peas do not require soaking before cooking.)
2. Bring about 2½ quarts water to a boil in a 5-quart casserole or saucepan, add the beans, and bring to a boil. Remove from heat, cover, and let stand 1 hour.
3. Pour off the soaking water and drain.*

To Cook:

1. Return the beans to the soaking pan and cover with water two to three times their volume.
2. Bring to a boil; reduce to a slow simmer, and cook until just tender, referring to the chart on page 130 for cooking time.

NOTE: Cool, drain, and freeze those beans not to be used in a few days in airtight plastic bags.

---

* It seems that flatulence is less of a problem if soaking water is not used to cook beans.

COOKING TIMES FOR DRIED PEAS, BEANS, AND LENTILS*

1 LB. DRIED BEANS	COOKING TIME AFTER SOAKING
Soybeans	3 to 3½ hours
Chick-peas (garbanzo beans)	2 to 3 hours
Black beans or turtle beans	1½ to 2 hours
Kidney or pinto beans	1½ to 2 hours
Black-eyed peas	1½ hours
Northern beans or navy beans	1½ hours
Lima beans (do not soak)	45 minutes to 1½ hours
Split peas or lentils (do not soak)	45 minutes

* 1⅓ cups uncooked dried beans, or 8 ounces = about 3 cups cooked beans.

COOKING TIMES AND MEASURES FOR GRAINS*

GRAIN	NUMBER OF SERVINGS	UNCOOKED AMOUNT	AMOUNT OF WATER	COOKING TIME	COOKED AMOUNT
Barley	4	½ cup (4 oz)	3 cups	50–60 minutes	2 cups
Buckwheat	4	⅔ cup (4 oz)	1⅓ cups	8–10 minutes	2 cups
Bulgur	4	¾ cup (4 oz)	1½ cups	15–20 minutes	2 cups
Brown rice	4	⅔ cup (4 oz)	1⅔ cups	50 minutes	2 cups
Converted rice	4	⅔ cup (4 oz)	1⅔ cups	20 minutes	2 cups
Quinoa†	5	1 cup (6 oz)	2 cups	10–15 minutes	2½ cups

* These weights and measures are approximate.
† A millet-like seed, with twice the protein of rice.

Basic Directions for Preparing Grains

Cereal grains today comprise the principal source of food for most of the world's people. Rice is the main food for half of the world's population. Grains are easily digested and rich in complex carbohydrates, B complex vitamins, and iron. They are low in fat and of course contain no cholesterol.

1. Rinse the uncooked grain in cold water; drain.

2. Refer to the chart opposite for the amount of cooking water needed. Bring the water to a boil in a saucepan over medium-high heat.

3. Add the grain and stir. Return to a boil, reduce heat to low, cover, and cook according to the time on the chart.

4. Fluff with a fork and serve or use in your favorite recipe. (If grain is not soft enough, add a small amount of hot water and cook a little longer. If liquid remains and grain is tender, remove lid and continue cooking until liquid evaporates.)

Soups

◆Old-Fashioned Bean Soup◆
Corn Bread
Apple and Pear Waldorf Salad

Old-Fashioned Bean Soup

Yield: about 30 cups (1¼ cups = 1 serving)

This hearty soup is newly recognized for its cholesterol-lowering qualities. Half a cup of cooked navy beans contains about 3.8 grams of soluble fiber. This soup freezes beautifully and tastes even better the next day.

1 pound navy beans, washed
1 pound soup bones
1 large onion, peeled and quartered
5 quarts cold water
2 whole carrots, sliced in 1-inch pieces
3 stalks celery with leaves, sliced in 1-inch pieces

Bouquet garni*
1 cup chopped onion
1 tablespoon extra-virgin olive oil
½ cup unbleached white flour
1 16-ounce can diced tomatoes with juice
1 16-ounce package frozen mixed vegetables (carrots, corn, beans, and peas)

1. Cover the beans with cold water, bring to a boil, cover, and let stand 1 to 2 hours off heat (or microwave on high for about 10 minutes and let stand). Drain.

2. Place the bones and quartered onion on a shallow baking pan and brown about 15 minutes in the upper third of a preheated 450° oven.

3. Cover the beans with 5 quarts cold water. Add the drained bones and onions, and the carrots, celery, and bouquet garni. Bring to a boil and simmer 1½ hours or until beans are tender.

4. In a nonstick skillet, sauté 1 cup chopped onion in 1 tablespoon extra-virgin oil until barely colored.

5. Add the flour and brown lightly. Stir the flour mixture into the soup and cook 30 minutes. Remove bones.

6. Add the tomatoes and frozen vegetables and cook 15 minutes more. Taste and adjust seasonings.

Per serving: 0 mg cholesterol, 0.17 gm saturated fat, 1 gm total fat, 2.8 gm fiber, 49 mg sodium, 99 calories

* *Bouquet garni:* Fresh parsley, thyme, bay leaf, and red pepper flakes tied in cheesecloth.

♦Hearty Eight-Bean Soup♦
Mixed Green and Red Cabbage Salad
Sourdough Rolls
Seasonal Fresh Fruit

Hearty Eight-Bean Soup

Yield: 16 cups (1½ cups = 1 serving as an entrée)

This soup is a meal in itself; all these beans and legumes are high in soluble fiber, which helps to lower cholesterol. Since the recipe makes a lot, freeze some for future use. Don't be concerned about having to buy all these different beans, for they can be stored dry or prepared and frozen for use in casseroles, salads, and other soups.

⅓ cup each dried lima beans, black beans, white Northern beans, kidney beans, and black-eyed peas
½ cup each lentils, barley, yellow split peas, and green split peas
3 quarts cold water
1 large onion, chopped
3 large carrots, chopped

3 stalks celery with leaves, chopped
1 bay leaf
Few grains crushed red pepper
1 28-ounce can Italian plum tomatoes with juice, chopped
2 tablespoons fresh basil, chopped, or 1½ teaspoons dried basil, crushed

1. Wash all the dried beans and lentils thoroughly. Place in a large bowl, cover with cold water, and soak 1 to 2 hours or overnight, or soak and cook in microwave (page 129).
2. Place the drained beans and all the other ingredients except the basil in an 8-quart saucepan.
3. Bring to a boil over high heat; reduce to simmer, and cook for 2½ to 3 hours. Add the basil just before serving; taste and adjust seasonings.

Variation: Any combination of your favorite beans or lentils may be used in preparing this soup as long as you have a total of about 3⅔ cups of the mixture.

Per serving: 0 mg cholesterol, 0.19 gm saturated fat, 1 gm total fat, 7.5 gm fiber, 151 mg sodium, 260 calories

♦Daal♦
Marinated Cucumber and Yogurt Salad
Whole Wheat Pita Bread
Lemon-Lime Yogurt Pie (page 236)

Daal (Indian Yellow Split Pea Soup)

Yield: 18 cups (1¼ cups = 1 serving)

The Indian seasonings give this hearty yellow split pea soup a very different taste from the traditional green split pea soup that we're accustomed to. Once again, you can freeze the leftovers for future use.

1 pound yellow split peas, soaked in cold water overnight (or microwaved on high for 10 minutes) and drained
4 large cloves garlic, chopped
3 celery stalks, chopped
4 carrots, chopped
3 onions, chopped
3 leeks, chopped
1½ red peppers, seeded and chopped
1½ green peppers, seeded and chopped
2 tablespoons extra-virgin olive oil or canola oil

1 16-ounce can peeled, diced tomatoes
1⅓ tablespoons turmeric
1⅓ tablespoons cumin
1 teaspoon coriander
¼ teaspoon freshly ground nutmeg
3½ quarts defatted sodium-reduced chicken stock or water
Juice of 2 limes

Chopped fresh cilantro, for garnish

1. In a large soup pot, sauté the garlic, celery, carrots, onion, leeks, and peppers in the oil for 2 to 3 minutes.
2. Add the tomatoes, spices, and yellow split peas, and sauté for 2 minutes.
3. Add the chicken broth and lime juice. Bring to a boil and simmer for about 1 hour, uncovered.
4. Remove from the heat, taste, and adjust seasonings as needed.
To Serve: Spoon into heated soup bowls and garnish with chopped cilantro.

Per serving: 0 mg cholesterol, 0.73 gm saturated fat, 4 gm total fat, 2.9 gm fiber, 75 mg sodium, 184 calories

◆Mother's Potato, Leek, and Carrot Soup◆
Salmon Salad Sandwich
Crudités: Radish, Green Pepper, Carrot, and Cucumber
Seasonal Fresh Fruit

Mother's Potato, Leek, and Carrot Soup

Yield: 10 cups (1 cup = 1 serving)

The flavor of this vegetarian soup is enhanced by a roux (a browned mixture of just a bit of polyunsaturated fat and flour). It adds a wonderful nutty flavor to the soup as well as thickening it just a bit. This soup keeps well in the refrigerator for a few days and may also be frozen for future use.

1 tablespoon canola or cold-pressed safflower oil
¼ cup unbleached white flour
1 small onion, grated
¼ teaspoon white pepper
7 cups cold water
2 teaspoons salt-free vegetable seasoning
Freshly ground pepper
1 teaspoon dried thyme, crushed

1 bay leaf
1 leek, washed and white part sliced, green part left whole
3 carrots, peeled and sliced
2 celery stalks with leaves, sliced
1 pound russet potatoes, peeled and cubed
1 6-ounce sweet potato, peeled and cubed
1 teaspoon Kosher salt (optional)

1. *To make the roux:* Place the oil in a nonstick 4-quart saucepan, add the flour and stir over medium heat until golden brown.
2. Add the grated onion and pepper and cook 2 to 3 minutes, stirring constantly.
3. Add the water, vegetable seasoning, pepper, thyme, and bay leaf and bring to a boil.
4. Add the remaining ingredients, stir, and bring to a boil.
5. Reduce to a simmer and cook 45 to 60 minutes or until vegetables are tender. Remove green part of leek and bay leaf. Taste and adjust seasonings.
To Serve: Spoon soup into heated bowls and serve immediately.

Per serving: 0 mg cholesterol, 0.18 gm saturated fat, 1.6 gm total fat, 1.4 gm fiber, 254 mg sodium, 97 calories

◆Country-Fresh Vegetable Soup◆
Whole Grain Bread
Baked Apple with Nonfat Milk

Country-Fresh Vegetable Soup

Yield: 20 cups (1½ cups = 1 serving as an entrée)

This soup doesn't freeze well, but it keeps in the refrigerator for 3 or 4 days.

1 large onion, finely chopped
3 large cloves garlic, minced
2 teaspoons extra-virgin olive oil
¾ cup barley, washed
1 cup small white beans plus 1 cup water, cooked in microwave on high 8 minutes (or cover with cold water, soak 1 to 2 hours or overnight and drain)
3½ quarts water or defatted sodium-reduced chicken broth
1 28-ounce can diced tomatoes with juice
3 tablespoons chopped fresh thyme, or 1 teaspoon dried thyme, crushed
1 teaspoon crushed red pepper flakes
2 bay leaves

1 parsnip, diced
1 turnip, diced
6 carrots, cut in ¾-inch slices
6 stalks celery, cut in ½-inch slices
1 leek (white part only), thinly sliced
2 zucchini, cut in ¼-inch slices
2 summer squash, cut in ¼-inch slices
2 crookneck squash, cut in ¼-inch slices
1 russet potato, diced
1 cup coarsely shredded cabbage
1½ cups fresh or frozen peas
6 fresh mushrooms, cut in ¼-inch slices
½ cup chopped fresh Italian parsley

1. Sauté the onion and garlic in oil in an 8-quart saucepan for 3 minutes.
2. Add the barley, beans, water, tomatoes, thyme, pepper flakes, and bay leaves. Bring to a boil, reduce heat, and simmer 45 minutes, stirring occasionally.
3. Add the parsnips, turnips, carrots, celery, and leek and simmer 20 minutes.
4. Add the squashes, potato, cabbage, peas, and mushrooms and simmer 20 minutes. Add the parsley and heat 5 minutes.

Per serving: 0 mg cholesterol, 0.26 gm saturated fat, 1.5 gm total fat, 6.2 gm fiber, 139 mg sodium, 175 calories

♦Hot Cabbage Borscht♦
with
Nonfat Plain Yogurt and Freshly Chopped Dill
Hearty Whole Grain Bread
Fresh Fruit Cup

Hot Cabbage Borscht Ⓠ Ⓜ

Yield: 16 to 18 cups (1½ cups = 1 serving as an entrée)

1 tablespoon canola oil
2 large onions, coarsely chopped
5 large cloves garlic, minced
4 leeks (white part only), washed and thinly sliced
3 stalks celery with leaves, coarsely chopped
½ cup chopped Italian parsley
2 cups canned diced tomatoes
3 cups crushed Italian plum tomatoes, in puree
1 1-pound head green cabbage, cut into 1-inch cubes
1 pound beef bones (visible fat removed), cut into 1-inch slices (optional)

2½ quarts cold water
2 bay leaves
2 teaspoons dried thyme, crushed
½ teaspoon dried oregano
1 teaspoon crushed red pepper flakes
2 cups fresh green beans, cut into 2-inch pieces (optional)

Nonfat plain yogurt and chopped fresh dill, for garnish

1. In a 6-quart nonstick saucepan, heat the oil; add the onions and garlic and sauté until wilted. Add the leek and cook 5 minutes, stirring occasionally.
2. Add the celery, parsley, tomatoes, cabbage, bones, water, bay leaves, thyme, oregano, and pepper flakes. Bring to a boil, reduce heat, cover, and simmer 1½ hours.
3. Add the green beans and continue to simmer for 1 hour more.
4. Remove the bones before serving.
To Serve: Place the soup in heated bowls and garnish with a dollop of nonfat plain yogurt and a sprinkle of dill.

Variation: Sometimes I brown 3 tablespoons of unbleached white flour in a 6-inch nonstick skillet and add it to soup with the water. This gives the soup a wonderful flavor, rather like a roux without fat.

Per serving: 0 mg cholesterol, 0.23 gm saturated fat, 1.9 gm total fat, 2.6 gm fiber, 219 mg sodium, 81 calories

Sandwiches

Low-Sodium V-8 Juice
♦Tuna Melt♦
Crudités: Radishes, Carrot and Zucchini Sticks
Seasonal Fresh Fruit

Tuna Melt Ⓠ

Yield: 4 sandwiches (1 sandwich = 1 serving)

1 6½-ounce can white-meat tuna in water, drained
1 teaspoon sweet pickle relish, drained
1 green onion, sliced
¼ green pepper, finely diced
3 tablespoons nonfat plain yogurt and 2 tablespoons finely shredded part-skim mozzarella cheese mixed with 1 teaspoon dried dill
8 slices whole grain bread (rye, whole wheat, or pumpernickel)

1. Flake the tuna in a bowl with a fork.
2. Add the relish, onion, pepper, and yogurt mixture and blend thoroughly.
3. Divide the tuna mixture onto four slices of bread, spread evenly, and top with remaining four slices of bread.
4. Place the sandwiches on a heated, nonstick griddle or skillet sprayed with butter-flavored nonstick spray and heat until browned.
5. Turn over and brown the remaining side.

To Serve: Cut the hot sandwiches in half and place on a serving plate garnished with fresh vegetable crudités.

Per serving: 24 mg cholesterol, 0.92 gm saturated fat, 3.2 gm total fat, 4.4 gm fiber, 457 mg sodium, 195 calories

Last-Minute Soup (page 268)
♦Open-Faced Eggplant and Mozzarella Sandwiches♦
Carrot and Pepper Sticks
Fresh Apples

Open-Faced Eggplant and Mozzarella Sandwiches Ⓠ Ⓜ

Yield: 4 sandwiches (1 sandwich = 1 serving)

1 1-pound eggplant, peeled and sliced about ¾ inch thick (8 slices)

1–2 large, ripe tomatoes, cut into ½-inch-thick slices (8 slices)

1 teaspoon dried Italian herb blend, crushed

⅓ cup shredded part-skim mozzarella cheese

8 slices Garlic Toast (page 328) or whole grain toast spread with Pesto Sauce (page 244)

Fresh basil sprigs, for garnish

1. Arrange the eggplant in a single layer in a microwave dish. Cover tightly with microwave plastic wrap and microwave on high for about 2 minutes.

2. Remove the plastic and drain juice.

3. Top each eggplant slice with one slice of tomato, sprinkle with the herbs and cheese, and microwave on medium for 1 minute to just melt the cheese.

4. Place one eggplant slice on each piece of garlic toast, garnish with basil, and serve immediately.

Per serving: 7 mg cholesterol, 2.24 gm saturated fat, 8.5 gm total fat, 3 gm fiber, 343 mg sodium, 270 calories

Tomato Bouillon (page 92)
♦Stuffed French Toast♦
Date Waldorf Salad (page 281)

Stuffed French Toast ⓠ

Yield: 4 sandwiches (1 sandwich = 1 serving)

8 slices whole wheat bread

Filling:
**⅔ cup 1%-fat cottage cheese
  blended until smooth**
**1 tablespoon sugar-free apricot or
  peach preserves**
1 teaspoon grated lemon zest

Batter:
⅔ cup nonfat evaporated milk
**2 extra-large egg whites, slightly
  beaten**
**2 tablespoons unsweetened frozen
  apple juice concentrate**
1 teaspoon pure vanilla extract

1. Blend the filling ingredients.
2. Spread the mixture onto four slices of bread and top with the remaining slices.
3. Combine the batter ingredients in shallow pan.
4. Dip the sandwiches into batter, coating both sides.
5. Brown sandwiches on both sides in a nonstick skillet or griddle sprayed with butter-flavored nonstick spray.
6. Cut the browned sandwich in half and serve immediately.

Per serving: 7 mg cholesterol, 0.3 gm saturated fat, 1.8 gm total fat, 4.3 gm fiber, 328 mg sodium, 202 calories

Red and Green Cabbage, Carrot, and Raisin Salad
♦Salmon Burgers with Tartar Sauce♦
on Whole Wheat Buns
Lettuce and Tomato Slices
Pears

Salmon Burgers ⓠ

Yield: 4 burgers (1 burger with about 2 ounces cooked fish = 1 serving)

This recipe provides a way to serve a fast food without the red meat or frying usually associated with fast foods. It also gives you one of your three fish meals for the week.

¼ cup dry breadcrumbs for coating patties

4 whole wheat buns, or English muffins, toasted

Burgers:

1 7½-ounce can salmon, skinned, boned, drained, and flaked

2 whole green onions, thinly sliced

2 tablespoons chopped celery

5 ounces frozen chopped spinach, thawed and squeezed dry

1 teaspoon Worcestershire sauce

½ cup nonfat plain yogurt

1 tablespoon chopped fresh dill

2 tablespoons lemon juice

Freshly ground pepper

¼ cup dry breadcrumbs mixed with 3 tablespoons oat bran

Tartar Sauce:

¼ cup nonfat plain yogurt

1 teaspoon grated onion

1 teaspoon sweet pickle relish

1. Place all the burger ingredients in a mixing bowl, blend thoroughly with a fork, and shape into four patties.
2. Coat the patties on both sides with breadcrumbs.
3. Place the patties on a nonstick baking sheet and bake in the upper third of a preheated 425° oven for 10 minutes; turn and bake 10 minutes more.
4. *To make the tartar sauce,* combine the three ingredients thoroughly.

To Serve: Place each warm burger on a toasted whole wheat bun and top with a dollop of tartar sauce. Serve with leaves of romaine and slices of tomato.

Per serving: 23 mg cholesterol, 1.01 gm saturated fat, 4.3 gm total fat, 2.3 gm fiber, 292 mg sodium, 181 calories

Country-Fresh Vegetable Soup (page 136)
♦Healthy Burgers on Whole Wheat Buns♦
Tomato Slices and Romaine Lettuce
Cole Slaw
Fresh Fruit

Healthy Burgers ⓠ

Yield: 5 burgers (1 burger with about 2½ ounces cooked turkey = 1 serving)

Actually, this menu is hearty enough to be used for dinner. When using ground turkey, it's better to buy a raw turkey breast and have it skinned, boned, and ground. Three ounces of skinned turkey breast contains less than 2 grams of saturated fat, whereas a 3-ounce patty of packaged already-ground turkey may contain as much as 9 grams.

1 pound ground raw turkey breast
1 extra-large egg white
½ small onion, chopped
½ green pepper, seeded and
   chopped
1 carrot, grated
½ cup sodium-reduced vegetable
   juice, or ½ cup defatted sodium-
   reduced chicken broth, with 1
   teaspoon fresh lemon juice

½ cup dry breadcrumbs
1 tablespoon Worcestershire sauce
¼ teaspoon dried thyme, crushed
Freshly ground pepper
5 whole wheat buns, toasted

   1. Combine all the burger ingredients in a mixing bowl, stirring with a fork. Do not overmix.
   2. Shape into five round patties.
   3. Heat a nonstick skillet coated with nonstick spray and grill patties 3 to 4 minutes on each side. Serve immediately.

To Serve: Place each warm burger on a toasted whole wheat bun with a slice of tomato, romaine lettuce, and Dijon mustard or Chopped Vegetable Spread (page 145). Grilled or raw red onion slices may be added.

NOTE: Unused patties may be wrapped in plastic wrap, placed in freezer bags, and frozen for future use. To serve, microwave the frozen patty in microwave plastic wrap on high for about 3 minutes, turning over halfway through cooking. If you do not have a microwave, defrost and reheat in a hot nonstick skillet.

Per serving: 47 mg cholesterol, 0.81 gm saturated fat, 2.7 gm total fat, 0.4 gm fiber, 160 mg sodium, 163 calories

Mixed Green Salad
♦Spicy Pita Rolls♦
Fresh Fruit

Spicy Pita Rolls ⓠ

Yield: 5 pita rolls (1 roll=1 serving)

Whether you are six or sixty, you'll love these easy, piquant pita rolls. Leftovers can be frozen for future use.

½ pound ground raw turkey breast (see page 142)
1 teaspoon spicy salt-free vegetable seasoning
About ⅓ cup green chili salsa
1 clove garlic, minced
2 whole green onions, sliced

5 6-inch whole wheat pita breads, warmed in the oven or microwave
4 tablespoons diced green chilis
¼ cup shredded part-skim mozzarella cheese

1. Crumble the turkey into a hot nonstick skillet coated with nonstick spray and sprinkle with the vegetable seasoning.
2. Cook several minutes over medium high heat, stirring constantly. If it sticks, add a bit of the salsa. Add the garlic and stir.
3. Add the green onion and salsa and stir.
4. Place one fifth of the turkey mixture on a warmed pita, layer with 1 scant tablespoon chilis and 1 scant tablespoon mozzarella cheese. Roll up tightly and serve.

NOTE: Wrap leftovers tightly in plastic wrap and refrigerate or freeze. To serve frozen rolls, heat on high in microwave for about 2 minutes.

Per serving: 26 mg cholesterol, 1.04 gm saturated fat, 3 gm total fat, 4.8 gm fiber, 145 mg sodium, 199 calories

Vegetarian Lentil Soup (page 84)
♦Pesto, Cheese, and Tomato Sandwich♦
Crudités: Green Pepper, Radish, and Carrot
Fresh Pear

Pesto, Cheese,
and Tomato Sandwich ⓠ

Serves: 1

In Italy, this is called a pannino, but to Americans it's just a sandwich. It's always a popular lunch or quick supper.

1 5-inch section sourdough or
  whole wheat baguette, halved
1 tablespoon Pesto Sauce (page
  244) or Chopped Vegetable
  Spread (page 145)

2 tablespoons shredded part-skim
  mozzarella cheese
1 fresh Italian plum tomato, sliced
4 fresh basil leaves

1. Spread pesto on both halves of the baguette.
2. Layer the cheese, tomato, and basil on half of the baguette; top with remaining half.
To Serve: Cut the sandwich in half and garnish with crudités.

Per serving: 10 mg cholesterol, 1.85 gm saturated fat, 3.8 gm total fat, 2.2 gm fiber, 380 mg sodium, 231 calories

Spicy Tomato Soup (page 85)
◆Chopped Vegetable Spread◆
on
Whole Grain Bread
Carrot Sticks
Seasonal Fresh Fruit

Chopped Vegetable Spread ⓠ

Yield: about 2½ cups (1 tablespoon = 1 serving)

This vegetable spread is great to use by itself on a sandwich, or instead of mayonnaise or mustard on a turkey or chicken sandwich. It also blends well with steamed rice. Try 1½ cups of vegetable spread mixed with 2 cups hot cooked rice.

2 medium fresh mushrooms
3 canned artichoke hearts, well
  drained and quartered
½ small red pepper, cored,
  seeded, and quartered
1 small zucchini, quartered
1 small summer squash, quartered
1 carrot, quartered
2 to 3 pepperocini peppers,
  drained

8 fresh basil leaves and 1 teaspoon
  extra-virgin olive oil, or 1 tablespoon Pesto Sauce (page 244) or
  commercial pesto sauce
1 Italian plum tomato, quartered
  (optional)

1. Place all the ingredients in the food processor and process only until finely chopped. *Do not puree.*

2. Pack into a container and cover tightly. This will keep nicely in the refrigerator for five to six days. Drain and stir before each use.

Per serving: 0 mg cholesterol, 0.02 gm saturated fat, 0.1 gm total fat, 0.2 gm fiber,
6 mg sodium, 7 calories

<u>*Salads*</u>

◆Michelle's Chinese Tuna Salad◆
with
Romaine and Tomatoes
Whole Wheat Baguette
Mandarin Oranges and Fresh Pineapple

Michelle's Chinese Tuna Salad ⓠ

Serves: 2

Just a bit of Oriental sesame oil gives this tuna salad a different twist.

1 6½-ounce can white-meat tuna in water, drained and flaked	4 romaine leaves
3 tablespoons chopped chives	4 cherry tomatoes, halved
Freshly ground pepper	2 teaspoons toasted sesame seeds (optional)
¼ to ½ teaspoon Oriental sesame oil	

1. Place the tuna and chives in a bowl. Sprinkle with ground pepper and oil.
2. Blend thoroughly with a fork.
To Serve: Arrange the tuna on romaine leaves, garnish with cherry tomato halves, and sprinkle with sesame seeds.

Per serving: 36 mg cholesterol, 0.46 gm saturated fat, 2.7 gm total fat, 0.8 gm fiber, 335 mg sodium, 155 calories

---

Hint: If you buy an oil-free dressing, you may add 1 tablespoon extra-virgin olive oil to the entire bottle for a more interesting flavor.

◆Pasta and Vegetable Salad with Fresh Salsa◆
Whole Wheat Roll
Sliced Peaches with Nonfat Vanilla Yogurt

Pasta and Vegetable Salad with Fresh Salsa ⓠ

Serves: 4 (as an entrée)

This pasta salad may be served cold or heated briefly in a microwave oven or saucepan before serving.

8 ounces fusilli, cooked *al dente* and well drained

½ red pepper, seeded and thinly sliced

½ green pepper, seeded and thinly sliced

1 cup frozen peas, defrosted

1 cup canned black beans or kidney beans, drained and rinsed, or 1 cup cooked beans (page 129)

1½ cups fresh broccoli, chopped and steamed, or 1 10-ounce package frozen broccoli flowerets, defrosted

2 cups Fresh Salsa (page 183) or canned salt-free salsa

1 tablespoon grated Parmesan cheese

1. Combine the pasta with the peppers, peas, beans, and broccoli. Toss lightly.
2. Add the salsa and mix with two forks.
3. Sprinkle with the cheese, toss lightly, and chill in refrigerator for 20 minutes before serving.

Variation: Shredded leftover bits of roast turkey or chicken may be added as additional protein for a heartier salad.

Per serving: 1 mg cholesterol, 0.43 gm saturated fat, 1.8 gm total fat, 6 gm fiber, 86 mg sodium, 304 calories
Per 1 tablespoon serving of salsa: 0 mg cholesterol, 0.004 gm saturated fat, 0.03 gm total fat, 1 gm fiber, 1.4 mg sodium, 4 calories

◆Turkey Chef's Salad
with
Green Goddess Dressing◆
Whole Wheat Bread Sticks
Fresh Fruit

Turkey Chef's Salad with Green Goddess Dressing Ⓟ

Serves: 4

8 cups torn or chopped, mixed salad greens: romaine, butter lettuce, endive, red-leaf lettuce, radicchio, or red cabbage
½ pound cooked turkey breast, cut into thin strips
1 small green pepper, seeded and cut into thin strips
1 small red pepper, seeded and cut into thin strips

½ cup Green Goddess Dressing (page 149; save the rest of the dressing for a salad to be served in the next few days)

Halved cherry tomatoes, sliced beets, radishes, and cucumber and carrot strips, for garnish.

1. Place the greens, turkey, and peppers in a large salad bowl.
2. Add the salad dressing and toss lightly with two forks.
3. Arrange the desired garnishes on top of salad in the bowl and serve immediately.

Variations: Arrange the greens, turkey, peppers, and garnishes on individual salad plates and serve the dressing on the side.

You may prefer to use Russian Dressing (page 262) or low-calorie vinaigrette dressing instead of Green Goddess.

Per serving: 41 mg cholesterol, 0.82 gm saturated fat, 3.2 gm total fat, 1.3 gm fiber, 86 mg sodium, 137 calories

Green Goddess Dressing ℚ

Yield: about 1¼ cups (1 tablespoon = 1 serving)

1 tablespoon light-style mayonnaise, or 2 tablespoons nonfat
dried milk

1 cup 1%-fat buttermilk, strained,
or nonfat plain yogurt

1 clove garlic, minced

1 tablespoon chopped fresh tarragon, or 1 teaspoon dried tarragon, crushed

2 tablespoons chopped fresh
parsley

1 tablespoon fresh lemon juice

½ teaspoon Dijon mustard

Pinch of white pepper

2 tablespoons mashed ripe avocado
(optional)

1. Stir the mayonnaise in a small bowl until smooth. Add the buttermilk
gradually while mixing.

2. Add the remaining ingredients and blend thoroughly.

3. Place in a tightly covered container and store in the refrigerator until
ready to use. It will keep for several weeks.

Per serving: 1 mg cholesterol, 0.09 gm saturated fat, 0.5 gm total fat, 0 gm fiber,
19 mg sodium, 10 calories

◆Pasta Salad with Seafood◆
Whole Wheat Rolls
Assorted Grapes

Pasta Salad with Seafood Ⓠ

Serves: 6

The complex carbohydrate supplied by the pasta and vegetables in this salad means you can use a smaller amount of seafood, limiting your intake of animal protein and cholesterol.

3 cups cooked penne or fusilli, cooked *al dente* and well drained

8 ounces cooked bay shrimp

8 ounces scallops, poached in ⅓ cup white wine until opaque

½ green pepper, seeded and diced

½ red pepper, seeded and diced

1 cup sliced celery

1 cup unpeeled diced English cucumber

1 large carrot, shredded

1 cup frozen petit peas, defrosted under cold running water

3 fresh plum tomatoes, diced

8 cups mixed shredded romaine and red cabbage

¾ cup low-calorie oil-free vinaigrette dressing mixed with 1 tablespoon raspberry vinegar, 1 teaspoon extra-virgin olive oil, and remaining poaching liquid, or Green Goddess Dressing (page 149)

1. In a salad bowl, combine all the ingredients except the romaine and cabbage and the dressing. Sprinkle with freshly ground pepper and toss lightly.

2. Drizzle with salad dressing and toss lightly to combine.

3. Refrigerate 30 minutes or longer before serving.

To Serve: Arrange the shredded cabbage and romaine on a large serving platter, mound the pasta and seafood mixture on top.

NOTE: If you can find vegetable pasta made without egg yolks, it makes an even more attractive presentation.

Per serving: 70 mg cholesterol, 0.28 gm saturated fat, 1.8 gm total fat, 3.6 gm fiber, 395 mg sodium, 243 calories

♦Warm New Potato and Green Bean Salad♦
Sliced Turkey Breast
Pumpernickel Bread
Crudités: Carrots, Green Pepper, Cucumber,
Radishes, and Tomato
Watermelon

Warm New Potato and Green Bean Salad Ⓠ Ⓜ

Serves: 6 to 8

2 pounds unpeeled small red new
   potatoes, quartered
4 cloves garlic, chopped
2 tablespoons extra-virgin olive oil
1 small red onion or mild-flavored
   white onion thinly sliced or
   chopped
3 tablespoons dry white wine
2 tablespoons defatted sodium-
   reduced chicken broth

1 tablespoon Worcestershire sauce
2 teaspoons each Dijon and coarse-
   grain mustard
¼ cup chopped fresh parsley
1 tablespoon chopped fresh thyme
   or 1 teaspoon dried thyme
½ pound fresh green beans, cut
   into 2-inch lengths and steamed

1. Microwave the potatoes, garlic, and 1 tablespoon of oil for 5 minutes on high in a shallow baking dish covered with microwave plastic wrap. Add onions, stir, cover and microwave on high for 5 to 6 minutes.

2. While the potatoes are cooking, combine the remaining tablespoon of oil, wine, broth, Worcestershire sauce, mustard, parsley, and thyme in a small jar. Shake well.

3. Place the warm potatoes, garlic, and onion in a large bowl, add the beans, sprinkle with the salad dressing, and toss gently so that liquid may be absorbed.

To Cook on Stove:

1. Steam whole potatoes and quarter them.

2. Sauté garlic and onions in oil for 2 to 3 minutes, then proceed as in Step 2 above.

Per serving: 0 mg cholesterol, 0.71 gm saturated fat, 5 gm total fat, 1.6 gm fiber, 59 mg sodium, 205 calories

Spicy Gazpacho with Croutons (page 256)
◆Layered Luncheon Salad◆
Whole Wheat Rolls
Papaya with Blueberries

Layered Luncheon Salad ⓠ

Serves: 6

This is a lovely salad that can be prepared hours ahead of time and just topped with its salad dressing so that it does not wilt. It makes a great dish for a buffet or to take to a potluck supper.

4 cups shredded romaine and red leaf lettuce

1 cup canned kidney beans, drained and rinsed, or 1 cup cooked beans (page 129)

1 cup canned corn

1 cup peeled, diced jicama, red radishes, or water chestnuts

1 cup defrosted frozen peas

¼ cup finely chopped red onion

3 chopped, hard-cooked, extra-large egg whites (*no yolks*)

1 cup thinly sliced celery

3 tablespoons chopped red pepper or pimiento

6 halved cherry tomatoes and 1 tablespoon chopped fresh thyme or parsley, for garnish

Dressing:

½ cup nonfat plain yogurt

1 tablespoon light-style mayonnaise

1 tablespoon salt-free tomato sauce

2 teaspoons sweet relish, drained

⅛ teaspoon white pepper

1. Place the shredded lettuce on the bottom of a 3-quart glass soufflé dish or salad bowl and sprinkle separate layers of beans, corn, jicama, peas, red onion, egg whites, celery, and red pepper or pimiento over the top.

2. Mix together the dressing ingredients and spread salad dressing mixture on top of salad.

3. Garnish with tomato halves and thyme and chill in refrigerator until serving time.

To Serve: Gently toss salad until mixture is coated lightly with dressing.

NOTE: Jicama is a brown-skinned tuberous root vegetable with crisp white flesh. It is best served raw as a crudité or in salads.

Per serving: 1 mg cholesterol, 0.11 gm saturated fat, 1.4 gm total fat, 3.1 gm fiber, 132 mg sodium, 134 calories

◆Marinated Mixed Vegetable Salad◆
Oysters or Clams on the Half-Shell with
Cocktail Sauce and/or Lime
Whole Grain Crackers
Cantaloupe

Marinated Mixed Vegetable Salad Ⓠ Ⓜ

Serves: 4

An easy supper for a warm summer evening.

4 cups mixed fresh vegetables (for
  example: cauliflower, broccoli,
  carrots, corn, and red peppers),
  coarsely chopped
1 cup canned kidney beans,
  drained and rinsed, or cooked
  kidney beans (page 129)
⅓ cup low-calorie oil-free vinaigrette dressing

1 teaspoon Dijon mustard
1 teaspoon finely chopped shallot
  or red onion
½ teaspoon dried fines herbes
1 teaspoon balsamic vinegar
4 cups shredded salad greens

1. Place the vegetables in a microwave-safe bowl, cover, and cook on high for 3 minutes or steam until just crisp. Add the beans and combine.
2. Mix the salad dressing with remaining ingredients and pour over vegetable-bean mixture. Toss lightly and let marinate 20 minutes or overnight in the refrigerator before serving.

To Serve: Place 1 cup of greens on each plate and top with ¼ of marinated vegetable mixture.

Per serving: 0 mg cholesterol, 0.11 gm saturated fat, 0.8 gm total fat, 4.1 gm fiber, 260 mg sodium, 114 calories

Spicy Tomato Soup (page 85)
♦Fresh Vegetable Salad with Japanese Noodles♦
Brown Rice Cakes with Oat Bran
Apples

Fresh Vegetable Salad with Japanese Noodles ⓠ

Serves: 4 to 6

Most whole wheat pasta cannot be cooked *al dente*; the Japanese pasta called *soba*, is an exception.

4 stalks bok choy, thinly sliced
1 medium zucchini, thinly sliced
1 crookneck squash, coarsely shredded
1 small red pepper, seeded and thinly sliced
1 carrot, thinly sliced
1 cup diced eggplant
3 whole green onions, thinly sliced
6 ounces soba noodles, cooked *al dente*, drained, rinsed in cold water, and drained again

1 cup fresh or frozen snow peas, defrosted, washed and cut into lengthwise strips, for garnish

Dressing:
2 teaspoons Oriental sesame oil
⅓ cup defatted sodium-reduced chicken broth or vegetable broth
2 cloves garlic, minced
½ teaspoon fresh ginger, peeled and grated
1 teaspoon Chinese Five Spice seasoning
2 teaspoons sodium-reduced soy sauce
2 tablespoons frozen unsweetened apple juice concentrate
¼ cup brown rice or apple cider vinegar
1 tablespoon rice wine or sherry
2 teaspoons Dijon mustard

1. Place the first seven ingredients in a salad bowl; toss lightly to combine.
2. Mix the dressing ingredients together, drizzle over the vegetables, and toss lightly.
3. Let stand 15 minutes at room temperature; then add the pasta and toss.

To Serve: Mound the mixture on a serving plate and sprinkle with snow pea strips. Serve at room temperature.

Per serving: 0 mg cholesterol, 0.71 gm saturated fat, 4.9 gm total fat, 6.9 gm fiber, 143 mg sodium, 257 calories

◆Italian Bean and Tuna Salad◆
Carrot Sticks
Whole Wheat Baguette
Kiwi and Strawberries

Italian Bean and
Tuna Salad ℚ

Serves: 4

2 cups cooked cannellini or kidney beans (page 129), or 1 16-ounce can, drained and rinsed
1 small red onion, finely chopped
1 tablespoon red wine or balsamic vinegar
2 tablespoons low-calorie oil-free Italian dressing
2 teaspoons extra-virgin olive oil
1 tablespoon lemon juice
1 teaspoon Dijon mustard
1 garlic clove, minced

Freshly ground pepper
2 tablespoons chopped fresh basil or 2 teaspoons dried basil, crushed
¼ cup chopped fresh parsley
3 cups shredded romaine and radicchio
1 6½-ounce can white-meat tuna in water, drained and flaked

2 large carrots, cut into strips, for garnish

1. Place the beans and onion in a mixing bowl.

2. Combine the vinegar, dressing, oil, lemon juice, mustard, garlic, pepper, basil, and parsley. Sprinkle over beans and toss lightly. Marinate for 15 minutes at room temperature.

3. Place the romaine and radicchio on a serving dish. Arrange the tuna on top of greens. Spoon the beans over the tuna and garnish with carrot sticks.

Per serving: 18 mg cholesterol, 0.48 gm saturated fat, 3.3 gm total fat, 4.8 gm fiber, 268 mg sodium, 236 calories

<u>*Casseroles and One-Dish Meals*</u>

Mixed Green Salad with Pinto Beans
♦Pastel de Calabacitas with Salsa♦
Pumpernickel Garlic Toast (page 328)
Melon Slices

Pastel de Calabacitas (Zucchini Pie) with Salsa

Serves: 6 to 8

The original recipe, which came from Lillian, a student studying at the University of Mexico, used chayote squash instead of zucchini. After several translations, the following recipe has become a hit with my family.

2 teaspoons canola or corn oil
2 large onions, coarsely chopped
3 cloves garlic, minced
½ teaspoon dried oregano, or 2 teaspoons chopped fresh oregano
Freshly ground pepper
2 teaspoons salt-free vegetable seasoning
4 large zucchini, coarsely chopped
3 extra-large egg whites, slightly beaten
1 teaspoon dried dill, or 1 tablespoon chopped fresh dill
1 cup 1%-fat cottage cheese blended until smooth, or part-skim ricotta cheese

1 teaspoon baking powder
½ cup yellow cornmeal
2 tablespoons finely shredded part-skim mozzarella cheese
1 tablespoon finely shredded Parmesan cheese

2 tablespoons chopped fresh cilantro for garnish and warm Fresh Salsa (page 183) or salt-free canned salsa

1. Put the oil in a 10-inch nonstick skillet; add the onions and garlic. Sprinkle with oregano, pepper, and vegetable seasoning, and sauté until the onions are wilted.

2. Add the zucchini and stir-fry 3 minutes. Remove from heat.

3. Blend the egg whites, dill, cottage cheese, and baking powder in a blender or food processor. Add to the zucchini mixture and mix.

4. Add the cornmeal and mozzarella cheese to the zucchini mixture and blend.

5. Pour into a 10-inch glass pie plate or quiche pan coated with nonstick corn oil cooking spray. Sprinkle with 1 tablespoon Parmesan cheese.

6. Bake in a preheated 350° oven for 40 to 45 minutes or until golden brown. Cool slightly and cut into wedges.

To Serve: Sprinkle with chopped cilantro and serve warm with heated salsa.

Per serving: 15 mg cholesterol, 2.7 gm saturated fat, 5.9 gm total fat, 2.2 gm fiber, 157 mg sodium, 166 calories

Mixed Green Salad with Shredded Carrot
♦Beef Skillet Supper♦
Hearty Whole Wheat Bread
Cut Green Beans
Poached Pear (page 347)

Beef Skillet Supper ⓠ

Serves: 4 (2 ounces cooked beef = 1 serving)

This one-dish meal is easy to prepare and requires minimal clean-up afterward. While the skillet dish is cooking, you can prepare the salad and bake the apples in your microwave. I have used very lean beef (top round) as a seasoning: only 2 ounces per person.

¾ pound ground lean top round of beef, visible fat removed before grinding

1 large onion, chopped

2 large cloves garlic, minced

1 green pepper, cut into 1-inch chunks

1¾ cups water

1 16-ounce can sodium-reduced tomatoes in juice, chopped

3 tablespoons tomato paste

1 cup converted rice

⅓ cup seeded dark raisins

3 tablespoons frozen unsweetened apple juice concentrate

1 tablespoon red wine vinegar

½ teaspoon ground cinnamon

Freshly ground pepper

4 ½-inch-thick slices beefsteak tomato

2 teaspoons shredded Parmesan cheese

2 sliced green onions, for garnish

1. In a large nonstick or iron skillet, heat the beef until pink. Add the onions and garlic and sauté 5 minutes.

2. Add all the remaining ingredients except the tomato and Parmesan cheese, cover, and simmer 20 minutes or until the rice is tender and liquid absorbed.

3. Arrange the tomato slices on top of the mixture, sprinkle with Parmesan cheese, and place under the broiler a few minutes, until lightly browned.

4. Sprinkle with green onions and serve.

Per serving: 16 mg cholesterol, 0.58 gm saturated fat, 2.1 gm total fat, 2.5 gm fiber, 44 mg sodium, 326 calories

Confetti Corn Soup (page 266)
♦Spinach Frittata♦
Snow Peas and Carrots
Sliced Fresh Strawberries with Yogurt

Spinach Frittata ⓠ

Serves: 1

½ 10-ounce package frozen
  chopped spinach, defrosted and
  squeezed dry
2 green onions, thinly sliced
1 fresh Italian plum tomato, diced
1 teaspoon fresh thyme or Italian
  parsley, chopped
Freshly ground pepper
3 extra-large egg whites, slightly
  beaten with 1 tablespoon nonfat
  milk

1 teaspoon shredded Parmesan
  cheese
½ teaspoon extra-virgin olive oil
½ slice Pritikin whole wheat or rye
  bread, cut into ½-inch cubes

1. Place the drained spinach, onions, tomato, seasonings, egg white mixture, and cheese in a bowl and stir well with a fork.
2. Coat an 8-inch nonstick skillet with nonstick cooking spray. Add the olive oil and spread over bottom of skillet. Heat the skillet, sprinkle the cubed bread over the bottom of pan, and sauté on medium heat for 1 minute until lightly toasted.
3. Pour the egg mixture over the bread and smooth the mixture.
4. Cook over medium heat until bottom of frittata is lightly browned. Turn and cook until lightly browned on second side.

To Serve: Flip frittata, bread side up, onto a serving plate and serve hot.

Per serving: 1 mg cholesterol, 0.81 gm saturated fat, 3.9 gm total fat, 6.9 gm fiber, 361 mg sodium, 176 calories

◆Chili Beans◆
Brown Rice Pilaf
Zucchini, Corn, and Red Peppers
Fresh Fruit Compote (page 319)

Chili Beans Ⓠ Ⓜ

Serves: 12 as a side dish (½ cup = 1 serving) or 6 as an entrée (1 cup = 1 serving)

2 15-ounce cans kidney or pinto beans, drained and rinsed, or 4 cups cooked beans (page 129)
1 14-ounce can tomatoes, chopped
1 cup defatted sodium-reduced chicken broth
1 large onion, chopped
1 4-ounce can chopped green chilis, drained

½ teaspoon ground coriander
½ teaspoon garlic powder
1–2 tablespoons chili powder
Chopped Maui, Walla Walla, or Vidalia onion, as topping (optional)

1. Combine all the ingredients in a 3-quart saucepan; mix well.
2. Bring to a simmer, cover, and cook 30 to 40 minutes. (Or cover with microwave plastic wrap and microwave on high for 6 minutes; reduce to medium and cook 10 minutes, stirring occasionally.)
3. Taste and adjust seasonings before serving.

Per serving: 0 mg cholesterol, 0.24 gm saturated fat, 1.3 gm total fat, 5.6 gm fiber, 26 mg sodium, 190 calories

Chilled Mixed Green Salad
♦Black Bean Chili♦
Corn Tortillas
Kiwi Slices with Mango Puree

Black Bean Chili

Serves: 12 (1 cup = 1 serving)

1 large onion, chopped
6 garlic cloves, minced
2 large carrots, chopped
1 green pepper, seeded and
   chopped
1 red pepper, seeded and chopped
2 teaspoons canola oil
1 cup sliced fresh mushrooms
1 pound ground turkey breast (see
   page 142)
2 teaspoons dried oregano,
   crushed
1 teaspoon ground cumin

1 to 2 tablespoons chili powder
Freshly ground pepper
2 28-ounce cans crushed Italian
   plum tomatoes in puree
2 15-ounce cans black beans,
   drained and rinsed, or 4 cups
   cooked beans (page 129)
1 teaspoon hot red pepper sauce

Fresh Salsa (page 183) or salt-free
   canned salsa and nonfat plain
   yogurt, for garnish

1. Sauté the vegetables for 3 minutes in the oil in a large nonstick saucepan.
2. Add the mushrooms and cook 3 minutes.
3. Add the turkey and all the seasonings and sauté until the meat is no longer pink.
4. Add the remaining ingredients, stir, and simmer over low heat for 30 minutes, stirring occasionally. Taste and adjust seasonings.

To Serve: Serve hot in warm bowls; pass the nonfat plain yogurt and fresh salsa as toppings.

Per serving: 19 mg cholesterol, 0.56 gm saturated fat, 2.7 gm total fat, 5.5 gm fiber, 253 mg sodium, 193 calories

Dinner

In North America, dinner, the largest meal, is generally served at the end of the workday, usually between six and eight o'clock. In many European countries, however, the largest meal is served at noon, with enough time off to enjoy the food, relax, and even take a siesta. There is a real advantage to this custom, for when dinner is eaten at midday there is ample time to work off the added calories. Certainly, if you are concerned about weight control, it is better to eat a lighter meal in the evening, with the larger meal at noon. Although for most of us this is not always practical, when it is, I recommend it—for example, the "business lunch" can be your main meal instead of getting a double dose of calories by later having dinner at home.

In the low-cholesterol menus that follow, you will notice that many meals start with a salad or light soup. When you fill up a bit on these items, you cut your need for a large entrée. Most of the entrées offer small portions of animal protein with larger servings of vegetables and complex carbohydrates. Simple fresh fruit desserts round out the meals, with an occasional dessert that may be a bit more caloric but is still low in cholesterol and saturated fat.

Recipes

Fish:

Sea Bass with Microwaved Vegetables
Savory Sole Provençal
Red Snapper with Curry Sauce
Salmon Loaf with Creole Sauce
Brochettes of Scallops and Scrod
Fish Curry with Condiments
Microwave-Poached Whitefish with Mustard Sauce in Lime Shells
Salmon Mousse with Dill
Tuna Curry
Seafood Jambalaya
Capellini with Clams in White Wine
Salmon Tetrazzini
Turbot with Spanish Sauce
Piquant Broiled Mahimahi with Mango Salsa
Tuna-Stuffed Mushrooms with Creole Sauce
Stir-Fried Scallops with Garlic, Mushrooms, and Snow Peas
Grilled Red Snapper and Tomato
Broiled Swordfish Paillard with Fresh Salsa
Mediterranean Fish Soup
Salmon, Spinach, and Rice Casserole
Grilled Salmon Scallops on Mixed Greens with Assorted Salsas
Cajun Blackened Redfish
Flounder with Creole Sauce
Perfect Petrale Sole
Helen's Orange Roughy with a Vegetable Mélange

Poultry:

Chunky Turkey Chili
Turkey Roulades Stuffed with Asparagus, Carrots, and Red Pepper
Mini Turkey Loaves with Piquant Salsa
Stuffed Peppers in the Pot
Turkey Ragout
Italian Turkey Sausage
Bernice's Roast Turkey Thigh
Turkey Chow Mein
Roast Chicken with Tomatillo Sauce
Poached Chicken with Braised Endive and Carrots
Citrus Chicken Breasts

Poached Chicken Breasts
Peasant Chicken Stew
Rosemary Chicken Breasts with Garlic and Lemon
Grilled Chicken Breasts with Apples Calvados
Chicken Enchiladas
Hot Cajun Chicken and Black Bean Salad
Orange-Glazed Cornish Hens
Cornish Game Hens with Fresh Raspberry Glaze

Beef:

Shabu Sukiyaki

Pastas:

Fusilli with Broccoli Flowerets, Garlic, and Hot Red Pepper Flakes
Vegetarian Lasagna Rolls
Sweet Pepper Pasta
Linguini with Red Clam Sauce
Lillian's Quick and Easy Manicotti
Pasta Shells with Mushrooms
Fresh Tomato, Basil, and Mozzarella Pasta

Vegetarian Dishes:

Eggplant Lasagna
Peppered Potato Patties
Quick Minestrone
Vegetable Lo Mein
Celery Root, Red Cabbage, and Orange Salad
Angela's Herbed Squash Medley
Lentil Vegetable Salad with Low-Calorie Tarragon Vinaigrette
Vegetarian Paella
Stanford Moroccan Vegetable Stew with Couscous and Spicy Red
   Pepper Sauce (2 recipes)
Ratatouille

Desserts:

Papaya Ambrosia
Fresh Peach Scallop
Baked Alaska Pears
Lemon-Lime Yogurt Pie
Chocolate Zucchini Cupcakes

<u>*Fish*</u>

Hearts of Romaine with Mustard-Yogurt Dressing
♦Sea Bass with Microwaved Vegetables♦
Slim Asparagus Spears
Steamed Baby New Potatoes
Pineapple Wedges with Fresh Sliced Strawberries

Sea Bass with Microwaved Vegetables Ⓠ Ⓜ

Serves: 4 (3 ounces cooked fish = 1 serving)

If you are lucky enough to find Chilean sea bass, use it; otherwise, sea bass or cod will do. This is one of our family favorites.

1 pound fillet of sea bass or cod, cut into 4 equal pieces
2 teaspoons extra-virgin olive oil
2 small onions, thinly sliced
2 cups fresh mixed carrots, cauliflower, and zucchini, coarsely chopped, or ½ 16-ounce package frozen mixed vegetables
1 teaspoon dried thyme, crushed

Freshly ground pepper
1 tablespoon sodium-reduced soy sauce
Juice of ½ lemon
1 teaspoon salt-free vegetable seasoning
1 large plum tomato, diced
½ pound fresh pencil-thin asparagus

1. Wash the fish in cold water, drain, and dry with paper towel.
2. Place the olive oil and onion slices in a 9-inch microwave dish, cover with microwave plastic wrap, and cook on high for 2 minutes.
3. Add the vegetables, thyme, pepper, and soy sauce. Stir, cover, and microwave on high 1 minute.
4. Place the fish in a microwave dish and sprinkle with the lemon juice and vegetable seasoning.
5. Spoon the vegetable mixture over the fish, sprinkle with the diced tomato, and lay the asparagus on the center of the fish. Cover with microwave plastic wrap and cook on high for 5 minutes, or until fish flakes with fork.

Per serving: 58 mg cholesterol, 1.14 gm saturated fat, 5.9 gm total fat, 2.4 gm fiber, 210 mg sodium, 186 calories

Orange and Cabbage Slaw
♦Savory Sole Provençal♦
Brown and Wild Rice Pilaf
Steamed Carrots and Peas
Chocoholic's Chocolate Cake (page 340)

Savory Sole Provençal Ⓠ Ⓜ

Serves: 4 (4 ounces cooked fish = 1 serving)

Sole and flounder are low-fat, mild fishes that lend themselves beautifully to this savory sauce.

4 5-ounce fillets of sole or flounder
Juice of ½ lemon (about 2 table-
    spoons)
Salt-free vegetable seasoning and
    pepper
2 large cloves garlic, minced

½ green pepper, slivered
1 cup diced Italian plum tomatoes
1 teaspoon olive oil

6 tablespoons chopped green
    onion, for garnish

1. Season the fish with the lemon juice, vegetable seasoning, and pepper, and place in a shallow microwave dish.
2. Mix the garlic, green pepper, and tomato with the olive oil and spoon the mixture over the fish.
3. Cover tightly with microwave plastic wrap and microwave on high for 5 minutes, or until fish flakes with fork.

To Serve: Place the fish on a serving plate and top with sauce and vegetables. Sprinkle with green onions.

Per serving: 54 mg cholesterol, 0.49 gm saturated fat, 2.6 gm total fat, 0.6 gm fiber, 97 mg sodium, 132 calories

Chinese Cabbage and Sliced Radish Slaw
♦Red Snapper with Curry Sauce♦
Brown Rice (page 130)
Steamed Zucchini Spears and Red Peppers
Mango Slices with Blueberries

Red Snapper with Curry Sauce ⓠ

Serves: 4 (4 ounces cooked fish = 1 serving)

Red snapper is a low-fat, delicate-flavored fish that is made even more appealing with this flavorful sauce.

4 5-ounce red snapper fillets
Juice of ½ lemon
½ teaspoon onion powder
1 teaspoon salt-free vegetable
  seasoning

2 green onions, sliced, for garnish

Curry Sauce:
2 teaspoons minced shallot
1 teaspoon Oriental sesame oil
½ cup nonfat plain yogurt
1–2 teaspoons curry powder
½ ripe banana, mashed

1. Sprinkle the fish with the lemon juice and seasonings and broil 5 minutes or until the fish flakes.

2. *To make the curry sauce,* in a 6-inch nonstick skillet, sauté the shallots in sesame oil 2 to 3 minutes. Do not brown. Remove the skillet from the heat, add the yogurt, 1 teaspoon curry powder, and banana. Blend well and taste. If desired, add more curry.

To Serve: Place the fish on a warm platter, top with curry sauce, and sprinkle with green onion slices.

Per serving: 43 mg cholesterol, 0.55 gm saturated fat, 2.9 gm total fat, 0.6 gm fiber, 96 mg sodium, 157 calories

Mixed Greens with Kidney Beans
◆Salmon Loaf with Creole Sauce◆
Baked Potatoes
Steamed Broccoli Spears
Fresh Melon with Lime Wedge

Salmon Loaf with Creole Sauce

Serves: 8 (1 slice = 1 serving)

Using salmon, egg whites, whole grain bread, vegetables, and even oat bran, the cholesterol content is just 28 milligrams.

½ onion, quartered
1 carrot, quartered
1 small zucchini, quartered
½ green or red pepper, seeded and quartered
3 slices whole wheat bread, crumbled and soaked in ¾ cup nonfat milk
¼ cup oat bran
2 extra-large egg whites
3 tablespoons lemon juice
2 teaspoons Worcestershire sauce

1 15½-ounce can pink salmon, drained, bones and skin removed
2 teaspoons baking powder

Creole Sauce:
1 15-ounce can sodium-reduced stewed or diced tomatoes, chopped
¼ green pepper, slivered
¼ red pepper, slivered
1 tablespoon cornstarch

1. Process the onion, carrot, zucchini, and pepper in a food processor until minced.
2. Add the soaked bread, oat bran, egg whites, lemon juice, and Worcestershire sauce. Blend well.
3. Add the salmon and baking powder and process just until combined.
4. Coat a 9 × 5-inch glass loaf pan with nonstick spray, press the salmon mixture into the pan, and bake in a preheated 400° oven for 45 minutes or until loaf is firm and browned.
5. *To make the creole sauce*, combine all the ingredients and heat in a 1-quart saucepan until shiny, stirring constantly.
To Serve: Allow the loaf to stand 10 minutes, then unmold on a heated platter, top with Creole Sauce, and surround with broccoli spears.

Variation: Layer 1½ cups chopped mixed vegetables (broccoli, carrots, and peas) in the center of the loaf mixture and baked as directed.

Per serving: 28 mg cholesterol, 0.95 gm saturated fat, 4.1 gm total fat, 2.3 gm fiber, 175 mg sodium, 149 calories

Carrot and Onion Soup with Chervil (page 269)
♦Brochettes of Scallops and Scrod♦
Bulgur Wheat Pilaf (page 312)
Steamed Broccoli
Kiwi and Orange Slices

Brochettes of Scallops and Scrod

Serves: 4 (1 brochette, 3 ounces cooked fish = 1 serving)

Since scallops are one of the shellfish relatively low in cholesterol (see chart page 22), this delectable dish may be served and enjoyed without worry.

8 1-ounce sea scallops, rinsed
8 ounces scrod, sea bass, or halibut, cut into 8 equal pieces
½ small green pepper, seeded and quartered
½ small red pepper, seeded and quartered
4 small wedges mild onion
1 small zucchini, cut into 4 chunks
8 mushroom caps, cleaned
4 fresh water chestnuts, rinsed, scrubbed, and peeled or 4 canned whole water chestnuts (optional)

4 bamboo skewers (soaked for 10 minutes in cold water)

Marinade:

2 tablespoons sodium-reduced soy sauce
3 tablespoons frozen unsweetened pineapple juice concentrate
1 teaspoon grated fresh ginger
½ teaspoon finely minced garlic
¼ teaspoon Oriental sesame oil
Few grains crushed red pepper flakes
¼ cup plum wine or sake

1. Combine all marinade ingredients in a plastic bag.
2. Wash all seafood under cold tap water, dry thoroughly with paper towels, and add fish with the vegetables to the plastic bag. Marinate several hours in the refrigerator. Remove 30 minutes before preparing.
3. Thread a mushroom, a scallop, an onion, a zucchini chunk, scrod, red pepper, another scallop, green pepper, scrod, and another mushroom onto a skewer. Repeat on the remaining three skewers.
4. Broil or barbecue 3 to 4 inches from high heat for 5 to 7 minutes, turning frequently. Brush with the remaining marinade while cooking. Do not overcook; marinated fish cooks more rapidly.

To Serve: Arrange the brochettes on a bed of wheat pilaf and surround with broccoli spears.

Per serving: 45 mg cholesterol, 0.28 gm saturated fat, 2 gm total fat, 0.8 gm fiber, 125 mg sodium, 135 calories

Tomato Bouillon (page 92) with Whole Wheat Bread Sticks
◆Fish Curry with Condiments◆
in a Ring of Steamed Brown Rice (page 130)
Steamed Cauliflower and Broccoli Flowerets
Lemon Sorbet

Fish Curry with Condiments ⓠ

Serves: 6 (1¼ cups = 1 serving)

1½ pounds sea bass, cod, and/or
monkfish, cut into 1-inch cubes
Juice of ½ lemon
Freshly ground white pepper
2 teaspoons salt-free vegetable
seasoning
1 large onion, finely chopped
1 clove garlic, finely chopped
2 celery stalks, thinly sliced
3 tablespoons dry white wine
½ pound fresh mushrooms, sliced
½ green pepper, seeded and cut
into 1-inch squares
½ red pepper, seeded and cut into
1-inch squares

1½ teaspoons curry powder, or to
taste
1½ cups defatted sodium-reduced
chicken or vegetable broth
1½ tablespoons cornstarch mixed
with ¼ cup vegetable or chicken
broth

Condiments:
Sliced green onion, plumped dark
raisins,* toasted almond slivers,
unsweetened banana flakes, and
chutney

1. Sprinkle the fish with the lemon juice, white pepper, and vegetable seasoning.
2. Sauté the onion, garlic, and celery in the white wine until transparent.
3. Add the mushrooms, peppers, and curry; stir to combine. Add the broth and continue to cook about 5 minutes.
4. Add the seasoned fish, bring to a simmer, and cook 5 minutes.
5. Stir in the cornstarch mixture and simmer until the sauce is shiny and coats the spoon. Taste and adjust seasonings.

To Serve: Spoon a ring of steamed brown rice onto a warm serving platter. Place the curried fish in the center, surround with cauliflower and broccoli flowerets, and accompany with condiments served in small separate bowls.

Per serving: 49 mg cholesterol, 0.2 gm saturated fat, 1.2 gm total fat, 0.9 gm fiber, 79 mg sodium, 145 calories

* To plump raisins, place 1 cup of raisins in a single layer on a plate and sprinkle with 2 tablespoons of fresh orange juice or apple juice. Cover tightly with microwave plastic wrap and cook on high for 1 minute.

Watercress and Shredded Carrot Salad with
Low-Calorie Orange Vinaigrette Dressing
♦ Microwave-Poached Whitefish
with
Mustard Sauce in Lime Shells ♦
French-Cut Green Beans
Steamed Sliced Beets
Parslied New Potatoes
Strawberries Topped with Yogurt

Microwave-Poached Whitefish with Mustard Sauce in Lime Shells Ⓠ Ⓜ

Serves: 4 (4 ounces cooked fish = 1 serving)

4 5-ounce whitefish or salmon
  fillets, skinned
Freshly ground white pepper
½ teaspoon dried thyme, or 1½
  teaspoons fresh thyme
1 small onion, coarsely chopped
1 carrot, coarsely chopped
1 stalk celery with leaves, coarsely
  chopped

Few sprigs fresh parsley
½ cup dry white wine

Mustard Sauce:
½ cup nonfat plain yogurt
½ teaspoon fines herbes
1 teaspoon Dijon mustard
2 limes, halved and juiced (save
  the juice for future use)

1. Place the fish in a 9- or 10-inch round glass baking dish (a pie plate will do nicely) and sprinkle with the pepper, thyme, and vegetables.

2. Pour the wine over the fish. Cover tightly with microwave plastic wrap and microwave on high for 5 minutes. Let stand in poaching liquid for 2 to 3 minutes before serving.

3. *To make the mustard sauce,* combine the first three ingredients and mix thoroughly. Cut a slice from the bottom of each lime half (so that they do not tip) and spoon sauce into the half lime shells.

To Serve: Remove fish with vegetables from the liquid and place on a heated platter. Surround with bundles of green beans, steamed new potatoes, and sliced beets. Garnish with mustard-sauce-filled lime shells.

Per serving: 64 mg cholesterol, 0.21 gm saturated fat, 5.2 gm total fat, 0.8 gm fiber, 116 mg sodium, 115 calories

◆Salmon Mousse with Dill◆
Steamed Asparagus Spears
Pickled Beets   Hearts of Palm and Corn Salad
Pumpernickel Bread
Fresh Fruit Compote (page 319)

Salmon Mousse with Dill

Serves: 6 as an entrée or 16 as an appetizer

1 15½-ounce can salmon, skinned, boned, and drained (save juice), or 1¼-pound salmon fillets, poached (page 172), save the liquid
1½ tablespoons plain gelatin
⅔ cup hot, defatted, sodium-reduced chicken broth or vegetable broth
½ cup nonfat plain yogurt
3 tablespoons light-style mayonnaise
1 tablespoon sweet relish
1 tablespoon white horseradish, drained

1 tablespoon lemon juice
2 tablespoons tarragon vinegar
2 tablespoons grated onion
1 teaspoon Worcestershire sauce
½ cup diced red pepper, or 1 2-ounce jar chopped pimientos, drained
¼ cup finely diced celery

2 tablespoons chopped fresh dill
2 bunches fresh dill, for garnish
1 bunch Belgian endive, 2 tablespoons nonfat plain yogurt, and 1 tablespoon chopped black olives, for garnish (optional)

1. Flake the salmon in a mixing bowl with a fork.
2. Soften the gelatin in the salmon juice or ½ cup poaching liquid; add the hot chicken broth and stir until liquefied.
3. Add the remaining ingredients to the salmon and blend.
4. Add the liquefied gelatin and mix thoroughly.
5. Turn the salmon mixture into a 3-cup fish mold coated with nonstick spray, cover with plastic wrap, and chill in the refrigerator for 5 to 6 hours until firm, or overnight.

To Unmold and Serve: Loosen the edges of the mousse with a metal spatula, invert the mold on a platter, and shake gently until mousse is unmolded. Sprinkle with chopped fresh dill and garnish with bunches of fresh dill. Surround the mousse with leaves of Belgian endive that have a dollop of yogurt and a dab of chopped black olives if you like.

Per serving as an entrée: 43 mg cholesterol, 0.46 gm saturated fat, 5 gm total fat, 0.3 gm fiber, 146 mg sodium, 141 calories
Per serving as an appetizer: 16 mg cholesterol, 0.17 gm saturated fat, 1.9 gm total fat, 0.1 gm fiber, 55 mg sodium, 53 calories

Tomato and Cucumber Salad with
Herbed Yogurt Dressing
♦Tuna Curry♦
Steamed Quinoa (page 130)
Julienned Green Beans with Toasted Almonds
Sliced Bananas and Blueberries in Orange Juice

Tuna Curry ⓠ

Serves: 4 (1½ ounces cooked fish = 1 serving)

2 teaspoons canola oil or cold-
pressed safflower oil
1 cup chopped onions
¼ cup unbleached white flour
2 cups defatted sodium-reduced
chicken broth
1–1½ teaspoons curry powder
⅛ teaspoon white pepper
1 15-ounce can kidney beans,
drained and rinsed, or 1½ cups
cooked beans (page 129)

1 large zucchini, cut into ¼-inch
slices
¼ red pepper, slivered
4 canned water chestnuts, sliced
1 6½-ounce can albacore tuna in
water, drained and flaked

2 tablespoons chopped green
onion, for garnish

1. Heat the oil in a 10-inch nonstick skillet, add the onions, and sauté until lightly browned.
2. Add the flour and heat briefly. Add the chicken broth and stir until sauce coats the spoon.
3. Stir in the curry, white pepper, beans, zucchini, red pepper, and water chestnuts. Cover and simmer 10 minutes.
4. Stir in the tuna and cook until just heated.
To Serve: Spoon the curry over a bed of quinoa and sprinkle with chopped green onions.

Per serving: 12 mg cholesterol, 0.4 gm saturated fat, 3.6 gm total fat, 3.3 gm fiber,
117 mg sodium, 213 calories

Hearts of Romaine and Hearts of Palm with
Chopped Red Pepper Vinaigrette
♦Seafood Jambalaya♦
Spinach
Pitted Bing Cherries with Brandy

Seafood Jambalaya

Serves: 6 to 8 (2 ounces cooked fish = 1 serving)

1 tablespoon unbleached white flour
2 teaspoons extra-virgin olive oil
2 medium onions, chopped
3 cloves garlic, minced
2 cups defatted sodium-reduced chicken broth or clam juice
1 28-ounce can chopped Italian plum tomatoes with juice
1 cup sodium-reduced vegetable juice
1 cup diced celery with leaves
1 green pepper, seeded and chopped
1 bay leaf
2 teaspoons dried thyme, crushed

Few grains crushed red pepper flakes
1 teaspoon hot pepper sauce or Tabasco
2 tablespoons Worcestershire sauce
⅓ cup chopped fresh Italian parsley
1 cup converted or brown rice
8 ounces monkfish or sea bass, cut into 1-inch cubes
8 ounces fresh or canned crab meat

1. Brown the flour in the oil in a 5-quart nonstick saucepan. Add onions and garlic and stir 5 minutes or until wilted.

2. Add the broth, stir, and cook until slightly thickened.

3. Add the tomatoes, vegetable juice, celery, green pepper, seasonings, and parsley, and mix well. Simmer for 30 minutes.

4. Add the rice, cover, and simmer for 20 minutes (40 minutes for brown rice).

5. Stir in the fish and cook about 10 minutes.

6. Add the crab meat, stir, heat, and adjust seasonings (remove bay leaf).

To Serve: Spoon into warm soup plates.

Variation: Jambalaya may be cooked without the rice, and served over steamed rice.

Per serving: 35 mg cholesterol, 0.61 gm saturated fat, 3.4 gm total fat, 1.8 gm fiber, 493 mg sodium, 201 calories

Roasted Pepper Salad
♦Capellini with Clams in White Wine♦
Braised Escarole
Hot Crusty Sourdough Bread
Ribière Grapes

Capellini with Clams in White Wine ⓠ

Serves: 6

The good news is that clams and mussels are both low in cholesterol as well as saturated fat.

1 tablespoon extra-virgin olive oil
2 shallots, finely chopped
3 large cloves garlic, finely minced
2 carrots, thinly sliced
½ teaspoon crushed red pepper flakes
4 dozen clams or mussels, well scrubbed under cold running water
¾ cup defatted sodium-reduced chicken broth
¾ cup dry white wine or apple cider
⅔ cup chopped fresh Italian parsley

2 tablespoons fresh oregano, finely chopped, or 1 tablespoon dried oregano, crushed
12 ounces capellini (angel hair pasta), cooked *al dente* and drained
2 tablespoons fresh basil, finely chopped, or 1 tablespoon dried basil, crushed
Freshly ground pepper
1 tablespoon shredded Parmesan cheese

1. Combine the olive oil, shallots, garlic, carrots, and red pepper flakes in a 4-quart nonstick saucepan or casserole and cook over medium heat until onions are soft, not browned.

2. Add the clams, chicken broth, wine, ½ cup of the parsley, and the oregano and stir to coat clams. Cover, bring to a boil, lower heat, and cook until clams are open (about 8 minutes). *Discard the clams that do not open.*

3. Add the drained pasta, basil, pepper, and cheese, and mix lightly.

To Serve: Divide the pasta mixture with liquid among four deep heated soup bowls. Surround with *open* clams, sprinkle with the remaining chopped parsley, and serve immediately with hot crusty bread.

Per serving: 55 mg cholesterol, 0.75 gm saturated fat, 4.9 gm total fat, 2.5 gm fiber, 121 mg sodium, 326 calories

Marinated Tomato and Onion Salad
◆Salmon Tetrazzini◆
Steamed Brussels Sprouts
Lemon Sorbet

Salmon Tetrazzini Ⓠ Ⓜ

Serves: 8 (2 ounces cooked fish = 1 serving)

2 teaspoons canola or cold-pressed safflower oil
1 medium onion, chopped
1 large clove garlic, minced
¼ teaspoon white pepper
⅓ cup unbleached white flour
1 teaspoon salt-free vegetable seasoning
¼ teaspoon freshly ground nutmeg
4 cups nonfat milk (including drained salmon liquid, if canned salmon is used)
2 teaspoons Worcestershire sauce
1 bay leaf
2 stalks celery, diced
1 small green pepper, seeded and diced
1 small red pepper, seeded and diced

1½ cups sliced fresh mushroom caps
2 tablespoons grated Parmesan cheese
8 ounces spaghettini, soba noodles, or linguini, cooked *al dente*
1 15½-ounce can salmon, drained (save liquid), skinned, and boned, or 1¼-pound salmon, poached (page 172, save the liquid)
1 tablespoon grated Parmesan cheese mixed with 2 tablespoons dry breadcrumbs

3 tablespoons chopped fresh dill, for garnish

1. Heat the oil in a 3-quart nonstick saucepan with the onion, garlic, and pepper. Sauté 3 minutes.
2. Add the flour and seasonings; stir to combine.
3. Add the milk, Worcestershire sauce, bay leaf, celery, peppers, mushrooms, and cheese and stir over medium heat until sauce coats the spoon. Remove the bay leaf.
4. Combine half the sauce with the cooked pasta and place in the bottom of a 3-quart shallow casserole.
5. Flake the salmon, stir into remaining sauce, and pour over pasta.
6. Sprinkle with the cheese mixture and bake in a preheated 350° oven for 25 to 30 minutes until bubbly, or microwave on high for 12 minutes.
To Serve: Sprinkle with chopped dill and serve hot.

Per serving: 33 mg cholesterol, 1.01 gm saturated fat, 4.6 gm total fat, 1.4 gm fiber, 172 mg sodium, 275 calories

Mixed Greens with Red Cabbage
♦Turbot with Spanish Sauce♦
Corn on the Cob
Snow Peas and Carrot Slices
Stewed Prunes with Fresh Pineapple Chunks

Turbot with Spanish Sauce Ⓠ Ⓜ

Serves: 6 (3½ ounces cooked fish = 1 serving)

1¾ pounds turbot, haddock or cod, cut into 6 portions
Juice of 1 lime
2 teaspoons extra-virgin olive oil
1 small onion, chopped
2 large cloves garlic, minced
2½ cups chopped Italian plum tomatoes (fresh or canned)
½ green pepper, seeded and thinly sliced
2 tablespoons tomato paste
¼ cup chopped fresh Italian parsley
½ teaspoon Italian herb blend, crushed
1 bay leaf
¼ cup dry white wine

1. Sprinkle the fish with the lime juice and set aside.
2. Place the oil, onions, and garlic in a round shallow glass dish, cover tightly with microwave plastic wrap, and microwave on high for 2 minutes.
3. Add the remaining ingredients except the fish, stir, and cover with plastic. Cook on high for 6 minutes, stirring one time during cooking.
4. Remove the bay leaf and add the fish to the sauce. Cover with plastic and microwave on high for about 6 minutes, or until fish flakes with fork.

To Serve: Arrange fish with sauce on heated platter and surround with pea pods and carrots.

Per serving: 47 mg cholesterol, 0.39 gm saturated fat, 2.6 gm total fat, 1.1 gm fiber, 78 mg sodium, 138 calories

Marinated Mushroom Salad
♦Piquant Broiled Mahimahi with Mango Salsa♦
Baked Potato with Yogurt and Chives
Summer Squash with Shredded Carrots
Angel Food Cake (page 324) with Sliced Fresh Strawberries

Piquant Broiled Mahimahi with Mango Salsa Q

Serves: 4 (3 ounces cooked fish = 1 serving)

This flavorful fish comes from the dolphin family (but not Flipper).
It is delicious grilled, sautéed, or baked.

2 teaspoons Worcestershire sauce	Juice of 1 lime
2 tablespoons white wine	Freshly ground pepper
1 garlic clove, minced	1 pound mahimahi or sea bass, cut
¼ teaspoon onion powder	into 4 pieces
½ teaspoon Dijon mustard	Mango Salsa (page 326)

1. Combine the first seven ingredients in a small jar or custard cup and blend thoroughly.
2. Brush the fish on one side with the sauce and broil or barbecue 4 inches from heat for 3 minutes.
3. Turn the fish and cook, basting frequently with sauce, until fish flakes with fork. (Total cooking time about 8 to 9 minutes per inch of thickness.)

To Serve: Place fish on platter, spoon salsa onto fish and surround with potatoes and summer squash with carrots.

Per serving: 43 mg cholesterol, 1.2 gm saturated fat, 4.4 gm total fat, 0 gm fiber,
132 mg sodium, 137 calories

Three-Bean Salad Vinaigrette
◆Tuna-Stuffed Mushrooms with Creole Sauce◆
Bulgur Wheat (page 130) with Peas
Persimmon Freeze (page 320)

Tuna-Stuffed Mushrooms with Creole Sauce ⓠ

Serves: 4 as an entrée (3 stuffed mushrooms = 1 serving)
or 1 as an appetizer (1 stuffed mushroom = 1 serving)

1 small onion, quartered
½ green pepper, seeded and quartered
1 stalk celery, quartered
1 large clove garlic
16 large mushrooms, cleaned and stemmed (save stems for vegetable mixture)
2 teaspoons extra-virgin olive oil
½ teaspoon dried Italian herb blend
2 ounces chopped pimiento, drained
½ cup soft whole wheat breadcrumbs

2 extra-large egg whites, slightly beaten
1 teaspoon Worcestershire sauce
1 6½-ounce can salt-reduced light-meat tuna in water, flaked, or 6½ ounces fresh or canned crab meat
Freshly ground pepper
1½ tablespoons shredded Parmesan cheese

Creole Sauce:
1½ cups salt-reduced canned tomatoes, chopped
1 teaspoon cornstarch

1. Chop the onion, green pepper, celery, garlic, and mushroom stems in the food processor.

2. Sauté the vegetable mixture in oil in a nonstick skillet for 5 minutes.

3. Add the herb blend, pimiento, breadcrumbs, egg whites, Worcestershire sauce, tuna, and pepper. Mix well with a fork.

4. Mound the mixture lightly into the mushroom caps and sprinkle with the cheese. Place in a shallow baking pan and bake in a preheated 400° oven 7 minutes or until lightly browned.

5. *To prepare the creole sauce:* Combine the tomatoes and cornstarch in a 1-quart saucepan and mix thoroughly. Stir over medium heat until shiny.

To Serve: Place the mushrooms on a serving platter, and spoon hot sauce over them.

Per serving: 13 mg cholesterol, 0.83 gm saturated fat, 3.9 gm total fat, 1.1 gm fiber, 191 mg sodium, 180 calories

Belgian Endive and Shredded Beet Salad
◆Stir-Fried Scallops with Garlic, Mushrooms, and Snow Peas◆
Steamed Wild Rice
Asparagus
Orange Sorbet

Stir-Fried Scallops with Garlic, Mushrooms, and Snow Peas ⓠ

Serves: 4 (3 ounces cooked scallops = 1 serving)

2 teaspoons extra-virgin olive oil
1 ounce dried shiitake mushrooms
   (soaked 20 minutes in warm
   water, drained, stems removed,
   and sliced)
4 whole green onions, sliced
1 tablespoon lemon juice
1 tablespoon sodium-reduced soy
   sauce

Freshly ground pepper
3 cloves garlic, minced
1 pound bay scallops, thoroughly
   rinsed and drained
⅓ cup dry white wine mixed with
   2 teaspoons cornstarch
1 cup fresh or frozen snow peas,
   halved lengthwise

1. Place the oil in a nonstick skillet and add the mushrooms and green onions; sprinkle with the lemon juice, soy sauce, and pepper and stir-fry 2 to 3 minutes.
2. Add the garlic and sauté 1 minute.
3. Add the scallops and stir-fry until opaque.
4. Add the wine and snow peas and cook for several minutes.
To Serve: Place a mound of rice on a warm serving platter, spoon the scallop mixture on top.

Per serving: 37 mg cholesterol, 0.43 gm saturated fat, 3.3 gm total fat, 1.7 gm fiber,
310 mg sodium, 182 calories

Salad of Spinach, Corn, and Hearts of Palm
◆Grilled Red Snapper and Tomato◆
Parslied Potatoes
Seasoned Green Beans
Cantaloupe and Blueberries with Yogurt

Grilled Red Snapper and Tomato ⓠ

Serves: 4 (3 ounces cooked fish = 1 serving)

4 4-ounce fillets red snapper, halibut, or Spanish mackerel
¼ cup low-calorie oil-free Italian dressing
Freshly ground pepper
1½ teaspoons dried oregano, crushed

1 tablespoon freshly grated Parmesan cheese
2 ripe medium tomatoes, cut in half
Watercress sprigs, for garnish

1. Brush the fish with half of the salad dressing and sprinkle with pepper, oregano, and Parmesan cheese.

2. Arrange fish seasoned-side-down on a heated nonstick griddle or sauté pan and cook 3 minutes.

3. Brush the fish with the remaining salad dressing and turn. Place the tomato halves cut-side-down alongside the fish and continue grilling for 2 to 3 minutes or until fish flakes when tested with a fork. *Do not overcook.*

To Serve: Place the red snapper and tomato halves on a heated serving plate and garnish with watercress.

Variation: Halibut, tuna, or salmon fillets may be substituted for the red snapper and served as a salad on shredded romaine with the grilled tomato and dilled steamed green beans.

Per serving: 41 mg cholesterol, 0.58 gm saturated fat, 2 gm total fat, 0.5 gm fiber, 237 mg sodium, 134 calories

Salad of Julienne Carrots and Jicama with Spinach
♦Broiled Swordfish Paillard
with Fresh Salsa♦
Peas and Artichoke Hearts
Warm Corn Tortillas
Fresh Raspberries with Mango Puree

Broiled Swordfish Paillard
with Fresh Salsa ℚ

Serves: 4 (3 ounces cooked fish = 1 serving)

Paillard refers to a thin slice of fish, poultry, or meat. It need only be broiled on one side. I serve swordfish very infrequently because it is believed to have excessive levels of methyl mercury.

4 4-ounce swordfish, ocean perch, or Spanish mackerel fillets, cut ½-inch thick
1½ tablespoons lime juice or balsamic vinegar
Salt-free vegetable seasoning
Freshly ground pepper

Fresh Salsa:
2 medium tomatoes, chopped
½ small onion, finely chopped
2 tablespoons canned chilis, chopped, or 1 fresh jalapeno pepper, chopped
1–2 tablespoons lime juice
3 tablespoons fresh chopped parsley or cilantro

1. Preheat the broiler. Brush the fish with the lime juice and sprinkle with vegetable seasoning and pepper.
2. Place the fish in a broiler pan and broil for 3 to 4 minutes on one side only. *Do not overcook.*
3. *To make the fresh salsa:* Combine all the ingredients in a bowl and blend with a fork.
To Serve: Place the fish on a platter and pass the salsa.

NOTE: Fresh Salsa is also wonderful served with warm corn tortillas as an appetizer or as a topping for broiled chicken or baked potatoes.

Per serving: 43 mg cholesterol, 1.23 gm saturated fat, 4.6 gm total fat, 0.8 gm fiber, 107 mg sodium, 155 calories

Marinated Broccoli and Red Pepper Salad
◆Mediterranean Fish Soup◆
Crusty Whole Wheat Baguette
Blueberries with Yogurt

Mediterranean Fish Soup Ⓠ

Serves: 6 (1½ cups = 1 serving)
Yield: about 8 to 9 cups

This easy-to-make dish can be partially prepared the day before. It is a wonderful choice for informal entertaining. Like most soups, this one tastes even better the next day.

3 shallots or 1 small onion, minced
4 cloves garlic, minced
2 teaspoons extra-virgin olive oil
1 28-ounce can crushed Italian plum tomatoes with juice
1 teaspoon chopped fresh oregano, or ½ teaspoon dried oregano
1 teaspoon chopped fresh thyme, or ½ teaspoon dried thyme
Few grains crushed red pepper flakes

1½ cups defatted sodium-reduced chicken broth
½ cup dry white wine
1 10-ounce package frozen corn
3 tablespoons chopped parsley
½ pound sea bass or red snapper, cubed
½ pound monkfish, cubed

1. In a large saucepan, sauté the shallots and garlic in the oil until lightly colored.

2. Add all the remaining ingredients except the fish, corn, and parsley and simmer uncovered about 20 minutes. This dish may be prepared ahead to this point and refrigerated until the next day.

3. Add the corn, parsley, and fish, cover, and cook about 8 minutes. Taste and adjust seasoning.

To Serve: Spoon into shallow heated soup bowls and serve with lots of crusty whole wheat bread.

Per serving: 42 mg cholesterol, 0.61 gm saturated fat, 3.5 gm total fat, 2.2 gm fiber, 267 mg sodium, 163 calories

Shredded Carrot and Zucchini Slaw
◆Salmon, Spinach, and Rice Casserole◆
Broiled Tomato Halves
Broccoli Spears
Seasonal Fresh Fruit

Salmon, Spinach, and Rice Casserole ⓠⓜ

Serves: 4

Casseroles always provide an easy, convenient method of serving because they can be prepared well ahead of time.

2 teaspoons canola oil or cold-pressed safflower oil
½ cup chopped onion
1 10-ounce package frozen chopped spinach, defrosted and drained
Freshly ground nutmeg
1 7½-ounce can salmon, drained (save liquid), bones removed, and flaked
2 cups cooked brown rice (page 130)
2 tablespoons lemon juice
½ cup chopped celery with leaves

½ cup chopped green pepper
½ cup chopped zucchini
2 whole green onions, sliced
2 teaspoons dried dill
2 extra-large egg whites, slightly beaten
½ cup part-skim ricotta cheese mixed with ¾ cup nonfat milk, drained salmon liquid, and 1 teaspoon dry or Dijon mustard
2 tablespoons dry breadcrumbs mixed with 1 tablespoon grated Parmesan cheese

1. Microwave the oil and onions on high in a 10-inch glass pie plate or quiche pan for 2 minutes (or sauté in nonstick skillet until wilted and place in pie plate). Top with spinach and sprinkle with nutmeg.
2. Combine the salmon, rice, lemon juice, celery, green pepper, zucchini, green onion, dill, egg whites, and ricotta cheese mixture in a bowl. Stir lightly with a fork to blend; spoon on top of the spinach.
3. Sprinkle with the breadcrumb and cheese mixture.
4. Cook uncovered in a microwave oven on high for 12 to 15 minutes or in a preheated 400° oven for 35 minutes.

Per serving: 34 mg cholesterol, 2.92 gm saturated fat, 7.5 gm total fat, 5.1 gm fiber, 252 mg sodium, 306 calories

Confetti Corn Soup (page 266)
Whole Wheat Bread Sticks
♦Grilled Salmon Scallops on Mixed Greens♦
with
Dijon Mustard, Chili Pepper, and Yogurt Sauce
Fresh Tomato and Green Pepper Salsa
Jicama and Orange Relish
Boysenberries with Vanilla Yogurt

Grilled Salmon Scallops on Mixed Greens with Assorted Salsas ⒬

Serves: 4 (3 ounces cooked fish = 1 serving)

8 cups torn assorted greens
½ cup low-calorie oil-free vinaigrette mixed with 1 teaspoon
extra-virgin olive oil
12 small leaves radicchio
16-ounce salmon fillet, sliced into
12 thin scallops
Juice of ½ lemon

Dijon Mustard, Chili Pepper,
and Yogurt Sauce:
¼ cup nonfat plain yogurt mixed
with 2 tablespoons finely diced
jalapeno peppers and 2 teaspoons Dijon mustard

Fresh Tomato and Green Pepper
Salsa:
3 diced Italian plum tomatoes
mixed with ¼ finely diced green
pepper, ¼ finely diced medium
white onion, and 1 tablespoon
lime juice

Jicama and Orange Relish:
1 large navel orange, peeled and
diced, mixed with ⅔ cup finely
diced jicama or water chestnuts

1. Prepare the salsas.
2. Toss the greens lightly with the vinaigrette dressing and divide among
four serving plates. Place three small radicchio leaves around the greens on
each plate and fill each leaf with a quarter of the prepared salsas.
3. Season the salmon scallops with the lemon juice and sear in a hot
nonstick skillet 1 minute on each side.
4. Place the hot salmon scallops on top of the dressed greens and serve.

Per serving: 45 mg cholesterol, 0.75 gm saturated fat, 4.9 gm total fat, 3.7 gm fiber,
131 mg sodium, 204 calories

♦Cajun Blackened Redfish♦
Roast Potatoes with Basil (page 306)
Steamed Broccoli and Carrots
Dilled Cucumber and Yogurt Salad
Raspberry Sorbet

Cajun Blackened Redfish Q

Serves: 4 (3½ ounces cooked fish = 1 serving)

Cajun food lovers should avoid catfish, even "farmed catfish," these days. The Center for Science in the Public Interest cautions us to avoid catfish and carp "since they are bottom feeders and are particularly vulnerable to contamination from tainted sediments." However, red snapper, pompano, or redfish are good substitutes.

4 5-ounce red snapper, pompano, or redfish fillets (about ½-inch thick)
Juice of ½ lemon
2 teaspoons Hungarian paprika*

½ teaspoon each white pepper, freshly ground black pepper, cayenne, celery seed, and garlic and onion powders*
1 teaspoon dried thyme, crushed*

1. Wash the fish in cold water. Sprinkle with lemon juice.
2. Blend the spices together, place on waxed paper, and press into both sides of each piece of fish.
3. Heat a heavy iron skillet coated with nonstick spray over high heat, add fish, and grill 3 to 4 minutes on each side, depending upon thickness of fish. Fish may also be cooked on the oiled grill of a barbecue. Serve immediately.

Per serving: 47 mg cholesterol, 0.41 gm saturated fat, 2 gm total fat, 0.5 gm fiber, 58 mg sodium, 137 calories

* Substitute 2 to 3 teaspoons salt-free commercial Cajun seasoning for all the spices listed if you like.

Chilled Mixed Greens with Jicama
♦Flounder with Creole Sauce♦
Steamed New Potatoes
Steamed Broccoli Spears
Pureed Rutabaga
Fresh Fruit Cup with Mint

Flounder with Creole Sauce ℚ

Serves: 4 (3 ounces cooked fish = 1 serving)

2 teaspoons extra-virgin olive oil
½ small onion, finely chopped
2 cloves garlic, minced
½ small green pepper, seeded and
    diced
1 cup sliced fresh mushrooms
⅓ cup dry white wine
3 fresh plum tomatoes, finely
    chopped
Few grains crushed red pepper
    flakes

1½ teaspoons Hungarian paprika
4 4-ounce flounder, sturgeon, or
    sea bass fillets
½ lemon
1 teaspoon salt-free vegetable
    seasoning
½ cup nonfat plain yogurt mixed
    with 1 teaspoon cornstarch
2 tablespoons chopped fresh
    parsley

1. Heat the oil in a nonstick saucepan. Add the onion, garlic, pepper, and mushrooms and sauté 2 minutes.

2. Add the wine, tomatoes, pepper flakes, and paprika and simmer 15 minutes to reduce. Remove from heat.

3. Sprinkle the flounder with the lemon juice and vegetable seasoning. Grill in a hot nonstick skillet (or broil) 3 to 4 minutes on each side.

4. Just after turning the fish, add the yogurt mixture and parsley to the tomato mixture and warm briefly. *Do not bring to a boil.*

To Serve: Spoon a quarter of the warm sauce onto each of four dinner plates and top with the hot fish.

Per serving: 58 mg cholesterol, 0.7 gm saturated fat, 4 gm total fat, 1.2 gm fiber, 122 mg sodium, 172 calories

Pickled Beet Salad
♦Perfect Petrale Sole♦
Baked Potato with Chives
Steamed Asparagus Spears
Broiled Grapefruit

Perfect Petrale Sole Ⓠ

Serves: 4 (3 ounces cooked fish = 1 serving)

½ cup nonfat plain yogurt
½ teaspoon salt-free vegetable
seasoning
½ teaspoon onion powder
¼ teaspoon garlic powder
⅛ teaspoon white pepper
1 pound petrale sole or flounder,
cut in 4 portions

⅔ cup dry breadcrumbs mixed
with 1 teaspoon salt-free vegetable seasoning, 3 tablespoons
chopped parsley, and 2 teaspoons grated Parmesan cheese

Lemon juice, lemon slices, and 1½
tablespoons rinsed capers, for
garnish (optional)

1. Combine the yogurt with the seasonings and coat the petrale sole on
both sides with the mixture. Then dip the sole into the breadcrumb mixture.

2. Place the sole on a nonstick baking sheet and bake in a preheated 450°
oven for 12 to 15 minutes or until golden brown.

To Serve: Place the sole on a warm serving platter, surround with asparagus
spears, and sprinkle with lemon juice, lemon slices, and capers.

Per serving: 62 mg cholesterol, 0.65 gm saturated fat, 2.2 gm total fat, 0.1 gm fiber,
224 mg sodium, 174 calories

Broccoli and Onion Soup (page 269)
◆Helen's Orange Roughy with a Vegetable Mélange◆
Steamed Zucchini Spears
Steamed New Potatoes
Poached Pears and Prunes (page 317)

Helen's Orange Roughy with a Vegetable Mélange Ⓠ Ⓜ

Serves: 4 (4 ounces cooked fish = 1 serving)

1 large onion, thinly sliced
½ green pepper, seeded and sliced
½ red pepper, seeded and sliced
1¼ pounds orange roughy, floun-
    der, or cod, cut into 4 portions
¼ teaspoon white pepper
½ teaspoon garlic powder

2 tablespoons dry vermouth
2 tablespoons fresh orange juice
8 mushroom caps, thinly sliced
8 slices dehydrated tomatoes, or
    4 cherry tomatoes, halved

1. Place the sliced onion in a 9-inch baking dish coated with nonstick cooking spray. Cover with microwave plastic wrap and microwave on high for 2 minutes.

2. Add the green and red pepper slices, cover, and microwave on high for 1 minute.

3. Season the fish with the white pepper and garlic powder and arrange fish over the onions, moving the pepper slices to top fish.

4. Pour the vermouth and orange juice over the fish; add the sliced mushrooms and tomatoes.

5. Cover and microwave on high for 4 minutes or until fish flakes with a fork.

Per serving: 35 mg cholesterol, 0.2 gm saturated fat, 8.1 gm total fat, 1 gm fiber, 74 mg sodium, 178 calories

Poultry

Crisp Green Salad with Shredded Red Cabbage
with Low-Calorie Vinaigrette Dressing
♦Chunky Turkey Chili♦
Sourdough Rolls
Bowl of Assorted Seasonal Fresh Fruit

Chunky Turkey Chili ©

Serves: 8 (1¼ cups = 1 serving)

Chili is always a favorite of mine for informal menus. This chili is particularly great not only because it tastes terrific, but also because the beans, high in soluble fiber, help to lower cholesterol. In this case the traditional ground beef is replaced by low-cholesterol low-fat turkey with no sacrifice in flavor.

1 small onion, quartered
3 garlic cloves
3 stalks celery, quartered
1 green pepper, quartered
2 teaspoons canola oil
8 ounces turkey breast fillet
(cooked or raw), diced
¼ cup dry white or red wine
1–2 tablespoons chili seasoning
1 teaspoon dried thyme, crushed
1 teaspoon dried oregano, crushed

1 teaspoon spicy salt-free vegetable seasoning
1 28-ounce can crushed Italian plum tomatoes, in puree
1 15½-ounce can kidney beans, drained and rinsed, or 2 cups cooked beans, (page 129)
1 15½-ounce can garbanzo beans, pinto beans, or black beans, drained and rinsed, or 2 cups cooked beans (page 129)

1. Coarsely chop the onion, garlic, celery, and green pepper in the food processor or blender; then sauté for 3 minutes in the oil in nonstick 2-quart saucepan.
2. Add the diced turkey and sauté for 5 minutes, stirring constantly.
3. Add the remaining ingredients, stir, and bring to a simmer. Taste and adjust seasonings.
4. Cover and simmer 20 minutes, stirring occasionally to prevent sticking.

Variation: To make vegetarian chili, substitute 1½ cups chopped carrots and 1½ cups chopped zucchini or 3 cups chopped eggplant for the turkey.

Per serving: 20 mg cholesterol, 0.59 gm saturated fat, 3.8 gm total fat, 4.4 gm fiber, 208 mg sodium, 216 calories

Tomato Bisque
♦Turkey Roulades Stuffed with
Asparagus, Carrots, and Red Pepper♦
Steamed Green Beans with Water Chestnuts
Wild Rice with Scallions
Poached Pear with Fresh Strawberry Sauce (page 316)

Turkey Roulades Stuffed with Asparagus, Carrots, and Red Pepper Ⓠ Ⓜ

Serves: 4 (2 roulades = 1 serving)

Ordinary turkey slices, sold in packages at your market (your butcher may also have turkey breast slices available), can be transformed into an extraordinary dinner for guests.

8 2-ounce slices raw turkey breast, ½ inch thick
Juice of ½ lemon
2 teaspoons salt-free vegetable seasoning
Freshly ground pepper
1 teaspoon extra-virgin olive oil
1 shallot, minced
½ 10-ounce package frozen chopped spinach, defrosted and drained
3 tablespoons part-skim ricotta cheese
1 tablespoon grated Parmesan cheese
Freshly ground nutmeg

Freshly ground pepper
16 thin asparagus spears
2 small carrots, quartered lengthwise
½ small red pepper, seeded and cut into 8 strips
⅓ cup crushed oat bran flake cereal mixed with 2 tablespoons oat bran, 1 tablespoon each dried parsley flakes and onion flakes, and ½ teaspoon each garlic powder and salt-free vegetable seasoning
Hungarian paprika

1. Flatten the turkey slices between sheets of plastic wrap to ¼-inch thickness. Remove the plastic and season the turkey with the lemon juice, vegetable seasoning, and pepper.

2. Microwave the oil and shallot on high in a 10-inch glass pie plate or quiche pan for 30 seconds.

3. Combine the shallot with the spinach, cheeses, nutmeg, and pepper and mix thoroughly.

4. Spread each turkey slice with about 1 tablespoon of the spinach mixture. Place two asparagus spears, one carrot stick, and one pepper strip crosswise on each fillet. Roll up and coat the roll with the oat mixture. Secure with a toothpick.

5. Arrange the roulades in a pie plate in spokelike fashion, sprinkle with paprika, cover tightly with microwave plastic wrap, and microwave on high for 6 minutes.

To Serve: Spoon hot barley pilaf onto serving platter, arrange roulades on top of barley, and surround with green beans and water chestnuts.

Per serving: 63 mg cholesterol, 1.93 gm saturated fat, 5.9 gm total fat, 3.5 gm fiber, 166 mg sodium, 244 calories

Cole Slaw with Yogurt Dressing
♦Mini Turkey Loaves with Piquant Salsa♦
Sweet Potato Chips (page 264)
Steamed Cauliflower, Carrots, and Corn
Blueberry Meringue (page 342)

Mini Turkey Loaves with Piquant Salsa

Yield: 6 loaves (1 miniloaf = 1 serving)

In this recipe, I have replaced ground beef with ground turkey breast, since white meat of turkey is the lowest in saturated fat of all meats.

1 small onion, chopped
½ small green pepper, seeded and chopped
1 large carrot, chopped
1 stalk celery with leaves, diced
1 large clove garlic, minced
2 teaspoons canola oil
1 teaspoon salt-free vegetable seasoning
Freshly ground pepper
1 pound ground turkey breast (ground from raw or leftover cooked—see page 142)
½ cup rolled oats, soaked in ½ cup nonfat milk or defatted sodium-reduced chicken broth
¼ cup oat bran

2 extra-large egg whites, slightly beaten
1 tablespoon Worcestershire sauce
2 teaspoons Dijon mustard
1 teaspoon fines herbes or thyme
Hungarian paprika

Watercress, for garnish

Piquant Salsa:
1 8-ounce jar salt-free salsa or 1 cup Fresh Salsa (page 183)
1 teaspoon cornstarch
3 tablespoons fresh cilantro, chopped

1. Place the onion, green pepper, carrot, celery, garlic, and oil in a non-stick skillet. Sauté 5 minutes; sprinkle with vegetable seasoning and pepper.
2. In a large mixing bowl, combine the turkey, the onion mixture, and the soaked oats, oat bran, egg whites, Worcestershire sauce, mustard, and fines herbes. Mix lightly with a fork until well blended.
3. Shape into six miniloaves and place in a shallow nonstick baking pan. Sprinkle lightly with paprika.

4. Bake in the upper third of a preheated 375° oven for 25 minutes.

5. *To prepare the salsa*, place the salsa and cornstarch in a saucepan and blend. Heat 2 to 3 minutes, stirring constantly, until shiny and thickened. Add the cilantro and mix.

To Serve: Arrange the hot turkey loaves on a serving platter, garnish with watercress, and top with hot salsa.

Per serving: 46 mg cholesterol, 0.97 gm saturated fat, 4.7 gm total fat, 2.4 gm fiber, 129 mg sodium, 210 calories

Mixed Green Salad with Kidney Beans
♦Stuffed Peppers in the Pot♦
Hearty Whole Grain Bread
Apple Crisp (page 315)

Stuffed Peppers in the Pot

Serves: 6 (1 pepper with 1⅓ ounces turkey = 1 serving)

A kidney bean salad, a soup with peppers stuffed with brown rice, vegetables, and a small amount of ground turkey, whole grain bread, and apples—all high-fiber, low-fat foods perfect for your low-cholesterol lifestyle. The stuffed peppers are even more delicious prepared the day before.

2 teaspoons extra-virgin olive oil
1 small onion, finely chopped
1 large carrot, finely chopped
1 stalk celery with leaves, finely chopped
1 zucchini, finely chopped
2 large cloves garlic, minced
1 teaspoon dried oregano
Freshly ground pepper
1 cup ground turkey or chicken breast (ground from raw or leftover cooked—see page 142)
1 cup fresh or frozen corn
2 teaspoons salt-free vegetable seasoning
1 tablespoon sodium-reduced soy sauce
¼ cup chopped fresh Italian parsley

1½ cups cooked brown rice (page 129)
3 each small green and red peppers, tops removed and cleaned inside
3 tablespoons unbleached white flour
1 28-ounce can crushed Italian plum tomatoes in puree
3 cups water or defatted sodium-reduced chicken broth
1 teaspoon crushed red pepper flakes
1 bay leaf
1 teaspoon dried thyme, crushed, or 1 tablespoon chopped fresh thyme

1. Heat the oil in a 6-inch nonstick skillet. Add the onion, carrot, celery, zucchini, garlic, oregano, and pepper and sauté until soft.

2. Place the turkey, corn, vegetable seasoning, soy sauce, parsley, cooked rice, and onion mixture into a mixing bowl and blend with a fork.

3. Fill the hollowed peppers with the turkey mixture.

4. Brown the flour in a 10-inch sauté pan or casserole until golden brown, stirring constantly. Add the tomatoes and water, stirring to blend in the flour. Bring to a boil.

5. Add the stuffed peppers, red pepper flakes, bay leaf, and thyme. Reduce heat, cover, and simmer 1½ to 2 hours over low heat, basting the peppers occasionally.

6. Taste and adjust seasonings before serving.

To Serve: Spoon into shallow heated soup plates, allowing one pepper for each serving, and serve immediately. If using a casserole, serve directly at the table. Additional rice may be served and added to the soup plates at the table.

Per serving: 16 mg cholesterol, 0.73 gm saturated fat, 3.9 gm total fat, 4.3 gm fiber, 333 mg sodium, 211 calories

Wild Rice and Corn Salad
♦Turkey Ragout♦
Braised Red Cabbage
Zucchini Circles
Whole Wheat Bread
Fruited Mousse (page 319)

Turkey Ragout Ⓠ

Serves: 8 (3 ounces cooked turkey = 1 serving)

We usually think of red meat in stews; however, this hearty peasant-style turkey ragout provides wonderful flavor without excess saturated fat and cholesterol. This recipe may be prepared a day ahead and reheated, or frozen for future use.

¼ cup flour mixed with 2 teaspoons salt-free vegetable seasoning and 2 teaspoons Hungarian paprika

2 pounds boned raw turkey breast or chicken breast, cut into 1-inch cubes

1 tablespoon extra-virgin olive oil

2 cloves garlic, minced

1 bay leaf

6 canned or peeled fresh Italian plum tomatoes, chopped

6 fresh mushrooms, quartered

½ red pepper, seeded and cut into chunks

½ green pepper, seeded and cut into chunks

1 cup small whole fresh or frozen onions

1 teaspoon dried tarragon, or 1 tablespoon chopped fresh tarragon

½ cup defatted sodium-reduced chicken broth

½ cup dry white wine

1 tablespoon Worcestershire sauce

Freshly ground pepper

1 strip orange zest

3 tablespoons chopped fresh tarragon, for garnish

1. Place the seasoned flour in a plastic or paper bag, add the turkey pieces, and shake to coat with flour.
2. Heat the oil in a nonstick pan and sauté the turkey to a golden brown.
3. Add the remaining ingredients, cover, and cook over low heat, stirring occasionally, for about 20 minutes or until tender (chicken will cook faster than turkey). Remove the bay leaf and orange strip.

To Serve: Place in a warmed casserole and sprinkle lightly with fresh tarragon.

Per serving: 68 mg cholesterol, 0.85 gm saturated fat, 3.8 gm total fat, 0.9 gm fiber, 143 mg sodium, 188 calories

Last-Minute Soup (page 268)
Spinach, Red Cabbage, and Orange Salad with
Oil-Free Vinaigrette Dressing
◆Italian Turkey Sausage◆
Sliced Tomatoes
Larry's Potatoes and Onions (page 303)
Kiwi and Strawberry Slices

Italian Turkey Sausage

Serves: 4 (1 patty = 1 serving)

Fennel and garlic give these sausages their Italian flavor. You may increase or eliminate any of the spices in the recipe to suit your palate.

1 pound ground turkey breast (see page 142) or lean veal (or a combination of the two)
1 extra-large egg white
¼ cup oat bran, soaked in ⅓ cup dry white wine or defatted sodium-reduced chicken broth
1 shallot, finely minced
1 teaspoon onion powder

1 teaspoon crushed fennel seeds
½ teaspoon ground sage
½ teaspoon dried oregano
3 cloves garlic, minced
½ teaspoon crushed red pepper flakes
¼ cup chopped fresh Italian parsley
¼ teaspoon salt (optional)

1. Place all the ingredients in a bowl, mix thoroughly with a fork, and chill for several hours to allow flavors to blend.
2. Shape into four patties.
3. Heat a nonstick skillet coated with nonstick cooking spray and sear the patties until browned, about 5 to 6 minutes on each side.

NOTE: These may be frozen for future use and reheated in your microwave oven.

Per serving: 59 mg cholesterol, 0.89 gm saturated fat, 3.4 gm total fat, 1.6 gm fiber, 69 mg sodium, 169 calories

Green Pea and Onion Soup (page 269)
♦Bernice's Roast Turkey Thigh♦
Steamed Rice (page 130)
French-Cut Green Beans
Cole Slaw Relish (page 277)
Peach Scallop (page 234)

Bernice's
Roast Turkey Thigh ⓠ ⓜ

Serves: 6 (3 ounces cooked meat = 1 serving)

A 3-ounce serving of roast *dark meat* of turkey contains about 2 grams of saturated fat, while a 3-ounce serving of roast beef may contain as much as 11 grams.

1 2-pound turkey thigh, boned, skinned, and fat removed
2 teaspoons salt-free vegetable seasoning
Freshly ground pepper
2 teaspoons Hungarian paprika
1 cup coarsely chopped onions
1 cup coarsely chopped celery

1 cup coarsely chopped carrots
2 large cloves garlic, minced
⅓ cup fresh dill, minced, or 2 tablespoons dried dill mixed with 3 tablespoons chopped fresh parsley
½ cup dry white wine

1. Place the turkey in a baking dish and season with the vegetable seasoning, pepper, and paprika.
2. Combine the vegetables with the garlic and dill and sprinkle over the turkey.
3. Cover and bake 30 minutes in a preheated 350° oven.
4. Uncover and add the wine. Continue baking, uncovered, 30 minutes, or until tender.

To Serve: Cut the turkey into thin slices, arrange over steamed rice, and top with the cooked vegetables.

To Microwave:

1. Follow Steps 1 and 2. Cover tightly with plastic wrap and microwave on high for 10 minutes.
2. Uncover, add wine, and continue cooking on high for 6 minutes until tender or turkey reaches temperature of 180°.

Per serving: 72 mg cholesterol, 2.09 gm saturated fat, 6.3 gm total fat, 0.8 gm fiber, 89 mg sodium, 184 calories

Chicken Broth with Bean Curd
♦Turkey Chow Mein♦
Steamed Brown Rice (page 130)
Steamed Broccoli Spears and Carrot Coins
Lichee Nuts

Turkey Chow Mein ⓠ

Serves: 4 to 6 (3 ounces cooked turkey = 1 serving)

2 teaspoons canola oil
1 large onion, thinly sliced and
separated
1 clove garlic, minced
2 stalks celery, cut into ½-inch
diagonal slices
½ red pepper, seeded and cut into
¼-inch strips
½ green pepper, seeded and cut
into ¼-inch strips
1 cup mushrooms, thinly sliced
1 6½-ounce can water chestnuts,
drained and thinly sliced
3 stalks bok choy, cut into ½-inch
slices or 2 cups frozen French-
cut green beans

2 cups fresh bean sprouts
1 teaspoon Chinese five-spice
seasoning
2 cups cooked turkey, cut into ¾-
inch chunks, or 1 pound packaged raw turkey breast slices,
cut into ½-inch strips
2 tablespoons sodium-reduced soy
sauce
1 cup defatted sodium-reduced
chicken broth
2 to 3 tablespoons cornstarch

3 tablespoons slivered toasted
almonds, for garnish

1. Heat the oil in a 10-inch nonstick skillet or wok. Add the onions and garlic and sauté 3 to 4 minutes; then add celery and sauté 3 minutes.
2. Add the peppers, mushrooms, water chestnuts, bok choy, and bean sprouts, stirring after each addition. Sprinkle with Chinese five-spice seasoning, add the turkey, cover and cook 5 to 7 minutes.
3. Combine the soy sauce, broth, and cornstarch and pour over the turkey mixture.
4. Bring to a simmer while stirring constantly and cook until mixture is shiny.

To Serve: Serve over steamed brown rice and sprinkle with almonds.

Variation: *To make this a vegetarian meal*, substitute ½ pound eggplant, cut into strips, and 1 cup diced tofu for the turkey.

Per serving: 32 mg cholesterol, 0.62 gm saturated fat, 3.4 gm total fat, 1.3 gm fiber, 237 mg sodium, 151 calories

Shredded Carrot Salad with Lemon Vinaigrette
♦Roast Chicken with Tomatillo Sauce♦
Brown Rice Pilaf with Chopped Tomatoes
Crookneck Squash
Cafe au Lait Custard (page 320)

Roast Chicken with Tomatillo Sauce Ⓠ Ⓜ

Serves: 4 (4 ounces cooked chicken = 1 serving)

½ pound fresh tomatillos, husks removed and quartered
4 cloves garlic, minced
2 ounces diced green chilis
½ bunch fresh cilantro, chopped
1 small onion, chopped

Freshly ground pepper
2 whole chicken breasts (about 14–16 ounces each), halved, skin and fat removed
4 red pepper rings

1. Puree the first six ingredients. Place in a 9-inch quiche pan or pie plate, cover with microwave plastic wrap, and microwave on high for 5 minutes. To cook on top of stove: place pureed ingredients in saucepan and simmer for 20 minutes.

2. Place the chicken in the sauce, flesh side up, with the thick side toward the outside of the dish. Baste with the sauce mixture.

3. Cover tightly with double plastic wrap and cook on high for 7 minutes. Uncover and cook on high for 2 minutes. Place a pepper ring on each piece of chicken, return to the oven, and microwave on high for 2 minutes more.

To Serve: Place the chicken on a bed of rice pilaf and coat with sauce.

To Bake in Oven: Spoon the sauce over the chicken, cover, and bake in a preheated 350° oven for 35 to 40 minutes.

Per serving: 85 mg cholesterol, 1.37 gm saturated fat, 4.9 gm total fat, 1.6 gm fiber, 97 mg sodium, 219 calories

Green Pea and Red Pepper Salad with
Red Onion-Yogurt Dressing
♦Poached Chicken with Braised Endive and Carrots♦
Barley Pilaf
Whole Wheat Baguette
Glazed Bananas with Blueberries

Poached Chicken with Braised Endive and Carrots

Serves: 4 (3 ounces cooked meat = 1 portion)

4 chicken legs (1½ pounds), skin and fat removed
Freshly ground pepper
1 teaspoon dried thyme, crushed
2 cloves garlic, minced
1 shallot, minced
1 cup vermouth or dry white wine
½ teaspoon celery seed
1 medium onion, peeled, halved, and thinly sliced

2 stalks celery with leaves, diagonally sliced ¾-inch thick
1 bay leaf
1¾ cups defatted sodium-reduced chicken broth
½ pound slim fresh carrots, peeled and cut in 4 pieces
2 heads fresh Belgian endive, halved lengthwise

1. Sprinkle the chicken with the pepper and thyme.
2. Place the garlic, shallot, and vermouth in a sauté pan or casserole; bring to a boil.
3. Add the seasoned chicken and sprinkle with the celery seed, onion, celery slices, and bay leaf. Cover with the chicken broth, bring to a boil, reduce to a simmer, and cook 15 minutes.
4. Baste the chicken with juices, add the carrots and endive, covering with liquid, and cook covered for 15 minutes, or until the juices in the chicken run clear.
5. Remove the vegetables and chicken to a heated platter and cover with foil.
6. Reduce the remaining broth to about half.
To Serve: Pour the hot sauce over the chicken and vegetables.

Per serving: 79 mg cholesterol, 2.49 gm saturated fat, 8.6 gm total fat, 1.8 gm fiber, 143 mg sodium, 252 calories

Radicchio, Romaine, and Mushroom Salad
◆Citrus Chicken Breasts◆
Bulgur Wheat Pilaf (page 312)
Snow Peas and Petit Peas
Pineapple and Strawberry Slices

Citrus Chicken Breasts Ⓠ Ⓜ

Serves: 4 (4 ounces cooked chicken = 1 serving)

3 tablespoons lemon juice
⅔ cup fresh orange juice
½ cup chopped green onions
2 tablespoons dry vermouth
1 tablespoon sodium-reduced soy
  sauce
2 teaspoons grated orange zest
1 teaspoon salt-free vegetable
  seasoning
2 teaspoons crushed caraway seeds

2 teaspoons freshly grated ginger
Freshly ground pepper
2 whole chicken breasts (about 14–
  16 ounces each), halved, boned,
  skin and fat removed

8 peeled orange slices, 4 lemon
  slices, and 1 teaspoon caraway
  seeds, for garnish

1. Combine all the ingredients except the chicken breasts in a plastic bag.
2. Add the chicken and marinate in the refrigerator for an hour, turning occasionally.
3. Place the chicken with marinade in a shallow microwave dish with the thick portion toward the outside of the dish. Cover with wax paper and microwave on high for 7 minutes.
4. Remove the chicken to a heated serving platter and cover to keep warm.
5. Microwave the sauce on high until reduced by one-third, about 3 minutes.

To Serve: Pour the sauce over the chicken, sprinkle with caraway seeds, and garnish with fresh orange and lemon slices.

Per serving: 84 mg cholesterol, 1.27 gm saturated fat, 4.7 gm total fat, 0.3 gm fiber,
200 mg sodium, 207 calories

Black Bean and Corn Salad (page 274)
♦Poached Chicken Breasts♦
Steamed Asparagus Spears
Nan's Quick Cubed Potatoes (page 306)
Whole Wheat Rolls
Fresh Strawberries with Yogurt

Poached Chicken Breasts Ⓠⓜ

Serves: 4 (4 ounces cooked chicken = 1 serving)

2 whole chicken breasts (about 14–
   16 ounces each), halved, boned,
   skin and fat removed
1 carrot, coarsely chopped
1 stalk celery, coarsely chopped
¼ small onion, coarsely chopped
1 clove garlic, crushed
1 bay leaf
4 sprigs fresh parsley
½ teaspoon dried thyme, or 2
   sprigs fresh thyme
Few grains crushed red pepper
   flakes

¼ cup dry vermouth
½ cup defatted sodium-reduced
   chicken broth
About 2 cups water, to barely
   cover chicken breasts, if cooked
   on top of stove

Minced chives and ¼ cup Spicy
   Red Pepper Sauce (page 231)

1. Arrange the chicken breasts in a 9- or 10-inch quiche dish or pie plate with the thick portion toward the outside of the dish. Top with the vegetables, seasonings, vermouth, and broth. Cover tightly with microwave plastic wrap and microwave on high for 5 minutes. For more even cooking, rotate the dish one quarter turn every 2 minutes.

2. Remove from heat, puncture plastic with a fork to allow steam to escape, remove plastic, and let chicken stand in the broth until ready to serve.

To Serve: Remove the chicken from the broth and cut each breast into four to five diagonal slices. Arrange on a heated platter, top with a dollop of Spicy Red Pepper Sauce, and sprinkle with chives. Surround with asparagus and potatoes.

To Cook on Stove: Combine all the ingredients except the chicken breasts in a heavy skillet and bring to a boil. Cover, reduce heat, and simmer 10 minutes. Add the chicken breasts, baste with cooking liquid, cover, and simmer 15 minutes, or until juices run clear .

Per serving: 84 mg cholesterol, 1.26 gm saturated fat, 4.4 gm total fat, 0.7 gm fiber,
105 mg sodium, 188 calories

Spinach and Shredded Beet Salad with
Cucumber-Buttermilk Dressing (page 271)
♦Peasant Chicken Stew♦
Pumpernickel
Fruit Sorbet

Peasant Chicken Stew

Serves: 8 (3 ounces cooked meat = 1 serving)

This one-dish meal may be cooked peasant-style; however, it is fit
for a king! The stew smells wonderful as it cooks—a pleasure that is
sometimes missed in microwave cooking, even if it is quicker. If any
of the vegetables are not available fresh, frozen may be used.

8 5-ounce chicken thighs, skinned
and defatted
2 teaspoons salt-free vegetable
seasoning
2 teaspoons Hungarian paprika
Freshly ground black pepper
2 teaspoons extra-virgin olive oil
1 large onion, chopped
1 shallot, minced
3 large cloves garlic, minced
½ cup dry white wine
4 carrots, sliced ½ inch thick
2 cups celery, sliced ½ inch thick
10 string beans, sliced into 1-inch
pieces

2 russet potatoes, cut into 1-inch
cubes
1 cup quartered fresh mushrooms
1½ teaspoons dried thyme,
crushed
2 cups defatted sodium-reduced
chicken broth
½ cup barley
2 cups fresh corn
1 cup fresh or frozen peas
1 cup fresh or canned Italian plum
tomatoes, cubed

1. Wash the chicken in cold water and dry with paper towels. Sprinkle
with seasoning, paprika, and pepper and sauté in oil in a 12-inch nonstick
sauté pan or an oven-proof casserole until lightly browned, about 3 to 5
minutes.

2. Add the onion, shallot, and garlic and sauté 2 to 3 minutes. Add the
wine and stir.

3. Add the carrots, celery, beans, potatoes, and mushrooms; sprinkle with
the thyme. Add the chicken broth, mix, and bring to a simmer.

4. Cover and bake in a preheated 300° oven for 30 minutes. (if you have
used a sauté pan, transfer to a casserole at this point.)

5. Lower the oven temperature to 250°, add the barley and corn, and bake about 1 hour or until barley is tender.

6. Add the peas and tomatoes for the last 10 minutes of cooking.

To Serve: If an attractive, oven-proof casserole is used for baking, you may use it to serve at the table; if not, transfer the stew to a covered tureen before serving.

Variation: *To make this a vegetarian meal,* substitute 1 cubed eggplant for the chicken thighs.

Per serving: 79 mg cholesterol, 2.57 gm saturated fat, 10.4 gm total fat, 3.8 gm fiber, 132 mg sodium, 343.5 calories

Tomato Salad with Chopped Red Onion
and Balsamic Vinegar
♦Rosemary Chicken Breasts with Garlic and Lemon♦
Brown and Wild Rice
Broccoli Puree and Carrot Coins
Poached Pears with Natural Juices

Rosemary Chicken Breasts with Garlic and Lemon

Serves: 4 (3 ounces cooked chicken = 1 serving)

Chicken is a popular and relatively inexpensive entrée to serve. The following is a delicious recipe that is quick and easy even though you do not use a microwave.

2 whole chicken breasts (about 14–16 ounces each), halved, boned, skin and fat removed

2 teaspoons extra-virgin olive oil

1 tablespoon dry rosemary, crushed

4 cloves garlic, minced

3 tablespoons lemon juice

1 teaspoon grated lemon zest

½ cup dry white wine or vermouth

1½ cups defatted sodium-reduced chicken broth

2 teaspoons arrowroot mixed with 3 tablespoons defatted sodium-reduced chicken broth

Rosemary or watercress, for garnish

1. Marinate the chicken breasts in the olive oil, rosemary, garlic, lemon juice, and zest in the refrigerator for 3 to 4 hours.

2. Heat an oven-proof skillet coated with butter-flavored nonstick spray and brown the breasts lightly on both sides. Add any remaining marinade.

3. Bake uncovered in a preheated 350° oven for 12 to 15 minutes.

4. Remove the chicken from the skillet and keep warm. Add the wine and broth to the skillet and simmer for 5 minutes.

5. Add the arrowroot mixture and thicken the sauce. Return the chicken to the sauce and heat for 5 minutes.

To Serve: Place the chicken breasts on a bed of rice, top with sauce, and garnish with watercress or rosemary.

Per serving: 72 mg cholesterol, 1.38 gm saturated fat, 6.2 gm total fat, 0.2 gm fiber, 70 mg sodium, 200 calories

COMPANY DINNER

Steamed Artichoke with Lemon
◆Grilled Chicken Breasts with Apples Calvados◆
Seasonal Vegetable Brochette
Brown Rice Pilaf
Today's Coffee Cake (page 336)
Fresh Fruit

Grilled Chicken Breasts with Apples Calvados Ⓠ

Serves: 4 (3 ounces cooked chicken = 1 serving)

4 4-ounce boned, skinned, and de-fatted chicken breasts
Juice of ½ lemon
1 teaspoon salt-free vegetable seasoning
1 teaspoon onion powder
2 teaspoons canola or cold-pressed safflower oil
2 tablespoons Calvados

2 cups peeled apples (Golden Delicious or McIntosh), sliced ⅔ inch thick
¼ cup frozen unsweetened apple juice concentrate, defrosted
1 tablespoon cornstarch

Watercress, for garnish

1. Season the chicken breasts with lemon juice, vegetable seasoning, and onion powder.
2. Place the oil in a 10-inch nonstick skillet and heat; add the chicken breasts and grill 3 minutes on each side.
3. Sprinkle the Calvados over the chicken and heat 2 minutes.
4. Arrange the apple slices over the chicken, pour the apple juice over the chicken and apples, and partially cover.
5. Cook 12 to 15 minutes or until chicken is tender. Baste halfway through cooking.
6. Remove the chicken and apples to a heated platter and keep warm. Add the cornstarch to the remaining liquid and stir over heat until shiny.

To Serve: Spoon the sauce over the chicken breasts and garnish with watercress.

Variation: Pears may be substituted for the apples and pear liqueur substituted for the Calvados.

Per serving: 72 mg cholesterol, 1.23 gm saturated fat, 6.3 gm total fat, 1.7 gm fiber, 68 mg sodium, 241 calories

Mixed Green Salad with Chopped Tomatoes
♦Chicken Enchiladas♦
Vegetarian Refried Beans
Steamed Brown Rice (page 130)
Papaya with Lime

Chicken Enchiladas Ⓠ Ⓜ

Serves: 4 (2 enchiladas = 1 serving)

1 medium onion, chopped
3 cloves garlic, minced
2 teaspoons canola oil
1 stalk celery, chopped
6 green tomatillos, husked and finely chopped
½ cup defatted sodium-reduced chicken broth
½ cup chopped fresh cilantro
1¼-pound boned, skinned, and defatted chicken breast, poached (page 142) or about 3 cups shredded leftover cooked chicken or turkey

2 tablespoons nonfat plain yogurt
8 corn tortillas, warmed in microwave oven for 10 seconds
1½ to 2 cups canned red enchilada sauce
3 tablespoons finely shredded part-skim mozzarella cheese

⅔ cup nonfat plain yogurt mixed with 2 tablespoons light-style sour cream, and chopped green onions, for garnish

1. Sauté the onion and garlic in the oil in a one-quart nonstick saucepan for 3 minutes. Add the celery, tomatillos, chicken broth, and cilantro and simmer 10 minutes.

2. Shred the chicken breasts and add with the yogurt to the tomatillo sauce.

3. Lay a tortilla flat and place a scant ½ cup of the chicken mixture along the center. Fold over the ends to cover the mixture and place seam-side-down in a 13 × 9 × 2-inch casserole that has a thin layer of enchilada sauce on the bottom. Repeat with the remaining tortillas.

4. Cover with enchilada sauce. Sprinkle with shredded mozzarella cheese* and bake in a preheated 350° oven for 20 to 25 minutes or until bubbly, or in microwave on high for 12 minutes.

To Serve: Garnish with the yogurt mixture topped with chopped green onions.

Per serving: 47 mg cholesterol, 1.22 gm saturated fat, 5.4 gm total fat, 1 gm fiber, 127 mg sodium, 218 calories

* At this point, the enchiladas may be wrapped and frozen for future use.

◆Hot Cajun Chicken and Black Bean Salad◆
Warm Corn Tortillas
Papaya Filled with Raspberries and
a Dollop of Yogurt

Hot Cajun Chicken and Black Bean Salad

Serves: 4 (3 ounces cooked chicken = 1 serving)

1 tablespoon chopped onion
1 large clove garlic, minced
1 teaspoon olive oil
½ cup dried black beans, soaked
  overnight and drained*
1½ cups defatted sodium-reduced
  chicken broth
1 tablespoon chopped canned
  green chilis
¼ cup fresh cilantro or parsley,
  chopped
4 6-ounce chicken breasts,
  skinned, boned, and flattened

Juice of 1 lemon
2 teaspoons Cajun spice seasoning
  or spicy vegetable seasoning

8 cups shredded red-leaf lettuce
1 cup diced tomato
1 cup fresh white or sodium-
  reduced canned kernel corn
1 cup salt-free canned salsa

1. In a nonstick saucepan, sauté the onion and garlic in oil until wilted.
2. Add the beans and sauté 1 minute.
3. Add the chicken broth, bring to a boil, reduce heat, cover, and simmer 45 minutes or until very tender. Add chilis and cilantro and set aside.
4. Season the chicken with the lemon juice and spicy seasoning. Grill on a hot nonstick skillet until browned on both sides. Cut each breast into six slices.

To Serve: Mound 2 cups of greens on each of four dinner plates. Pour a quarter of the hot black beans over the lettuce. Sprinkle with a quarter of the chopped tomatoes and corn. Top with hot chicken slices and serve with salsa on the side.

Per serving: 72 mg cholesterol, 1.48 gm saturated fat, 6.4 gm total fat, 5.9 gm fiber, 103 mg sodium, 333 calories

* One can of black beans or 2 cups cooked beans (page 129) may be substituted for the dry beans. In this case, reduce the amount of chicken broth to ⅔ cup and cook uncovered 20 minutes. Then proceed as in recipe.

Watercress, Endive, and Mushroom Salad
♦Orange-Glazed Cornish Hens♦
Bulgur Wheat Pilaf (page 312)
Succotash
Marbled Angel Food Cake (page 324)

Orange-Glazed Cornish Hens

Serves: 4 (4 ounces cooked meat = 1 serving)

2 1-pound Cornish game hens,
   halved, skin and fat removed
Juice of ½ lemon
2 teaspoons salt-free vegetable
   seasoning
1 teaspoon onion powder
Freshly ground pepper
1 medium onion, chopped

1 6-ounce can frozen unsweetened
   orange juice or pineapple-
   orange juice (not reconstituted)

8 orange wedges and 1 large
   bunch grapes, for garnish
   (optional)

1. Season both sides of the hens with the lemon juice, vegetable seasoning, onion powder, and pepper.

2. Sprinkle the chopped onion over the bottom of an 8 × 11-inch glass baking dish coated with nonstick cooking spray. Place the hens flesh-side-down on top of the onions.

3. Spoon 1 tablespoon of the orange juice over each half.

4. Bake uncovered in a preheated 350° oven for 15 minutes. Turn the hens over and cover with the remaining juice.

5. Continue to bake for 30 minutes or until nicely browned and tender. If the juice dries out during cooking, add a bit of chicken broth or water to the pan.

To Serve: Mound pilaf on a serving platter and spoon the onions and sauce over it. Arrange the hens on top and garnish with orange wedges, and grapes.

Per serving: 101 mg cholesterol, 2.33 gm saturated fat, 8.6 gm total fat, 0.4 gm fiber, 102 mg sodium, 305 calories

COMPANY DINNER
Mixed Greens and Fennel with Low-Calorie Balsamic Vinaigrette
◆Cornish Game Hens with Fresh Raspberry Glaze◆
Broccoli Crown Vinaigrette (page 299)
Diced Sweet Potatoes and Peas
Wild Rice Pilaf with Scallions
Lemon-Lime Yogurt Pie (page 236)

Cornish Game Hens
with Fresh Raspberry Glaze

Serves: 8 (4 ounces cooked meat = 1 serving)

1 shallot, finely minced
3 cups fresh or frozen raspberries
(if fresh, reserve ½ cup for
garnish)
1 cup raspberry wine vinegar
¼ cup frozen unsweetened apple
juice concentrate
2 bay leaves
2 teaspoons dried thyme
1 cup defatted sodium-reduced
chicken broth

4 1-pound Cornish game hens,
halved, skin and fat removed
Salt-free vegetable seasoning
Freshly ground pepper
½ cup dry white wine mixed with
1½ tablespoons cornstarch

Watercress, for garnish

The Day Before: 1. Combine the shallot, raspberries, vinegar, apple juice concentrate, bay leaves, thyme, and chicken broth in a saucepan. Bring to a boil, remove from heat and cool.

2. Pour the cooled mixture over the hens in a shallow casserole. Add seasonings.

3. Cover and marinate overnight in the refrigerator, turning occasionally.

The Next Day: 1. Remove hens from marinade and place on a baking sheet. Broil until lightly browned on each side.

2. In a saucepan, combine the remaining marinade with the wine and cornstarch mixture. Stir and bring to a boil.

3. Pour the sauce over the hens and bake in a preheated 350° oven for 20 to 25 minutes or until tender.

To Serve: Arrange the hens on a warm serving platter, coat with sauce, and garnish with fresh watercress and fresh raspberries.

Per serving: 101 mg cholesterol, 2.33 gm saturated fat, 8.7 gm total fat, 3.6 gm fiber,
102 mg sodium, 272 calories

Beef

Marinated Cucumbers
◆Shabu Sukiyaki◆
Steamed Rice (page 130)
Mandarin Oranges

Shabu Sukiyaki ⓠ

Serves: 4 (1½ ounces cooked beef=1 serving)

½ pound beef tenderloin, visible
fat removed, chilled in freezer
and cut across grain into ⅛-inch
slices
½ cup white wine or sake
2 tablespoons sodium-reduced soy
sauce
2 tablespoons unsweetened frozen
apple juice concentrate
2 onions
3 carrots
2 stalks celery
⅓ pound fresh mushrooms
6 thin green onions
1 16-ounce package washed fresh
spinach, rinsed, stems removed
2 teaspoons canola oil
1½ cups defatted sodium-reduced
chicken broth
2 ounces uncooked vermicelli,
broken in thirds

1. Marinate the steak slices in the wine, soy sauce, and apple juice concentrate while preparing the vegetables.
2. Cut the onions, carrots, celery, and mushrooms into ⅛-inch-thick slices.
3. Cut the green onions into 2-inch lengths. Tear the spinach into bite-sized pieces.
4. Heat the oil in a 12-inch nonstick skillet. Add the onions, carrots, celery, mushrooms, and green onions. Stir-fry 2 minutes.
5. Drain the marinade from the meat and add to the skillet with the broth and vermicelli. Bring to a boil and simmer 5 minutes.
6. Stir in the meat and cook until it loses its red color.
7. Add the spinach, stir, and cook 30 seconds.
To Serve: Spoon into a warm serving bowl and serve with steamed rice.

Variation:
For a vegetarian sukiyaki, add 4 stalks sliced bok choy, 2 cups marinated diced tofu, and 1 cup frozen or fresh snow peas instead of meat.

Per serving: 36 mg cholesterol, 1.8 gm saturated fat, 7.1 gm total fat, 6.5 gm fiber, 412 mg sodium, 289 calories

Pasta

Artichoke Heart, Tomato, and Onion Salad with
Low-Calorie Sweet Basil Vinaigrette Dressing
♦Fusilli with Broccoli Flowerets,
Garlic, and Hot Red Pepper Flakes♦
Sourdough Rolls
Fresh Figs with Yogurt

Fusilli with Broccoli Flowerets, Garlic, and Hot Red Pepper Flakes

Serves: 4

Here's a recipe that combines complex carbohydrates with a high fiber vegetable in a delicious and colorful mixture.

1 tablespoon extra-virgin olive oil
3 large cloves garlic, minced
4 cups chopped broccoli flowerets, steamed until barely tender, or microwaved 3 minutes on high
Few grains crushed red pepper flakes

8 ounces fusilli, cooked *al dente* and drained
1 tablespoon shredded Parmesan cheese

1. Heat the oil in a 10-inch nonstick skillet, add the garlic, and cook 2 minutes; do not brown. Add the broccoli and heat 2 minutes over medium heat.

2. Add the red pepper flakes and hot cooked pasta; stir with a wooden fork 2 to 3 minutes or until heated through.*

To Serve: Spoon onto a heated platter and sprinkle with Parmesan cheese. Pass more crushed hot red pepper flakes for heartier souls.

Per serving: 1 mg cholesterol, 0.85 gm saturated fat, 4.8 gm total fat, 2.7 gm fiber, 49 mg sodium, 273 calories

* If the pasta mixture is not as moist as you like, add a bit of chicken broth.

Chilled Greens with Corn and Kidney Beans
◆Vegetarian Lasagna Rolls◆
Steamed Fresh Asparagus
Strawberries Sprinkled with Balsamic Vinegar

Vegetarian Lasagna Rolls Ⓠ Ⓜ

Serves: 8 (2 rolls = 1 serving)

1 small onion, finely chopped
2 cloves garlic, minced
½ red pepper, seeded and finely chopped
2 teaspoons salt-free vegetable seasoning
1 teaspoon dried Italian herb blend, crushed
2 teaspoons extra-virgin olive oil
1 cup coarsely shredded carrot
1 cup chopped zucchini
1 cup thinly sliced fresh mushrooms
1 10-ounce package frozen chopped spinach, defrosted and squeezed dry

1 cup part-skim ricotta cheese
2 extra-large egg whites, slightly beaten
8 lasagna noodles (7 to 8 ounces), cooked, drained, rinsed, drained, and halved lengthwise
2½ cups salt-free marinara sauce, tomato sauce, or Garden Vegetable Marinara Sauce (page 283)
3 fresh Italian plum tomatoes, sliced crosswise (16 slices)
3 tablespoons shredded part-skim mozzarella cheese (optional)
Fresh basil leaves, for garnish

1. Sauté the onion, garlic, red pepper, and seasonings in the olive oil in a nonstick skillet for about 2 to 3 minutes.
2. Add the carrot, zucchini, and mushrooms and sauté 3 minutes.
3. Remove from heat and add the spinach, ricotta cheese, and egg whites. Blend well.
4. Spread one sixteenth of the mixture on each lasagna strip and roll up in jelly roll fashion.
5. Place the rolls (filled-side-up) into a shallow baking dish (13 × 9 × 2 inches). Spoon the marinara sauce over the rolls.
6. Top each roll with a tomato slice and sprinkle with mozzarella cheese if desired.
7. Bake uncovered on high in a microwave oven for about 15 minutes, or covered in a preheated 350° oven for 30 to 35 minutes.
To Serve: Garnish with leaves of fresh basil and serve hot.

Per serving: 10 mg cholesterol, 1.76 gm saturated fat, 4.2 gm total fat, 3 gm fiber, 105 mg sodium, 206 calories

Green Bean, Tomato, and Red Onion Salad Vinaigrette
♦Sweet Pepper Pasta♦
Whole Wheat Baguette
Mixed Fresh Fruit Cup

Sweet Pepper Pasta ⓠ

Serves: 4

1 tablespoon extra-virgin olive oil
½ small onion, thinly sliced
4 large cloves garlic, chopped fine
1 small red pepper, seeded and
cut into ½-inch strips
1 small yellow pepper, seeded and
cut into ½-inch strips
1 small green pepper, seeded and
cut into ½-inch strips
1 small orange pepper, seeded and
cut into ½-inch strips (optional)
1 teaspoon salt-free vegetable
seasoning
½ cup dry white wine or vermouth
⅔ cup defatted sodium-reduced
chicken broth

1 tablespoon sodium-reduced soy
sauce
1 teaspoon grated peeled fresh
ginger
⅛ teaspoon crushed red pepper
flakes or freshly ground pepper
to taste
½ teaspoon Oriental sesame oil
8 ounces capellini or spaghettini
pasta, cooked 3 to 4 minutes or
al dente and drained

2 tablespoons sliced green onions,
for garnish

1. Coat a nonstick skillet with nonstick spray; add the olive oil and heat over medium heat.
2. Separate the onion slices, add to the pan, and sauté quickly about 3 minutes. Add the garlic and sauté quickly about 1 minute, stirring constantly.
3. Add the peppers and vegetable seasoning and sauté 1 minute more.
4. Stir in the wine, chicken broth, soy sauce, ginger, and pepper flakes. Bring the mixture to a boil, reduce the heat, cover, and simmer 3 minutes.
5. Uncover and continue cooking over high heat about 3 minutes. Sprinkle with sesame oil.
6. Combine the pepper mixture with the hot cooked pasta.
To Serve: Mound the hot pasta mixture onto a warm serving platter and sprinkle with sliced green onions.

Variation: Three fresh shiitake or oyster mushrooms may be added with the peppers.

Per serving: 0 mg cholesterol, 0.69 gm saturated fat, 5 gm total fat, 2.4 gm fiber, 128 mg sodium, 286 calories

Mixed Greens and Fennel with
Balsamic Vinaigrette
♦Linguini with Red Clam Sauce♦
Crisp Whole Wheat Rolls
Poached Pears and Raspberries (page 317)

Linguini with Red Clam Sauce ⓠ

Serves: 6

The sauce in this recipe may be prepared earlier in the day, or you may use 3½ cups of the Garden Vegetable Marinara Sauce on page 283.

12 ounces linguini, cooked *al dente* and drained

Red Clam Sauce:
6 cloves garlic, minced
½ small onion, minced
1 tablespoon extra-virgin olive oil
1 28-ounce can crushed Italian plum tomatoes
½ cup dry red wine
⅔ cup chopped celery
1 strip orange zest
1 teaspoon dried oregano, crushed, or 1 tablespoon fresh oregano, chopped

1 teaspoon dried thyme, crushed, or 1 tablespoon fresh thyme, chopped
Freshly ground pepper
½ teaspoon crushed red pepper flakes
¼ cup chopped fresh Italian parsley leaves
4 dozen fresh clams, *well scrubbed and washed* under cold running water

1. Sauté the garlic and onion in the oil in a 4-quart saucepan until wilted.
2. Add all the remaining sauce ingredients except the parsley and clams. Bring to a boil, reduce heat, and simmer for 20 minutes, stirring occasionally.
3. Add the clams and parsley and steam, covered, over medium heat, shaking the pan occasionally, for 5 to 7 minutes or until the shells are opened. *Discard any unopened clams* and remove the orange zest.

To Serve: Place the drained linguini in a large serving bowl and spoon the sauce and clams over the pasta. Serve immediately.

Per serving: 54 mg cholesterol, 0.63 gm saturated fat, 4.9 gm total fat, 2.9 gm fiber, 321 mg sodium, 336 calories

Three-Bean Salad
◆Lillian's Quick and Easy Manicotti◆
Steamed Zucchini Spears
Lemon Sorbet with Raspberry Sauce

Lillian's Quick and Easy Manicotti Ⓜ

Serves: 6 (2 manicotti = 1 serving)

15 ounces part-skim ricotta cheese
1 10-ounce package frozen chopped spinach, defrosted and drained
2 whole green onions, sliced
2 extra-large egg whites, or ¼ cup egg substitute

1 tablespoon dried dill, or 2 tablespoons chopped fresh dill
¼ teaspoon freshly ground nutmeg
About 8 ounces uncooked egg-free manicotti shells (12)
3 cups marinara sauce

1. Combine the ricotta cheese, drained spinach, onions, egg whites, dill, and nutmeg. Mix thoroughly.
2. Stuff the *uncooked* manicotti shells with the mixture.
3. Coat an 11 × 14 × 2-inch glass baking pan with corn oil cooking spray.
4. Cover the bottom of the pan with a layer of marinara sauce. Arrange the stuffed manicotti shells next to each other in the pan and cover with the remaining sauce.
5. Cover the pan tightly, first with plastic wrap, then with aluminum foil. Bake in a preheated 350° oven for 1 hour.

NOTE: This dish may be prepared ahead or frozen for future use. To serve if frozen, place in a cold oven and bake 1½ hours at 350°.

To Microwave:
1. Spread half of the *heated* sauce on the bottom of a baking dish.
2. Lay filled shells over sauce and top with remaining sauce.
3. Cover dish tightly with plastic wrap and microwave on high for 10 minutes.
4. Turn each shell over, cover and microwave on medium high for 15 minutes.
5. Remove plastic and let stand 12 to 15 minutes before serving.

Per serving: 17 mg cholesterol, 2.88 gm saturated fat, 5 gm total fat, 2.4 gm fiber, 138 mg sodium, 227 calories

Salad of Chilled Mixed
Radicchio, Red Lettuce, and Butter Lettuce
with Low-Calorie Balsamic Vinaigrette
♦Pasta Shells with Mushrooms♦
Steamed Broccoli
Mixed Berries with Creme Topping (page 314)

Pasta Shells with Mushrooms

Serves: 4

Use pasta shells about one inch in size in preparing this recipe, not the ones that are large enough for stuffing.

½ cup minced onion
1 tablespoon extra-virgin olive oil
1 ounce dried Porcini mushrooms, soaked in 1 cup dry white wine for 30 minutes (save the strained liquid)
1½ cups thinly sliced fresh mushroom caps

½ teaspoon dried Italian herb blend, or 2 teaspoons chopped fresh basil
8 ounces 1-inch pasta shells, cooked *al dente* and drained

1 tablespoon grated Parmesan cheese (optional)

1. Sauté the onion in the oil in a nonstick 1-quart saucepan for several minutes until wilted.
2. Slice the drained Porcini mushrooms and add to onions with the sliced fresh mushroom caps and herbs. Sauté 3 minutes.
3. Add the strained soaking liquid and cook 5 minutes.
4. Add the hot cooked pasta shells to the mushroom mixture and mix thoroughly.

To Serve: Mound pasta mixture on a heated serving platter and sprinkle with Parmesan cheese.

Per serving: 0 mg cholesterol, 0.61 gm saturated fat, 4.3 gm total fat, 2.8 gm fiber, 7 mg sodium, 291 calories

Assorted Greens and Sliced Fresh Asparagus with
Low-Calorie Lemon Vinaigrette Dressing
♦Fresh Tomato, Basil, and Mozzarella Pasta♦
Crisp Sourdough Baguette
Cantaloupe Cubes with Fresh Strawberry Sauce (page 317)

Fresh Tomato, Basil, and Mozzarella Pasta Ⓠ

Serves: 2

There is no oil added in this recipe, and the tomatoes in the dish
are not cooked—just heated to give a wonderful, fresh taste.

4 ounces spaghettini, cooked *al
dente* and drained
⅓ cup defatted sodium-reduced
chicken broth
2 tablespoons dry white wine
Freshly ground pepper
2 fresh Italian plum tomatoes,
diced

2 ounces part-skim mozzarella
cheese, diced
1 tablespoon chopped fresh basil
leaves

1. While the pasta is cooking, bring the broth, wine, and pepper to a
boil. Add the tomatoes and heat *1 minute*. Add the cheese and stir.
2. Immediately pour the tomato mixture and basil over the drained hot
pasta and toss to blend.
To Serve: Place on warm plates and serve while hot.

Per serving: 16 mg cholesterol, 2.99 gm saturated fat, 5.4 gm total fat, 2.5 gm fiber,
144 mg sodium, 312 calories

Vegetarian Dishes

Mixed Green Salad with Garbanzo Beans and
Oil-Free Vinaigrette Dressing
◆Eggplant Lasagna◆
Lemony Brussels Sprouts
Baked Sweet Potatoes
Whole Grain Rolls
Fresh Strawberries with Yogurt

Eggplant Lasagna Ⓠ Ⓜ

Serves: 6

Many people accustomed to cooking meat-and-potato meals are stymied by the thought of preparing a vegetarian dinner. The following recipe is simple to make and high in fiber and satisfying flavors.

1 1-pound eggplant, cut into 18 slices
1 tablespoon extra-virgin olive oil
8 ounces part-skim ricotta cheese
2 carrots, coarsely shredded
2 green onions, thinly sliced
1 tablespoon chopped fresh parsley
2 extra-large egg whites, slightly beaten

1 tablespoon grated Parmesan cheese
Freshly ground pepper
2 cups salt-free marinara sauce or tomato sauce, mixed with 6 sliced fresh mushrooms and 1 tablespoon chopped fresh basil
3 Italian plum tomatoes, cut into 12 thin slices

1. Place the eggplant slices on a nonstick cookie sheet and brush one side lightly with olive oil. Broil until lightly colored on both sides.

2. Combine the ricotta cheese, carrots, onion, parsley, egg whites, 1½ teaspoons of the Parmesan cheese, and the freshly ground pepper.

3. Spoon ⅓ cup of the marinara sauce mixture on the bottom of an 8 × 11 × 3-inch baking pan. Arrange a layer of six slices of eggplant on the sauce; top each eggplant slice with 1 tablespoon of the ricotta cheese mixture, 1 tomato slice, and 1 tablespoon of the marinara sauce mixture.

4. Repeat for a second layer, then top with the remaining slices of eggplant and the remaining marinara sauce. Sprinkle with the Parmesan cheese and cover with wax paper.

5. Bake on high in a microwave oven for 10 minutes or in a preheated 375° oven for 30 to 35 minutes. Let stand 10 minutes before serving.

Per serving: 12 mg cholesterol, 2.38 gm saturated fat, 5.9 gm total fat, 2.8 gm fiber, 594 mg sodium, 153 calories

Hearty Eight-Bean Soup (page 133)
♦Peppered Potato Patties♦
Steamed Zucchini Spears
Broiled Tomato
Whole Wheat Rolls
Fresh Fruit

Peppered Potato Patties ℚ

Serves: 4 (2 patties = 1 serving)

For a flavorful appetizer, save the potato skins, brush with a bit of safflower oil, and bake in a hot oven until crisp. Serve with fresh salsa and a dab of nonfat plain yogurt.

2 8-ounce baked russet potatoes, halved and pulp removed
⅓ cup nonfat plain yogurt or buttermilk
¼ teaspoon salt (optional)
¼ teaspoon white pepper
3 green onions, sliced
½ green pepper, seeded and chopped

½ red pepper, seeded and chopped
2 large broccoli spears, chopped and steamed until crisp
¼ cup yellow cornmeal
2 teaspoons canola or cold-pressed safflower oil

1. Mash the potato pulp in a mixing bowl; add the yogurt, salt, and pepper.
2. Add the vegetables and blend. Taste and adjust the seasonings.
3. Shape into eight round 3-inch patties and coat both sides with the cornmeal.
4. Brush a nonstick skillet with the oil; heat and add the patties.
5. Cook over medium-high heat about 3 minutes on each side or until golden brown.

To Serve: Arrange on a platter and surround with zucchini spears and broiled tomatoes.

Variation: Instead of making patties, return the potato mixture to the potato skins, sprinkle lightly with cornmeal, and bake in a preheated 375° oven for 15 to 20 minutes.

Per serving: 0 mg cholesterol, 0.2 gm saturated fat, 2.6 gm total fat, 1.6 gm fiber, 22 mg sodium, 140 calories

Steamed Artichokes with Lemon
♦Quick Minestrone♦
Whole Wheat Sourdough Rolls
Fusilli with Marinara Sauce
Mixed Fresh Fruit Cup

Quick Minestrone Ⓠ Ⓜ

Yield: 6 to 7 cups (1 cup = 1 serving)

3 fresh mushrooms, sliced
1 small zucchini, diced
½ cup green beans, cut into
  ½-inch pieces
¼ onion, diced
½ stalk celery with leaves, thinly
  sliced
1 small carrot, thinly sliced
1 stalk bok choy, coarsely chopped
½ cup shredded rinsed fresh
  spinach
3 cups defatted sodium-reduced
  chicken broth
¼ teaspoon dried thyme, crushed

Freshly ground white pepper
1 tablespoon chopped fresh basil,
  or ½ teaspoon dried basil,
  crushed
2 fresh or canned Italian plum tomatoes, diced
½ cup canned kidney beans,
  drained and rinsed

6 ¼-inch-thick slices sourdough
  baguette, sprinkled lightly with
  1 tablespoon Parmesan cheese
  and toasted, for garnish

1. Place the first ten ingredients in a 2-quart microwave casserole.
2. Cover and microwave on high for 10 minutes.
3. Add the pepper, basil, tomatoes, and kidney beans and microwave on high for 3 minutes. Taste and adjust seasonings.

To Serve: Ladle the hot soup into warm bowls and garnish each bowl with one slice of toast.

Per serving: 0 mg cholesterol, 0.04 gm saturated fat, 0.3 gm total fat, 1.5 gm fiber,
22 mg sodium, 51 calories

Bean Curd and Spinach Soup (page 266)
♦Vegetable Lo Mein♦
Steamed Bok Choy with Mushrooms
Fresh Orange Wedges

Vegetable Lo Mein Ⓠ

Serves: 4

Chinese-style cooking lends itself nicely to meals low in calories, saturated fat and cholesterol without any animal protein added. Try using a wok to prepare the combination of vegetables, whether alone or with a small amount of chicken, tofu, beef, or pasta.

1 tablespoon canola oil
1 medium onion, thinly sliced and separated
1 stalk celery, thinly sliced
2 carrots, thinly sliced with vegetable peeler
1 large zucchini, cut into 2-inch julienne strips
2 cups chopped broccoli
1 4-ounce can water chestnuts, drained and thinly sliced (optional)

1 cup fresh snow peas or frozen peas
2 tablespoons sodium-reduced soy sauce
8 ounces linguini, cooked *al dente* and drained
1 teaspoon Oriental sesame oil (optional)
3 green onions, cut into 2-inch julienne strips

1. Heat a wok or a nonstick skillet over high heat. Add the oil, swirling it around the pan.
2. Add the onions and stir-fry 2 to 3 minutes.
3. Add the celery and carrots, stir-fry for 2 minutes. Add the zucchini, broccoli, water chestnuts, and pea pods and stir-fry for 2 minutes more.
4. Add the soy sauce; heat 1 minute.
5. Add the hot, well-drained linguini to the vegetable mixture, sprinkle with sesame oil and green onions, and mix until heated through.

Per serving: 0 mg cholesterol, 0.36 gm saturated fat, 4.5 gm total fat, 4.2 gm fiber, 279 mg sodium, 305 calories

◆Celery Root, Red Cabbage, and Orange Salad◆
Breast of Chicken Roasted with
Onions and Leeks
Brown Rice Pilaf
Steamed Brussels Sprouts
Raisin Bread Pudding (page 321)

Celery Root, Red Cabbage, and Orange Salad ⊛

Serves: 4

Three high-fiber winter vegetables join forces to make a deliciously different salad.

1 cup celery root, peeled and shredded

2 cups shredded red cabbage

1 large navel orange, peeled and cubed

2 green onions, thinly sliced, for garnish

Dressing:

¼ cup low-calorie oil-free vinaigrette dressing

3 tablespoons fresh orange juice

¼ teaspoon celery seed

2 teaspoons balsamic vinegar

1. Place the celery root, red cabbage, and oranges in a mixing bowl. Toss and chill.
2. Combine the dressing ingredients and blend thoroughly.
3. Just before serving, sprinkle the salad with dressing and toss gently with two forks.

To Serve: Arrange on individual salad plates and sprinkle with sliced green onions.

Per serving: 0 mg cholesterol, 0.05 gm saturated fat, 0.3 gm total fat, 1.7 gm fiber, 45 mg sodium, 52 calories

*Assorted Muffins
(Cranberry and Blueberry)*

Quick Breakfast Beverage

Oat Bran Waffles

Marinated Broccoli, Corn,
Artichoke Hearts, and Red Peppers
Sweet Pepper Pasta
Vegetable Lo Mein
Gingered Pineapple Carrots
Vegetable Paella with Clams

Blueberry Meringue Cobbler
Chocoholic's Chocolate Cake
Almost Edie's Coffee Cake
Poached Pears "en Croute"
Fresh Peach Scallop
with Creme Anglaise
Oatmeal Cookies
Oat Nut Slices with Jam
Great Date Brownies

Stir-Fried Scallops with Garlic,
Mushrooms, and Snow Peas

Tuscan Minestrone

Tamale Pie

Hot Cajun Chicken and Black Bean Salad

Grilled Salmon Scallops on Mixed Greens with Salsa

Pasta Salad with Seafood
Parsley and Tomato Salad
with Basil Vinaigrette
Black Bean and Corn Salad
Warm New Potato Salad

Hearts of Romaine and Shredded Carrot Salad with
Mustard-Yogurt Dressing
Broiled Orange Roughy
Baked Russet Potatoes
♦Angela's Herbed Squash Medley♦
Red and Green Grapes

Angela's
Herbed Squash Medley ⓆⓂ

Serves: 8 to 10

This vegetable dish makes a large amount (great for guests) and
may be prepared in the morning to be cooked and served for dinner.

4 teaspoons extra-virgin olive oil
6–8 crookneck squash, cut into
¼-inch slices
4 large cloves garlic, minced, and
1 bunch green onions, thinly
sliced, mixed together
1 pint cherry tomatoes, halved, or
6 plum tomatoes, chopped
¼ cup chopped fresh basil, ¼ cup
chopped fresh Italian parsley,
and 1 tablespoon chopped fresh
thyme, mixed together

Freshly ground pepper
Salt-free vegetable seasoning
1 large beefsteak tomato, thinly
sliced
1 tablespoon grated Parmesan
cheese mixed with 3 tablespoons
dry whole wheat breadcrumbs

1. Coat a 2-quart shallow oval casserole with butter-flavored nonstick
spray. Sprinkle with 1 teaspoon of the olive oil.
2. Arrange a third of the squash slices in one layer, sprinkle with a third
of the onion and garlic mixture; cover with a third of the tomatoes, sprinkle
with a third of the herb mixture, freshly ground pepper, and vegetable
seasoning. Sprinkle 1 teaspoon of the olive oil over the top. Repeat two
times.
3. Top with the sliced tomatoes and the cheese mixture.
4. Cover tightly with microwave plastic wrap and microwave on high for
12 to 15 minutes. (Using a carousel in your microwave oven makes it unnecessary to rotate the dish a quarter turn after half the cooking time.)

Per serving: 1 mg cholesterol, 0.5 gm saturated fat, 2.9 gm total fat, 1.5 gm fiber,
41 mg sodium, 70 calories

Tomato-Rice Soup
♦Lentil Vegetable Salad with
Low-Calorie Tarragon Vinaigrette♦
Baked Russet Potato with Nonfat Plain Yogurt
Sliced Fall Fruits with Papaya Puree

Lentil Vegetable Salad with Low-Calorie Tarragon Vinaigrette

Serves: 4

Lentils are a good source of protein and soluble fiber, and this salad makes a nice entrée for a vegetarian meal.

1 cup dried lentils, washed and drained
2 cups water
2 teaspoons dried thyme, crushed
1 bay leaf
Few grains crushed red pepper
1 large carrot, chopped
2 celery stalks, chopped
½ cup chopped red onion
1 small red or green pepper, seeded and thinly sliced

2 tablespoons chopped fresh Italian parsley
⅓ cup low-calorie oil-free vinaigrette dressing mixed with
1 tablespoon tarragon vinegar and 1 teaspoon extra-virgin olive oil

8 leaves butter lettuce and 1 cup alfalfa sprouts, for garnish

1. Place the lentils, water, thyme, bay leaf, and crushed pepper in a 2-quart saucepan. Bring to a boil, reduce heat, cover, and simmer 30 to 45 minutes. (*The lentils should be cooked but firm.*)

2. Drain the excess water, remove the bay leaf, and place the lentils in a salad bowl.

3. Add salad dressing and all the vegetables to the lentils; toss lightly and cool at room temperature.

To Serve: Line individual plates with butter lettuce, mound the salad on top of lettuce, and if desired, garnish with alfalfa sprouts.

Per serving: 0 mg cholesterol, 0.28 gm saturated fat, 1.9 gm total fat, 6.9 gm fiber, 34 mg sodium, 206 calories

Endive, Arugula, and Romaine Salad with
Yogurt Dressing (page 89)
♦Vegetarian Paella♦
Whole Wheat Rolls
Poached Peaches with Raspberry Sauce

Vegetarian Paella

Serves: 6 to 8

1½ tablespoons extra-virgin olive oil

2 large onions, thinly sliced

4 garlic cloves, minced

2 cups brown rice, washed

1 small eggplant (about 1 pound), cubed, or 4 Japanese eggplant, cut crosswise into ¼-inch slices

1 large red pepper, seeded and sliced

4½ cups vegetable or defatted sodium-reduced chicken stock

2 celery stalks with leaves, chopped

6 peeled Italian plum tomatoes, diced

1 can quartered artichoke hearts, rinsed and drained

Freshly ground pepper

⅛ teaspoon crushed saffron threads dissolved in 2 teaspoons hot water

1 cup frozen peas

½ cup chopped fresh parsley

2 tablespoons sliced green onions and 2 tablespoons slivered toasted almonds, for garnish (optional)

1. In a 3-quart nonstick saucepan, heat the oil; add the onions and garlic and sauté 5 minutes or until the onions are wilted. Add the rice and stir until opaque.

2. Add the eggplant and red pepper and sauté 3 to 5 minutes.

3. Add the stock, bring to a boil, and reduce the heat to a simmer.

4. Stir in the celery, tomatoes, artichoke hearts, pepper, and saffron.

5. Cover and simmer 35 to 40 minutes or until the rice is tender. Add the peas and parsley and cook 3 to 4 minutes, just until peas are cooked.

To Serve: Turn the paella into a warm serving dish and garnish with sliced green onions and almonds if desired.

Variation: *To make paella with animal protein,* add 8 skinned chicken thighs (about 1½ pounds) seasoned and broiled, and 1 16-ounce can sodium-reduced stewed tomatoes in Step 4. If desired, instead of chicken add 18 clams in Step 5 with the peas and parsley.

Per serving: 0 mg cholesterol, 0.65 gm saturated fat, 3.8 gm total fat, 3.5 gm fiber, 51 mg sodium, 255 calories

Chilled Mixed Green Salad
♦Stanford Moroccan Vegetable Stew with Couscous and
Spicy Red Pepper Sauce♦
Fresh Fruit
Oat Nut Slices with Jam (page 345)

Stanford Moroccan Vegetable Stew with Couscous and Spicy Red Pepper Sauce

Yield: 6 servings (2 tablespoons sauce = 1 serving)

This dish is my adaptation of a recipe from the *Sunset International Vegetarian Cookbook.*

1 tablespoon extra-virgin olive oil
1 large onion, finely chopped
1½ teaspoons ground coriander
¾ teaspoon ground cinnamon
2 medium-sized yams or sweet potatoes, peeled and cut into ½-inch cubes
1 small rutabaga (about 1 cup), peeled and cut into ½-inch cubes
2–3 large tomatoes, peeled and chopped
1¼ cups water or defatted sodium-reduced chicken broth
2 tablespoons lemon juice
½ teaspoon powdered saffron
2 cups cooked, drained chick-peas (garbanzo beans, page 129), or 1 15-ounce can chick-peas, drained and rinsed

Salt (optional)
2 medium-sized zucchini, cut diagonally into ½-inch slices
1 cup chopped broccoli flowerets
1 large red pepper, seeded and chopped
1 large green pepper, seeded and chopped
4 cups cooked whole wheat couscous, prepared according to package directions (without added fat)

Spicy Red Pepper Sauce (page 231)

1. Heat the oil in a 5-quart kettle over medium heat; add the onion, coriander, and cinnamon, and cook, stirring occasionally, until the onion is soft (about 5 minutes).

2. Stir in the sweet potatoes and rutabagas and cook, stirring often, for 2 minutes.

3. Add the tomatoes, water or broth, lemon juice, saffron, and garbanzos. Add salt to taste, if desired. Cover, reduce heat, and simmer for 15 minutes, or until the sweet potatoes are nearly tender.

4. Mix the zucchini, broccoli, and red and green peppers into the potato mixture and cook, covered, until all the vegetables are tender but still crisp (about 7 minutes).

To Serve: Spread the hot couscous around the edges of a deep platter and spoon the vegetable mixture into the center. Pass the Spicy Red Pepper Sauce.

Variation: Hot cooked brown rice, bulgur, buckwheat, quinoa, or millet, prepared according to directions on page 130, can be used instead of couscous.

Per serving: 0 mg cholesterol, 0.77 gm saturated fat, 5.1 gm total fat, 7.8 gm fiber, 25 mg sodium, 345 calories

Spicy Red Pepper Sauce Ⓠ Ⓜ

Yield: about 1½ cups (1 tablespoon = 1 serving)

This sauce will keep for weeks in a tightly closed jar in the refrigerator and may be used as a topping on steamed potatoes, broccoli, or chicken.

3 red peppers, seeded and
  quartered
1½ teaspoons commercial hot red
  pepper sauce, or 1 teaspoon
  cayenne pepper mixed with
  1 teaspoon ground cumin and
  3 cloves garlic

About ½ cup vegetable liquid or
  defatted sodium-reduced chicken
  broth (optional)

1. In a covered dish, microwave the peppers with seasonings for 10 minutes or until soft. Turn dish twice while cooking.

2. Puree the peppers in a food processor or blender. Taste and adjust seasonings.

3. If desired, you may thin the sauce with liquid from vegetables or with chicken broth.

Per serving: 0 mg cholesterol, 0.04 gm saturated fat, 0.3 gm total fat, 0.6 gm fiber, 11 mg sodium, 15 calories

Confetti Corn Soup (page 266)
♦Ratatouille♦
Steamed Carrot Spears
Quinoa with Peas
Baked Apple with Blueberry Sauce (page 314)

Ratatouille Ⓠ Ⓜ

Serves: 8 (1¼ cups = 1 serving)

This menu presents a lovely vegetarian meal for winter. Ratatouille itself, whether served hot as part of a vegetarian meal or as a vegetable side dish with chicken, is a versatile dish that can be made ahead.

1 large onion, coarsely chopped
3 large cloves garlic, minced
2 teaspoons extra-virgin olive oil
½ pound fresh mushrooms, sliced
1 green pepper, cut into ½-inch slices
1 red or yellow pepper, cut into ½-inch slices
1 pound eggplant with skin, cut into ¾-inch cubes
1 medium zucchini, cut into ½-inch slices

4 peeled Italian plum tomatoes, cubed, or 8 cherry tomatoes, halved
⅓ cup dry white wine
⅓ cup sodium-reduced vegetable juice
2 tablespoons tomato paste
1 tablespoon Worcestershire sauce
2 tablespoons chopped fresh oregano, thyme, or basil, or 2 teaspoons dried herb
Freshly ground pepper

1. In a large nonstick skillet, sauté the onion and garlic in the oil for several minutes over medium heat.

2. Add the remaining vegetables, stir, and reduce the heat. Combine the remaining ingredients. Add to the vegetables and stir.

3. Cover and simmer the vegetable mixture 35 minutes, stirring occasionally.

To Serve: Serve warm or cold.

To Microwave: Combine the onion, garlic, and oil in a 3-quart oval casserole and cook on high for 3 minutes. Add the remaining ingredients, stir, cover with microwave plastic wrap, and cook on high for about 15 minutes. Mix twice during the cooking time. Let stand, covered, for 10 minutes before serving.

Per serving: 0 mg cholesterol, 0.22 gm saturated fat, 1.6 gm total fat, 2 gm fiber, 29 mg sodium, 62 calories

Desserts

COMPANY DINNER
Sautéed Mushrooms on Greens with Balsamic Vinaigrette
Broiled Fish with Mustard and Capers
Corn on the Cob
Steamed French-Cut Green Beans
♦Papaya Ambrosia♦

Papaya Ambrosia ⓠ

Serves: 4 (¼ papaya = 1 serving)

This is a busy-day company dinner that allows you to enjoy your guests. Corn is a readily available vegetable, fresh or frozen, that is high in soluble fiber and this refreshing fruit dessert requires little preparation.

2 papayas, quartered and seeded
½ cup small red seedless grapes
½ cup unsweetened pineapple tidbits
½ cup nonfat plain yogurt mixed with 1 teaspoon pure vanilla extract

2 tablespoons toasted slivered almonds, for garnish (optional)

1. Using a grapefruit knife, remove the papaya meat from the shells (reserve the shells) and cube.
2. Combine the papaya, grapes, and pineapple in a bowl and toss lightly to combine.
3. Add the yogurt mixture to the fruit and stir lightly with a fork. Place in the refrigerator to chill.
To Serve: Just before serving, spoon the fruit mixture into the papaya shells and, if desired, sprinkle with toasted almonds.

Per serving: 1 mg cholesterol, 0.12 gm saturated fat, 0.4 gm total fat, 1.6 gm fiber, 26 mg sodium, 92 calories

Parsley and Tomato Salad
in Basil Vinaigrette (page 94)
Roast Turkey Breast
Stir-Fried Vegetables with Sesame Seeds
Steamed Brown and Wild Rice with Scallions
♦ Peach Scallop ♦

Fresh Peach Scallop Ⓠ Ⓜ

Serves: 8

Take advantage of fruits that are in season; they are more flavorful and less expensive. Nectarines, plums, pears, pineapples, or apples may be substituted for the peaches in this delicious dessert.

2 pounds fresh Freestone peaches, cut into ¾-inch slices (about 4 cups sliced)
2 tablespoons minute tapioca
1½ tablespoons lemon juice
2 tablespoons frozen unsweetened apple juice concentrate
1 tablespoon peach brandy or Amaretto

Topping:
3 tablespoons rolled oats, chopped
3 tablespoons sugar-free cold cereal (corn flakes, wheat flakes, or oat bran flakes), crushed
2 teaspoons brown sugar
½ teaspoon ground cinnamon
2 tablespoons chopped almonds

⅓ cup nonfat plain yogurt mixed with 1 teaspoon peach brandy or Amaretto, for garnish

1. Sprinkle the peaches with the tapioca, lemon juice, apple juice concentrate, and brandy.
2. Arrange the peaches in a 10-inch round glass pie plate or quiche pan.*
3. Combine the topping ingredients and blend with your fingers until crumbly.
4. Sprinkle over the peaches and microwave uncovered on high for 6 minutes or bake in a preheated 350° oven for 25 to 30 minutes.

To Serve: Serve warm with a dollop of flavored yogurt, a pitcher of nonfat milk, or Creme Topping (page 314).

Per serving: 0 mg cholesterol, 0.2 gm saturated fat, 1.9 gm total fat, 2.1 gm fiber, 3 mg sodium, 118 calories

---

* Round or oval is the better shape for the microwave because it gives more even cooking.

COMPANY DINNER

Mixed Greens with Shredded Carrots and
Basil Vinaigrette Dressing (page 94)
Broiled Salmon with Balsamic Vinegar
Baked Potatoes with Salsa
Summer Squash
♦Baked Alaska Pears♦

Baked Alaska Pears ℚ

Serves: 4

2 large, ripe pears, peeled,
halved, and cored, or 4 pear
halves canned in juice
2 tablespoons frozen unsweetened
apple juice concentrate
3 extra-large egg whites, at room
temperature
¼ teaspoon cream of tartar

3 tablespoons confectioner's sugar*
1 teaspoon hazelnut liqueur
(Frangelica)
2 tablespoons chopped hazelnuts

4 large unhulled strawberries, for
garnish

1. Place the pear halves in a shallow baking dish and sprinkle with the apple juice concentrate. Cover with microwave plastic wrap and microwave on high for 3 minutes. (This may be prepared in the morning or the day before.) If you are using canned pears, omit this step.
2. Drain the pears on paper towels and place on a baking sheet.
3. Beat the egg whites and cream of tartar with an electric mixer until soft peaks start to form. Add the sugar, 1 tablespoon at a time, while beating constantly, until stiff peaks form. Add the liqueur and blend.
4. Cover each pear *completely* with the meringue mixture and sprinkle with chopped hazelnuts.
5. Brown quickly in a preheated 400° oven for 5 minutes or until golden brown.

To Serve: Slide a broad spatula under the pears and place on individual dessert plates. Garnish with a fresh unhulled strawberry and serve immediately.

Per serving: 0 mg cholesterol, 0.18 gm saturated fat, 2.6 gm total fat, 2.2 gm fiber,
61 mg sodium, 114 calories

* You can prepare the meringue without any sugar; however, the texture and taste of the meringue will be affected.

Raddichio and Romaine Salad with Vinaigrette Dressing
Broiled Red Snapper with Balsamic Vinegar and Garlic
Diced Sweet Potatoes and Peas
◆Lemon-Lime Yogurt Pie◆

Lemon-Lime Yogurt Pie

Serves: 12 (1 slice = 1 serving)

Crust:

1 cup graham cracker crumbs (no animal fat or coconut or palm oils)

4 tablespoons frozen unsweetened apple juice concentrate

1 teaspoon cinnamon

1½ cups fresh raspberries and/or blueberries and 2 limes, thinly sliced, for garnish

Filling:

2 envelopes unflavored gelatin*

⅓ cup fresh orange juice

8 ounces 1%-fat small-curd cottage cheese

3 8-ounce cartons nonfat lemon-flavored yogurt

Grated zest and juice of 1½–2 limes

To Make Crust: 1. Combine the graham cracker crumbs, apple juice concentrate, and cinnamon; mix well with a fork to blend.

2. Sprinkle on the bottom of an 8-inch springform pan coated with butter-flavored nonstick spray. Pat into place.

3. Bake in a preheated 375° oven for 5 to 6 minutes.

To Make Filling: 1. Sprinkle the gelatin over the fresh orange juice in a saucepan. Stir over low heat or hot water until the gelatin is dissolved.

2. Blend the cottage cheese in a food processor or blender *until smooth*.

3. Add the remaining ingredients, including the dissolved gelatin, to the processor and blend until smooth and well combined.

4. Pour the filling into the crust, cover, and chill 1 hour or overnight before serving.

To Serve: Loosen the pie around the edges with a metal spatula and remove the ring from the springform pan. Place the pie on a serving plate and arrange fresh berries and lime slices around the perimeter.

Variation: Save 2 tablespoons graham cracker crumb mixture from the crust to sprinkle on top of the pie.

Per serving: 3 mg cholesterol, 0.45 gm saturated fat, 1.2 gm total fat, 0.8 gm fiber, 171 mg sodium, 84 calories

* If there is gelatin in your brand of yogurt, use only 1½ tablespoons gelatin instead of two envelopes.

Celery Root, Red Cabbage, and Orange Salad (page 226)
Broiled Chicken Breast
Orzo with Peas and Red Peppers
Steamed Spinach
♦Chocolate Zucchini Cupcake♦

Chocolate Zucchini Cupcakes

Yield: 24 cupcakes (1 cupcake = 1 serving)

What a treat to be able to enjoy a no-cholesterol no-saturated-fat chocolate cupcake!

4 extra-large egg whites
⅓ cup sugar
¼ cup canola or cold-pressed safflower oil
1 12-ounce can nonfat evaporated milk
2 teaspoons pure vanilla extract
2 cups unbleached white flour or whole wheat pastry flour
¼ cup oat bran, processed in blender until fine

1 teaspoon baking soda
2 teaspoons baking powder
1½ teaspoons ground cinnamon
¼ cup unsweetened cocoa
2 cups shredded zucchini
½ cup seeded dark raisins (microwave on high with 2 tablespoons fresh orange juice for about 1 minute)

1. Preheat the oven to 350°. Line two 12-cup muffin tins with paper baking cups.
2. Add the egg whites, sugar, oil, milk, and vanilla to a food processor with a steel blade and process 30 seconds.
3. Combine the flour, oat bran, baking soda, baking powder, cinnamon, and cocoa in a mixing bowl. Blend thoroughly. Add to the food processor and process until smooth.
4. Add the zucchini and raisins and process 5 seconds.
5. Fill the cups with batter and bake at 350° for about 20 minutes or until a toothpick comes out clean.
6. Remove the cupcakes from the tins and cool on a wire rack.

Variation: Mix ¼ cup finely chopped almonds with 1 tablespoon sugar and ½ teaspoon ground cinnamon and sprinkle ½ teaspoon of the mixture on top of each cupcake *before* baking.

Per serving: 1 mg cholesterol, 0.27 gm saturated fat, 2.7 gm total fat, 0.8 gm fiber, 87 mg sodium, 99 calories

Twelve Menus
for Special Occasions

Any meal becomes a special occasion if you give a little extra thought to your menu planning and food preparation. Healthful foods that are both delicious and attractively served are not the impossible dream. To prove it, here are some menus for celebrations and get-togethers to share with family and friends. With these menus and recipes your guests will come away feeling satisfied but comfortable, and you can be sure that the foods you serve are in everyone's best interest.

MENUS AND RECIPES

AN OUTDOOR BARBECUE	*Confetti Corn Relish*
A CHINESE DINNER	*Lion's Head Chinese Meatballs with Chinese Cabbage*
A FRENCH DINNER	*Chicken Breasts, Mushrooms, and Water Chestnuts in Wine Sauce*
AN ITALIAN DINNER	*Pasta with Pesto*
A MEXICAN DINNER	*Tamale Pie*
AFTER THE GAME	*Manhattan Clam Chowder*
A COMPANY CASSEROLE DINNER	*Penny's Tarragon Chicken and Rice Velouté*
FAMILY FAVORITES FOR OLD FRIENDS	*Down-Home Meat Loaf*
IT'S YOUR BIRTHDAY DINNER	*Grilled Marinated Flank Steak*
LOTS-OF-COMPANY DINNER	*Mustard-Baked Chicken Breasts*
THANKSGIVING DINNER (without the turkey)	*Pumpkin Pie Cheesecake*
LATE FOR DINNER	*Cold or Hot Spicy Gazpacho*

AN OUTDOOR BARBECUE

Spicy Gazpacho (page 256) and Crudités
Grilled Chicken with Rosemary
Grilled Mixed Squash Kabobs
♦Confetti Corn Relish♦
Baked Potatoes with Assorted Toppings (page 304)
Watermelon Slices
Chocoholic's Chocolate Cake (page 340)

Confetti Corn Relish

Yield: about 4 cups (½ cup = 1 serving)

A cookout always officially introduces the start of summer. Instead of hot dogs and hamburgers, this menu offers a small amount of chicken or fish and lots of vegetables. To cut your grilling time and ensure juicy meat, partially cook your chicken in the microwave oven for about 9 minutes on high. This corn relish uses fresh or canned corn and keeps in the refrigerator for 3 or 4 days.

2 tablespoons nonfat plain yogurt
2 cups cream-style canned corn
½ teaspoon balsamic vinegar
Freshly ground pepper
2 cups fresh or frozen (steamed 1 minute) or canned kernel corn
½ small red pepper, seeded and diced

½ small green pepper, seeded and diced
4 whole green onions, thinly sliced
2 teaspoons dried fines herbes

1. Stir the yogurt in a small bowl until smooth; add the cream-style corn and blend. Season with balsamic vinegar and pepper.
2. Add the corn, peppers, onions, and fines herbes and mix thoroughly. Chill at least 1 hour before serving.

Per serving: 0 mg cholesterol, 0.16 gm saturated fat, 1 gm total fat, 1.4 gm fiber, 255 mg sodium, 111 calories

A CHINESE DINNER
Dry Bean Thread Soup (page 267)
♦Lion's Head Chinese Meatballs with Chinese Cabbage♦
Snow Peas and Red Peppers
Steamed Rice (page 130)
Lichee Nuts and Orange Wedges
Fortune Cookies

This dish originated in Shanghai, but today it is equally at home in Chicago. The oversized meatballs were supposed to be reminiscent of lions' heads. Traditionally, ground pork is used, but I have substituted ground turkey or chicken, which lowers the saturated fat and cholesterol content without sacrificing flavor. Fortune cookies are included in the menu, but enjoy the fortune and forget the cookie.

Lion's Head Chinese Meatballs with Chinese Cabbage

Serves: 6 (about 2 ounces cooked meat = 1 serving)

4 dried shiitake mushrooms (1 ounce), soaked in hot water 20 minutes, drained, and stems removed and discarded
1 pound ground turkey or chicken breast (see page 142), skin and fat removed
2 extra-large egg whites, slightly beaten
5 finely chopped fresh or canned water chestnuts
2 whole green onions, thinly sliced
1 large clove garlic, minced
2 teaspoons grated fresh ginger root

2 tablespoons dry sherry or dry white wine
1 tablespoon sodium-reduced soy sauce
1 tablespoon cornstarch
1 cup defatted sodium-reduced chicken broth mixed with 1 tablespoon dry sherry
½ fresh Chinese cabbage or bok choy, cut into 6 portions
Freshly ground pepper

6 small green onions, cut into brushes, for garnish

1. Mince the drained mushroom caps.
2. Combine the mushrooms with the turkey, egg whites, water chestnuts, green onions, garlic, ginger, sherry, soy sauce, and cornstarch, mixing thoroughly. Shape into six equal-sized large meatballs.

3. Brown the meatballs in a hot nonstick skillet coated with nonstick cooking spray.

4. Add the broth and sherry mixture. Bring to a boil, reduce heat, cover, and simmer 20 minutes.

5. Remove the meatballs from the sauce. Layer the Chinese cabbage in the sauce, season with pepper, and then top with the meatballs, basting with sauce.

6. Bring the sauce to a boil, reduce heat, cover, and simmer about another 8 to 10 minutes.

To Serve: Arrange the cooked Chinese cabbage on a warm serving platter, top with the meatballs, and pour sauce over all. Garnish with green onion brushes.

Per serving: 39 mg cholesterol, 0.59 gm saturated fat, 1.9 gm total fat, 1.3 gm fiber, 198 mg sodium, 144 calories

A FRENCH DINNER

Red and Green Lettuce Salad with
Dijon Mustard and Shallot Vinaigrette Dressing
♦Chicken Breasts, Mushrooms, and
Water Chestnuts in Wine Sauce♦
Steamed Wild Rice
Asparagus Spears   Baby Carrots
Meringue Shells (page 323) with
Raspberries and Creme Topping (page 314)

Chicken Breasts, Mushrooms, and Water Chestnuts in Wine Sauce

Serves: 8 (3½ ounces cooked chicken = 1 serving)

It is always convenient to have a company dish that's not a casserole and yet can be prepared ahead of time or the day before. To complete this meal before your guests arrive, you have only to prepare a salad of mixed greens, generous amounts of rice and vegetables, and raspberries or some other fresh seasonal fruit to serve with meringue shells for dessert. The meringue shells can also be made in advance.

4 whole chicken breasts (about 14–16 ounces each), halved, skinned, boned, and flattened*
2 teaspoons salt-free vegetable seasoning
2 teaspoons Hungarian paprika
Freshly ground pepper
2 teaspoons extra-virgin olive oil
3 large cloves garlic, minced
2 shallots, minced
1 small onion, finely chopped
1 green pepper, seeded and diced
1 cup sliced fresh or drained canned water chestnuts
2½ cups sliced fresh mushroom caps

1 10-ounce package frozen small whole onions
1½ tablespoons fresh thyme, chopped, or 1 teaspoon dried thyme, crushed
2 cups canned crushed plum tomatoes in puree
¼ cup white wine
¼ cup dry red wine

Chopped fresh thyme, for garnish

1. Dry the flattened chicken breasts with paper towel and season both sides with vegetable seasoning, paprika, and ground pepper.

2. Coat a 12-inch sauté pan with nonstick spray; add the olive oil and heat the pan.

3. Place chicken breasts in the hot pan and brown lightly on both sides over moderate heat. Remove the chicken to a shallow oven-proof casserole.

4. Add the garlic, shallots, and onion to the sauté pan and sauté, stirring constantly, for 2 to 3 minutes. (If necessary, add a bit of chicken broth.)

5. Add the green pepper, water chestnuts, mushrooms, and whole onions, and sauté 5 minutes.

6. Add the thyme, tomatoes, and wine; stir and bring to a boil. Simmer 5 minutes.

7. Pour the vegetable mixture over the chicken in the shallow baking dish† and cook, uncovered, 25 minutes in a preheated 350° oven.

To Serve: Sprinkle fresh thyme or parsley over the chicken just before serving.

Per serving: 84 mg cholesterol, 1.48 gm saturated fat, 6.1 gm total fat, 1.4 gm fiber, 181 mg sodium, 247 calories

* *To flatten chicken breasts,* place a boned breast half between two pieces of waxed paper or plastic wrap and pound with a mallet until it is about ½ inch thick.

† May be prepared a day ahead to this point and refrigerated. If chilled, add 15 minutes to the baking time.

AN ITALIAN DINNER
Panzanella (page 265)
Vegetarian Lentil Soup (page 84)
♦Pasta with Pesto♦
Zucchini, Red Peppers, and Mushrooms
Garlic Toast (page 328)
Compote of Fresh Fruit with Amaretto

Panzanella (a salad using leftover bread and fresh vegetables), a full-bodied vegetarian lentil soup, pasta and pesto, and Amaretto liqueur are all favorites in Italian-style cooking.

Pesto, or basil sauce, is a tradition in Genoa in the northwest part of Italy. If you are fortunate enough to be able to grow your own fresh basil, it should go right from your garden to your food processor. If not, many markets are now selling packaged fresh herbs for your convenience. This flavorful low-fat recipe has much less oil than commercial pesto, and no pine nuts. It is not only wonderful as a sauce with pasta, but a dab enhances the taste of minestrone, steamed or baked potatoes, sliced tomato and onion salad, sandwiches, or warm toast. Fresh pesto will keep for six weeks in the refrigerator in a tightly closed jar, or may be frozen for future use.

Pasta with Pesto Ⓠ

Serves: 4 (2 tablespoons pesto = 1 serving)

Pesto:
3 cloves garlic
1 shallot
1 packed cup fresh parsley leaves
  without stems
2½ packed cups fresh basil leaves
  without stems
2 tablespoons extra-virgin olive oil

Few grains crushed red pepper
1 tablespoon freshly grated Parmesan cheese

8 ounces capellini (angel hair pasta), cooked *al dente* and drained

1. Place the garlic, shallot, and parsley in a food processor or blender and chop. Add the basil and process the mixture until chopped.
2. Add the oil, pepper, and cheese, and process until finely blended.
3. Add about half of the sauce to the hot, drained pasta, and stir to blend. (Reserve the rest of the sauce for future use.)

4. Serve immediately while hot, and pass additional Parmesan cheese if desired.

Variations: Two diced peeled Italian plum tomatoes may be added with the pesto sauce before blending with the pasta.

Two and one half cups fresh spinach leaves and 2 tablespoons dried basil may be substituted for the fresh basil in the Pesto Sauce. However, it won't be nearly as delicious.

Per serving: 1 mg cholesterol, 1.28 gm saturated fat, 8.3 gm total fat, 3 gm fiber,
34 mg sodium, 311 calories
Per 2 tablespoons pesto: 1 mg cholesterol, 1.18 gm saturated fat, 7.5 gm total fat, 1.8 gm fiber,
33 mg sodium, 99 calories

A MEXICAN DINNER
Quesadilla (page 92)
Sweet Potato Chips (page 264) and Crudités
with Fresh Salsa (page 183)
♦Tamale Pie♦
Mixed Green Salad
Mango Fruited Mousse (page 319)

Mexican-style cooking *can* be low-fat and low-cholesterol, as this tamale pie proves.

Tamale Pie

Serves: 8

1 recipe Chunky Turkey Chili (page 191); if necessary, add 1 can chili beans with chili gravy to equal 6½ cups total chili mixture
1 cup canned cream-style corn
1 cup fresh corn (about 2 ears) or canned salt-free corn
2 teaspoons dried Italian herb blend, crushed

2 cups cold water
2 cups cold nonfat milk
1¼ cups yellow cornmeal
Freshly ground pepper
1 tablespoon shredded Parmesan cheese

3 tablespoons chopped fresh cilantro or Italian parsley, for garnish

1. Combine the chili, cream-style corn, corn, and 1 teaspoon of the Italian herb blend. Mix thoroughly and pour into a 13 × 9 × 2-inch baking dish coated with nonstick spray.
2. Place the cold water and milk in a 1½-quart saucepan. Add the cornmeal, the remaining teaspoon Italian herb blend, and the pepper. Mix. Cook over medium heat until thick and stiff (about 7 minutes), stirring frequently.
3. Top the chili with eight heaping portions of the cornmeal mixture and flatten with the back of a spoon. Sprinkle each portion of cornmeal with a bit of Parmesan cheese.
4. Bake in a preheated 350° oven for 25 to 30 minutes.
To Serve: Sprinkle with cilantro or parsley and serve hot.

Variation: To make a vegetarian meal, use the vegetarian chili recipe on page 191 as a base instead of the Chunky Turkey Chili.

Per serving: 21 mg cholesterol, 0.87 gm saturated fat, 4.8 gm total fat, 6.9 gm fiber, 346 mg sodium, 352 calories

AFTER THE GAME
◆Manhattan Clam Chowder◆
Crusty Sourdough Rolls
Salad Trio:
Bristol Farms Fantastic Corn and Eggplant Fiesta (page 278)
Three-Bean Salad   Mixed Fresh Fruit Salad
Oven-Toasted Wheat Chex
Whole Wheat Raisin Bread Pudding (page 321)
with Creme Topping (page 314)

This menu will score with family or guests. The tomato-based chowder is filled with vegetables and just enough clams to give a wonderful flavor.

Manhattan Clam Chowder Ⓜ

Yield: 16 cups (1½ cups = 1 serving as an entrée)

1 large onion, chopped
1 large leek (white part only), washed and chopped
6 stalks celery, chopped
6 large carrots, coarsely chopped
2 large peeled russet potatoes, coarsely chopped
⅓ cup chopped fresh Italian parsley
1 28-ounce can crushed Italian plum tomatoes in puree
4 cups water
½ teaspoon crushed red pepper flakes
1 bay leaf

2 teaspoons dried oregano, crushed
1 teaspoon dried thyme, crushed
2 cloves garlic, chopped
3 tablespoons unbleached white flour
1 cup sodium-reduced canned chopped tomatoes
½ cup dry white wine
2 7½-ounce cans chopped clams with juice (no MSG or preservatives added)
1 8-ounce bottle clam juice (optional)

1. Place the onions, leek, celery, carrots, potatoes, parsley, Italian plum tomatoes, water, and seasonings in a 4½-quart saucepan. Bring to a boil, reduce to a simmer, cover, and cook 1 hour, stirring occasionally.

2. Lightly brown the flour in a nonstick skillet, stirring constantly. Add the browned flour to the soup and mix thoroughly.

3. Add the chopped tomatoes, wine, and clams and clam juice, and simmer 30 minutes.

Per serving: 18 mg cholesterol, 0.11 gm saturated fat, 0.9 gm total fat, 1.8 gm fiber, 141 mg sodium, 99 calories

COMPANY CASSEROLE DINNER
Spicy Tomato Soup (page 85)
Curly Endive, Romaine, and Red Lettuce Salad with
Low-Calorie Salad Dressing (page 272)
◆Penny's Tarragon Chicken and Rice Velouté◆
Assorted Whole Grain Rolls
Broccoli Crown (page 299)   Parslied Carrot Coins
Poached Pear "en Croute" (page 347) with
Blueberry Sauce (page 314)

Whether cooking for four or forty, your preparation for entertaining should allow you time to enjoy your guests. This chicken and rice casserole may be prepared the day before, and the rest of the menu is simple yet satisfying.

Penny's Tarragon Chicken and Rice Velouté

Serves: about 10

4 cups defatted sodium-reduced chicken broth (1 cup dry vermouth or dry white wine may be substituted for 1 cup chicken broth)
1 bay leaf
1 teaspoon dried thyme, crushed
½ teaspoon white pepper
2 teaspoons salt-free vegetable seasoning
2½ pounds skinless and boneless chicken breasts
½ cup dry nonfat milk
½ cup unbleached white flour
2 large shallots, minced
3 tablespoons shredded Parmesan cheese
3 tablespoons chopped fresh tarragon, or 1 tablespoon fines herbes

2–3 tablespoons lemon juice
2 tablespoons tomato paste
Few drops hot pepper sauce
1½ cups fresh or frozen peas
1½ cups diced celery with leaves
1 small red pepper, seeded and diced
3½ cups cooked brown rice (page 130)
1½ tablespoons each shredded Parmesan cheese and shredded part-skim mozzarella cheese mixed with 3 tablespoons dry breadcrumbs

1. Place the first five ingredients in a 10-inch skillet and bring to a boil. Add the chicken breasts, return to a boil, reduce heat, cover, and simmer 6 minutes.

2. Remove the chicken breasts and cut into 1-inch cubes.

3. Remove the bay leaf from the broth and add the dry milk. Blend thoroughly.

4. Place the flour and shallots in a 2-quart saucepan and add the broth mixture gradually, whisking constantly. Place over low heat, stirring constantly until mixture coats the spoon. (*Do not boil.*)

5. Add the cheese, tarragon, lemon juice, tomato paste, and hot pepper sauce. Blend, taste, and adjust seasonings. Add the peas, celery, red pepper, and cubed chicken and blend thoroughly.

6. Spread the cooked rice in the bottom of a 13 × 9 × 2-inch casserole. Add the chicken mixture. Sprinkle with the cheese mixture* and bake in a preheated 375° oven for 35 to 40 minutes.

Per serving: 75 mg-cholesterol, 1.74 gm saturated fat, 5.3 gm total fat, 1.8 gm fiber, 353 mg sodium, 309 calories

* At this point, the casserole may be covered with plastic wrap and refrigerated for one to two days before using. If so, add 15 minutes to cooking time.

FAMILY FAVORITES FOR OLD FRIENDS

Cole Slaw with Yogurt Dressing
♦Down-Home Meat Loaf♦
Mashed Potatoes with Scallions
Braised Kale
Succotash
Bowl of Fresh Seasonal Fruit
Oatmeal Cookies (page 344)

Considering the resurgence of interest in American cooking, no recipe collection would be complete without a meat loaf recipe. I have added oat bran or rolled oats instead of breadcrumbs to provide more soluble fiber and an assortment of vegetables for added flavor. My mother added rolled oats fifty years ago without having any special reason except that it tasted good.

The traditional American recipes in this menu can be adjusted by using nonfat plain yogurt dressing for the cole slaw and 1% fat milk, some Butter Buds, and/or perhaps some sliced scallions in the mashed potatoes. And of course, the cholesterol and saturated fat content will be lower if you use ground turkey breast instead of ground round of beef.

Down-Home Meat Loaf

Serves: 6 (2 slices = 1 serving)

2 extra-large egg whites
½ cup nonfat milk or sodium-reduced vegetable juice
⅔ cup oat bran or rolled oats
1 tablespoon Worcestershire sauce
Freshly ground pepper
1 small onion, quartered
1 large carrot, quartered
½ green pepper, quartered
1 zucchini, quartered
2 cloves garlic, peeled
½ cup fresh parsley, coarse stems removed

1 pound ground turkey (see page 142) or lean ground round or half ground turkey and half ground round

Glaze:
¼ cup salt-free tomato sauce
2 tablespoons frozen unsweetened apple juice concentrate
1 teaspoon Dijon mustard or 3 tablespoons sodium-reduced ketchup mixed with ½ teaspoon dry mustard

1. In a mixing bowl, beat the egg whites slightly with a fork. Add the milk, oat bran, Worcestershire sauce, and pepper, and let stand 5 to 10 minutes.

2. Place the onion, carrot, green pepper, zucchini, garlic, and parsley in a food processor or blender and chop fine.

3. Add the vegetable mixture and the ground meat to the egg white mixture and mix lightly with a fork (or clean hands) to combine.

4. Mound the meat mixture into a 9-inch square pan coated with nonstick spray and shape into an 8-inch loaf.

5. Bake in a preheated 375° oven for 35 minutes.

6. Mix the glaze ingredients together, brush over the meat loaf, return to the oven, and bake 10 minutes longer.

7. Remove from the oven and let stand 10 minutes before slicing.

To Serve: Cut the meat loaf into twelve slices and arrange on a heated serving platter. Surround with mashed potatoes with scallions.

To Microwave:

1. Pack meat mixture into a 9 × 5 × 3-inch glass loaf pan and microwave uncovered on high for 7 minutes.

2. Drain juice and cover with glaze. Microwave uncovered on high for 2 minutes.

Per serving: 40 mg cholesterol, 0.63 gm saturated fat, 3 gm total fat, 3.3 gm fiber, 108 mg sodium, 175 calories

IT'S YOUR BIRTHDAY DINNER
Clam Dip with Crudités (page 262)
♦Grilled Marinated Flank Steak♦
Grilled New Potatoes
with Spicy Red Pepper Sauce (page 231)
Sally's Zucchini (page 309)
Pumpernickel Garlic Toast (page 328)
Chocoholic's Chocolate Cake (page 340)
with Nonfat Frozen Vanilla Yogurt

In our family, on your birthday you choose your dinner menu. Grilled Marinated Flank Steak is my daughter Sally's choice. If you prefer, you can substitute firm-fleshed fish such as salmon or sea bass.

Grilled Marinated Flank Steak

Serves: 4 (3 ounces cooked meat = 1 serving)

Marinade:
¼ cup fresh orange juice
1 tablespoon lime juice
1 tablespoon sodium-reduced soy
sauce
2 tablespoons plum or rice wine or
sherry
2 teaspoons chili powder
2 teaspoons ground cumin
2 teaspoons grated orange zest
2 cloves garlic, minced

1 pound flank steak (grade Good)

Sliced grilled papaya, pineapple
and/or orange, for garnish

1. Combine the marinade ingredients and pour over the flank steak in a plastic bag. Marinate overnight in the refrigerator, turning meat several times to coat with marinade.
2. Remove the meat from the refrigerator just 30 minutes before grilling. Reserve any remaining marinade.
3. Broil or grill about 4 minutes on each side.
4. Heat the reserved marinade. Slice the steak diagonally into thin slices after letting it stand for 5 minutes.
To Serve: Place the sliced meat on a heated platter, top with heated marinade, and surround with grilled fruit slices. Serve immediately.

Per serving: 60 mg cholesterol, 5.45 gm saturated fat, 12.8 gm total fat, 0.1 gm fiber, 105 mg sodium, 212 calories

LOTS-OF-COMPANY DINNER

Cold Spicy Gazpacho (page 256)
♦Mustard-Baked Chicken Breasts♦
and/or
Oven-Baked Chinese Chicken Legs (page 292)
Fresh Asparagus Salad (page 272)   Assorted Mixed Green Salad
Roast Potatoes with Basil (page 306)
Lemon-Lime Yogurt Pie (page 236)
Oat Nut Slices with Jam (page 345)

Somehow when I start inviting guests for dinner, it always ends up a crowd—and I love it. The Mustard-Baked Chicken Breasts and Oven-Baked Chinese Chicken Legs give variety without exhausting the hostess.

Mustard-Baked Chicken Breasts ⓠ

Serves: 12 (3 ounces cooked chicken = 1 serving)

½ cup dry white wine
½ cup defatted sodium-reduced chicken broth
2 tablespoons each Dijon mustard and coarsely ground mustard
1⅓ cups fine, dry breadcrumbs
2 tablespoons grated Parmesan cheese

⅓ cup chopped fresh Italian parsley
12 4-ounce halved boned, skinned, and defatted chicken breasts

Watercress and cherry tomatoes, for garnish

1. Mix the wine, broth, and mustard together in a shallow bowl.
2. Mix the breadcrumbs, cheese, and parsley together in separate shallow bowl.
3. Coat the chicken with the wine mixture, then dip in the breadcrumbs on one side only. Place chicken, unbreaded-side-down, on a nonstick baking sheet. Bake in the upper third of a preheated 475° oven for 15 to 20 minutes or until lightly brown and tender.
To Serve: Place the chicken breasts on a heated platter on bed of watercress and garnish with cherry tomatoes.

Per serving: 74 mg cholesterol, 1.36 gm saturated fat, 4.8 gm total fat, 0.1 gm fiber, 229 mg sodium, 200 calories

<u>THANKSGIVING DINNER (*Without the Turkey*)</u>

Confetti Corn Soup (page 266)
with Whole Wheat Bread Sticks
Watercress, Radicchio, and Spinach Salad
Orange-Glazed Cornish Hens (page 212)
Cranberry-Pineapple Freeze (page 326)
Different Stuffed Potatoes (page 307)
Stir-Fried Squash and Red Pepper (page 308)
Steamed Tender Whole Green and Yellow Stringbeans
♦Pumpkin Pie Cheesecake♦

For a delicious change at Thanksgiving, I have combined my cheesecake and pumpkin pie recipes.

Pumpkin Pie Cheesecake

Yield: 1 8-inch cheesecake
Serves: 12 to 14

Graham Cracker Crust:
1¼ cups graham cracker crumbs (with *no* animal or hydrogenated fat, or coconut or palm oil)
¼ cup ground hazelnuts
1 teaspoon ground cinnamon
Freshly ground nutmeg
3 tablespoons frozen unsweetened apple juice concentrate
2 tablespoons cornstarch

Pumpkin-Cheese Filling:
16 ounces part-skim ricotta cheese
¼ cup brown sugar

2 extra-large egg whites, slightly beaten
½ cup nonfat evaporated milk
1 1-pound can pumpkin pie filling
1 teaspoon pure vanilla extract

Yogurt-Cream Topping:
1 cup nonfat plain yogurt
2 teaspoons pure vanilla extract
2 tablespoons light-style sour cream

To Prepare Crust:
1. Combine the crumbs, hazelnuts, cinnamon, and nutmeg.
2. Moisten the crumb mixture with the apple juice concentrate, mixing with a fork. Reserve 2 to 3 tablespoons of the crumb mixture for garnish.
3. Press the remainder of the crumb mixture firmly into the bottom of an 8-inch springform pan lightly coated with nonstick spray.

To Prepare Filling and Topping:

1. In a food processor or blender blend the cheese, sugar, and cornstarch until smooth.

2. Add the egg whites and blend. Add the milk, pumpkin, and vanilla and blend thoroughly.

3. Pour into the prepared crust and bake in a preheated 300° oven for 1 hour or until firm.

4. Cool the pie slightly on a rack for about 10 to 15 minutes. Meanwhile, blend the topping ingredients.

5. Cover the pie with the yogurt-cream topping and sprinkle with the reserved crumb mixture. Cover and chill until serving time.

To Serve: For an especially festive feeling, place a mini pumpkin on the center of the pie before presenting your dessert.

Per serving: 10 mg cholesterol, 1.85 gm saturated fat, 4.5 gm total fat, 1.3 gm fiber, 109 mg sodium, 129 calories

LATE FOR DINNER
♦Cold or Hot Spicy Gazpacho♦
Broiled Salmon with Dijon Mustard and Capers
Parslied Potatoes
Steamed Broccoli and Carrots
Fresh Berries Topped with Nonfat Vanilla Yogurt

We have all been in the position of realizing that there's "nothing at home for dinner," or that we'll be getting home too late to prepare it. In Europe, it's not an uncommon practice to stop at the market, see what's available, and use that for the evening meal. With this in mind, if you pick up some fresh salsa for soup, some fresh fish for the entrée, a few fresh vegetables and potatoes, for the microwave and some fresh seasonal fruit—dinner will be ready thirty minutes after you get home!

This spicy gazpacho is fantastic served either cold or hot, and is so easy to make. Make certain that you buy salsa with no preservatives added. It will keep about a week in your refrigerator.

Cold or Hot Spicy Gazpacho Ⓠ

Serves: 4 to 5 (¾ cup = 1 serving)

16 ounces Fresh Salsa (page 183) or salt-free or canned mild salsa (no preservatives added)
1 large clove garlic
2 6-ounce cans sodium-reduced vegetable juice
2–3 tablespoons red wine vinegar

½ teaspoon dried oregano or Italian herb blend
Few drops hot pepper sauce, or to taste

Thinly sliced cucumbers and nonfat plain yogurt, for garnish

1. Place all the ingredients except the garnish in a food processor or blender and process until smooth. Taste and adjust seasonings.

2. Either pour into a storage container, cover, and chill in the freezer for about 20 minutes before serving, or heat and serve hot.

To Serve: Pour into cups or bowls, garnish with cucumber slice and a dollop of nonfat yogurt.

Per serving: 0 mg cholesterol, 0.04 gm saturated fat, 0.2 gm total fat, 1.5 gm fiber, 11 mg sodium, 35 calories

◆ 6 ◆

Mix and Match: More
Low-Cholesterol Dishes

The recipes in this chapter may be exchanged for comparable recipes in the menus in the previous chapters and you will still be assured
of a cholesterol-controlled diet. For example, you may decide that
you prefer one of the soups or salads in Mix and Match to one of
those listed in a menu. Or you may choose one of the fish, poultry,
or pasta entrées in this chapter as an exchange for a similar entrée
listed in a menu. (All portions of protein are within the guidelines
for a low-cholesterol lifestyle.) Instead of fruit for dessert, you may
have the time or taste for one of the many tempting desserts from
this chapter or, occasionally, even a luscious one from Chapter 7.

Whatever you decide, aim for variety to make your mealtimes
special. There's no reason that a low-cholesterol lifestyle can't be a
treat for your palate as well as good for your health.

You can also put together complete menus of your own, based
on the patterns of the menus in Chapters 4 and 5. A sample low-
cholesterol dinner could include:

Soup and/or Salad
4-ounce Cooked Portion of Fish or Poultry
or a Pasta or Casserole Recipe
Complex Carbohydrate such as Potatoes,
Rice, Barley, or Corn*
Green or Yellow Vegetable
Dessert (generally fruit)

Just remember that animal protein should be served at either lunch
or dinner, *not at both*, and try to have two vegetarian days a week.

* If the entrée is not a pasta.

Remember the meal plan goal

Total calories: ♦ at least 65 to 70 percent from complex carbohydrates
♦ no more than 15 percent from animal protein
♦ no more than 15 to 20 percent from fat

Recipes

Appetizers:

Spicy Artichoke Hearts
Clam Dip
Russian Dressing Dip
Beth's Eggplant Spread
Sweet Potato Chips
Tex-Mex Mini Quiches
Panzanella

Soups:

Bean Curd and Spinach Soup
Confetti Corn Soup
Dry Bean Thread Soup
Last-Minute Soup
Tuscan Minestrone
Potato and Onion Soup
Chilled Papaya Soup

Salads and Salad Dressings:

Cucumber-Buttermilk Dressing
Low-Calorie Salad Dressing
Fresh Asparagus Salad
Sliced Beet and Orange Salad
Black Bean and Corn Salad
Green Bean Salad Piquant with Ginger
Cabbage, Bean Sprout, Tomato, and Carrot Slaw

Cole Slaw Relish Salad
Bristol Farms Fantastic Corn and Eggplant Fiesta
Kasha and Corn Salad
Radish, Celery, and Cucumber Salad
Spinach and Pear Salad
Date Waldorf Salad
Vegetable Antipasto

Entrées:

Pasta with Garden Vegetable Marinara Sauce
Turkey Chili and Macaroni
Deviled Turkey Fillets
Grilled Hawaiian Fish with Pineapple Sauce
Red Snapper with Spicy Tomato Sauce
Foil-Baked Fish with Vegetables
Soft Tuna Tacos
Stir-Fried Tuna and Vegetables
Chicken Breasts in Phyllo
Oven-Baked Chinese Chicken Legs
Margie's Pasta with Sun-Dried Tomatoes
Pasta Pizza Pie
Corn Crêpes with Cheese and Spinach or Vegetable Filling

Vegetarian Dishes:

Broccoli Crown
Easy Eggplant Parmesan
Eggplant in Spicy Brown Sauce
Gingered Pineapple Carrots
Larry's Potatoes and Onions
Sherry's Stuffed Potatoes (with Seven Toppings)
Nan's Quick Cubed Potatoes
Roast Potatoes with Basil
Different Stuffed Potatoes
Stir-Fried Squash and Red Pepper
Sally's Zucchini

Pasta and Grain Side Dishes:

Sweet Pasta Pudding
Cracked Wheat and Tomato Salad
Bulgur Wheat Pilaf
Buckwheat Kernels and Pasta

Desserts:

Creme Topping
Blueberry Sauce
Apple Crisp
Poached Pear with Fresh Strawberry Sauce (2 recipes)
Poached Pears and Prunes
Individual Fresh Apple Tarts with Apricot Glaze
Fresh Fruit Compote
Fruited Mousse
Persimmon Freeze
Café au Lait Custard
Raisin Bread Pudding
Bing Cherry Clafouti
Meringue Shells with Fruit
Angel Food Cake

Accompaniments:

Mango Salsa
Cranberry-Pineapple Freeze
Cheese Berry Spread
Garlic Toast
High-Fiber Whole Grain Onion Bread
Bran Berry Loaf
The Great Pumpkin Muffins

Snacks:

Yogurt-Fruit Shake
Orange-Yogurt Popsicles

Appetizers

Spicy Artichoke Hearts

Serves: 8

A piquant low-calorie starter.

2 cans quartered artichoke hearts, rinsed and squeezed dry, or 2 9-ounce packages frozen artichoke hearts, cooked in microwave

2 cups Fresh Salsa (page 183) or salt-free canned salsa

1 clove garlic, minced

½ cup salt-free tomato sauce

1 teaspoon Italian herb blend, crushed

Few drops hot pepper sauce

1 tablespoon chopped fresh cilantro or Italian parsley, for garnish

1. Combine all the ingredients except the cilantro in a bowl. Stir to blend.
2. Sprinkle with cilantro and chill for at least 1 hour in refrigerator before serving.

Per serving: 0 mg cholesterol, 0.05 gm saturated fat, 0.3 gm total fat, 1.5 gm fiber, 48 mg sodium, 50 calories

Clam Dip

Yield: 1½ cups (2 tablespoons = 1 serving)

A tasty starter to serve with assorted vegetables.

1 cup nonfat plain yogurt or 1%-fat cottage cheese processed until smooth
1 tablespoon sodium-reduced ketchup
1 teaspoon lemon juice
1 teaspoon dried minced onion flakes, or 1 tablespoon grated onion
⅛ teaspoon white pepper

½ teaspoon Worcestershire sauce
½ teaspoon dried horseradish
1 tablespoon chopped fresh Italian parsley
1 tablespoon capers, rinsed and drained (optional)
½ cup steamed clams, chopped, or 4 ounces canned chopped clams without preservatives, drained

1. Combine all the ingredients in a small bowl.
2. Chill at least 30 minutes before serving.

To Serve: Serve with raw vegetables for dipping, such as broccoli flowerets; carrot, zucchini, green and red pepper sticks, jicama, cherry tomatoes.

Variation: Substitute ½ cup chopped fresh crab meat or ½ cup scallops poached in 3 tablespoons dry white wine and 1 teaspoon chopped shallot, for the clams.

Per serving: 4 mg cholesterol, 0.03 gm saturated fat, 0.1 gm total fat, 0 gm fiber, 23 mg sodium, 17 calories

Russian Dressing Dip ⓠ

Yield: 1⅓ cups (1 tablespoon = 1 serving)

This dip may also be used as a salad dressing.

1 cup 1%-fat cottage cheese
¼ cup nonfat plain yogurt
1 minced shallot
½ cup minced green pepper and/or celery

2 tablespoons red wine vinegar
1½ tablespoons chili sauce
Freshly ground pepper
1 tablespoon rinsed capers (optional)

1. Blend the cottage cheese in a blender or food processor until smooth.
2. Add the remaining ingredients and blend just 2 to 3 seconds.
3. Place in a serving bowl, cover, and chill 1 hour or more.
To Serve: Serve cold with assorted raw vegetables.

Per serving: 0 mg cholesterol, 0.07 gm saturated fat, 0.1 gm total fat, 0.1 gm fiber, 22 mg sodium, 12 calories

Beth's Eggplant Spread Ⓠ Ⓜ

Yield: 4 cups (2 tablespoons=1 serving)

Even ten-year-olds have ideas for healthy cooking! This simple appetizer, invented by my niece Beth, may be prepared several days before serving. The recipe makes a generous amount, but leftovers keep well refrigerated for up to a week. You may also use it as a sandwich filling on whole wheat pita bread.

1 tablespoon extra-virgin olive oil
1 large eggplant (about 1 pound), cubed
1 cup chopped onion
1 cup diced seeded green pepper
2 cloves garlic, minced

1 6-ounce can salt-free tomato paste
⅓ cup red wine vinegar
3 fresh Italian plum tomatoes, diced

1. Mix all the ingredients except the tomatoes together in a microwave casserole, cover tightly with plastic wrap, and microwave on high for 12 minutes.
2. Stir, add tomatoes, and blend.
3. Microwave on high for 5 minutes more or until vegetables are tender.
4. Cover and chill for several hours or overnight before serving.
To Serve: Bring to room temperature and serve with warmed or toasted whole wheat pita bread wedges, or try Sweet Potato Chips, page 264, as a change.

Per serving: 0 mg cholesterol, 0.07 gm saturated fat, 0.5 gm total fat, 0.4 gm fiber, 5 mg sodium, 17 calories

Sweet Potato Chips Ⓠ

Serves: 6

Whether served as a snack with Fresh Salsa (page 183), salt-free canned salsa, or store-bought salsa or as an accompaniment in a meal, these sweet potato chips are delicious. They can be frozen for future use and reheated briefly.

2 pounds yams or sweet potatoes, scrubbed and sliced ⅛ inch thick
2 tablespoons cold-pressed saf- flower oil

2 tablespoons spicy salt-free vege- table seasoning

1. Place the sliced potatoes in a bowl, sprinkle with oil, and mix thoroughly.
2. Spread the potatoes in a single layer on a nonstick baking sheet and sprinkle with vegetable seasoning.
3. Bake in the upper third of a preheated 450° oven for 12 to 15 minutes, or until nicely browned. Serve immediately.

Variation: Russet potatoes can be used instead of sweet potatoes.

Per serving: 0 mg cholesterol, 0.21 gm saturated fat, 3.5 gm total fat, 2.9 gm fiber, 12 mg sodium, 150 calories

Tex-Mex Mini Quiches Ⓠ

Yield: 30 mini quiches (1 quiche = 1 serving)

Since you might make this hours ahead of time, to reheat, place on a cookie sheet and bake in a preheated 425° oven for 2 to 3 minutes.

4 extra-large egg whites, slightly beaten
½ cup nonfat evaporated milk
½ cup shredded part-skim mozza- rella cheese
½ teaspoon chili powder
½ teaspoon ground cumin

2 teaspoons Worcestershire sauce
4 ounces chopped, canned green chilis, drained
2 fresh plum tomatoes, diced
2 whole green onions, sliced
8 6-inch corn tortillas, cut into 30 2½-inch rounds

1. *To make the quiche filling*, place all the ingredients except the tortillas into a mixing bowl and blend thoroughly with a fork.

2. Heat the tortilla circles in a microwave oven for about 1 minute on medium, or until softened or sprinkle with 1½ tablespoons of water, wrap lightly in foil, and heat in a 375° oven for 5 minutes.

3. Press the tortilla circles into 2½-inch nonstick mini muffins tins.

4. Fill the tortilla-lined cups with quiche filling and bake in a preheated 425° oven for 10 to 12 minutes. Serve warm.

Per serving: 1 mg cholesterol, 0.23 gm saturated fat, 0.6 gm total fat, 0.1 gm fiber, 41 mg sodium, 32 calories

Panzanella Ⓠ

Serves: 8

This delicious no-cholesterol appetizer is often served in Italian restaurants as a first course, and it can easily be prepared at home.

6 Italian plum tomatoes, cut into chunks
½ red or white onion, diced
½ cucumber, peeled, halved lengthwise, seeded and sliced
½ green pepper, seeded and sliced
2 tablespoons extra-virgin olive oil
1–2 tablespoons red wine vinegar or balsamic vinegar

1 clove garlic, minced (optional)
Freshly ground pepper
½ cup chopped fresh Italian parsley or chopped fresh basil
1 tablespoon capers, rinsed
4 slices day-old baguette, cubed

1. Place all the ingredients except the bread in a mixing bowl. Mix lightly but thoroughly with a fork.

2. Chill 30 minutes before serving to marry flavors, but serve at room temperature—it tastes better.

To Serve: Place the bread on a platter, top with the tomato mixture, and serve.

Per serving: 0 mg cholesterol, 0.55 gm saturated fat, 3.8 gm total fat, 1 gm fiber, 147 mg sodium, 81 calories

<u>*Soups*</u>

Bean Curd and Spinach Soup Ⓠ

Serves: 6 (¾ cup = 1 serving)

4 cups defatted sodium-reduced chicken broth
⅔ cup cubed bean curd (tofu)
1 teaspoon sodium-reduced soy sauce
Freshly ground pepper

1½ cups raw spinach leaves, washed and shredded
2 whole green onions, finely chopped

1. Place the chicken broth, bean curd, soy sauce, and pepper into a saucepan. Bring to a boil and cook for 1 minute.
2. Add the spinach, turn off heat, and stir.
3. Add the green onions and serve immediately.

Per serving: 0 mg cholesterol, 0.2 gm saturated fat, 1.4 gm total fat, 0.7 gm fiber, 43 mg sodium, 49 calories

Confetti Corn Soup Ⓠ

Yield: 7 cups (⅔ cup = 1 serving)

1 15½-ounce can salt-free cream-style corn
1 cup fresh or canned salt-free corn
1½ cups defatted sodium-reduced chicken broth
2 tablespoons nonfat dried milk
2 green onions, sliced
2 teaspoons chopped fresh thyme

Few grains crushed red pepper flakes
½ cup frozen petit peas
¼ cup finely diced seeded red pepper
Spicy Red Pepper Sauce (page 231—optional)

1. Mix the corn, broth, and milk together in a saucepan. Bring to a boil.
2. Add the remaining ingredients, return to a boil, cover, and remove from heat. Let stand 10 minutes before serving.
To Serve: Place the hot soup in a heated tureen and garnish with a dollop of Spicy Red Pepper Sauce if desired.

Per serving: 1 mg cholesterol, 0.11 gm saturated fat, 0.6 gm total fat, 1.1 gm fiber, 22 mg sodium, 100 calories

Dry Bean Thread Soup ⓠ

Serves: 4 (1 cup=1 serving)

1 quart water
2 ounces dry bean threads (saifun)
2 whole green onions, thinly sliced
½ cup frozen peas
⅓ small cucumber, peeled, halved,
  seeded, and cut into thin slices

3 cups defatted sodium-reduced
  chicken broth
1 tablespoon sodium-reduced soy
  sauce

1. In a 2-quart saucepan, bring the water to a boil. Add the noodles, stir to separate, remove from heat, and let soak until soft (about 15 minutes). Drain and cut into 3-inch lengths.

2. Return the cut noodles to the saucepan and add the remaining ingredients. Bring to a boil.

3. Remove from heat and serve immediately.

Per serving: 0 mg cholesterol, 0.1 gm saturated fat, 0.3 gm total fat, 1 gm fiber, 143 mg sodium, 77 calories

Last-Minute Soup Ⓠ

Serves: 4 (1 cup = 1 serving)

When a hearty hot soup seems to be in order, try this one instead of a canned soup that is high in fat and sodium.

3 cups defatted sodium-reduced chicken broth
½ stalk celery, thinly sliced
1 carrot, thinly sliced
3 fresh mushroom caps, thinly sliced

⅛ teaspoon white pepper
3 tablespoons small macaroni or orzo
4 tablespoons frozen peas

1. Combine the chicken broth, celery, carrot, mushrooms, and pepper in a saucepan.
2. Bring to a boil, reduce heat to simmer, cover, and cook 10 minutes.
3. Add the macaroni and cook 10 minutes.
4. Add the peas and cook 3 minutes.

Per serving: 0 mg cholesterol, 0.02 gm saturated fat, 0.2 gm total fat, 1.1 gm fiber, 24 mg sodium, 54 calories

Tuscan Minestrone

Yield: about 3½ quarts (1½ cups = 1 serving as entrée)

This soup is a hearty meal-in-one, and it's one of my favorites.

1 cup dry kidney beans
1 tablespoon extra-virgin olive oil
3 cloves garlic, minced
1 bay leaf
½ teaspoon crushed red pepper flakes
1 onion, coarsely chopped
2½ quarts water or defatted sodium-reduced chicken broth
1 leek (white part only), sliced
3 large carrots, sliced
3 stalks celery with leaves, sliced
2 potatoes, peeled and cubed
1 cup sliced fresh green beans
1½ cups salt-free tomato sauce

1 tablespoon dried Italian herb blend, crushed
Freshly ground pepper
2 zucchini, coarsely chopped
1½ cups canned cannellini or garbanzo beans, drained and rinsed
1 14½-ounce sodium-reduced stewed tomatoes or peeled tomatoes, chopped
½ cup small macaroni or orzo
1 10-ounce package frozen chopped spinach, defrosted and drained, or 2 cups washed and shredded fresh spinach or Swiss chard

1. Cover the beans with water and soak overnight, or cook in microwave (page 129).

2. Place the oil in a 6-quart saucepan, add the drained beans, garlic, bay leaf, red pepper flakes, and onion; sauté 5 minutes.

3. Add the water or broth, bring to a boil, and simmer for 1 hour.

4. Add the leek, carrots, celery, potatoes, green beans, tomato sauce, herb blend, and pepper and cook 30 minutes.

5. Add the zucchini, beans, and tomatoes and cook 15 minutes.

6. Add the macaroni and spinach and cook 15 minutes.

Per serving: 0 mg cholesterol, 0.31 gm saturated fat, 2.2 gm total fat, 4.6 gm fiber, 42 mg sodium, 188 calories

Potato and Onion Soup Ⓠ Ⓜ

Serves: 4 to 5 (1 cup = 1 serving)

This soup has all of the flavor but none of the saturated fat or cholesterol found in canned or traditional homemade cream soups.

1¼ pounds potatoes, peeled and sliced
1¾ cups nonfat milk
1 medium onion, peeled and sliced, or 2 leeks (white part only), sliced
3 tablespoons chopped fresh celery leaves

1 bay leaf
1 shallot, chopped
½ teaspoon dried thyme
⅛ teaspoon ground white pepper
Pinch of coarse salt (optional)

Chopped fresh Italian parsley or thyme, for garnish

1. Place all the ingredients except the parsley in a 1½-quart saucepan and simmer, covered, until very soft (about 40 to 45 minutes). Remove bay leaf.

2. Pour into a blender or food processor and process until smooth. If the mixture appears to be too thick, add nonfat milk or chicken broth to suit.

To Serve: Serve hot in bowls or cups, garnished with fresh Italian parsley or thyme.

Variation: Substitute 2½ cups raw corn, carrots, broccoli, green peas, and/or zucchini, or celery root (celeriac), or any leftover vegetables for the potatoes.

To Microwave: Place all the ingredients except the parsley in a 2-quart microwave casserole, cover tightly with microwave plastic wrap, and microwave on high for about 12 to 15 minutes.

Per serving: 1 mg cholesterol, 0.14 gm saturated fat, 0.3 gm total fat, 0.8 gm fiber, 49 mg sodium, 137 calories

Chilled Papaya Soup ⓠ

Serves: 4 (⅔ cup = 1 serving)

A refreshing soup for those hot summer days. If the soup appears too thick after chilling, add a bit more orange juice or milk.

2 whole papayas, halved and
  seeded
½ cup nonfat lemon yogurt
About ½ cup nonfat milk
1 teaspoon grated orange zest

Fresh lemon or orange juice for
  seasoning (optional)

4 strawberry halves and mint
  leaves, for garnish

1. Remove the pulp from the papayas with a grapefruit knife or a spoon, leaving the shell intact with ⅛ inch of pulp. Reserve the shells for serving.

2. Puree the pulp in a food processor. Add the yogurt, milk, and zest and blend. If the soup is too thick, add a bit more milk. Chill for 25 minutes.

3. Before serving, taste and adjust seasoning with lemon or orange juice.

To Serve: Spoon the chilled soup into the papaya shells and garnish each with a strawberry half and a sprig of mint.

Per serving: 1 mg cholesterol, 0.12 gm saturated fat, 0.3 gm total fat, 1 gm fiber,
41 mg sodium, 66 calories

Salads and Salad Dressings

Cucumber-
Buttermilk Dressing ⓠ

Yield: 1½ cups (1 tablespoon = 1 serving)

This salad dressing provides a welcome change from the usual low-calorie vinaigrette. It keeps for 2 weeks in the refrigerator.

½ cup 1%-fat cottage cheese
1 5-inch slice hothouse cucumber, cubed, or regular cucumber, peeled and seeded
1 slice green onion
1 clove garlic

¾ cup buttermilk (fat removed) or nonfat yogurt
¼ teaspoon dried thyme
¼ teaspoon dried basil
1 tablespoon white wine vinegar
⅛ teaspoon white pepper

1. Puree the cottage cheese, cucumber, onion, and garlic in a blender.
2. Add the remaining ingredients and process until well blended and smooth.
3. Taste and adjust seasonings. Store in a tightly closed jar in the refrigerator.

NOTE: Hothouse cucumbers are long thin-skinned cucumbers that are not waxed and need not be peeled before using. They generally come wrapped in plastic.

Per serving: 0 mg cholesterol, 0.07 gm saturated fat, 0.1 gm total fat, 0 gm fiber, 9 mg sodium, 8 calories

Low-Calorie Salad Dressing ⓠ

Yield: about 1½ cups (1 tablespoon = 1 serving)

12 ounces sodium-reduced vegetable juice
3 tablespoons fresh lemon juice
2 tablespoons red wine vinegar
1 tablespoon finely chopped onion or shallot
1 tablespoon fresh parsley, minced
1 large clove garlic, minced

½ teaspoon honey, sugar, or apple juice concentrate (optional)
¼ teaspoon celery seed
½ teaspoon dried basil, crushed
Freshly ground pepper
1 teaspoon arrowroot powder
Few drops red pepper sauce (optional)

1. Combine all the ingredients in jar; shake to blend.
2. Pour into a small saucepan and bring to a boil over medium heat, while stirring, until slightly thickened (about 3 minutes).
3. Cool, return to jar, and refrigerate. It keeps for about 3 weeks.

Per serving: 0 mg cholesterol, 0 gm saturated fat, 0 gm total fat, 0.1 gm fiber, 2 mg sodium, 4 calories

Fresh Asparagus Salad ⓠⓜ

Serves: 4

If you are an asparagus lover, as I am, you'll enjoy this flavorful salad as an accompaniment to either hot or cold chicken breasts.

1 pound fresh asparagus
2 tablespoons water
2 teaspoons extra-virgin olive oil
1 tablespoon dry sherry
2–3 tablespoons brown rice vinegar
1 tablespoon lemon juice
2 teaspoons sodium-reduced soy sauce

1 clove garlic, minced
½ small red onion, minced
½ red pepper, seeded and thinly sliced
½ cup canned water chestnuts, drained and thinly sliced

1. With a vegetable peeler, remove the thin outer skin of the asparagus. Remove the tough ends of the stalks. Cut the stalks into 1½-inch diagonal pieces.

2. Place the asparagus in a microwave dish, add the water, cover, and cook on high for 3 minutes. Drain, rinse under cold water, and drain again.

3. Combine the oil, sherry, vinegar, lemon juice, soy sauce, and garlic in a serving bowl.

4. Add the onion, pepper, water chestnuts, and asparagus. Mix lightly and chill 20 minutes before serving.

Per serving: 0 mg cholesterol, 0.4 gm saturated fat, 2.7 gm total fat, 1.5 gm fiber, 89 mg sodium, 83 calories

Sliced Beet
and Orange Salad ⓠ

Serves: 4

2 bunches watercress, washed and
   heavy stems removed
6 cooked beets, peeled and sliced
2 large navel oranges, peeled and
   sliced

Strips of zest of 1 orange, for
   garnish

Dressing:
3 tablespoons low-calorie oil-free
   vinaigrette dressing
1 tablespoon white wine vinegar
1 teaspoon extra-virgin olive oil
1 teaspoon Dijon mustard

1 teaspoon frozen unsweetened
   apple juice concentrate
½ teaspoon chopped fresh
   tarragon

1. Arrange a bed of watercress on a shallow serving plate.

2. Overlap sliced beets with sliced oranges on the watercress.

3. Combine the dressing ingredients, spoon over the beets and oranges, and garnish with strips of orange zest.

Per serving: 0 mg cholesterol, 0.2 gm saturated fat, 1.5 gm total fat, 2.8 gm fiber, 121 mg sodium, 106 calories

Black Bean and Corn Salad ⓠ

Serves: 4

In addition to being wonderfully flavorful, beans and corn are both high in complex carbohydrates and soluble fiber.

1 tablespoon cold-pressed safflower oil or soy or corn oil

2 tablespoons sherry or white wine vinegar

2 tablespoons chopped onions or shallots

1 tablespoon frozen unsweetened apple juice concentrate

¼ teaspoon dry ground mustard

¼ teaspoon ground cumin

About ¼ teaspoon hot pepper sauce

2 cups cooked black beans (page 129), or 1 15-ounce can black beans, drained and rinsed

1 12-ounce can sodium-reduced corn, or 1¾ cups fresh corn cooked for 1 minute on high in microwave

½ sweet red pepper, seeded and finely diced

2 tablespoons chopped fresh cilantro

4 cups shredded romaine

1. Place the first seven ingredients in a mixing bowl; blend well.
2. Add the beans, corn, red pepper, and cilantro, and toss.
3. Chill 20 minutes in the refrigerator and then bring to room temperature before serving.

To Serve: Place 1 cup shredded romaine on each salad plate and top with a quarter of the salad mixture.

Per serving: 0 mg cholesterol, 0.5 gm saturated fat, 3.8 gm total fat, 9 gm fiber, 16 mg sodium, 282 calories

Green Bean Salad
Piquant with Ginger ⓠ

Serves: 4

3 cloves garlic, minced
2 green onions, finely chopped
1–2 tablespoons grated fresh ginger root
2 teaspoons canola oil
½ teaspoon crushed red pepper flakes
2 tablespoons brown rice vinegar

1 tablespoon hoisin sauce
1 pound Chinese long beans or young, tender green beans, cut into 3-inch lengths

2 peeled roasted red peppers, for garnish

1. Place the garlic, onion, ginger, oil, and pepper flakes in 9- or 10-inch round glass baking dish. Microwave uncovered on high for 2 minutes.

2. Add the vinegar, hoisin sauce, and beans and stir to combine. Cover tightly with microwave plastic wrap and microwave on high for 4 to 5 minutes. Mix and cook 4 to 5 minutes more.

3. Remove from oven, stir, cover, and chill at least 30 minutes before serving.

To Serve: Place on a serving platter and garnish generously with roasted red pepper strips. Or, to serve as individual salads, arrange green bean bundles in roasted red pepper halves.

Per serving: 0 mg cholesterol, 0.21 gm saturated fat, 2.7 gm total fat, 2.2 gm fiber, 125 mg sodium, 69 calories

Cabbage, Bean Sprout, Tomato, and Carrot Slaw ℚ

Serves: 4

Winter vegetables can also make interesting salad combinations varied to suit your palate.

1½ cups shredded red cabbage
1½ cups shredded green cabbage
4 ounces fresh bean sprouts,
  washed and drained
4 plum tomatoes, diced
3 carrots, shredded

4 thin slices avocado, for garnish
  (optional)

Salad Dressing:
½ cup low-calorie vinaigrette
  dressing
2 teaspoons Hungarian paprika
2 tablespoons frozen unsweetened
  apple juice concentrate
2 teaspoons white wine vinegar

1. Combine the cabbages, bean sprouts, tomatoes, and carrots and toss lightly in a bowl.

2. Mix the dressing ingredients together, pour over the salad, and toss lightly.

To Serve: Mound the salad on chilled plates and garnish each with a thin slice of avocado.

Per serving: 0 mg cholesterol, 0.09 gm saturated fat, 0.7 gm total fat, 3.4 gm fiber, 42 mg sodium, 91 calories

Cole Slaw Relish Salad ⑨

Serves: 16 (½ cup = 1 serving)

This salad goes particularly well with chicken, turkey, or meat loaf. Using your food processor for chopping will really speed up the preparation time.

1 small head (about 1 pound) green cabbage, finely chopped
½ small head red cabbage, finely chopped
½ cup chopped seeded green pepper
½ cup chopped seeded red pepper
1 cup chopped carrots
½ small onion, finely chopped

1½ teaspoons celery seed
Freshly ground pepper
3 tablespoons light-style mayonnaise mixed with ¾ cup nonfat plain yogurt and 2 tablespoons lemon juice
3 tablespoons chopped fresh dill (optional)

1. Combine the vegetables. Add the celery seed and freshly ground pepper to taste.
2. Add the yogurt mixture and stir well.
3. Cover and refrigerate at least 2 hours before serving.

Per serving: 1 mg cholesterol, 0.05 gm saturated fat, 1.2 gm total fat, 1.5 gm fiber, 47 mg sodium, 45 calories

Bristol Farms Fantastic Corn and Eggplant Fiesta

Serves: about 10 (⅔ cup = 1 serving)

Bristol Farms Market sells this delicious, habit-forming salad in their takeout section. This is my adaptation to make it a more viable recipe for home use.

10 ears fresh corn* (about 5 cups), or 5 cups canned (if fresh is unavailable)
⅔ pound eggplant, diced into about ½-inch cubes
1 tablespoon extra-virgin olive oil
1 red pepper, seeded and diced
1 green pepper, seeded and diced
1 small red onion, finely chopped
1 2-ounce can chopped green chilis, drained, or 2 Anaheim chilis, roasted, peeled, and diced

¼ cup chopped fresh Italian parsley
½ bunch fresh cilantro, chopped

Dressing:
¼ cup fresh lemon juice
1 tablespoon extra-virgin olive oil
1 tablespoon cold-pressed safflower oil
Freshly ground pepper

1. Remove the kernels from the cob with a sharp knife and place in a bowl and microwave on high for 2 minutes.
2. Place the eggplant on a nonstick baking sheet and brush lightly with the 1 tablespoon olive oil. Place under the broiler and brown lightly.
3. Add the diced eggplant and all the salad remaining ingredients to the corn. Mix to combine.
4. Combine the dressing ingredients and sprinkle over the corn mixture. Blend thoroughly. Taste and adjust seasonings.
5. Cover and refrigerate for at least 1 hour before serving.

Per serving: 0 mg cholesterol, 0.6 gm saturated fat, 5.1 gm total fat, 2.1 gm fiber, 16 mg sodium, 124 calories

* If you can, use fresh white corn; it's divine.

Kasha and Corn Salad ⓠ

Serves: 6 (½ cup = 1 serving)

This hearty dish—high in complex carbohydrates, B-complex vitamins, and iron—may be served as a side dish or a salad.

½ cup cooked buckwheat (kasha), quinoa, or millet (page 130)
1 cup (about 2 ears) cooked fresh corn (save cooking liquid) or sodium-reduced canned corn
⅓ cup sliced green onion
⅓ cup minced fresh Italian parsley
½ cup chopped carrots
⅓ cup chopped celery
1 tablespoon extra-virgin olive oil
2 tablespoons lemon juice
3 tablespoons juice from corn or Low-Calorie Salad Dressing (page 272)

1½ teaspoons chopped fresh basil, or ½ teaspoon dried basil
1 teaspoon chopped fresh oregano, or ½ teaspoon dried oregano

Thinly sliced hothouse cucumber, for garnish
2 Italian plum tomatoes, chopped, for garnish

1. Place the first six ingredients in a mixing bowl and toss lightly.
2. Combine the oil, lemon juice, vegetable juice, basil, and oregano in a small jar and shake to combine.
3. Pour over the corn mixture and toss to blend. Marinate at least 15 minutes.

To Serve: Arrange on a platter and garnish with cucumber slices and chopped tomato.

Per serving: 0 mg cholesterol, 0.38 gm saturated fat, 2.7 gm total fat, 1.2 gm fiber, 53 mg sodium, 70 calories

Radish, Celery, and Cucumber Salad ⓠ

Serves: 4

2 cups red radishes, trimmed and halved
3 celery stalks, cut into ¼-inch slices
1 cup diced hothouse cucumber or regular cucumber, peeled and seeded
1 teaspoon chopped fresh chervil
1 teaspoon chopped fresh tarragon or ⅓ teaspoon dried tarragon
Freshly ground pepper

Butter lettuce, for lining plates
2 tablespoons chopped almonds, for garnish (optional)

Dressing:
½ cup nonfat plain yogurt
1 tablespoon light-style mayonnaise
1 tablespoon apple cider vinegar

1. Combine the radishes, celery, and cucumbers in a bowl. Sprinkle with the chervil, tarragon, and pepper; toss lightly.
2. Blend the dressing ingredients, add to the radish mixture, and combine.

To Serve: Line a platter with butter lettuce and mound the salad mixture on top. Sprinkle with chopped almonds if desired.

Per serving: 2 mg cholesterol, 0.07 gm saturated fat, 1.6 gm total fat, 0.8 gm fiber, 86 mg sodium, 47 calories

Spinach and Pear Salad ⓠ

Serves: 4

Pears are high in soluble fiber; however, since fruits always have better flavor when in season, you may substitute nectarines or peaches in their season.

4 cups spinach leaves, washed thoroughly, dried, and torn
2 cups red leaf lettuce, washed thoroughly, dried, and torn
3 tablespoons low-calorie vinaigrette dressing

1 tablespoon lemon juice
2 tablespoons orange juice
½ teaspoon Dijon mustard
Freshly ground pepper
2 small ripe pears or papaya, halved, cored, and sliced

1. Toss the spinach and lettuce together in a bowl. Divide evenly among four plates.

2. Combine the dressing, lemon and orange juices, mustard, and pepper. Beat with a fork to blend.

3. Arrange a quarter of the pear slices in a fan shape on the greens on each plate.

4. Sprinkle with dressing and serve.

NOTE: The salad may be prepared ahead (sprinkle the fruit *lightly* with lemon juice to prevent discoloring). Cover with plastic wrap and refrigerate. Drizzle with dressing just before serving.

Per serving: 0 mg cholesterol, 0.06 gm saturated fat, 0.6 gm total fat, 4.6 gm fiber, 56 mg sodium, 73 calories

Date Waldorf Salad ⓠ

Serves: 4

This combination of ingredients is a pleasant change from the traditional Waldorf salad.

2 large red apples, cored and diced
2 teaspoons lemon juice
1 raw turnip, peeled and shredded

8 dates, pitted and chopped
¼ cup nonfat lemon yogurt

2 carrots, shredded, for garnish

1. Combine the apples, lemon juice, turnips, and dates in a bowl; toss lightly.

2. Add the yogurt and blend with a fork.

To Serve: Place on a platter and surround with shredded carrot.

Per serving: 0 mg cholesterol, 0.09 gm saturated fat, 0.3 gm total fat, 3.7 gm fiber, 21 mg sodium, 96 calories

Vegetable Antipasto Ⓜ

Serves: 8

An easy and attractive salad, first course, or buffet dish for entertaining.

¼ cup white wine vinegar
3 tablespoons water
½ tablespoon extra-virgin olive oil
½ teaspoon Dijon mustard
Freshly ground pepper
1 tablespoon chopped fresh thyme, or 1 teaspoon crushed dried thyme
3 cups combined fresh broccoli and cauliflower flowerets and sliced carrots
1 cup French-cut green beans

½ green pepper, seeded and cut into thin strips
½ red pepper, seeded and cut into thin strips
¼ cup sliced black olives
½ mild white onion, thinly sliced

Butter lettuce, for lining platter
2 plum tomatoes, diced, and 1 tablespoon chopped fresh thyme or parsley, for garnish

1. Place the first six ingredients in a microwave casserole and combine.
2. Add all the vegetables except the peppers. Stir, cover tightly with plastic wrap, and microwave on high for 3 to 5 minutes.
3. Stir. Add the peppers, olives, and onion slices.
4. Toss, cover, or place in a plastic bag, seal, and chill 2 hours or overnight.
To Serve: Remove the vegetable mixture with a slotted spoon to a platter lined with butter lettuce and sprinkle with chopped tomato and chopped fresh thyme.

Variations: A 16-ounce package of any frozen vegetable mixture of your choice may be substituted for the broccoli mixture.

Instead of the first six ingredients, use ½ cup oil-free low-calorie Italian dressing plus 1 teaspoon olive oil and ½ teaspoon Dijon mustard.

Per serving: 0 mg cholesterol, 0.23 gm saturated fat, 1.5 gm total fat, 1.5 gm fiber, 57 mg sodium, 38 calories

Entrées

Pasta with Garden Vegetable Marinara Sauce

Serves: about 10

Yield: 5 to 6 cups sauce (⅔ cup = 1 serving)

This meatless sauce for pasta helps make a vegetarian dinner special. It may be prepared ahead of time and frozen for future use. Any egg-free pasta may be used.

Sauce:

1 medium onion, finely chopped
3 cloves garlic, minced
1 tablespoon extra-virgin olive oil
2 carrots, finely chopped
1 stalk celery with leaves, finely chopped
1 medium zucchini, coarsely chopped
1 crookneck squash, coarsely chopped
½ green pepper, seeded and finely chopped
1 28-ounce can chopped plum tomatoes in puree
3 tablespoons tomato paste

1 teaspoon dried Italian herb blend, crushed
½ teaspoon crushed dried basil, or 1½ teaspoons chopped fresh basil
½ teaspoon crushed dried red pepper flakes

1¼ pounds angel hair pasta or linguini, cooked *al dente* and drained
Freshly grated Parmesan cheese (optional)

1. Sauté the onions and garlic in the oil in a 3-quart saucepan for 3 to 5 minutes, stirring constantly.
2. Add the carrots, celery, zucchini, squash, and pepper. Stir and sauté 5 minutes.
3. Add the tomatoes, tomato paste, herbs, and pepper flakes.
4. Bring to a boil, reduce to a simmer, and cook for 30 minutes. Place hot pasta in large pasta bowl. Spoon one half of the sauce over hot pasta and blend. Serve remaining sauce at the table and allow each person to use with cheese as desired.

Per serving: 0 mg cholesterol, 0.29 gm saturated fat, 2 gm total fat, 2.5 gm fiber, 119 mg sodium, 217 calories

Turkey Chili and Macaroni

Serves: 6 (1½ ounces cooked turkey = 1 serving)

A meal in one.

10 ounces ground turkey breast
(see page 142)
1 14½-ounce can sodium-reduced
stewed or chopped tomatoes
2 6-ounce cans sodium-reduced
vegetable juice
1 cup chopped onion
2 cloves garlic, minced
1 tablespoon chili powder
½ teaspoon ground cumin

1 teaspoon dried oregano, crushed
Freshly ground pepper
1 bay leaf
1½ cups cooked kidney beans
(page 129) or canned beans,
drained and rinsed
2 cups fresh or frozen mixed
vegetables
6 ounces elbow macaroni, cooked
al dente and drained

1. Put the turkey into a 4-quart nonstick saucepan and cook until the meat is no longer pink, stirring frequently.
2. Add the tomatoes, juice, onion, garlic, and seasonings. Simmer, covered, for 20 minutes. Remove the bay leaf.
3. Add the beans and vegetables and simmer, covered, for 12 minutes.
4. Add the cooked macaroni and heat 5 minutes.
To Serve: Serve with mixed green salad and crisp sourdough rolls, with fruit for dessert.

Per serving: 28 mg cholesterol, 0.44 gm saturated fat, 2 gm total fat, 5.7 gm fiber, 90 mg sodium, 307 calories

Deviled Turkey Fillets

Serves: 4 (3 ounces cooked turkey = 1 serving)

2 8-ounce turkey breast fillets
Juice of ½ lemon
2 teaspoons onion powder
2 teaspoons salt-free vegetable
seasoning
2 tablespoons Dijon mustard
2 tablespoons dry white wine

½ teaspoon red pepper sauce
2 teaspoons Worcestershire sauce
1 cup dry whole wheat or rye
breadcrumbs

Watercress and cherry tomatoes,
for garnish

1. Sprinkle the fillets with the lemon juice and seasonings, cover, and let stand in the refrigerator for 30 minutes or overnight.

2. Combine the mustard, wine, red pepper sauce, and Worcestershire sauce.

3. Brush the fillets with the mustard sauce and coat one side with breadcrumbs.

4. Place on a nonstick baking sheet, crumbed-side-up, and bake in the upper third of a preheated 375° oven for about 20 minutes or until lightly browned.

To Serve: Cut the turkey into sixteen diagonal slices and arrange on a platter with watercress and tomatoes.

Per serving: 60 mg cholesterol, 0.9 gm saturated fat, 4.1 gm total fat, 0.2 gm fiber, 322 mg sodium, 222 calories

Grilled Hawaiian Fish with Pineapple Sauce ⓠ

Serves: 4 (4 ounces cooked fish = 1 serving)

The fish of Hawaii is combined tastefully with its native fruit.

1 cup fresh or canned crushed pineapple with its juice
2 teaspoons cornstarch
½ teaspoon crushed red pepper flakes
1 tablespoon chopped fresh cilantro

1 tablespoon chopped fresh parsley
4 5-ounce fillets of ahi, mahimahi, or hebi (halibut or tuna may be substituted for Hawaiian fish)

1. Combine the first three ingredients in a saucepan and bring to a boil. Add the cilantro and parsley.

2. Grill or broil the fish about 3 minutes on each side.

To Serve: Place fish on a heated serving platter and top with warmed sauce. Accompany with fresh broccoli and wild rice.

Per serving: 62 mg cholesterol, 0.2 gm saturated fat, 1.1 gm total fat, 0.5 gm fiber, 90 mg sodium, 163 calories

Red Snapper with
Spicy Tomato Sauce ⓠ

Serves: 4 (3½ ounces cooked fish = 1 serving)

4 5-ounce red snapper, pollock, or
ocean perch fillets
2 teaspoons extra-virgin olive oil
¼ cup dry breadcrumbs mixed
with 2 teaspoons salt-free vegetable seasoning and ⅛ teaspoon
white pepper

1 tablespoon chopped fresh cilantro or parsley, for garnish

Spicy Tomato Sauce:
2 cups crushed Italian plum tomatoes in puree
1 large shallot, finely minced
2 cloves garlic, finely minced
2 tablespoons chopped fresh
cilantro
Few grains crushed red pepper
flakes
Few drops red pepper sauce

1. Combine the sauce ingredients in a saucepan and bring to a boil. Set
aside.

2. Coat a baking dish with nonstick butter-flavored cooking spray, arrange
the fish fillets in the pan, and brush lightly with the olive oil. Bake in a
preheated 375° oven for 5 minutes.

3. Sprinkle the fish with the seasoned breadcrumbs, return to the oven,
and bake 10 minutes or until lightly browned.

To Serve: Spoon ½ cup hot tomato sauce onto each dinner plate. Top
with a fish fillet and sprinkle with chopped cilantro.

Per serving: 40 mg cholesterol, 0.73 gm saturated fat, 4.3 gm total fat, 1 gm fiber,
294 mg sodium, 189 calories

Foil-Baked Fish
with Vegetables Ⓠ

Serves: 2 (3 ounces cooked fish = 1 serving)

This dish may be prepared en papillote (in parchment paper) but it works quite well with foil. It can be prepared and refrigerated hours ahead.

Sauce:

1 shallot, minced

2 teaspoons extra-virgin olive oil

2 green onions, cut into matchstick slices 2 inches long

1 leek (white part only), well washed, cut into matchstick slices 2 inches long

1 teaspoon peeled grated fresh ginger root

1 carrot, cut into matchstick slices 2 inches long

1 small zucchini, cut into matchstick slices 2 inches long

4 fresh mushroom caps, thinly sliced

4 canned water chestnuts, thinly sliced

1 tablespoon fresh lime or lemon juice

2 teaspoons sodium-reduced soy sauce

Freshly ground white pepper

2 4-ounce halibut, salmon, or monkfish fillets

Parslied lemon wedges, for garnish

1. Sauté shallot in the oil for ½ minute. Add the green onions, leek, and ginger root and cook 1 minute.

2. Add the carrot, zucchini, mushrooms, and water chestnuts, stirring over heat for about 2 minutes.

3. Add the lime or lemon juice, soy sauce, and pepper.

4. Place the fish fillets on a 20 × 12-inch piece of lightweight foil and top each fillet with half of the vegetable mixture. Fold the foil over the fish-vegetable mixture and crimp the edges to seal the packet.

5. Place on a baking sheet and bake in a preheated 450° oven for 8 to 10 minutes per inch of thickness of the fish.

To Serve: Place the packet on a heated plate, slit open, slide the fish and vegetables onto the plate, remove from the foil, and serve immediately with parslied lemon wedges.

Per serving: 35 mg cholesterol, 1.32 gm saturated fat, 9.6 gm total fat, 1.7 gm fiber, 242 mg sodium, 239 calories

Soft Tuna Tacos ⓠ

Serves: 4 (1 taco = 1 serving)

This is a satisfying dish to serve when the family is home for lunch.

1 6½-ounce can albacore tuna in
　water, drained and flaked
⅔ cup Fresh Salsa (page 183) or
　canned salt-free salsa mixed
　with 1 tablespoon lime juice
4 6-inch corn tortillas
1 cup chopped cucumber, drained

1 cup sliced seeded green pepper
½ cup chopped fresh tomatoes
½ cup chopped fresh cilantro
2 cups shredded lettuce
Taco sauce to taste

1. Combine the tuna with the salsa and lime juice.
2. Warm the tortillas briefly in the microwave oven or wrap in foil and heat in a 375° oven for 3 minutes.
3. Place the tortillas in the center of a large serving platter and surround with separate bowls of each vegetable and a bowl of taco sauce.

To Serve: Each person fills a tortilla with his choice of fillings, sprinkles the fillings with taco sauce if desired, and folds the tortilla in half to eat.

Per serving: 19 mg cholesterol, 0.48 gm saturated fat, 2.6 gm total fat, 1.6 gm fiber, 246 mg sodium, 165 calories

Stir-Fried Tuna and Vegetables Q

Serves: 4

This tuna dish is a convenient fish meal that can be prepared in minutes. Remember to always use tuna packed in water because it has only a trace of fat, whereas there are about 18 grams of fat in a 3½-ounce can of tuna packed in oil.

2 teaspoons cold-pressed safflower oil

3 cloves garlic, minced

1 teaspoon grated fresh ginger root

3 cups chopped fresh broccoli flowerets, or 1 16-ounce package frozen broccoli, red peppers, and corn, defrosted and drained

1 small red onion, thinly sliced into rings

3 tablespoons defatted sodium-reduced chicken broth

1 cup fresh snow peas

2 cups sliced fresh mushrooms

1 6½-ounce can albacore tuna in water, drained and flaked

1–2 tablespoons sodium-reduced soy sauce

3 cups hot steamed brown rice (page 130)

1. Heat the oil in a nonstick skillet. Add the garlic and ginger and stir-fry briefly.
2. Add the broccoli and onion rings and stir-fry 3 minutes.
3. Add the chicken broth, snow peas, and mushrooms and stir-fry 3 minutes more.
4. Add the tuna and soy sauce, and stir-fry just to heat.

To Serve: Mound the hot rice on a warm serving platter, spoon the hot tuna and vegetables over the top, and serve immediately.

Per serving: 19 mg cholesterol, 0.51 gm saturated fat, 3.9 gm total fat, 2.1 gm fiber, 323 mg sodium, 143 calories

Chicken Breasts
in Phyllo

Serves: 4 (3 ounces cooked chicken = 1 serving)

I used to teach a version of this elegant and delicious dish years ago in my French cooking classes. Of course, then each leaf of phyllo was drenched with melted butter.

4 4-ounce boned, skinned, and de-fatted chicken breasts, flattened (see page 142)
Juice of ½ lemon
Freshly ground pepper
1 tablespoon chopped fresh thyme, or 1 teaspoon dried thyme
1 shallot, minced
1 large clove garlic, minced
¾ cup each chopped onion, chopped celery, and chopped fresh mushrooms, mixed to-gether (reserve ½ cup mixture for sauce)
2 teaspoons extra-virgin olive oil
2 tablespoons defatted sodium-reduced chicken broth mixed with 1 tablespoon dry white wine and ½ teaspoon fines herbes

8 sheets phyllo, defrosted if frozen
Butter-flavored nonstick cooking spray
Extra-virgin olive oil (optional)

Sauce:
½ cup reserved vegetable mixture
½ cup defatted sodium-reduced chicken broth
1 tablespoon dry white wine
Pinch dried Herbes de Provence

1. Season the chicken with the lemon juice, pepper, and thyme.
2. Sear the chicken in a heated nonstick skillet coated with nonstick spray, cooking about 2 minutes on each side. Cool.
3. Sauté the shallot, garlic, and mixed vegetables in the oil in a separate skillet for about 2 minutes. Add the broth mixture and cook 3 minutes or until excess moisture evaporates. Save ½ cup for sauce.
4. Coat a nonstick baking sheet with nonstick spray. Place a sheet of phyllo on the counter and coat with butter-flavored nonstick spray. Fold in half; coat with a light layer of spray. Place 1 chicken breast on the folded phyllo, 4 inches from the bottom. Spread a quarter of the vegetable mixture

on the chicken. Fold the sides of the phyllo over the chicken and roll up, enclosing chicken entirely in phyllo.* Place the phyllo packet on the baking sheet seam-side-down. Repeat for the remaining chicken and phyllo.

5. Coat the phyllo packets with a light layer of cooking spray or brush them lightly with olive oil and bake in a preheated 425° oven for 12 to 15 minutes until golden brown.

To Make Sauce:

1. Puree the vegetables with the broth in a food processor or blender until smooth.

2. Place in a saucepan, add the wine and herbs. Bring to a simmer, taste, and adjust seasonings.

To Serve: Serve immediately with a selection of crisp cooked fresh vegetables such as snow peas, carrots, and zucchini and stir-fried cherry tomatoes with chives. Serve sauce on side.

Per serving: 72 mg cholesterol, 1.42 gm saturated fat, 6.3 gm total fat, 0.7 gm fiber, 88 mg sodium, 206 calories

* Phyllo packets may be prepared several hours ahead of time to this point and refrigerated or frozen for future use. Defrost in the refrigerator for several hours before baking.

Oven-Baked Chinese Chicken Legs

Serves: 6 (2 legs = 1 serving)

These chicken legs are a favorite of mine. They are delicious served hot or cold at a picnic with potato or rice salad.

12 chicken drumsticks, skin and fat removed (cut tendon at tip of leg to prevent splitting)

Juice of 1 large lemon (about 3 tablespoons)

2 tablespoons sodium-reduced soy sauce

1 clove garlic, minced

2 tablespoons dry sherry or rice wine

2 tablespoons hoisin sauce

1. Place the drumsticks in a plastic bag. Combine the remaining ingredients and add to the chicken. Coat the chicken thoroughly and marinate overnight in the refrigerator, turning the bag from time to time to distribute the marinade.

2. Drain the drumsticks, place on a nonstick baking sheet, and bake in the upper third of a preheated 425° oven, turning and basting occasionally with marinade, about 25 to 30 minutes, or until golden brown.

Per serving: 80 mg cholesterol, 1.27 gm saturated fat, 4.9 gm total fat, 0 gm fiber, 243 mg sodium, 154 calories

Margie's Pasta with Sun-Dried Tomatoes Ⓠ

Serves: 6

This pasta makes a wonderful entrée for one of your vegetarian meals. Start with a large salad and end with fresh fruit.

2 tablespoons extra-virgin olive oil
1 red or white onion, sliced and separated into rings
3 cloves garlic, minced
Freshly ground pepper
3 ounces sun-dried tomatoes, covered with defatted sodium-reduced chicken broth, white wine, or water and heated on high in microwave for 1 to 2 minutes

12 ounces penne, cooked *al dente* and drained
2 tablespoons Pesto Sauce (page 244)

¼ cup chopped fresh basil, as garnish

1. Heat the oil in a nonstick skillet. Add the onion rings, garlic, and pepper, and sauté until transparent but not wilted.
2. Cut the reconstituted tomatoes into ½-inch slices and add to the onion mixture with the liquid.
3. Heat thoroughly, then add the hot cooked pasta and the pesto. Toss to blend, garnish with basil, and serve immediately.

Per serving: 0 mg cholesterol, 0.94 gm saturated fat, 6.7 gm total fat, 3 gm fiber, 16 mg sodium, 297 calories

Pasta Pizza Pie

Serves: 10 to 12

Instead of taking the time to make a pizza crust, I use pasta as the crust and fill it with a generous tomato-vegetable filling. Add an easy salad and fresh fruit for dessert and it fills the bill for lunch or dinner.

Filling:
1 small onion, finely chopped
2 cloves garlic, minced
2 teaspoons extra-virgin olive oil
½ red pepper, seeded and thinly sliced
½ green pepper, seeded and thinly sliced
1 small zucchini, diced
1 crookneck squash, diced
1 Japanese eggplant, diced
1 cup thinly sliced fresh mushrooms
1 28-ounce can crushed Italian plum tomatoes in puree
2 tablespoons dry red wine
2 tablespoons chopped fresh basil, or 1 teaspoon dried Italian herb blend

2 plum tomatoes, cut crosswise into 10 to 12 slices, for top
Fresh basil leaves, for garnish

Crust:
½ cup dry breadcrumbs
1 green onion, thinly sliced
2 extra-large egg whites, slightly beaten
Few drops red pepper sauce
Freshly ground pepper
¼ cup shredded part-skim mozzarella cheese mixed with 2 tablespoons shredded Parmesan cheese
⅓ cup filling
About 2 cups (4 ounces dry) cooked capellini (angel hair pasta), drained

To Make the Filling:
1. Sauté the onion and garlic in the oil in a nonstick saucepan for 2 to 3 minutes.
2. Add the peppers, squashes, eggplant, and mushrooms and sauté 3 minutes.
3. Add the remaining ingredients except the garnishes, bring to a boil, reduce to a simmer, and cook 15 minutes, stirring occasionally.

To Make the Crust:
1. Combine all the ingredients except the sauce and the pasta in a large

mixing bowl. Add ⅓ cup sauce and blend with a fork; add the pasta and blend.

2. Coat a 10-inch glass pie plate with nonstick spray. Spread the pasta mixture around the bottom and sides of the plate.

3. Pour the vegetable filling into the crust and arrange the tomato slices on top.

4. Bake in the upper third of a preheated 425° oven for about 20 minutes.

To Serve: Let stand 20 minutes; garnish with basil leaves and cut into 10 or 12 pie-shaped pieces and serve.

Per serving: 2 mg cholesterol, 0.61 gm saturated fat, 1.9 gm total fat, 1.3 gm fiber, 177 mg sodium, 89 calories

Corn Crêpes with Cheese and Spinach or Vegetable Filling

Yield: about 15 crêpes

(2 filled crêpes = 1 serving as entrée; 1 crêpe = 1 serving as appetizer)

These crêpes are easy to make and extremely versatile. With a filling they make a wonderful entrée to serve with soup, salad, and dessert. Or they may be used in any recipe instead of tortillas. They may also be sprinkled lightly with Parmesan cheese, folded into quarters, heated in a microwave, and served as an accompaniment to chicken or turkey.

4 extra-large egg whites
1½ cups nonfat milk
1 tablespoon cold-pressed safflower or corn oil
½ cup whole wheat flour or cornmeal
1 cup unbleached white flour
⅛ teaspoon white pepper
1 teaspoon dried thyme
Pinch of salt (optional)
1 tablespoon grated onion

2 tablespoons canned chopped green chilis
1 cup fresh corn kernels (about 2 ears corn) or sodium-reduced canned corn
4 tablespoons chopped fresh cilantro or Italian parsley (optional)

Cheese and Spinach Filling (page 298) or Vegetable Filling (page 297)

To Make the Batter:

1. Place the egg whites, milk, oil, flours, pepper, thyme, and salt in a blender or the food processor. Blend until smooth.

2. Add the onion, green chilis, corn, and cilantro. Blend just to combine, not until smooth.

3. Place in a bowl, cover, and chill at least 1 hour before preparing crêpes.

To Prepare the Crêpes:

1. Heat a 6-inch nonstick skillet coated with nonstick spray until hot. (A few drops of water will dance on the skillet.)

2. Stir the batter and pour ¼ scant cup (about 3 tablespoons) onto the hot skillet, tilting to cover the bottom.

3. Brown the bottom of the crêpe; turn and just dry the second side.

4. Flip the hot crêpe onto a flat clean dish towel before cooking the next one. Do not stack the warm crêpes.

5. If you plan to use the crêpes right away, cover them loosely with dish towels to keep them warm and pliable. Fill and bake as directed in the filling recipes below.

6. If you plan to use the crêpes later, let them cool. As the crêpes are cooled, stack them in layers using wax paper or plastic bags between them to prevent sticking. Then wrap the stacked crêpes in foil. They will keep in the refrigerator for 2 to 3 days or the freezer for 6 to 8 weeks.

To Freeze for Future Use: Seal the foil-wrapped crêpes in a freezer bag. *To defrost*, heat the foil packet of crêpes in a 350° oven for 5 to 7 minutes or remove the foil and defrost in the microwave on medium for 2 minutes.

Per crêpe: 0 mg cholesterol, 0.16 gm saturated fat, 1.2 gm total fat, 0.7 gm fiber, 31 mg sodium, 73 calories

Vegetable Filling for 8 Corn Crêpes:

1 tablespoon canola or cold-pressed safflower oil
1 small onion, chopped
1 clove garlic, minced
4 carrots, cut into julienne strips
2 zucchini, cut into julienne strips
1 red pepper, seeded and cut into julienne strips
Freshly ground pepper
1 teaspoon dried marjoram
2 tablespoons grated Parmesan cheese

1. Place the oil, onion, and garlic in a 9-inch glass pie plate. Microwave on high for 2 minutes, or sauté in a nonstick skillet for 5 minutes.

2. Add the remaining vegetables, stir, cover with plastic, and microwave on high for 3 minutes, or stir-fry for about 2 minutes and cook covered for 6 minutes.

3. Season with pepper and marjoram. Place ⅛ of the mixture on each of 8 crêpes, roll, and place seam-side-down in the pie plate.

4. Top each crêpe with 1 scant teaspoon of cheese and microwave on high for 1 minute.

To Serve: Place 2 crêpes on a warm plate and accompany with broccoli spears and broiled tomato half.

Per crêpe: 0 mg cholesterol, 0.08 gm saturated fat, 0.7 gm total fat, 1.3 gm fiber, 14 mg sodium, 32 calories

Cheese and Spinach Filling for 8 Crêpes:

1½ cups part-skim ricotta cheese

½ 10-ounce package frozen chopped spinach, defrosted and squeezed dry

3 green onions, finely chopped

2 tablespoons chopped fresh cilantro (optional)

About 1½ cups Fresh Salsa (page 183) or salt-free canned salsa

1. Place all the ingredients except the salsa in a bowl and stir to blend.

2. Spread about 3 tablespoons onto each crêpe and fold the crêpe into thirds.

3. Arrange in a shallow baking pan, spoon 2 tablespoons fresh salsa over each crêpe, and bake in a preheated 375° oven for 5 to 7 minutes to heat before serving.

To Serve: Place 2 hot crêpes on a serving dish, top with salsa, and accompany with steamed broccoli and carrots.

Per crêpe: 15 mg cholesterol, 2.28 gm saturated fat, 3.8 gm total fat, 1 gm fiber, 75 mg sodium, 76 calories

Vegetables

Broccoli Crown Ⓠ Ⓜ

Serves: 4

This colorful dish may be served hot or cold, as part of a vegetable plate or as a salad. Broccoli is high in insoluble fiber, and also a great source of calcium and vitamin A.

1½ pounds fresh broccoli, or
  ¾ pound fresh broccoli and
  ¾ pound fresh cauliflower
½ red pepper, seeded and cut into
  1-inch squares
1 tablespoon water

2 tablespoons Low-Calorie Salad
  Dressing (page 272—optional)

Sliced tomatoes or broiled halved
  tomatoes, for garnish

1. Peel the broccoli stems and remove the flowerets. Cut the stems into 1-inch pieces.
2. Sprinkle the red pepper pieces into the bottom and sides of a 2-quart glass mixing bowl.
3. Arrange the broccoli flowerets, stem-side-up, around the bowl. Sprinkle with the water and fill the center with the remaining broccoli stems.
4. Cover tightly with microwave plastic wrap and microwave on high for 6 minutes. Puncture holes in the plastic with a fork to allow steam to escape.
5. Place a 2-pound can on top of the plastic to mold the broccoli and let stand 10 minutes before serving or chilling for future use.

To Serve: Remove the plastic and drain the bowl of any liquid. Unmold on a serving plate and drizzle with salad dressing if desired. Surround with sliced tomatoes or broiled halved tomatoes.

Per serving: 0 mg cholesterol, 0.1 gm saturated fat, 0.6 gm total fat, 2.3 gm fiber, 46 mg sodium, 50 calories

Easy Eggplant Parmesan Ⓠ Ⓜ

Serves: 4 as an entrée, 8 as a vegetable

1 1½-pound eggplant, cut into 16 ½-inch slices with the skin
3 tablespoons part-skim ricotta cheese
4 plum tomatoes, cut into 16 lengthwise slices

⅔ cup salt-free tomato sauce mixed with ½ teaspoon dried Italian herb blend
1 tablespoon grated Parmesan cheese

1. Place the sliced eggplant in an 11 × 14 × 2-inch microwave baking dish and cover tightly with microwave plastic wrap.

2. Microwave on high for about 2 minutes, or broil in the broiler until lightly browned on both sides.

3. Remove the plastic wrap and spread 8 slices of the eggplant lightly with about 1 teaspoon ricotta cheese each, then top with 2 tomato slices each and the remaining slices of eggplant.

4. Spoon the sauce over the eggplant and sprinkle with the Parmesan cheese.

5. Bake on high in the microwave oven for 5 minutes, or uncovered in a preheated 375° oven for 15 to 20 minutes.

Per serving as an entrée: 5 mg cholesterol, 1.31 gm saturated fat, 5.1 gm total fat, 3.8 gm fiber, 61 mg sodium, 134 calories

Per serving as a vegetable: 2 mg cholesterol, 0.66 gm saturated fat, 0.86 gm total fat, 1.9 gm fiber, 2 mg sodium, 52 calories

Eggplant in
Spicy Brown Sauce ©

Serves: 4

2 teaspoons canola or cold-pressed safflower oil
1 pound eggplant, stem removed, halved lengthwise, and cut into 1½-inch-thick strips
¾ cup defatted sodium-reduced chicken broth
1 tablespoon sodium-reduced soy sauce

1 teaspoon peeled grated fresh ginger root
Few grains crushed red pepper flakes
1 teaspoon cornstarch mixed with ¼ cup defatted sodium-reduced chicken broth and ½ teaspoon chopped garlic

1. Place the oil in a nonstick skillet. Heat, add the eggplant slices, cut-side-down, and brown. Turn and brown the skin side.

2. Combine the broth, soy sauce, ginger, and pepper, and add to the eggplant. Cover and simmer until quite tender (about 10 minutes).

3. Remove the eggplant with a slotted spoon to a serving dish and add the cornstarch mixture to the remaining juices in the skillet. Cook until the mixture boils and thickens, stirring constantly. Pour the sauce over the eggplant and serve immediately.

Per serving: 0 mg cholesterol, 0.23 gm saturated fat, 2.4 gm total fat, 1.7 gm fiber, 127 mg sodium, 61 calories

Gingered
Pineapple Carrots Ⓠ Ⓜ

Serves: 6

6 medium carrots, cut into
   3 × ½-inch spears
2 tablespoons water
1 8-ounce can sugar-free crushed
   pineapple with juice

2 teaspoons cornstarch
¼ teaspoon ground ginger
¼ teaspoon freshly grated nutmeg

1. Microwave the carrots in the water in a tightly covered casserole on high for 3 minutes or until barely tender.

2. Mix the remaining ingredients, add to the carrots, stir, and microwave on high for 2 to 3 minutes or until the juice is slightly thickened.

To Serve: Place on a warm platter and serve immediately.

Per serving: 0 mg cholesterol, 0.04 gm saturated fat, 0.2 gm total fat, 2 gm fiber, 25 mg sodium, 57 calories

Larry's Scalloped Potatoes and Onions

Serves: 6 to 8

When our family embarked on a low-cholesterol lifestyle, I thought my son would never get over the trauma of my not preparing his favorite scalloped potatoes. He did, and indeed, now even prefers these to my archaic fat- and calorie-laden old recipe!

1 onion, halved and thinly sliced
1 large clove garlic, minced
2 teaspoons extra-virgin olive oil
3 unpeeled russet potatoes, scrubbed and cut into ¼-inch slices
Freshly ground pepper
1 teaspoon dried thyme, or 1 tablespoon chopped fresh thyme

2 teaspoons salt-free vegetable seasoning
1½ cups defatted sodium-reduced chicken broth
1 tablespoon shredded Parmesan cheese

1. Sauté the onions and garlic in the oil in a nonstick skillet briefly, for about 2 to 3 minutes.
2. Place the sliced potatoes in a 9-inch glass baking dish. Add the wilted onions and garlic, mix, and sprinkle with pepper, thyme, and vegetable seasoning.
3. Pour the broth over the potato mixture and sprinkle with cheese.
4. Bake in a preheated 425° oven for 30 to 40 minutes or until lightly browned and tender.

Per serving: 0 mg cholesterol, 0.3 gm saturated fat, 1.4 gm total fat, 0.4 gm fiber, 17 mg sodium, 73 calories

Sherry's
Stuffed Potatoes Ⓠ Ⓜ

Serves: 4 (2 halves = 1 serving)

4 6-ounce russet baking potatoes, scrubbed

1 cup chopped cooked turkey breast

1 4-ounce can chopped green chilis, drained

1 cup coarsely chopped steamed broccoli

2 whole green onions, sliced

About 1¼ cups Fresh Salsa (page 183) or canned salt-free salsa

3 tablespoons shredded part-skim mozzarella cheese

2 Italian plum tomatoes, sliced

1 tablespoon grated Parmesan cheese

1. Pierce the potatoes with a fork and microwave on high for about 12 to 15 minutes or until soft to the touch, or bake in a preheated 425° oven for about 45 minutes.

2. Slice the potatoes lengthwise; scoop out the pulp into a mixing bowl and mash.

3. Add the turkey, chilis, broccoli, green onions, salsa, and mozzarella cheese. Mix well.

4. Fill the potato skins with the mixture; top each half with 2 slices of tomato and sprinkle with Parmesan cheese.

5. Place in a shallow microwave-safe round dish and bake on high for 10 minutes or in a 350° oven for 25 to 30 minutes.

Variations: Instead of stuffing your potatoes, try serving split baked potatoes with one or several of the following toppings:

Per serving: 31 mg cholesterol, 1.46 gm saturated fat, 3.6 gm total fat, 3.7 gm fiber, 107 mg sodium, 347 calories

SEVEN TOPPINGS FOR SPLIT BAKED POTATOES
(MEASUREMENTS ARE FOR 1 POTATO)

START WITH	ADD	SEASON WITH
½ cup 1%-fat cottage cheese, blended until smooth	3 tbsp. chopped fresh broccoli 1 tbsp. chopped red pepper	Freshly ground pepper 1 tsp. chopped fresh dill

START WITH	ADD	SEASON WITH
⅓ cup nonfat plain yogurt	3 tbsp. shredded carrots 1 tbsp. chopped chives	Freshly ground pepper 1 tsp. Parmesan cheese
⅓ cup nonfat plain yogurt	1 tbsp. chopped green onion ½ clove garlic, chopped 3 tbsp. frozen peas, defrosted	Freshly ground pepper About 1 tsp. curry powder ½ tsp. Worcestershire sauce
½ cup chopped fresh tomato	1 tbsp. chopped onion 1 tbsp. chopped green chilis ½ tbsp. lime juice	¼ tsp. dried oregano Freshly ground pepper Top with nonfat plain yogurt and chopped fresh cilantro
½ small red onion, sliced, with 1 tsp. olive oil Microwave covered in a 1-cup measure on high for 1 min.	3 fresh mushrooms, sliced 2 tbsp. chopped green pepper 1 tbsp. defatted sodium-reduced chicken broth *or* 1 chopped Italian plum tomato Microwave all together on high for ½ min. in 1-cup glass measure	Salt-free vegetable seasoning Freshly ground pepper Few drops red pepper sauce
1 tbsp. each: chopped green & red peppers, zucchini, & 1 small clove garlic in 1 tbsp. defatted sodium-reduced chicken broth Microwave on high for 1 min. and place on split potato	1 tbsp. shredded part-skim mozzarella cheese sprinkled over potato Microwave on high for 30 seconds	Spicy vegetable seasoning Chopped chives
¼ cup salt-free canned salsa or Fresh Salsa (page 183)	2 tbsp. nonfat plain yogurt	Chopped fresh cilantro

Nan's
Quick Cubed Potatoes Ⓠ Ⓜ

Serves: 6

3 russet or new potatoes (1½ pounds), scrubbed and cut into 1½-inch cubes
1 teaspoon onion powder
1 teaspoon salt-free vegetable seasoning

Freshly ground pepper
1½ teaspoons Hungarian paprika
3 cloves garlic, minced, or 1 teaspoon garlic powder
¼ cup chopped chives

1. Place the cubed potatoes in a microwave dish and sprinkle with onion powder, vegetable seasoning, and pepper. Mix lightly with a fork.

2. Sprinkle with paprika, cover with microwave plastic wrap and microwave on high for 6 minutes.

3. Remove plastic, add minced garlic or garlic powder, and stir. Recover tightly and microwave on high for 5 to 6 minutes.

4. Sprinkle with chopped chives and serve.

Per serving: 0 mg cholesterol, 0.03 gm saturated fat, 0.2 gm total fat, 0.4 gm fiber, 4 mg sodium, 63 calories

Roast Potatoes with Basil

Serves: 6

1 recipe Basil Vinaigrette (page 94)
1 tablespoon extra-virgin olive oil
½ small onion, finely chopped
3 pounds small new potatoes, scrubbed and quartered

Freshly ground pepper
Hungarian paprika

1. Combine the vinaigrette, olive oil, and onions and place in a shallow nonstick roasting pan.

2. Add the potatoes and stir to coat potatoes. Sprinkle with pepper and paprika.

3. Roast the potatoes in a preheated 425° oven for 35 to 40 minutes, stirring occasionally, until browned and tender.

Per serving: 0 mg cholesterol, 0.25 gm saturated fat, 1.5 gm total fat, 0.6 gm fiber, 12 mg sodium, 136 calories

Different Stuffed Potatoes Ⓜ

Serves: 8 (½ potato = 1 serving)

By combining sweet and white potatoes, this recipe takes on an interesting new taste. For special occasions, use a pastry tube to fill the potato shells.

4 6-ounce russet potatoes, scrubbed
8 ounces sweet potatoes, scrubbed
About ⅔ cup nonfat milk
¼ cup nonfat plain yogurt

1 teaspoon ground cinnamon
¼ teaspoon freshly grated nutmeg
¼ teaspoon white pepper
2 whole green onions, thinly sliced
1 cup frozen peas

1. Pierce the russet potatoes with a fork and microwave with the sweet potatoes on high for about 15 minutes, or bake in a preheated 425° oven for about 1 hour.

2. Halve and scoop out the centers of the russet potatoes, leaving ¼-inch shells. Scoop out the pulp of the sweet potatoes and discard the skins.

3. Mash the white potato and sweet potato pulp together.

4. Add the remaining ingredients and combine well.

5. Mound the mixture into the russet potato shells* and heat in a 450° oven for 10 to 15 minutes or until reheated and lightly browned or heat on high in microwave for 5 minutes.

Per serving: 1 mg cholesterol, 0.09 gm saturated fat, 0.3 gm total fat, 2.3 gm fiber, 43 mg sodium, 150 calories

* May be prepared ahead of time to this point, or frozen for future use.

Stir-Fried Squash and Red Pepper Ⓠ Ⓜ

Serves: 6

I particularly enjoy this recipe because squash is so delicious, and it cooks so quickly! You may, of course, use other combinations of vegetables in stir-frying.

2 teaspoons canola oil or 3 tablespoons defatted sodium-reduced chicken broth
2 summer squash, sliced ¼ inch thick
2 crookneck squash, sliced ¼ inch thick

2 zucchini, cut into 3-inch spears
¼ red pepper, seeded and sliced ¼ inch thick
1 teaspoon onion powder
Freshly ground pepper

1. Heat the oil or broth in a 12-inch nonstick skillet over medium-high heat.
2. Add the squashes and stir-fry 2 to 3 minutes. Add the pepper and seasonings and stir.
3. Cover and cook 3 to 5 minutes.

To Microwave: Place all the ingredients in a microwave dish, cover, and cook on high for 3 minutes. Mix and cook 1 additional minute.

NOTE: If you have any vegetables left over, add to a mixed green salad the next day, or serve by themselves with a bit of oil-free vinaigrette dressing.

Per serving: 0 mg cholesterol, 0.14 gm saturated fat, 1.8 gm total fat, 1.5 gm fiber, 2 mg sodium, 36 calories

Sally's Zucchini ⓆⓂ

Serves: 4 (2 halves = 1 serving)

4 whole zucchini (about 1 pound), steamed or microwaved until barely tender and halved lengthwise

2 teaspoons salt-free vegetable seasoning

Freshly ground pepper

¼ cup nonfat plain yogurt

2 tablespoons shredded part-skim mozzarella cheese

Fresh thyme sprigs or watercress, for garnish

1. Remove a ½-inch strip from the center of each zucchini with a grape-fruit spoon or knife.

2. Sprinkle with vegetable seasoning and pepper.

3. Spoon 2 teaspoons of the yogurt down the center of each zucchini half; sprinkle with cheese.

4. Place on a microwave-safe dish and microwave on medium for 1 minute or until the cheese is melted. Top with fresh thyme.

Per serving: 2 mg cholesterol, 0.41 gm saturated fat, 0.8 gm total fat, 0.6 gm fiber, 33 mg sodium, 36.5 calories

Pasta and Grain Side Dishes

Sweet Pasta Pudding

Serves: 8 (1 wedge = 1 serving)

A pleasant change from rice or potatoes with roast turkey or chicken.

8 ounces whole wheat linguini or capellini (angel hair pasta), cooked *al dente* and drained

4 extra-large egg whites, beaten until slightly thickened

½ cup frozen unsweetened apple juice concentrate, or 3 tablespoons brown sugar

1 teaspoon ground cinnamon

½ cup dark seeded raisins

1½ tablespoons canola oil

1. Combine all the ingredients except the oil in a mixing bowl and blend well.

2. Heat the oil in a 10-inch glass pie plate in a preheated oven. Add the hot oil to the pasta mixture and blend well.

3. Pour the mixture into the hot pie plate that has been coated with oil from heating. Bake in a preheated 375° oven for 30 to 40 minutes or until the bottom is golden brown.

To Serve: Invert the pudding on a serving dish, unmold, and cut into eight wedges.

Per serving: 0 mg cholesterol, 0.34 gm saturated fat, 4 gm total fat, 3.1 gm fiber, 37 mg sodium, 189 calories

Cracked Wheat
and Tomato Salad Ⓠ

Serves: 6

Grain dishes like this one offer an inexpensive source of complex carbohydrates, B complex vitamins, and iron.

1⅓ cups cracked wheat, soaked in cold water 20 minutes and drained

4 tablespoons chopped fresh parsley

2 tablespoons chopped fresh mint

4 green onions, sliced

4 plum tomatoes, diced

3 tablespoons lemon juice

1½ tablespoons extra-virgin olive oil

1 teaspoon freshly ground pepper

Romaine leaves, for lining salad bowl

12 cucumber slices and 1 quartered tomato, for garnish

1. Place the cracked wheat, parsley, mint, green onions, and tomatoes in a bowl and mix with a fork.

2. Combine the lemon juice, olive oil, and pepper. Blend with a fork and sprinkle over the wheat mixture.

To Serve: Line a salad bowl with romaine, add the cracked wheat mixture, and garnish with sliced cucumbers and tomato wedges.

Per serving: 0 mg cholesterol, 0.56 gm saturated fat, 4.1 gm total fat, 3.1 gm fiber, 8 mg sodium, 136 calories

Bulgur Wheat Pilaf

Serves: 4

There are some packaged wheat pilaf mixes that may be prepared without added fat. But in case you can't find one at your market, here's a recipe that can be made from scratch.

1 small onion, finely chopped
2 teaspoons extra-virgin olive oil
¾ cup bulgur wheat (cracked wheat), washed
1 stalk celery, thinly sliced
1 carrot, thinly sliced
½ green pepper, seeded and thinly sliced
1 teaspoon salt-free vegetable seasoning

⅛ teaspoon white pepper
1 13¾-ounce can defatted sodium-reduced chicken broth or water

¼ cup slivered almonds, lightly toasted, for garnish (optional)

1. In a 2-quart saucepan, sauté the onion in the olive oil for 3 to 5 minutes or until wilted. Add the bulgur and cook, stirring constantly, for 2 to 3 minutes.
2. Stir in the celery, carrot, green peppers, seasoning, and pepper. Add the chicken broth and bring to a boil.
3. Reduce to a simmer, cover, and cook over low heat 25 minutes.
4. Remove from heat and let stand until all the liquid is absorbed.
5. Fluff with a fork and serve, sprinkling with almonds if desired.

Variation: After removing from heat, add ½ cup muscat raisins, chopped dates, or frozen peas.

Per serving: 0 mg cholesterol, 0.39 gm saturated fat, 2.9 gm total fat, 3.7 gm fiber, 18 mg sodium, 157 calories

Buckwheat Kernels
and Pasta Q M

Serves: 2

1 large clove garlic, chopped
1 small onion, finely chopped
½ green pepper, seeded and diced
2 teaspoons cold-pressed safflower
  oil
½ 10-ounce package frozen peas

1 cup cooked buckwheat (prepared
  according to package directions)
4 ounces farfalle (macaroni bows),
  cooked *al dente* and drained
Freshly ground pepper, to taste

1. Microwave the garlic, onions, peppers, and oil on high until soft (about
2 minutes). Add the frozen peas.
2. Combine with the hot cooked buckwheat, toss with the cooked pasta,
season with pepper, and serve.

Variation: For Black-Eyed Peas and Tomatoes with Pasta, substitute ⅔ cup
cooked black-eyed peas and 1 cup chopped tomatoes for the frozen peas and
buckwheat.

Per serving: 0 mg cholesterol, 0.64 gm saturated fat, 6 gm total fat, 4.3 gm fiber,
257 mg sodium, 310 calories

Desserts

Creme Topping Ⓠ

Yield: 1 cup (1 tablespoon = 1 serving)

This low-calorie sauce makes a delicious no-fat, no-cholesterol topping for fruit or pudding to use instead of whipped cream or heavy cream (remember them?).

½ cup nonfat powdered skim milk   **¼ cup *very* cold water**
¼ cup frozen unsweetened apple
  juice concentrate

1. Place all the ingredients into a chilled 2-cup measure.
2. Beat with Bamix, Krupps, or Braun mini-mixer until thick.
3. Store in the refrigerator until serving time—up to 1½ hours.

Variation: Your favorite chilled fruit juice may be substituted for the apple juice concentrate.

Per serving: 1 mg cholesterol, 0.02 gm saturated fat, 0 gm total fat, 0 gm fiber, 21 mg sodium, 21 calories

Blueberry Sauce Ⓜ

Yield: 1½ cups (3 tablespoons = 1 serving)

This may be used as a topping for frozen nonfat vanilla yogurt, sliced pears, or angel food cake as dessert, or without the liqueur, on pancakes, French toast, or waffles.

1 pint fresh blueberries, washed,   **2 tablespoons pear brandy or**
  or 2 cups frozen unsweetened   **Grand Marnier**
  blueberries
2 tablespoons frozen unsweetened
  apple juice concentrate, or 1 ta-
  blespoon sugar

1. Combine the blueberries with the apple juice concentrate in a 4-cup glass measure.

2. Cover tightly with microwave plastic wrap and microwave on high for 3 minutes.

3. Add the brandy and stir to blend. Store in tightly covered container in refrigerator until serving time.

Per serving: 0 mg cholesterol, 0.01 gm saturated fat, 0.2 gm total fat, 1.1 gm fiber, 3 mg sodium, 36 calories

> Melted frozen nonfat vanilla yogurt makes a tasty topping for fruit and fruit desserts.

Apple Crisp Ⓠ Ⓜ

Serves: 8

4 medium apples (McIntosh or Golden Delicious) or pears, peeled, cored, and cut into ½-inch slices

3 tablespoons unsweetened papaya juice or frozen unsweetened apple juice concentrate mixed with ½ teaspoon ground cinnamon and ½ teaspoon freshly ground nutmeg

Topping:
⅓ cup rolled oats, chopped
3 tablespoons whole wheat flour
1 tablespoon brown sugar
½ teaspoon cinnamon
1 teaspoon cold-pressed safflower oil
2 tablespoons chopped pecans or walnuts (optional)

1. In a mixing bowl, toss the apples and juice mixture together.

2. Place in 8-inch round* or square microwave baking dish.

3. Combine the topping ingredients and blend with your fingers until crumbly. Sprinkle over the apples.

4. Bake on high in a microwave oven for 12 to 15 minutes, or in a preheated 350° oven for 35 to 40 minutes.

To Serve: Serve warm with a pitcher of nonfat cold milk or Creme Topping (page 314).

Per serving: 0 mg cholesterol, 0.17 gm saturated fat, 1.1 gm total fat, 2.2 gm fiber, 2 mg sodium, 81 calories

* Use of a round baking dish or a turntable in the microwave gives more even cooking.

Poached Pear with
Fresh Strawberry Sauce Ⓠ Ⓜ

Serves: 4 (1 pear = 1 serving)

This is a repeat performance of the popular Perfect Pear recipe found in my book *Deliciously Low*. It makes such a special dessert that it bears repeating, and this time around it sits on a bed of pureed fresh strawberries. Of course, you may just serve it with some of its cooking liquid if you wish. A microwave is the only way to cook these pears (and apples, too, for that matter).

4 ripe Bosc, Bartlett, or d'Anjou
   pears
3 tablespoons fresh orange juice or
   papaya nectar
½ teaspoon ground cinnamon
½ teaspoon freshly ground nutmeg

1 cup Fresh Strawberry Sauce
   (page 317)
Lemon or camelia leaves, for
   garnish

1. Core each pear starting at the bottom, leaving the stem intact, and peel.
2. Place the pears upright in a microwave dish; sprinkle with the juice, cinnamon, and nutmeg.
3. Cover the dish with microwave plastic wrap (airtight but not stretched) and microwave on high for about 5 to 6 minutes or until barely fork-tender. *Do not overcook.*

To Serve: Spoon ¼ cup strawberry sauce on each of four flat dessert plates. Place a warm or chilled pear in the center of each plate and garnish with a green lemon or camelia leaf or fresh mint leaves.

Variation: Pears may also be served with the Blueberry Sauce on page 314 or nonfat vanilla yogurt and Wax Orchards Fudge Topping (see footnote page 325).

Per serving: 0 mg cholesterol, 0.10 gm saturated fat, 0.6 gm total fat, 3.1 gm fiber, 0 mg sodium, 82 calories

Fresh Strawberry Sauce ⓠ

Yield: 1 cup (¼ cup = 1 serving)

This sauce may be used with fresh cantaloupe cubes or peaches, as a sauce over nonfat frozen yogurt, or as a topping on angel food cake.

1¼ cups fresh strawberries, washed and hulled

Frozen unsweetened apple juice concentrate or Grand Marnier

1. Place the strawberries in a food processor or blender and puree until smooth.
2. Taste and adjust the flavor with apple juice concentrate or Grand Marnier. Store in a covered container in the refrigerator until ready to use, or freeze for future use.

Per serving: 0 mg cholesterol, 0.12 gm saturated fat, 1 gm total fat, 5.2 gm fiber, 1 mg sodium, 121 calories

Poached Pears and Prunes ⓠⓜ

Serves: 4

2 Bartlett pears, peeled, cored, and cut into a total of 12 slices in all
12 pitted prunes
3 tablespoons frozen unsweetened apple juice concentrate

½ teaspoon ground cinnamon

1 lemon or lime, quartered, for garnish

1. Place the pears and prunes in a 1½-quart microwave casserole.
2. Sprinkle with the apple juice concentrate and cinnamon. Cover and microwave on high for about 4 minutes.
3. Serve warm or at room temperature.

Per serving: 0 mg cholesterol, 0.04 gm saturated fat, 0.5 gm total fat, 6.2 gm fiber, 4 mg sodium, 132 calories

Individual Fresh Apple Tart with Apricot Glaze Ⓠ Ⓜ

Yield: 6 tarts (1 tart = 1 serving)

6 Granny Smith or Golden Delicious apples, peeled, cored, and sliced ½ inch thick
1 cup papaya nectar or fresh orange juice
1 tablespoon Grand Marnier
2 teaspoons honey
1 teaspoon orange zest
½ teaspoon ground cinnamon

Freshly ground nutmeg
9 sheets frozen phyllo, thawed
Butter-flavored nonstick cooking spray

Glaze:
6 pitted fresh apricots
¼ cup apple juice
½ split vanilla bean

1. Place the apples in a microwave dish. Mix the juice, Grand Marnier, honey, zest, and spices together and pour over the apples. Microwave on high for 3 minutes, drain the juice, return the juice to the microwave, and reduce to ¼ cup.

2. Fold the phyllo leaves in half and cut out two 6-inch circles from each.

3. Place six circles of phyllo on a nonstick baking sheet, coat with butter-flavored nonstick spray. Place another phyllo circle on each of the six circles and spray. Repeat with the last six circles.

4. Arrange the drained apple pieces on each of the six phyllo stacks. Pour 2 tablespoons reduced sauce over each apple tart.

5. Bake in a preheated 425° oven for 5 to 7 minutes or until lightly browned.

6. *To make the glaze*, cook the apricots with the apple juice and vanilla bean in a saucepan for about 15 minutes until tender. Remove the vanilla bean and puree in the food processor. If necessary, use apple juice to thin the glaze.

To Serve: Drizzle the warm apricot glaze over the apple tarts and serve immediately.

Variations: Use fresh peaches or nectarines instead of apples and Amaretto instead of Grand Marnier.

For a quick glaze, use sugar-free apricot preserves thinned with apple juice.

To Microwave: Cook all the ingredients in a 3-cup glass measure covered with microwave plastic wrap for 5 minutes on high. Then proceed as above.

Per serving: 0 mg cholesterol, 0.12 gm saturated fat, 0.7 gm total fat, 4.3 gm fiber, 3 mg sodium, 147 calories

Fresh Fruit Compote ⓠ

Serves: 8

1 cup diced fresh pineapple
1 orange, peeled and cubed
1 peach or nectarine, cubed
1 banana, sliced

1 apple, cored and cubed
1 cup red or green seedless grapes
½ cup unsweetened papaya nectar

1. Place all the fruits in a bowl and toss lightly.
2. Sprinkle with papaya nectar, cover, and chill at least 20 minutes before serving.

Per serving: 0 mg cholesterol, 0.09 gm saturated fat, 0.4 gm total fat, 2.2 gm fiber, 2 mg sodium, 71 calories

Fruited Mousse ⓠ

Serves: 8

This fresh fruit dessert is a wonderful light ending to a meal. It is best if served within 1 hour of preparation. You may use frozen mangos, papayas, strawberries, or nectarines instead of peaches.

12 ounces frozen unsweetened
  peaches (packaged, or flash-
  freeze your own in season)
2 extra-large egg whites
1 tablespoon fresh lemon juice

2–3 tablespoons frozen unsweet-
  ened apple juice concentrate
1 teaspoon almond extract, or
1 tablespoon Amaretto

1. Chop the frozen fruit with the metal blade of a food processor or in a blender.
2. Add the remaining ingredients and process until thick and fluffy, about 3 to 4 minutes.

To Serve: Spoon into 8 wine glasses or glass fruit coupes and serve or chill up to 1 hour before serving.

Per serving: 0 mg cholesterol, 0 gm saturated fat, 0.1 gm total fat, 0.6 gm fiber, 16 mg sodium, 32 calories

Persimmon Freeze ⓠ

Serves: 4

This wonderful fresh fruit sorbet is made by simply freezing ripe persimmons when they're in season. The taste is incredibly delicious!

4 ripe persimmons, unwashed and
   frozen solid

4 teaspoons frozen unsweetened
   apple juice concentrate, defrosted, Cointreau, or Creme
   Topping (page 314)

1. Defrost the frozen persimmons at room temperature for about 1 hour (depending on the size of the persimmon) until slightly soft.

2. Peel the defrosted persimmons in petal-like fashion and place in a fruit dish or on dessert plates.

3. Drizzle each persimmon with 1 teaspoon apple juice concentrate and serve with a grapefruit spoon.

Per serving: 0 mg cholesterol, 0 gm saturated fat, 0.1 gm total fat, 0.4 gm fiber, 2 mg sodium, 41 calories

Café au Lait Custard

Serves: 10 (⅓ cup = 1 serving)

Baked custard has always been one of my husband's favorite desserts, and since it is easy to prepare, it appeared frequently as a family dessert in our "prior life." However, when we converted to a low-cholesterol lifestyle, I thought "Never again."

A traditional custard conjures up visions of lots of egg yolks and cream but not so with my Café au Lait Custard, which uses egg whites and nonfat evaporated milk. It sets up beautifully and has a delectable velvety texture and delicious flavor.

6 extra-large egg whites, or
   3 extra-large egg whites and
   ½ cup egg substitute
⅓ cup sugar or frozen unsweetened apple juice concentrate
1½ cups brewed decaffeinated
   coffee

2 teaspoons pure vanilla extract
1½ cups nonfat evaporated milk,
   scalded
2 teaspoons cocoa mixed with a
   dash of ground cinnamon
   (optional)

1. Beat the egg whites lightly; add sugar, coffee, and vanilla.
2. Slowly add the scalded milk, stirring constantly.
3. Pour into 10 custard cups or 5-ounce soufflé dishes, and if desired, sprinkle with the cocoa mixture. Place the cups in a rectangular pan containing very hot water to just below the level of the custard.
4. Bake in a preheated 375° oven for 20 minutes or until a knife comes out clean when inserted in the custard. Cool slightly, cover, and refrigerate at least 1 hour before serving.

NOTE: If you use apple juice concentrate instead of sugar, the custard will weep a bit when chilled.

Per serving: 2 mg cholesterol, 0.05 gm saturated fat, 0.1 gm total fat, 0 gm fiber, 81 mg sodium, 71 calories

Raisin Bread Pudding

Serves: 12 (½ cup = 1 serving)

1 red apple with skin, cored and shredded
5 cups day-old whole wheat raisin bread, cubed
1¼ cups nonfat milk
1 12-ounce can nonfat evaporated milk
¼ cup frozen unsweetened apple juice concentrate

2 teaspoons pure vanilla extract
1 teaspoon ground cinnamon
4 extra-large egg whites, slightly beaten with a fork
½ teaspoon freshly grated nutmeg
2 tablespoons chopped walnuts (optional)

1. Coat an 8-inch-square glass baking dish with butter-flavored cooking spray.
2. Mix the apple with the bread cubes and spread in the baking dish.
3. Combine the milks, apple juice concentrate, vanilla, and half of the cinnamon with the egg whites. Beat with a fork to blend.
4. Pour the milk mixture over the bread and let soak 10 minutes.
5. Sprinkle with the remaining cinnamon, nutmeg, and nuts if desired and bake in a preheated 350° oven for 40 to 45 minutes.
To Serve: While warm or at room temperature, spoon into serving dishes. Accompany with Creme Topping (page 314) or Fresh Strawberry or Blueberry Sauce (pages 317 and 314).

Per serving: 2 mg cholesterol, 0.14 gm saturated fat, 0.5 gm total fat, 1.3 gm fiber, 114 mg sodium, 74 calories

Bing Cherry Clafouti

Serves: 12

1½ pounds (about 4 cups) fresh pitted black bing cherries or frozen unsweetened cherries, thawed and drained

Zest of 1 orange

1 tablespoon Grand Marnier

1⅓ cups nonfat milk

2 teaspoons pure vanilla extract

4 extra-large egg whites

1 cup whole wheat unbleached white flour

⅓ cup sugar

Confectioner's sugar (optional)

1. Preheat the oven to 400°.
2. Macerate the cherries with the zest and Grand Marnier in a bowl for about 5 to 10 minutes.
3. Place the milk, vanilla, egg whites, flour, and sugar in a blender or food processor and blend until smooth, or mix by hand.
4. Pour a third of the mixture into a 9-inch-round nonstick baking pan or springform pan.
5. Spread the cherries over the batter; pour the remaining batter over the cherries.
6. Bake at 400° for 5 minutes; lower the temperature to 375° and bake for about 45 minutes or until a knife comes out clean.

To Serve: Cool about 30 minutes. Sprinkle with confectioner's sugar if desired, and serve while still warm.

Per serving: 2 mg cholesterol, 0.38 gm saturated fat, 0.8 gm total fat, 0.9 gm fiber, 36 mg sodium, 107 calories

Meringue Shells with Fruit

Yield: 12 shells (1 shell = 1 serving)

Although this dessert has more sugar than I normally use or recommend, it is fat- and cholesterol-free and makes a lovely occasional dessert treat. When watching your cholesterol, you sometimes need something a little sweet so that you don't feel completely deprived.

5 extra-large egg whites, *at room temperature*
¼ teaspoon cream of tartar
2 teaspoons pure vanilla extract
1 cup extra-fine granulated sugar

6 cups fresh blueberries or sliced strawberries, peaches, pears, or nectarines

Blueberry Sauce (page 314) or Fresh Strawberry Sauce (page 317), optional

1. Preheat the oven to 200°. Lightly coat a nonstick cookie sheet with nonstick cooking spray; then coat it lightly with flour, shaking off any excess.
2. Combine the egg whites, cream of tartar, and vanilla in the large bowl of an electric mixer and beat until the egg whites form soft peaks.
3. Gradually add the sugar, a tablespoon at a time, while beating continually.
4. Beat until the meringue is shiny and forms very stiff (not dry) peaks.
5. Using a tablespoon, shape the meringue into twelve individual shells on the prepared baking sheet, pressing the centers with the back of a spoon to form nests.
6. Bake at 200° for 30 minutes. For optimum texture and taste, the meringues should be totally dry and not change color. (Technically, meringues are dried, not baked.)
7. Turn off the heat, leave the oven door partially ajar, and leave the meringues in the oven until cool. Remove carefully with a spatula.

To Serve: Fill the meringue shells with fruit and serve with Blueberry Sauce or Strawberry Sauce if you like.

Variation: For extra soluble fiber, you may gently fold in 1½ cups oat bran flakes after the meringue is shiny and stiff. Then bake as directed.

NOTE: These meringue shells may be made in advance, placed in a container or plastic bag (not airtight), and stored for up to a week at room temperature or for several months in the freezer.

Per serving: 0 mg cholesterol, 0.01 gm saturated fat, 0.3 gm total fat, 1.7 gm fiber, 30 mg sodium, 62 calories

Angel Food Cake

Serves: 16 to 20

No collection of recipes for a low-cholesterol lifestyle would be complete without a recipe for angel food cake. In my prior life, angel food cake was not one of my favorites. I used to lust for a piece of rich homemade pound cake. I'd settle for chiffon cake made with oil or sponge cake made with lots of egg yolks! Today, it's old faithful angel food cake that I can have in the freezer and serve with fresh fruit or fresh fruit sauce for dessert. You can vary the recipe by adding cocoa or spices, or you can top the cake with Wax Orchards Fudge Topping—a wonderful, virtually fat-free chocolate sauce (only 16 calories in a teaspoon). If you'd rather use a commercial cake mix, the result will be the same nutritionally, but the taste will not be nearly as good.

1 cup cake flour, or 1 cup unbleached white flour less 2 tablespoons
½ cup granulated sugar
1½ cups egg whites† (about 10–12), at room temperature
1 teaspoon cream of tartar
1½ teaspoons pure vanilla extract
½ teaspoon pure almond extract
¾ cup sugar

Fresh Strawberry Sauce (page 317), Blueberry Sauce (page 314), or heated Wax Orchards Fudge Topping* (optional)

1. Sift the flour and ½ cup sugar together.
2. Place the egg whites into the large bowl of an electric mixer, beat until frothy, and add the cream of tartar and extracts. Beat until stiff, not dry, then gradually add the remaining ¾ cup sugar, 2 tablespoons at a time. Beat well after each addition.
3. Continue beating until the meringue forms stiff peaks and is glossy (the whites will not slide in the bowl).
4. Gradually sprinkle the flour-sugar mixture over the meringue, 3 tablespoons at a time, and fold in gently with a rubber spatula to combine.
5. Quickly but gently push the batter into an *ungreased* 10-inch tube pan.
6. Bake in a preheated 375° oven for 30 to 35 minutes or until the cake springs back when touched with fingers.
7. Remove from the oven, invert the pan onto a vinegar or soda bottle, and cool upside-down for about 1 hour.
To Serve: When cool. loosen the cake from the sides, bottom, and tube

of the pan with a long knife and invert onto a platter. Pass fruit sauce or chocolate sauce if desired.

Hint: Use a serrated knife to cut the cake so that the slices are not squashed.

Variations:

Marble Angel Food Cake:

Follow the basic recipe, omitting the almond extract. Divide the batter in half and fold in 3 tablespoons sifted cocoa to one half. Put alternate spoonfuls of white and dark batter into the pan. Cut through the batter with a knife to make swirls of dark and light batter, and bake as directed in the basic recipe.

Spicy Angel Food Cake:

Add 2½ teaspoons pumpkin pie spice to the sifted flour mixture and stir lightly to blend. Proceed as in the basic recipe.

Per serving: 0 mg cholesterol, 0.01 gm saturated fat, 0 gm total fat, 0.1 gm fiber, 38 mg sodium, 76 calories

---

* This delicious sauce is made from fruits only. Use it hot on frozen nonfat yogurt with a few almonds, and would you believe—a hot fudge sundae! I almost feel guilty eating it, and my guests still don't believe it when I say it has no cholesterol or saturated fat. The sauce may be available at specialty food stores in your area, or contact the manufacturer: Wax Orchards, Route 4–320, Vashon Island, WA 98070.

---

† Separate the eggs when cold (it's easier), then let the whites stand to reach room temperature. *Caution:* When separating the eggs, do not get a speck of egg yolk into the whites or they will not beat stiff.

Mango Salsa

Yield: 1½ cups (2 tablespoons = 1 serving)

A lovely fruited salsa to serve with grilled chicken, turkey breast slices, or broiled fish. It tastes better if it marinates for 30 minutes before being served.

1 large mango, halved and seeded
½ small red onion, diced
1 small clove garlic, finely minced

1 tablespoon finely diced jalapeno pepper, seeds removed, or 2 plum tomatoes, seeded and chopped
Juice of 1 lime

1. Remove the mango pulp with a grapefruit knife and dice.
2. Add all the remaining ingredients to the diced mango and combine thoroughly. Chill in a covered container in the refrigerator for 30 minutes before serving.

Variation: A fresh papaya and 1 small ripe pear may be substituted for the mango.

Per serving: 0 mg cholesterol, 0.01 gm saturated fat, 0 gm total fat, 0.2 gm fiber, 0 mg sodium, 9 calories

Cranberry-Pineapple Freeze

Yield: 24 foil cups (1 foil cup = 1 serving)

Freezes are delicious served either as an accompaniment to roast chicken or turkey or as a dessert. In my book *Deliciously Low*, I prepared this recipe with fresh cranberries; however, there are now available delicious sugar-free cranberry or cranberry-orange marmalades that make it even easier to prepare. This revised recipe can be made in minutes.

2 8-ounce jars sugar-free cranberry or cranberry-orange marmalade
1 20-ounce can crushed unsweetened pineapple, drained

1 pint nonfat plain or fruited yogurt
¼ cup chopped almonds (optional)

1. Combine all the ingredients in a mixing bowl and stir with a fork.
2. Line muffin tins with foil cupcake liners and fill each cup two-thirds full with the yogurt mixture.
3. Freeze for several hours or until firm.
To Serve: Remove from freezer 15 minutes before serving.

To Freeze for Future Use: When firmly frozen, remove the foil cups from the muffin tins and store in an airtight container in the freezer.

Per serving: 0 mg cholesterol, 0.03 gm saturated fat, 0.1 gm total fat, 0.4 gm fiber, 17 mg sodium, 73 calories

Cheese Berry Spread

Yield: about 1¼ cups (1 tablespoon = 1 serving)

A delicious low-fat, low-cholesterol spread to use on your daily Oat Bran Muffins or on whole wheat toast or English muffins. This is also excellent as a sandwich spread instead of the usual peanut butter and jelly.

8 ounces part-skim ricotta cheese   **3 tablespoons sugar-free strawberry or raspberry preserves**

1. Process the ricotta cheese in a food processor or blender until smooth.
2. Add the preserves and process until smooth.
3. Place in a covered container and chill at least 1 hour before serving. This keeps up to a week in the refrigerator.

Per serving: 4 mg cholesterol, 0.56 gm saturated fat, 0.9 gm total fat, 0 gm fiber, 14 mg sodium, 18 calories

Garlic Toast ⓠ

Yield: 8 slices (1 slice = 1 serving)

8 slices whole wheat or pumpernickel bread or sourdough
baguette
2 tablespoons extra-virgin olive oil
mixed with 3 cloves garlic,
minced, and 1 teaspoon fines
herbes

3 tablespoons shredded Parmesan
cheese (optional)

1. Arrange the bread slices on a baking sheet and brush one side lightly with the olive oil mixture.
2. Sprinkle each slice with 1 teaspoon of the Parmesan cheese.*
3. Place under a preheated broiler until lightly browned. Serve immediately.

Variation: For an oil-free toast, toast the bread lightly in the toaster and rub with cut garlic cloves while the toast is still hot, so that the garlic melts into the bread.

Per serving: 1 mg cholesterol, 0.58 gm saturated fat, 3.8 gm total fat, 0.3 gm fiber, 109 mg sodium, 86 calories

* Bread may be prepared ahead of time through Step 2 and just broiled at serving time.

High-Fiber Whole Grain Onion Bread

Yield: 1 loaf cut into 20 slices

This bread freezes well and is terrific toasted. It is great for sandwiches or just spread with part-skim ricotta cheese.

4 tablespoons dehydrated onion flakes or rolled oats, or a combination of the two
1 cup 7-grain cereal
2 cups whole wheat flour
1 cup rolled oats
½ cup oat bran

2 tablespoons brown sugar
½ cup lightly toasted onion flakes
1 envelope quick-rising yeast
1 teaspoon salt
2 cups *hot* water or nonfat milk (130°)

1. Preheat the oven to 425°. Coat a 9 × 5 × 4-inch loaf pan with butter-flavored nonstick spray and sprinkle with 2 tablespoons of the onion flakes. Reserve the remaining 2 tablespoons onion flakes for topping.

2. Place the remaining dry ingredients in a mixing bowl and combine with a fork or your fingers.

3. Add the liquid ingredients to the dry and stir with a wooden spoon until all the flour is completely moistened.

4. Put the batter into the prepared pan and sprinkle with the remaining onion flakes. Cover with a towel and allow to rise in a warm place for 20 minutes or until the dough reaches the top of the pan.

5. Lower the oven temperature to 400° and bake for 45 minutes.

6. Remove the bread from the pan and cool on a rack before slicing.

To Freeze for Future Use: Slice and wrap the cool bread in an airtight plastic bag.

Per serving: 0 mg cholesterol, 0.09 gm saturated fat, 0.7 gm total fat, 2.1 gm fiber, 134 mg sodium, 83 calories

Bran Berry Loaf

Yield: 1 loaf cut into 18 slices (1 slice = 1 serving)

This lovely loaf provides a pleasant change from Oat Bran Muffins; however, it does not contain quite as much soluble fiber per serving.

¾ cup whole wheat flour
½ cup unbleached white flour
1 cup oat bran
1 tablespoon baking powder
½ teaspoon baking soda
3 tablespoons brown sugar
1½ teaspoons cinnamon
2 extra-large egg whites, slightly
  beaten

1 tablespoon safflower oil
¾ cup fresh orange juice
1 teaspoon grated orange zest
¼ cup nonfat evaporated milk
1 cup fresh or frozen blueberries
  (do not defrost before using)

1. Preheat the oven to 350° and coat a 9 × 5 × 4-inch loaf pan with nonstick spray.
2. Combine the first seven ingredients in a mixing bowl and blend thoroughly.
3. In a separate bowl, mix together the egg whites, oil, orange juice, zest, and milk.
4. Add the liquid ingredients to the dry and stir until the dry ingredients are completely moistened.
5. Add the blueberries and blend gently.
6. Pour into the prepared loaf pan and bake at 350° for 50 minutes, or until loaf is lightly browned and starts to pull from sides of pan. Cool before slicing. This freezes nicely for future use.

Per serving: 0 mg cholesterol, 0.10 gm saturated fat, 1.4 gm total fat, 1.8 gm fiber, 84 mg sodium, 70 calories

The Great Pumpkin Muffins

Yield: 12–14 muffins (1 muffin = 1 serving)

There is no need to wait for Thanksgiving to savor the special flavor of pumpkin. These muffins are delicious for breakfast or with meals. In fact, they are so delicious you can even serve them as dessert. The pumpkin muffins you prepare from this recipe are different from the ones you buy commercially, since they contain *no* cholesterol and are *low* in fat and *high* in good soluble fiber.

1 cup whole wheat flour
1½ cups oat bran
½ cup barley flour or an additional
  ½ cup oat bran
1½ tablespoons baking powder
2 tablespoons brown sugar
2 teaspoons ground cinnamon
½ teaspoon ground nutmeg
½ cup dark raisins or chopped
  dates
3 extra-large egg whites, slightly
  beaten

1¼ cups canned pumpkin
½ cup frozen unsweetened apple
  juice concentrate
1 cup nonfat evaporated milk
2 tablespoons canola or cold-
  pressed safflower oil
1 teaspoon pure vanilla extract
¼ cup chopped nuts and/or dark
  raisins (optional)

1. Preheat the oven to 425° and coat muffin tins with nonstick spray or line with paper cupcake liners.
2. Mix the first eight ingredients together in a bowl; blend thoroughly with a fork.
3. Combine the liquid ingredients in another bowl and blend thoroughly.
4. Add the pumpkin mixture to the dry ingredients and stir with a fork until all the flour disappears and is moistened.
5. Fill the prepared muffin tins, place in oven, and lower temperature to 400°. Bake for 20 to 25 minutes or until lightly browned.
6. Cool slightly on a rack before serving.

Per serving: 1 mg cholesterol, 0.22 gm saturated fat, 3.5 gm total fat, 4.7 gm fiber, 137 mg sodium, 164 calories

Snacks

Yogurt-Fruit Shake ©

Serves: 1

A refreshing, nutritious drink that's great for a mid-afternoon snack.

½ cup sliced fresh strawberries, peaches, nectarines, bananas, or mango

½ cup nonfat plain yogurt
1 teaspoon pure vanilla extract
7 ice cubes

Place all the ingredients in a blender and combine until smooth and fluffy. Serve immediately.

Per serving: 2 mg cholesterol, 0.15 gm saturated fat, 0.5 gm total fat, 1.7 gm fiber, 87 mg sodium, 82.5 calories

Orange-Yogurt Popsicles

Yield: 8 popsicles (1 popsicle = 1 serving)

A wonderful snack—and not just for children!

16 ounces nonfat plain yogurt
1 ripe banana, sliced
6 ounces frozen unsweetened orange juice, pear-grape juice, or pineapple-orange juice concentrate

2–3 teaspoons pure vanilla extract
8 4-ounce paper cups
8 wooden popsicle sticks or tongue depressors*

1. Place the yogurt, banana, orange juice, and vanilla in a food processor or blender and blend thoroughly until smooth.
2. Pour into the paper cups, place in the freezer, and chill.
3. When half frozen, add the popsicle sticks or tongue depressors and freeze until solid.

To Serve: Place the cup in hot water *briefly* to just loosen the paper.

Variation: Instead of using paper cups, for smaller popsicles you can use plastic ice cube trays, pouring the yogurt mixture into each ice cube cup and using plastic stirrers for sticks.

Per serving: 1 mg cholesterol, 0.1 gm saturated fat, 0.2 gm total fat, 0.5 gm fiber, 44 mg sodium, 74 calories

* Ask your doctor or pharmacist.

• 7 •

Family Favorites
Made Healthful

When it comes to dessert, fruit is obviously the most nutritionally sound selection, but realistically, everyone wants an occasional indulgence. The day I decided it was past time for my family to change to a low-cholesterol lifestyle, I started to look at some of our favorite recipes—ones that I made "by popular request." I had thought I had been cooking in a healthful manner until I really examined some of these recipes more closely, particularly the desserts. What I found were high-fat, high-cholesterol killers. What I soon discovered was that all the fat, egg yolks, chocolate, and sugar I had previously added were unnecessary to produce a delicious product. By making substitutions, I proved that we could enjoy delicious desserts without feeling guilty *or* clogging our arteries.

In the following pages I have included some of our favorite desserts, changed to satisfy our revised style of eating as well as our palates. And to help you begin converting your own recipes, I am sharing a few tricks of the trade in the chart on page 335—substitutions that will cut the cholesterol and saturated fat content of baked goods dramatically.

334   ADOPTING THE CHOLESTEROL-CONTROL LIFESTYLE

Recipes

Today's Coffee Cake
Almost Edie's Coffee Cake
Carrot-Raisin Bread
Spiced Honey Tea Loaf
Chocoholic's Chocolate Cake
Chocolate Trifle
Blueberry Meringue Cobbler
Great Date Brownies
Oatmeal Cookies
Oat Nut Slices with Jam
Pineapple Cake
Poached Pear "en Croute"
Apple Streudel

SIMPLE TRICKS OF THE TRADE
FOR BAKING AND DESSERT MAKING

INSTEAD OF:	USE:
Butter, margarine, or vegetable shortening	Canola, sunflower, or cold-pressed safflower oil
Sugar	Frozen unsweetened apple juice concentrate, date sugar. Or cut amount of sugar in recipe by ⅓ to ½ of the amount listed. You can use smaller amounts of brown sugar when used instead of white sugar
Sour cream	Nonfat plain yogurt and/or strained buttermilk or at most plain low-fat yogurt
Whole milk	Nonfat milk or nonfat evaporated milk (also called skim)
Egg yolks or whole eggs	Egg whites (2 extra-large egg whites equal 1 whole egg) or low-cholesterol egg substitute
Chocolate	Cocoa (3 tablespoons cocoa plus 1 tablespoon canola or cold-pressed safflower oil equal 1 ounce chocolate)
All white flour	Whole wheat or sometimes a combination of whole wheat and unbleached white flour. Substitute some oat bran for some of the flour when possible in cookies, cakes, sweet breads, and plain breads.
Melted butter or margarine	Butter-flavored nonstick spray for coating pans. Use slightly beaten egg white as glaze or a base for spreading filling on coffee cakes.
Nuts in cake or cookies (See chart on nuts, page 20)	Crushed cereals, dried fruits (e.g., raisins and dates). Or reduce the amount of nuts.

For many years, I prepared a quick and easy coffee cake for my family and unexpected guests. It, like most of the baking in my "previous life," started with butter, eggs, sour cream or whole milk, and lots of sugar! But that was long ago. Today, I am much wiser and we all feel much healthier. This recipe uses egg whites—no yolks; safflower oil—no butter; skim milk instead of whole milk, and a third less sugar!

Today's Coffee Cake

Yield: 1 cake cut into 30 squares (1 square = 1 serving)

1⅓ cups unbleached white flour
1⅓ cups whole wheat pastry flour
½ cup oat bran
½ cup granulated sugar
¾ cup brown sugar, firmly packed
½ cup cold-pressed safflower oil
1 teaspoon freshly ground nutmeg
½ cup rolled oats, chopped

⅓ cup chopped walnuts
1 teaspoon ground cinnamon
1½ tablespoons baking powder
1 12-ounce can nonfat evaporated milk
4 extra-large egg whites, slightly beaten

1. Preheat the oven to 350°. Coat a 9 × 13-inch metal* baking pan with butter-flavored nonstick spray.

2. Combine the first seven ingredients in the large mixing bowl of an electric mixer. Blend well.

3. Remove ⅔ cup of the mixture and combine with the oats, nuts, and cinnamon to be used as topping. Set aside.

4. Combine the baking powder, milk, and eggs, and beat slightly with a fork. Add to the remaining flour mixture and beat thoroughly with electric beater on medium speed.

5. Pour half of the batter into the prepared baking pan and sprinkle half of the oat mixture evenly over the batter. Add the remaining batter and sprinkle with the remaining oat mixture.

6. Bake about 30 minutes or until cake springs back when lightly touched or a toothpick comes out clean.

7. Cool slightly in pan on a rack before cutting and serving.

NOTE: This cake freezes quite well. Sometimes I bake the recipes in two 9-inch loaf pans (baking time reduced to about 25 minutes) and freeze one for future use.

Per serving: 0 mg cholesterol, 0.34 gm saturated fat, 4.8 gm total fat, 0.8 gm fiber, 73 mg sodium, 121 calories

* If you use a glass baking dish, lower the oven temperature to 325°.

The tricks in this delicious and healthful coffee cake? I've cut the sugar in the original recipe by 1 cup, added whole wheat flour, and substituted yogurt for sour cream, egg whites for whole eggs, and light margarine for stick margarine (or you can use ⅓ cup canola oil instead).

Almost Edie's Coffee Cake

Yield: 1 cake cut into 40 slices (1 slice = 1 serving)

¼ pound light margarine
1⅔ cups sugar
3 teaspoons pure vanilla
6 extra-large egg whites
1¾ cups whole wheat pastry flour
1¾ cups unbleached white flour
1 tablespoon baking powder
2 teaspoons baking soda
1 pint nonfat plain yogurt

1 cup seeded Monukka raisins and/or sun-dried apricots, plumped in 2 tablespoons apricot brandy or fresh orange juice*

Streusel:
½ cup finely chopped hazelnuts or walnuts
⅓ cup finely chopped rolled oats
2 tablespoons brown sugar
2 teaspoons cinnamon

1. Preheat the oven to 375°. Coat a 10-inch tube pan (angelfood cake pan) with butter-flavored nonstick spray.
2. Cream the margarine in the bowl of an electric mixer. Add the sugar and beat until smooth. Add the vanilla and blend.
3. Add the egg whites gradually and beat for 3 minutes.
4. In a separate bowl, combine the flours, baking powder, and baking soda and mix thoroughly.
5. Alternately place a third of the flour mixture, then half of yogurt, into the batter, starting and ending with flour. Beat until smooth after each addition.
6. Mix together the streusel ingredients.
7. Place a third of the batter in the bottom of the prepared tube pan. Sprinkle with a third of the streusel and half of the raisins. Repeat; then top with the remaining third of batter and streusel.
8. Bake at 375° for 25 minutes. Lower the temperature to 325° and bake for about 30 minutes more or until the cake starts to pull away from sides of pan.
9. Cool in the pan on a rack and then loosen with a metal spatula and remove from pan. May be frozen for future use.

Per serving: 0 mg cholesterol, 0.33 gm saturated fat, 2.2 gm total fat, 0.9 gm fiber, 110 mg sodium, 102 calories

* Put in microwave for 1 minute on high, covered tightly with microwave plastic wrap. If your raisins are really fresh, just combine with hot brandy or juice.

Remember when you ate carrot and raisin cake because you thought it was healthful? After all, carrots are high in vitamin A and raisins are high in iron. But what about all the butter and eggs that sent your cholesterol soaring? And the loads of sugar that raise triglycerides? Instead, try a tasty loaf made more healthful with ¼ cup oil instead of 1 cup oil or butter, no egg yolks, only ⅓ as much sugar, and added oat bran that is high in cholesterol-lowering soluble fiber.

Carrot-Raisin Bread

Yield: 1 loaf cut into 12 slices (½ slice = 1 serving)

1 cup shredded raw carrots
⅓ cup brown sugar
1 teaspoon baking soda
¼ cup cold-pressed safflower oil
½ cup frozen unsweetened apple
  juice concentrate
1 cup boiling water
3 extra-large egg whites, slightly
  beaten

1 tablespoon baking powder
1½ cups unbleached white flour
½ cup oat bran
1 cup whole wheat pastry flour
⅔ cup dark seeded raisins
½ cup chopped nuts (optional)

1. Preheat the oven to 350°. Coat a 9 × 5-inch loaf pan with nonstick spray.
2. Place the carrots, sugar, baking soda, oil, apple juice concentrate, and boiling water in a mixing bowl. Mix thoroughly and let cool.
3. Add the remaining ingredients to the cooled mixture, stir, and beat until well blended.
4. Pour the batter into the prepared loaf pan and bake at 350° for 1 hour.
5. Cool in the pan on a rack 5 minutes, loosen, unmold, and finish cooling on a rack before slicing.

Per serving: 0 mg cholesterol, 0.26 gm saturated fat, 3.6 gm total fat, 1.3 gm fiber, 72 mg sodium, 103 calories

I have changed my traditional recipe by cutting the amount of sugar in half, the amount of oil in half, using egg whites only, and substituting part whole wheat flour and part oat bran for all white flour. This no-cholesterol, low-fat loaf is lovely to serve with tea or as a light dessert with fresh fruit.

Spiced Honey Tea Loaf

Yield: 2 loaves cut into 36 slices and halved (½ slice = 1 serving)

1 cup honey
1⅓ cups hot decaffeinated coffee
2 cups unbleached white flour
1 cup whole wheat pastry flour
½ cup oat bran
1 tablespoon baking powder
1 teaspoon baking soda
2 teaspoons cinnamon
½ teaspoon allspice

¼ cup canola, sunflower, or cold-pressed safflower oil
2 extra-large egg whites
6 tablespoons granulated sugar
4 extra-large egg whites, at room temperature
¼ teaspoon cream of tartar

¼ cup sliced almonds, for garnish

1. Preheat the oven to 350°. Lightly coat the bottoms of two 9 × 5 × 4-inch loaf pans with nonstick spray and line with wax paper.
2. Dissolve the honey in the hot coffee and cool.
3. Combine the flours, oat bran, baking powder, baking soda, cinnamon, and allspice and mix together with a spoon.
4. Beat the coffee mixture, oil, 2 egg whites, and 3 tablespoons of the sugar in the bowl of an electric mixer. Add the dry ingredients and mix until smooth.
5. In a separate bowl, beat the 4 egg whites with the cream of tartar until slightly thick. Add the remaining 3 tablespoons sugar, a tablespoon at a time, and beat until stiff (the whites will not slide in the bowl).
6. Fold the beaten egg whites into the cake mixture gently, just until blended.
7. Pour into the prepared loaf pans, sprinkle the tops of the loaves with the almonds, and bake at 350° for about 1 hour or until the cake starts to pull away from the sides of the pans.
8. Invert the pans onto a cake rack to cool completely.
9. Loosen the sides of the loaves with a spatula and remove from the pans. Remove the wax paper and slice.

To Freeze for Future Use: Wrap the sliced loaf in plastic wrap, then foil.

Per serving: 0 mg cholesterol, 0.05 gm saturated fat, 0.9 gm total fat, 0.4 gm fiber, 30 mg sodium, 47 calories

Devil's food cake has always been a favorite in our house. In fact, I made it as a standard birthday cake. How could I sacrifice this tradition? Happily I don't have to since I concocted this delicious, moist cake which we all just love. I fight being a chocoholic; however, when I do use chocolate, it's in the form of cocoa powder, not chocolate squares that are high in saturated fat (which raises cholesterol). This cake has no cholesterol and virtually no saturated fat so that you can enjoy each mouthful. It also freezes beautifully.

Chocoholic's Chocolate Cake

Yield: 1 cake cut into 20 pieces (1 piece = 1 serving)

¾ cup unbleached white flour or cake flour

¾ cup whole wheat pastry flour

⅓ cup unsweetened cocoa

½ cup sugar (or ¼ cup sugar and ¼ cup brown sugar)

2 teaspoons baking powder

1 teaspoon baking soda

2 extra-large egg whites, slightly beaten

⅓ cup canola or cold-pressed safflower oil

1 cup cold water or fresh orange juice

2 teaspoons pure vanilla extract

2 tablespoons white or raspberry wine vinegar

2 tablespoons Kahlua (optional)

Cocoa and confectioner's sugar, for sifting over cooled cake (optional)

1. Preheat the oven to 375° and spray the bottom of an 8 × 8 × 2-inch baking pan or an 8-inch round pan (for a fudgier cake) with butter-flavored nonstick cooking spray.

2. Combine the flours, cocoa, sugar, baking powder, and baking soda in a mixing bowl and blend thoroughly with a slotted spoon.

3. Combine the egg whites, oil, water, vanilla, vinegar, and Kahlua (if desired) in a separate bowl, and beat thoroughly with a fork.

4. Add the liquid ingredients to the dry and mix quickly with a slotted spoon until all the flour is moistened and the batter is smooth.

5. Pour the batter into the prepared baking pan immediately and bake at 375° for 20 to 25 minutes, or until the cake starts to shrink from the sides of the pan.

6. Cool on a rack. Sift the cocoa powder on the top of half of the cake and confectioner's sugar onto the remaining half if you like.

Variation: Drizzle 2 tablespoons of Wax Orchards Fudge Topping (see page 324) over hot cake before cooling.

Per serving: 0 mg cholesterol, 0.38 gm saturated fat, 4.1 gm total fat, 0.5 gm fiber, 78 mg sodium, 94 calories

Personally, I really never cared much for trifle as a dessert, but I did prepare it as a family tradition for holiday dinners. When I look back on the ingredients, I cringe: eggs in the cake, eggs in the custard, and heavy cream on top of all that! How could anybody who cooked like that change her culinary habits enough to make something that looked good, tasted delicious, and didn't perpetuate atherosclerosis? Well, I did—and so can you, while you bask in your family's approval!

Chocolate Trifle ℚ

Serves: about 16

⅓ Chocoholic's Chocolate Cake (page 340), cut into ½-inch slices
3 tablespoons sugar-free raspberry preserves mixed with 1 tablespoon Framboise liqueur
1 pint frozen nonfat vanilla yogurt
1 pint frozen nonfat chocolate yogurt
2 tablespoons chopped toasted almonds (optional)

1. Place a layer of chocolate cake slices on the bottom of a glass soufflé dish or a crystal bowl.
2. Spread the cake with half of the raspberry preserve mixture.
3. Cover the preserves with half of the vanilla and chocolate yogurt, giving a marbled or checkerboard effect.
4. Repeat the procedure and sprinkle the top with chopped almonds, if desired.
5. Cover with plastic wrap and place in the freezer until serving time, or until solid.

To Serve: Remove from freezer 20 to 30 minutes before serving.

Variation: This may be served with a fresh raspberry sauce and/or fresh raspberries.

Per serving: 1 mg cholesterol, 0.2 gm saturated fat, 1.5 gm total fat, 0.3 gm fiber, 70 mg sodium, 69 calories

An all-time family favorite for dessert in our home for many years was the traditional blueberry cobbler. Since cobblers have only a top crust, I thought that by not making my usual pie (with 387 calories and 17 grams of fat per serving), I was really cutting calories and fat. However, I now realize that was not nearly enough. The cobbler was made with three cans of blueberry pie filling and a topping of a very short and flaky (albeit delicious) pastry crust. Per serving, it was "reduced" to a whopping 320 calories and 12.8 grams of fat. As if this weren't bad enough, we frequently added a blob of French vanilla ice cream! I can hardly believe I made this, let alone ate it and fed it to my family.

Since we now realize that this calorically dense dessert is nutritionally unacceptable, I have come up with a delicious version of a cobbler that can be served and savored without qualms. It does have some sugar, but as a healthy dessert trade-off, it wins hands-down.

Blueberry Meringue Cobbler ℚ

Serves: 8

1 can blueberry pie filling
3 cups fresh or frozen blueberries, unsweetened
½ teaspoon ground cinnamon
4 extra-large egg whites, at room temperature

¼ teaspoon cream of tartar
⅓ cup sifted confectioner's sugar
1 teaspoon pure vanilla extract

1. Combine the blueberry filling with the fresh blueberries in a saucepan and bring to a boil, stirring constantly. Pour into an 8-inch-square glass baking dish and sprinkle lightly with cinnamon.

2. Place the egg whites and cream of tartar in the bowl of an electric mixer and beat until frothy.

3. Gradually beat in the sugar, a tablespoon at a time. Continue beating until stiff and glossy (not dry).

4. Pile the meringue by spoonfuls onto the blueberries and *seal the meringue to the edges of the dish all around to prevent shrinking*. Swirl with back of a spoon or spatula for a decorative top.

5. Bake in a preheated 425° oven for 5 to 7 minutes or until delicately browned. Cool gradually, away from drafts, before serving.

To Serve: Take the dessert to the table (it looks so pretty) and spoon onto dessert plates, with a portion of meringue on top of each serving.

Per serving: 0 mg cholesterol, 0.02 gm saturated fat, 0.3 gm total fat, 1.7 gm fiber, 41 mg sodium, 127 calories

As in many American families, brownies are a favorite in our home. My old recipe contained 12 ounces of chocolate and 1⅓ sticks of butter—both ingredients high in saturated fat—whole eggs (a total to 550 milligrams of cholesterol), and lots of sugar! Since we all do love an occasional chocolate treat, I came up with this healthier recipe for brownies, using cocoa instead of chocolate and canola oil instead of butter, virtually eliminating saturated fat. I use only the egg whites, so the cholesterol is eliminated completely, and I use apple juice concentrate and dates instead of sugar. I'm certain that the delicious, virtually cholesterol-free result will meet with your approval, as it does my family's.

Great Date Brownies ⓠ

Yield: 20 bars (1 bar = 1 serving)

⅓ cup unbleached white flour
½ cup whole wheat pastry flour
¼ cup oat bran, processed until fine as flour (see page 106)
¼ cup unsweetened cocoa
2 teaspoons baking powder
¼ teaspoon baking soda
½ cup chopped dates
2 extra-large egg whites

½ cup nonfat milk
6 ounces frozen unsweetened apple juice concentrate
2 tablespoons Kahlua (coffee liqueur)
⅓ cup canola oil
2 teaspoons vanilla
½ cup chopped almonds (optional)

1. Preheat the oven to 375°. Coat an 8 × 8 × 2-inch baking dish with butter-flavored nonstick spray.
2. Place the first six ingredients in a mixing bowl and blend thoroughly with a spoon. Add the dates and mix.
3. In a separate bowl, beat the egg whites with a fork until foamy. Add the milk, apple juice concentrate, Kahlua, oil, and vanilla. Mix thoroughly.
4. Add the liquid ingredients to the dry and stir until the flour is completely absorbed.
5. Spread in the prepared baking dish, sprinkle with nuts, and bake at 375° for 20 minutes.
6. Cool and cut into twenty bars.

Per serving: 0 mg cholesterol, 0.35 gm saturated fat, 4.1 gm total fat, 1 gm fiber, 51 mg sodium, 92 calories

Whether they're six or sixty, everybody likes to eat a cookie occasionally. This is an adaptation of a cookie that I made years ago. Then, I thought it was especially healthy, because I used rolled oats. I didn't count the half-pound of butter, the egg yolks, and the huge amount of sugar I used! This revised recipe *is* healthy, *and* high in soluble fiber. It is cholesterol-free and *low* in fat, though not fat-free; however, the fat I do use is polyunsaturated safflower oil, and the amount is *greatly* reduced (about 1 gram in each cookie!).

Oatmeal Cookies

Yield: about 60–65 cookies (1 cookie = 1 serving)

4 extra-large egg whites, slightly beaten

½ cup brown sugar, firmly packed, and ½ cup granulated white sugar

3 tablespoons canola or cold-pressed safflower oil

2 teaspoons pure vanilla extract

½ cup whole wheat flour

2 teaspoons ground cinnamon

1 teaspoon freshly ground nutmeg

4 teaspoons baking powder

3 cups quick cooking rolled oats

½ cup oat bran

½ cup finely chopped hazelnuts

1. Preheat the oven to 375°. Coat a nonstick cookie sheet with butter-flavored nonstick spray.
2. Combine the egg whites, sugar, oil, and vanilla in a bowl. Beat in electric mixer for 2 minutes or until thick.
3. In a separate bowl, combine the flour, cinnamon, nutmeg, baking powder, oats, oat bran, and nuts and mix thoroughly with a spoon.
4. Add the dry ingredients to the egg whites and blend until the flour disappears.
5. Drop rounded teaspoonfuls of cookie mixture onto cookie sheet.
6. Bake at 375° for 10 to 12 minutes or until lightly browned.
7. Loosen the cookies from the cookie sheet and cool. Store in a container that is *not* airtight, so that the cookies remain crisp.

Per serving: 0 mg cholesterol, 0.1 gm saturated fat, 1 gm total fat, 0.4 gm fiber, 23 mg sodium, 37 calories

There was a marvelous cookie I made years ago called the "thumb-print cookie." It contained butter, eggs, nuts, and all those terrible things. I have adjusted the recipe to eliminate *any* added fat or short-ening and egg yolks. The result is a super-delicious, cholesterol-free sliced bar with jam that brings rave reviews. Caution: These cookies may be habit-forming. Remember, they still have calories.

Oat Nut Slices with Jam

Yield: 32 ½-inch slices (1 slice = 1 serving)

¾ cup ground nuts (hazelnuts and/or almonds)

¾ cup rolled oats, chopped

¼ cup oat bran

¼ cup sugar

2 extra-large egg whites and 1 tea-spoon pure vanilla extract, slightly beaten with a fork

About 2 tablespoons sugar-free preserves (apricot, strawberry, or raspberry)

1. Preheat the oven to 350° and coat a nonstick baking sheet with butter-flavored nonstick spray.

2. Mix the nuts, oats, and oat bran with the sugar.

3. Add enough of the egg white and vanilla mixture to just make a mixture firm enough so that the nuts, oats, and sugar all adhere.

4. Shape two rolls 1½ inches in diameter and about 12 inches long and place on the prepared baking sheet.

5. Dip your finger in cold water and make a deep ridge down the center of each roll.

6. Bake for 15 to 20 minutes or until lightly browned.

7. Remove from the oven, spoon jam into each ridge, and cool.

8. When cool, cut into ½-inch slices.

Variation: Use Wax Orchards Fudge Topping (page 324) instead of jam.

Per serving: 0 mg cholesterol, 0.14 gm saturated fat, 1.9 gm total fat, 0.4 gm fiber, 4 mg sodium, 35 calories

We have a family friend whose nemesis was pineapple upside-down cake. One slice was always just a beginning to his eating orgy. With all the butter and eggs in the recipe, I had to make a change before I could serve this to him without regret. This no-cholesterol cake tastes rather like the traditional pineapple upside-down cake but has a delicious flavor of its own. Although there is no added fat or cholesterol, the fat in the nuts still makes it necessary to limit the portion size (even though it is principally a polyunsaturated fat).

Pineapple Cake

Yield: 28 pieces (1 piece = 1 serving)

2 cups unbleached white flour mixed with ⅔ cup finely chopped hazelnuts
1 cup whole wheat pastry flour
1 teaspoon cinnamon
¾ teaspoon allspice
¼ teaspoon freshly ground nutmeg
½ cup dark raisins
4 extra-large egg whites, at room temperature

¼ teaspoon cream of tartar
1¼ cups sugar
2 teaspoons pure vanilla extract
2 teaspoons each lemon and orange zest
1 20-ounce can crushed pineapple in natural juice
2 teaspoons baking soda mixed with ¼ cup pineapple juice drained from crushed pineapple

1. Lightly coat the bottom only of a 13 × 9 × 2-inch glass baking pan with butter-flavored nonstick cooking spray, and preheat the oven to 325°.
2. Combine the flours, nuts, spices, and raisins and mix until well combined.
3. Beat the egg whites with the cream of tartar until frothy. Gradually add the sugar, a tablespoon at a time, beating until the mixture forms soft peaks.
4. Add the vanilla, zests, baking soda mixture, and crushed pineapple with its remaining juice and blend.
5. Add the flour mixture to the pineapple mixture, and stir gently until the flour disappears.
6. Pour the batter into the prepared baking pan and bake 35 to 40 minutes or until the cake starts to pull from the sides of the pan.
7. Cool in the pan on a rack. Cut into 28 serving pieces.

Variations: This cake may be served with Creme Topping (page 314) that is made with chilled pineapple juice instead of apple juice concentrate, and topped with sliced strawberries.

Per serving: 0 mg cholesterol, 0.16 gm saturated fat, 1.8 gm total fat, 1 gm fiber, 70 mg sodium, 113 calories

My daughter always loved fruit, especially when it was combined with a rich pastry. My new Pear "en Croute" recipe is her favorite now that she too has changed to a healthier lifestyle. She doesn't mind the reduction in calories that goes with it either. I've taken "culinary license" by referring to this recipe as "en croute." Obviously, we can't use flaky puff pastry with all its fat and cholesterol. I have substituted phyllo dough, which is nothing more than flour and water but results in a delicate, crisp packet in which to enclose the fruit. When a peeled, poached apple is substituted for the pear, it resembles a fancy apple turnover.

Poached Pear "en Croute" ⓠ

Serves: 4 (1 pear = 1 serving)

4 phyllo leaves
4 small poached pears, drained
Butter-flavored nonstick cooking
  spray
1 cup papaya, mango, strawberry,
  or blueberry puree mixed with
  1 tablespoon Grand Marnier
  or pear poaching liquid

Lemon leaf or fresh mint, as
  garnish

1. Lightly coat the phyllo with butter-flavored nonstick cooking spray and fold in half. Coat again. Place a poached pear in the center of the folded leaf.
2. Wrap the pear tightly, twisting at the stem. Lightly coat the outside of the phyllo with butter-flavored cooking spray.
3. Repeat for the other three pears.
4. Place on a nonstick baking sheet and bake in a preheated 350° oven about 5 to 7 minutes, until the phyllo is crisped and lightly colored.
5. Spoon ¼ cup puree onto each of four dessert plates, place a hot pear in the center of the sauce, and garnish with a lemon leaf or fresh mint.

Variation: Strawberry Sauce (page 317) or Blueberry Sauce (page 314) may be used instead of the puree.

Per serving: 0 mg cholesterol, 0.12 gm saturated fat, 0.7 gm total fat, 3.4 gm fiber, 1 mg sodium, 106 calories

It's not exactly like Mama used to make, but in fact, I think it's even better without all the melted butter.

Apple Streudel ⓠ

Serves: 8

½ cup frozen unsweetened apple
  juice concentrate
3 cups thinly sliced McIntosh,
  Golden Delicious, or Granny
  Smith apples
½ cup seeded dark raisins
1 tablespoon brown sugar
½ teaspoon grated lemon zest
1 teaspoon ground cinnamon
¼ teaspoon freshly ground nutmeg

3 sheets phyllo pastry
Butter-flavored nonstick cooking
  spray or 2 tablespoons cold-
  pressed safflower oil
2 tablespoons dry breadcrumbs

Creme Topping (page 314), for
  serving

1. Heat the apple juice concentrate, add the apples, and sauté until tender, about 10 minutes.

2. Add the raisins, brown sugar, lemon zest, cinnamon, and nutmeg and mix well. Cool.

3. Coat each phyllo sheet lightly with cooking spray and lay phyllo sheets on top of one another on plastic wrap. Sprinkle lightly with breadcrumbs.

4. Spoon the apple mixture along the short edge of the phyllo and roll up into a long roll.

5. Place the roll on a nonstick baking sheet. Coat lightly with cooking spray. Score the top diagonally into eight equal sections with a knife.

6. Bake in a preheated 400° oven for 15 to 20 minutes. Remove from oven and cut into eight diagonal serving portions.

To Serve: Serve warm on individual dessert plates with Creme Topping.

Per serving: 0 mg cholesterol, 0.08 gm saturated fat, 0.3 gm total fat, 1.8 gm fiber, 17 mg sodium, 93 calories

Appendix

In 1988, C. Everett Koop, M.D., the U.S. Surgeon General, issued the first report on nutrition and disease. He urged the public to increase its consumption of fresh fruit, vegetables, and whole grain products and to decrease the consumption of dietry fat. He observed that "your diet can influence your long-term health prospects more than any other action you may take."

Besides limiting the intake of cholesterol, the most important change the average person can make in his diet is to reduce the amount of total fat he eats, *especially saturated fat*. Ideally, only 15 to 20 percent of the total calories in your diet should come from fat. If you know your total daily intake of calories, you can determine the total amount of fat and the total calories from fat you should eat daily from the table on page 350. For example, if you consume 1200 calories a day, only 240 of those calories should be from fat (using the more comfortable 20 percent figure). That means that you are allowed 26 grams of fat per day (there are about 9 calories in each gram of fat). Remember that of this amount, *no more than 7 percent of your daily calories* should come from saturated fat.

The recipes in this book, which focus on helping you lower your total fat intake as well as your cholesterol intake, give you the number of grams of fat they contain per serving. The table beginning on page 351 will help you determine how many grams of fat and what types of fat a given food or commercial product contains per serving as well as the sodium and cholesterol content and calorie count. Food labels can also help you find out how many grams of fat are contained in packaged foods.

Finally, you can increase the amount of fiber you eat daily by being aware of the fiber content of the foods you eat. The table starting on page 382 will help you.

GUIDE TO REDUCING TOTAL DIETARY FAT

PERCENT OF CALORIES DESIRED FROM FAT:	TOTAL CALORIES FROM FAT SHOULD NOT EXCEED:	TOTAL GRAMS OF FAT SHOULD NOT EXCEED:	TOTAL GRAMS OF SATURATED FAT SHOULD NOT EXCEED:
For a 1200 calorie diet:			
20 percent	240 calories	26 grams	8 grams
15 percent	180 calories	20 grams	8 grams
For a 1500 calorie diet:			
20 percent	300 calories	33 grams	10 grams
15 percent	225 calories	25 grams	10 grams
For a 2000 calorie diet:			
20 percent	400 calories	45 grams	13 grams
15 percent	300 calories	33 grams	13 grams
For a 2500 calorie diet:			
20 percent	500 calories	55 grams	16 grams
15 percent	375 calories	42 grams	16 grams

THE CALORIE, FAT, SODIUM, AND CHOLESTEROL CONTENT
OF COMMONLY USED FOODS

	PORTION	K CAL (CALORIES)	TOTAL FAT (gm.)	SATU-RATED FAT (gm.)	SODIUM (mg.)	CHOLES-TEROL (mg.)
Beverages						
Alcoholic:						
Beer:						
regular	12 fl. oz.	150	0	0	18	0
light	12 fl. oz.	95	0	0	18	0
Gin, Rum, Vodka, & Whiskey:						
80 proof	1½ fl. oz.	95	0	0	0	0
86 proof	1½ fl. oz.	105	0	0	1	0
90 proof	1½ fl. oz.	110	0	0	1	0
Wines:						
Champagne	4 fl. oz.	84	0	0	0	0
Red table wine	3½ fl. oz.	76	0	0	10	0
White table wine	3½ fl. oz.	80	0	0	7	0
Sweet dessert wine	3½ fl.oz.	153	0	0	7	0
Dry dessert wine	3½ fl. oz.	126	0	0	7	0
Sherry	2 fl.oz.	84	0	0	2	0
Carbonated:						
Club soda	12 fl. oz.	0	0	0	78	0
Perrier or comparable mineral water	8 fl. oz.	0	0	0	5	0
Colas:						
Regular	12 fl. oz.	160	0	0	20	0
Diet (artificially sweetened)	12 fl. oz.	TR	0	0	33	0
Ginger ale	12 fl. oz.	125	0	0	29	0
Grape soda	12 fl. oz.	180	0	0	48	0
Lemon-lime soda	12 fl. oz.	155	0	0	33	0
Orange soda	12 fl. oz.	180	0	0	52	0
Root beer	12 fl. oz.	165	0	0	48	0
Cocoa & chocolate-flavored beverages (See *Dairy Products*)						
Coffee:						
brewed	6 fl. oz.	TR	TR	TR	2	0
instant	6 fl. oz.	TR	TR	TR	TR	0

References: *Agriculture Handbooks Numbers* 8–11, 8–13, 8–15, 8–16 revised 1982–1987. USDA, *Nutritive Value of Foods*, Home & Garden Bulletin No. 72, revised 1981; Pennington and Church, *Bowes and Church's Food Values of Portions Commonly Used*, 14th edition, 1985.

TR = nutrient present in trace amount
NA = not available

THE CALORIE, FAT, SODIUM, AND CHOLESTEROL CONTENT OF COMMONLY USED FOODS

	PORTION	K CAL (CALORIES)	TOTAL FAT (gm.)	SATU-RATED FAT (gm.)	SODIUM (mg.)	CHOLES-TEROL (mg.)
Beverages (cont.)						
Tea:						
brewed	8 fl. oz.	TR	TR	TR	1	0
instant, unsweetened	8 fl. oz.	TR	TR	TR	1	0
instant, sweetened	8 fl. oz.	85	TR	TR	TR	0
Breads & Grain Products						
Breads:						
Bagels, plain or water*	1	200	2	0.3	245	0
Biscuits, baking powder (from mix)	1	95	3	0.8	262	TR
Boston brown bread, canned	1 slice	95	1	0.3	113	3
Breadcrumbs, enriched, dry	1 cup	390	5	1.5	736	5
Bread stuffing, prepared from mix:						
dry	1 cup	500	31	6.1	1,254	0
moist	1 cup	420	26	5.3	1,023	67
French or Vienna bread	1 slice	100	1	0.3	203	0
Italian bread, enriched	1 slice	85	TR	TR	176	0
Mixed grain bread, enriched	1 slice	65	1	0.2	106	0
Oatmeal bread, enriched	1 slice	65	1	0.2	124	0
Pita	1 6″ pita	165	1	0.1	339	0
Pumpernickel	1 slice	80	1	0.2	177	0
Raisin bread, enriched	1 slice	65	1	0.2	92	0
Rye	1 slice	65	1	0.2	175	0
Sourdough bread	1 slice	68	0.5	0	139	0
Wheat, enriched	1 slice	65	1	0.2	138	0
White, enriched	1 slice	65	1	0.3	129	0
Whole wheat	1 slice	70	1	0.4	180	0

* Egg bagels have 45 mg. cholesterol per bagel.

TR = nutrient present in trace amount
NA = not available

THE CALORIE, FAT, SODIUM, AND CHOLESTEROL CONTENT OF COMMONLY USED FOODS

	PORTION	K CAL (CALORIES)	TOTAL FAT (gm.)	SATU-RATED FAT (gm.)	SODIUM (mg)	CHOLES-TEROL (mg.)
Breakfast Cereals, Hot, Cooked:						
Corn (hominy grits):						
regular & quick	1 cup	145	TR	TR	0	0
instant, plain	1 packet	80	TR	TR	343	0
Cream of Wheat:						
regular, quick, instant	1 cup	140	TR	0.1	46	0
mix & eat	1 packet	100	TR	TR	241	0
Malt-o-Meal	1 cup	120	TR	TR	2	0
Oat Bran	1⅓ cups, cooked	110	2	TR	0	0
Oatmeal or Rolled Oats:						
regular, quick, instant	1 cup	145	2	0.4	2	0
instant, fortified	1 packet	105	2	0.3	285	0
Breakfast Cereals, Cold (all 1-ounce equivalents):						
All-Bran	⅓ cup	70	1	0.1	320	0
Cap'n Crunch	¾ cup	120	3	1.7	213	0
Cheerios	1¼ cups	110	2	0.3	307	0
Corn Flakes (Kellogg)	1¼ cups	110	TR	TR	351	0
40% Bran Flakes:						
Kellogg	¾ cup	90	1	0.1	264	0
Post	⅔ cup	90	TR	0.1	260	0
Crispy Oats (Kölln)	½ cup	120	2	TR	2	0
Fruit Loops	1 cup	110	1	0.2	145	0
Golden Grahams	¾ cup	110	1	0.7	346	TR
Grapenuts	¼ cup	100	TR	TR	197	0
Honey Nut Cheerios	¾ cup	105	1	0.1	257	0
Lucky Charms	1 cup	110	1	0.2	201	0
Nature Valley Granola	⅓ cup	125	5	3.3	58	0
100% Natural Cereal	¼ cup	135	6	4.1	12	TR
Oatios (New Morning)	1¼ cups	110	2	TR	0	0
Product 19	¾ cup	110	TR	TR	325	0
Raisin Bran:						
Kellogg	¾ cup	90	1	0.1	207	0
Post	½ cup	85	1	0.1	185	0

THE CALORIE, FAT, SODIUM, AND CHOLESTEROL CONTENT
OF COMMONLY USED FOODS

	PORTION	K CAL (CALORIES)	TOTAL FAT (gm.)	SATU-RATED FAT (gm.)	SODIUM (mg.)	CHOLES-TEROL (mg.)
Breakfast Cereals, Cold (cont.)						
Rice Krispies	1 cup	110	TR	TR	340	0
Shredded Wheat	⅔ cup	100	1	0.1	3	0
Special K	1⅓ cups	110	TR	TR	265	TR
Super Sugar Crisps	⅞ cup	105	TR	TR	25	0
Sugar Frosted Flakes (Kellogg)	¾ cup	110	TR	TR	230	0
Sugar Smacks	¾ cup	105	1	0.1	75	0
Super Bran Flakes (New Morning)	1 cup	100	1	TR	0	0
Total	1 cup	100	1	0.1	352	0
Trix	1 cup	110	TR	0.2	181	0
Wheaties	1 cup	100	TR	0.1	354	0
Breads & Grain Products, Miscellaneous:						
Barley, pearled & uncooked	1 cup	700	2	0.3	6	0
Bulgur, uncooked	1 cup	600	3	1.2	7	0
Corn chips	1 oz.	155	9	1.4	150	0
Cornmeal: whole ground, unbolted, dry	1 cup	435	5	0.5	1	0
degermed, enriched, cooked	1 cup	120	TR	TR	1	0
Crackers:						
Cheese: plain	10 - 1" squares	50	3	0.9	112	6
sandwich-type	1	40	2	0.4	90	1
Graham plain	2 - 2½" squares	60	1	0.4	86	0
Melba toast	1	20	TR	0.1	44	0
Rye wafers, whole grain	2	55	1	0.3	115	0
Saltines	4 crackers	50	1	0.5	165	4
Wheat thins	4 crackers	35	1	0.5	69	0
Whole wheat wafers	2 crackers	35	2	0.5	59	0
Croissant	1	235	12	3.5	452	13

TR = nutrient present in trace amount
NA = not available

THE CALORIE, FAT, SODIUM, AND CHOLESTEROL CONTENT OF COMMONLY USED FOODS

	PORTION	K CAL (CALORIES)	TOTAL FAT (gm.)	SATU-RATED FAT (gm.)	SODIUM (mg.)	CHOLES-TEROL (mg.)
Danish pastry:						
packaged ring, plain, without fruit or nuts	1 - 12-oz. ring	1,305	71	21.8	1,302	292
1 pastry	4¼" diam.	220	12	3.6	218	49
Doughnut:						
cake-type, plain	1	210	12	2.8	192	20
yeast-leavened, glazed	1	235	13	5.2	222	21
English muffin, plain	1	140	1	0.3	378	0
Flours (wheat):						
All-purpose, unsifted	1 cup	455	1	0.2	119	0
Cake or pastry, sifted	1 cup	350	1	0.1	91	0
Self-rising, unsifted	1 cup	440	1	0.2	1,349	0
Whole wheat, stirred	1 cup	400	2	0.3	4	0
French toast	1 slice	155	7	1.6	112	257
Macaroni, cooked:						
firm	1 cup	190	1	0.1	1	0
tender	1 cup	155	1	0.1	1	0
Muffins, commercial:						
blueberry	1 muffin	140	5	1.4	225	45
bran	1 muffin	140	4	1.3	385	28
corn	1 muffin	145	6	1.7	291	42
Noodles, egg, cooked	1 cup	200	2	0.5	3	50
Noodles, chow mein, canned	1 cup	220	11	2.1	450	5
Pancakes, from mix:	1 - 4" diam.					
buckwheat		55	2	0.9	125	20
plain	1 - 4" diam.	60	2	0.5	160	16
Popcorn:						
air-popped, unsalted	1 cup	30	TR	TR	TR	0
popped in vegetable oil, salted	1 cup	55	3	0.5	86	0
Pretzels:						
sticks	10	10	TR	TR	48	0
twisted, Dutch	1	65	1	0.1	258	0
twisted, thin	10	240	2	0.4	966	0
Rice:						
brown, cooked	1 cup	230	1	0.3	0	0
white, cooked	1 cup	225	TR	0.1	0	0

THE CALORIE, FAT, SODIUM, AND CHOLESTEROL CONTENT OF COMMONLY USED FOODS

	PORTION	K CAL (CALORIES)	TOTAL FAT (gm.)	SATURATED FAT (gm.)	SODIUM (mg)	CHOLESTEROL (mg.)
Breads & Grain Products (cont.)						
Rolls (commercial):						
dinner	1	85	2	0.5	155	TR
frankfurter or						
hamburger	1	115	2	0.5	241	TR
hard	1	155	2	0.4	313	TR
hoagie or submarine	1	400	8	1.8	683	TR
Spaghetti, cooked:						
firm (*al dente*)	1 cup	190	1	0.1	1	0
tender	1 cup	155	1	0.1	1	0
Tortilla, corn	1 tortilla	65	1	0.1	1	0
Waffles, from mix	1 waffle	205	8	2.7	515	59
Dairy Products						
Butter, see *Fats & Oils*						
Cheese, natural:						
Blue	1 oz.	100	8	5.3	396	21
Camembert	1⅓ oz.	115	9	5.8	320	27
Cheddar	1 oz.	115	9	6	176	30
Cottage cheese, creamed, 4% fat	1 cup	235	10	6.4	911	34
Cottage cheese, creamed, 2% fat	1 cup	205	4	2.8	918	19
Cream cheese	1 oz.	100	10	6.2	84	31
Feta cheese	1 oz.	75	6	4.2	316	25
Mozzarella:						
whole milk	1 oz.	80	6	3.7	106	22
part skim	1 oz.	72	4.5	2.9	150	16
Muenster	1 oz.	105	9	5.4	178	27
Parmesan, grated	1 tbsp.	25	2	1	93	4
Provolone	1 oz.	100	8	4.8	248	20
Ricotta:						
whole milk	1 cup	430	32	20.4	207	124
part skim	1 cup	340	19	12.1	307	76
Swiss	1 oz.	105	8	5	74	26
Pasturized process cheese:						
American	1 oz.	105	9	5.6	406	27

TR = nutrient present in trace amount
NA = not available

THE CALORIE, FAT, SODIUM, AND CHOLESTEROL CONTENT OF COMMONLY USED FOODS

	PORTION	K CAL (CALORIES)	TOTAL FAT (gm.)	SATU-RATED FAT (gm.)	SODIUM (mg.)	CHOLES-TEROL (mg.)
Swiss	1 oz.	95	7	4.5	388	24
Pasteurized cheese food:						
American	1 oz.	95	7	4.4	337	18
Pasteurized process cheese spread:						
American	1 oz.	80	3	3.8	381	16
Cream, sweet:						
Half & half	1 cup	315	28	17.3	98	89
	1 tbsp.	20	2	1.1	19	6
Light coffee or table	1 cup	470	46	28.8	95	159
	1 tbsp.	30	3	1.8	6	10
Whipping, unwhipped (volume double when whipped), heavy	1 cup	820	88	54.8	89	326
	1 tbsp.	50	6	3.5	6	21
Whipped topping, pressurized	1 cup	155	13	8.3	78	46
	1 tbsp.	10	1	0.4	4	2
Cream, sour	1 cup	495	48	30	123	102
	1 tbsp.	25	3	1.6	6	5
Cream Substitutes, imitation (made with vegetable fat):						
Sweet Creamers:						
liquid (frozen)	1 tbsp.	20	1.5	1.4	12	0
powdered	1 tsp.	10	1	0.7	4	0
whipped topping, frozen	1 cup	240	19	16.3	19	0
	1 tbsp.	15	1	0.9	1	0
powdered, whole milk	1 cup	150	10	8.5	53	8
pressurized	1 cup	185	16	13.2	43	0
	1 tbsp.	10	1	0.8	2	0
Sour dressings (non butterfat)	1 cup	415	39	31.2	113	13
	1 tbsp.	20	2	1.6	6	1
Ice cream, See *Milk Desserts, frozen*						
Ice milk, See *Milk Desserts, frozen*						
Milk, Fluid:						
Whole, 3.3% fat	1 cup	150	8	5.1	120	33

THE CALORIE, FAT, SODIUM, AND CHOLESTEROL CONTENT OF COMMONLY USED FOODS

	PORTION	K CAL (CALORIES)	TOTAL FAT (gm.)	SATU-RATED FAT (gm.)	SODIUM (mg.)	CHOLES-TEROL (mg.)
Milk, Fluid (cont.)						
Lowfat, 2%, no milk solids added	1 cup	120	5	2.9	122	18
Lowfat, 1%, no milk solids added	1 cup	100	3	1.6	123	10
Nonfat (skim), no milk solids added	1 cup	85	TR	0.3	126	4
Buttermilk	1 cup	100	2	1.3	257	9
Milk, Canned:						
Condensed, sweetened	1 cup	980	27	16.8	389	104
Evaporated:						
whole	1 cup	340	19	11.6	267	74
skim	1 cup	200	1	0.3	293	9
Milk, Dried:						
Buttermilk	1 cup	465	7	4.3	621	83
Nonfat, instantized	1 envel. (3.2 oz.)	325	1	0.4	499	17
Milk Beverages:						
Chocolate (commercial)						
regular	1 cup	210	8	5.3	149	31
lowfat (1%)	1 cup	160	3	1.5	152	7
Egg nog (commercial)	1 cup	340	19	11.3	138	149
Milk shakes, thick:						
chocolate	10 oz.	335	8	4.8	314	30
vanilla	10 oz.	315	9	5.3	270	33
Milk Desserts, frozen:						
Ice cream, vanilla (16% fat)	1 cup	350	24	14.7	108	88
Ice milk, vanilla (4% fat)	1 cup	185	6	3.5	105	18
Sherbet (2% fat)	1 cup	270	4	2.4	88	14
Frozen yogurt, nonfat (Heidi's, vanilla)	3 oz.	46	0.16	NA	64	4.8
Yogurt:						
whole milk	8 oz.	140	7	4.8	105	29
lowfat milk:						
fruit flavored	8 oz.	230	2	1.6	133	10

TR = nutrient present in trace amount
NA = not available

THE CALORIE, FAT, SODIUM, AND CHOLESTEROL CONTENT OF COMMONLY USED FOODS

	PORTION	K CAL (CALORIES)	TOTAL FAT (gm.)	SATU-RATED FAT (gm.)	SODIUM (mg.)	CHOLES-TEROL (mg.)
plain	8 oz.	145	4	2.3	159	14
nonfat milk	8 oz.	90	TR	0.3	135	4
Eggs:						
raw, large:						
whole without shell	1	80	6	1.7	69	213
white	1	15	TR	0	50	0
yolk	1	65	6	1.7	8	213
cooked:						
fried in butter	1 egg	95	7	2.7	320	217
poached	1 egg	80	6	1.7	146	213
scrambled (milk added, in butter); also omelettes	1 egg	110	8	3.2	176	223
Egg substitute (Egg Beaters)	¼ cup	25	0	0	80	0
Fats and Oils						
Butter (4 sticks per pound)						
1 stick, salted	½ cup	810	92	57.1	933	247
1 tablespoon	1 tbsp.	100	11	7.1	116	31
1 pat	1" square	35	4	2.5	41	11
Fats, cooking (vegetable shortening)	1 cup	1,810	205	51.3	0	0
Lard	1 cup	1,850	205	80.4	0	195
Margarine:						
Imitation (about 40% fat), soft, salted	1 tbsp.	50	5	1.1	134	0
Regular (about 80% fat):						
Hard (4 sticks/lb.						
1 stick, salted	½ cup	810	91	17.9	1,066	0
1 tbsp.	1 tbsp.	100	11	2.2	132	0
Soft, salted	1 tbsp.	100	11	1.9	151	0
Oils, salad or cooking (see chart p. 25)						
Salad dressings, commercial:						
Bleu Cheese	1 tbsp.	75	8	1.5	164	3
French: regular	1 tbsp.	85	9	1.4	188	0
reduced calorie	1 tbsp.	25	2	0.2	306	0

THE CALORIE, FAT, SODIUM, AND CHOLESTEROL CONTENT OF COMMONLY USED FOODS

	PORTION	K CAL (CALORIES)	TOTAL FAT (gm.)	SATU-RATED FAT (gm.)	SODIUM (mg.)	CHOLES-TEROL (mg.)
Salad dressings, commercial (cont.)						
Italian: regular	1 tbsp.	80	9	1.3	162	0
low calorie	1 tbsp.	5	TR	TR	136	0
Mayonnaise, regular	1 tbsp.	100	11	1.7	80	8
imitation	1 tbsp.	35	3	0.5	75	4
Tartar sauce	1 tbsp.	75	8	1.2	182	4
Thousand Island, regular	1 tbsp.	60	6	1.0	112	4
reduced calorie	1 tbsp.	25	2	0.2	150	2
Finfish						
Anchovies, canned in oil, drained	5 anchovies	42	1.94	0.44	734	NA
Bass, striped, raw	3 oz.	82	1.98	.43	59	68
Bluefish, raw	3 oz.	105	3.6	.77	51	50
Carp, raw	3 oz.	108	4.76	.92	42	56
Catfish, raw	3 oz.	99	3.62	.83	54	49
breaded & fried	3 oz.	194	11.3	2.79	289	69
Caviar, black & red granular	1 tbsp.	40	2.86	NA	240	94
Cod, Atlantic, raw	3 oz.	70	0.57	0.11	46	37
Croaker, Atlantic, raw	3 oz.	89	2.69	0.92	47	52
Dolphin, raw	3 oz.	73	0.60	0.16	74	62
Eel, raw	3 oz.	156	9.91	2.00	43	107
Fish portions & sticks frozen & reheated	1 stick (28 gm.)	76	3.42	0.88	163	31
Gefilte fish, commercial, sweet recipe	1 piece (42 gm.)	35	0.73	0.17	220	12
Grouper, raw	3 oz.	78	0.86	0.19	45	31
Haddock, raw	3 oz.	74	0.61	0.11	58	49
Halibut, cooked (dry heat)	3 oz.	119	2.49	0.35	59	35
Herring, Atlantic raw	3 oz.	144	7.68	1.73	76	51
kippered (40 gm.)	1 pc. (40 gm.)	87	4.95	1.11	367	33

TR = nutrient present in trace amount
NA = not available

THE CALORIE, FAT, SODIUM, AND CHOLESTEROL CONTENT OF COMMONLY USED FOODS

	PORTION	K CAL (CALORIES)	TOTAL FAT (gm.)	SATU-RATED FAT (gm.)	SODIUM (mg.)	CHOLES-TEROL (mg.)
pickled	3 oz.	190	13	4.3	850	85
Ling cod, raw	3 oz.	72	0.90	0.16	50	44
Mackerel, Atlantic, raw	3 oz.	174	11.81	2.76	76	60
Monkfish, raw	3 oz.	64	1.29	NA	16	21
Mullet, striped, raw	3 oz.	99	3.22	0.94	55	42
Ocean perch, Atlantic, raw	3 oz.	80	1.39	0.20	64	36
Pike, Northern, raw	3 oz.	75	0.58	0.10	33	33
Pike, Walleye, raw	3 oz.	79	1.03	0.21	43	73
Pollock, Atlantic, raw	3 oz.	78	.83	0.11	73	60
Pompano, Florida, raw	3 oz.	140	8.05	2.98	55	43
Rockfish, Pacific, raw	3 oz.	80	1.33	0.31	51	29
Roughy, orange, raw	3 oz.	107	5.95	0.11	54	17
Sablefish, smoked	3 oz.	218	17.12	3.58	626	55
Salmon, Chinook, raw	3 oz.	153	8.88	2.13	40	56
smoked	3 oz.	99	3.67	.79	666	20
Salmon, pink, canned	3 oz.	118	5.14	1.3	471	37
Salmon, sockeye, canned	3 oz.	130	6.21	1.39	458	37
Sardines, Atlantic (canned in oil, drained solids with bone)	1 sardine (24 gm.)	50	5.91	.36	121	34
Sardines, Pacific (canned in tomato sauce, drained solids with bone)	1 sardine (38 gm.)	68	4.55	1.17	157	23
Sea bass, raw	3 oz.	82	1.7	0.43	58	35
Shark, raw	3 oz.	111	3.83	0.78	67	43
Smelts, raw	3 oz.	83	2.06	0.38	51	60
Snapper, raw	3 oz.	85	1.14	0.24	54	31
Sturgeon, raw	3 oz.	90	3.43	0.77	NA	NA
Sucker, raw	3 oz.	79	1.97	0.38	34	35
Surimi (from Pollock)	3 oz.	84	0.77	NA	95	8
Swordfish, raw	3 oz.	103	3.41	0.93	76	33
Trout, rainbow, raw	3 oz.	100	17.46	0.55	23	48

THE CALORIE, FAT, SODIUM, AND CHOLESTEROL CONTENT OF COMMONLY USED FOODS

	PORTION	K CAL (CALORIES)	TOTAL FAT (gm.)	SATU-RATED FAT (gm.)	SODIUM (mg.)	CHOLES-TEROL (mg.)
Finfish (cont.)						
Tuna, light (canned in oil, drained)	3 oz.	169	6.98	1.30	301	15
Tuna, light (canned in water, drained)	3 oz.	111	0.43	0.13	303	15
Tuna, white (canned in oil, drained)	3 oz.	158	6.87	NA	336	26
Tuna, white (canned in water, drained)	3 oz.	116	2.09	0.55	333	35
Tuna, bluefin, raw	3 oz.	122	4.17	1.06	33	32
Turbot, raw	3 oz.	81	2.51	NA	127	NA
Whitefish, raw	3 oz.	114	4.98	0.77	43	51
smoked	3 oz.	92	0.79	0.19	866	28
Whiting, raw	3 oz.	77	1.12	0.21	61	57
Yellowtail, raw	3 oz.	124	4.45	NA	133	NA
Shellfish—Crustaceans						
Crab, Alaska king, raw	3 oz.	71	0.51	NA	711	35
Crab, blue, canned	3 oz.	84	1.04	0.21	283	76
Crab, Dungeness, raw	3 oz.	73	0.83	0.11	251	50
Crayfish, cooked	3 oz.	97	1.15	0.19	58	151
Lobster, northern, cooked	3 oz.	83	0.50	0.09	323	69
Shrimp, canned	3 oz.	102	1.67	0.31	143	147
cooked from raw	3 oz.	84	.92	0.06	190	166
breaded and fried	3 oz.	206	10.44	1.77	292	150
Spiny lobster, raw	3 oz.	95	1.29	0.2	150	60
Shellfish—Mollusks						
Abalone, raw	3 oz.	89	0.64	0.12	255	72
Clams, raw	3 oz.	63	0.83	0.08	47	29
canned, drained	3 oz.	126	1.65	0.16	95	57
Mussels, cooked	3 oz.	147	3.81	0.72	313	48
Oysters, raw	6	58	2.08	0.53	94	46
fried	6	173	11.07	2.81	367	72
Scallops, raw	3 oz.	75	0.64	0.06	137	28

TR = nutrient present in trace amount
NA = not available

THE CALORIE, FAT, SODIUM, AND CHOLESTEROL CONTENT OF COMMONLY USED FOODS

	PORTION	K CAL (CALORIES)	TOTAL FAT (gm.)	SATU-RATED FAT (gm.)	SODIUM (mg.)	CHOLES-TEROL (mg.)
Squid, raw	3 oz.	78	1.18	0.03	37	198
Fruits and Fruit Juices						
Apples, raw:	1 apple					
unpeeled, cored	(2¾″ diam.)	80	TR	0.1	TR	0
peeled, sliced	1 cup	65	TR	0.1	TR	0
Apple juice	1 cup	115	TR	TR	7	0
Applesauce, canned:						
sweetened	1 cup	195	TR	0.1	8	0
unsweetened	1 cup	105	TR	TR	5	0
Apricots:						
raw, pitted	3	50	TR	TR	1	0
canned in heavy						
syrup	1 cup	215	TR	TR	10	0
juice pack	1 cup	120	TR	TR	10	0
Apricots, dried:						
uncooked	1 cup	310	1	TR	13	0
cooked, unsweetened	1 cup	210	TR	TR	8	0
Apricot nectar, canned	1 cup	140	TR	TR	8	0
Avocado, raw, with skin & seed:						
California (8 oz.)	1	305	30	4.5	21	0
Florida (8 oz.)	1	170	13.5	2.6	8	0
Banana, whole	1 6-inch	105	1	0.2	1	0
sliced	1 cup	140	1	0.3	2	0
Blackberries	1 cup	80	1	TR	9	0
Blueberries, raw	1 cup	80	1	TR	9	0
Cantaloupe	½ melon (5″ diam)	95	1	0.1	24	0
Cherries, sweet, raw	10	50	1	0.1	TR	0
Cranberry juice cocktail, sweetened	1 cup	145	TR	TR	10	0
Cranberry sauce, sweetened	1 cup	420	TR	TR	80	0
Dates, pitted, whole	10	230	TR	0.1	2	0
chopped	1 cup	490	TR	0.3	21	0
Figs, dried	10	475	2	0.4	21	0
Fruit cocktail, canned						
in heavy syrup	1 cup	185	TR	TR	15	0
juice pack	1 cup	115	TR	TR	10	0

THE CALORIE, FAT, SODIUM, AND CHOLESTEROL CONTENT OF COMMONLY USED FOODS

	PORTION	K CAL (CALORIES)	TOTAL FAT (gm.)	SATU- RATED FAT (gm.)	SODIUM (mg.)	CHOLES- TEROL (mg.)
Fruit and Fruit Juices (cont.)						
Grapefruit, fresh	half	40	TR	TR	TR	0
canned sections,						
with syrup	1 cup	150	TR	TR	TR	0
Grapefruit juice, fresh	1 cup	95	TR	TR	2	0
canned,						
unsweetened	1 cup	95	TR	TR	5	0
canned, sweetened	1 cup	115	TR	TR	5	0
Grapes:						
Thompson seedless	10	35	TR	0.1	1	0
Tokay & Emperor,						
seeded	10	40	TR	0.1	1	0
Grape juice, canned or						
bottled	1 cup	155	TR	0.1	8	0
Honeydew melon	1/10 melon (6" diam.)	45	TR	TR	13	0
Kiwi, raw	1	45	TR	TR	4	0
Lemon juice, fresh	1 cup	60	TR	TR	51	0
Mango, raw	1	135	1	0.1	4	0
Nectarine, fresh	1	65	1	0.1	TR	0
Orange, whole fresh	1	60	TR	TR	TR	0
sections, no						
membrane	1 cup	85	TR	TR	TR	0
Orange juice, fresh	1 cup	110	TR	0.1	5	0
Papaya, fresh	1 cup	65	TR	0.1	9	0
Peaches, fresh, whole	1	35	TR	TR	TR	0
fresh, sliced	1 cup	75	TR	TR	TR	0
canned, heavy syrup	1/2 cup	60	TR	TR	10	0
canned, juice pack	1/2 cup	35	TR	TR	3	0
Pears, fresh:						
Bartlett, cored	1	100	1	TR	TR	0
Bosc, cored	1	85	1	TR	TR	0
D'Anjou, cored	1	85	1	TR	TR	0
canned:						
in heavy syrup	1/2 cup	60	TR	TR	4	0
juice pack	1/2 cup	40	TR	TR	3	0
Pineapple, fresh, diced	1 cup	75	1	TR	2	0
canned, heavy syrup	1 cup	200	TR	TR	1	0
canned, juice pack	1 cup	150	TR	TR	1	0

TR = nutrient present in trace amount
NA = not available

THE CALORIE, FAT, SODIUM, AND CHOLESTEROL CONTENT OF COMMONLY USED FOODS

	PORTION	K CAL (CALORIES)	TOTAL FAT (gm.)	SATU-RATED FAT (gm.)	SODIUM (mg.)	CHOLES-TEROL (mg.)
Pineapple juice, unsweetened	1 cup	140	TR	TR	3	0
Plantains, raw	1	220	1	0.3	8	0
Plums, fresh, pitted	1 (2⅛" diam.)	35	TR	TR	TR	0
canned, heavy syrup	3	120	TR	TR	25	0
canned, juice pack	3	55	TR	TR	1	0
Prunes, dried, uncooked	4 ex-lg.	115	TR	TR	2	0
cooked, unsweetened, fruit & liquid	1 cup	225	TR	TR	10	0
Prune juice, canned	1 cup	180	TR	TR	10	0
Raisins, seedless, not packed	1 cup	435	1	0.2	17	0
1 packet	½ oz.	40	TR	TR	2	0
Raspberries, fresh	1 cup	60	1	TR	3	0
Rhubarb, cooked, sweetened	1 cup	280	TR	TR	2	0
Strawberries, raw, whole	1 cup	45	1	TR	1	0
Tangerine, fresh	1	35	TR	TR	1	0
Watermelon, fresh	1 slice (4"×8")	155	2	0.3	10	0
diced	1 cup	50	1	0.1	3	0

Legumes
Beans, dry, cooked & drained:

	PORTION	K CAL (CALORIES)	TOTAL FAT (gm.)	SATU-RATED FAT (gm.)	SODIUM (mg.)	CHOLES-TEROL (mg.)
Black beans	1 cup	225	1	0.1	1	0
Black-eyed peas	1 cup	190	1	0.2	20	0
Chick-peas (garbanzo beans)	1 cup	270	4	0.4	11	0
Great Northern beans	1 cup	210	1	0.1	13	0
Lima beans	1 cup	260	1	0.2	4	0
Navy beans	1 cup	225	1	0.1	13	0
Pinto beans	1 cup	265	1	0.1	3	0
Soy beans	1 cup	235	10	1.3	4	0

Beans, canned, solids & liquids:

	PORTION	K CAL (CALORIES)	TOTAL FAT (gm.)	SATU-RATED FAT (gm.)	SODIUM (mg.)	CHOLES-TEROL (mg.)
Red kidney beans	1 cup	230	1	0.1	968	0

THE CALORIE, FAT, SODIUM, AND CHOLESTEROL CONTENT OF COMMONLY USED FOODS

	PORTION	K CAL (CALORIES)	TOTAL FAT (gm.)	SATU- RATED FAT (gm.)	SODIUM (mg.)	CHOLES- TEROL (mg.)
Beans, canned, solids & liquids (cont.)						
Lentils, dry, cooked	1 cup	215	1	0.1	26	0
Peas, split, dry, cooked	1 cup	230	1	0.1	26	0
Refried beans, canned	1 cup	295	3	0.4	1,228	0
Nuts & Seeds (See chart page 20)						
Meat and Meat Products						
Beef (all grades, lean, trimmed):						
Brisket, flat cut,						
braised	3 oz.	223	13.48	5.31	66	77
Chuck:						
arm pot roast,						
braised	3 oz.	196	8.48	3.22	56	85
blade pot roast,						
braised	3 oz.	230	12.98	5.29	60	90
Flank steak, broiled	3 oz.	207	12.72	5.43	70	60
Ground beef:						
lean, broiled	3 oz.	231	15.69	6.16	65	74
extra lean, broiled	3 oz.	217	13.88	5.45	59	71
Rib:						
roast, lean, trimmed	3 oz.	201	11.48	4.87	64	68
steak, trimmed and						
broiled	3 oz.	188	9.53	4.03	58	68
Round:						
bottom round,						
braised	3 oz.	189	8.21	2.92	44	81
eye of round,						
roasted	3 oz.	155	5.53	2.12	52	59
top of round, broiled	3 oz.	162	5.26	1.84	51	72
round tip, roasted	3 oz.	162	6.37	2.33	55	69
Short ribs, braised	3 oz.	251	15.41	6.58	50	79
Sirloin steak, broiled	3 oz.	232	14.76	6.16	53	77
Tenderloin steak,						
broiled	3 oz.	174	7.89	3.08	54	72
Lamb (lean, trimmed):						
Chops (3 per lb. with						
bone):						
Arm, braised						
lean only	1.7 oz.	135	7	2.9	36	59

TR = nutrient present in trace amount
NA = not available

THE CALORIE, FAT, SODIUM, AND CHOLESTEROL CONTENT
OF COMMONLY USED FOODS

	PORTION	K CAL (CALORIES)	TOTAL FAT (gm.)	SATU- RATED FAT (gm.)	SODIUM (mg.)	CHOLES- TEROL (mg.)
Loin, broiled						
lean and fat	2.8 oz.	235	16	7.3	62	78
lean only	2.3 oz.	140	6	2.6	54	60
Leg, roasted:						
lean only	2.6 oz.	140	6	2.4	50	65
Rib rack, roasted						
lean only	2 oz.	130	7	3.2	46	50
lean & fat	3 oz.	315	26	12.1	60	77
Pork, cured, cooked:						
Bacon: regular	3 slices	110	9	3.3	303	16
Canadian style	2 slices	85	4	1.3	711	27
Ham:						
lean & fat, roasted	3 oz.	205	14	5.1	1,009	53
lean only	2.4 oz.	105	4	1.3	902	37
canned, roasted	3 oz.	140	7	2.4	908	35
Luncheon meat:						
Chopped ham (8 slices per 6-oz. package)	2 slices	95	7	2.4	576	21
Cooked ham (2 slices):						
regular	2 oz.	105	6	1.9	751	32
extra lean	2 slices	75	3	0.9	815	27
Pork, fresh, cooked:						
Chopped loin (3 per lb. with bone):						
broiled, lean only	2.5 oz.	165	8	2.6	56	84
pan fried, lean only	2.4 oz.	180	11	3.7	57	72
Leg roasted, lean only	2.5 oz.	160	8	2.7	46	68
Rib roasted, lean only	2.5 oz.	175	10	3.4	33	56
Shoulder cut, braised, lean only	2.4 oz.	165	8	2.8	68	76
Sausages:						
brown and serve	1 link	50	5	1.7	105	9
pork link (16 per lb)	1 link	50	4	1.4	168	11
pork, fresh	1 patty (1 oz.)	100	8.4	2.9	349	22
Spare ribs, roasted	6 med.ribs	396	35	NA	NA	NA
Tenderloin, lean, roasted	3 oz.	141	4.1	NA	50	79

THE CALORIE, FAT, SODIUM, AND CHOLESTEROL CONTENT OF COMMONLY USED FOODS

	PORTION	K CAL (CALORIES)	TOTAL FAT (gm.)	SATU-RATED FAT (gm.)	SODIUM (mg.)	CHOLES-TEROL (mg.)
Meat and Meat Products (cont.)						
Veal						
Breast, lean, braised	2½ oz.	256	18.6	NA	64	NA
Cutlet, braised or broiled	3 oz.	185	9	4.1	56	109
Loin chop, lean only, broiled	3½ oz.	234	13.4	1.9	80	90
Rib, roasted	3 oz.	230	14	6.0	57	109
Venison, roasted	3½ oz.	146	2.2	NA	70	79
Sausages, Franks, and Luncheon Meats						
Blood sausage	1 slice (1 oz.)	95	8.6	3.3	NA	30
Bockwurst (raw pork, veal, etc.)	1 link (2 oz.)	200	17.9	6.6	NA	NA
Bologna:						
beef, 1 slice	1 oz.	72	6.5	2.7	230	13
beef & pork, 1 slice	1 oz.	73	6.5	2.5	234	13
turkey	1 oz.	60	4.5	1.4	222	20
Bratwurst (cooked pork)	1 link (3 oz.)	256	22	7.9	473	51
Braunschweiger (pork, beef)	1 slice (⅔ oz.)	65	5.8	2	206	28
Bratwurst (pork, beef)	1 link (2½ oz.)	226	19.5	7.0	778	44
Chorizo (pork, beef)	1 link (2 oz.)	265	23	8.6	NA	NA
Frankfurter:						
beef (1¾ oz.)	1 frank	145	13.2	5.4	461	22
beef & pork (1¾ oz.)	1 frank	144	13.1	4.8	75	22
chicken	1 frank	116	8.8	2.5	617	45
pork & beef, battered & fried (corn dog)	1 frank	330	20	8.4	1,252	37
turkey	1 frank	100	8.1	2.7	472	39
Ham (See chart page 367)						
Italian sausage, pork, cooked	1 link	216	17.2	6.1	618	52

TR = nutrient present in trace amount
NA = not available

THE CALORIE, FAT, SODIUM, AND CHOLESTEROL CONTENT OF COMMONLY USED FOODS

	PORTION	K CAL (CALORIES)	TOTAL FAT (gm.)	SATU-RATED FAT (gm.)	SODIUM (mg.)	CHOLES-TEROL (mg.)
Kielbasa—Kolbassy (pork & beef)	1 slice (1 oz.)	81	7.1	2.6	280	17
Knockwurst (pork & beef)	1 link	209	18.9	6.9	687	39
Liver cheese (pork liver)	1 slice	115	9.7	3.4	465	66
Mortadella (beef & pork)	1 slice (½ oz.)	47	3.8	1.4	187	8
Pepperoni	1 slice (¼ oz.)	27	2.4	0.9	112	NA
Salami: cooked beef	2 slices (2 oz.)	145	11	4.6	607	37
cooked turkey	1 slice (1 oz.)	50	3.4	1.0	251	20
dried/hard (Italian, pork & beef)	1 slice (⅓ oz.)	42	3.4	1.2	186	8
Turkey, breast meat loaf (8 slices per 6 oz.)	2 slices	45	1	0.2	608	17
Miscellaneous						
Baking powder	1 tsp.	5	0	0	329	0
low sodium	1 tsp.	5	0	0	TR	0
Black pepper	1 tsp.	5	TR	TR	1	0
Celery seed	1 tsp.	10	1	TR	3	0
Chili powder	1 tsp.	10	TR	0.1	26	0
Chocolate, bitter or baking	1 oz.	145	15	9.0	1	0
semisweet (See Sugars & Sweets, Candy)						
Cinnamon	1 tsp.	5	TR	TR	1	0
Curry powder	1 tsp.	5	TR	TR	1	0
Dried chipped beef	2.5 oz.	145	4	1.8	3,053	46
Garlic powder	1 tsp.	10	TR	TR	1	0
Gelatin, dry	1 envelope	25	TR	TR	6	0
Ketchup	1 tbsp.	15	TR	TR	156	0
reduced sodium and reduced calorie	1 tbsp.	8	0	0	110	0
Mustard, prepared, yellow	1 tsp. (or 1 packet)	5	TR	TR	63	0

THE CALORIE, FAT, SODIUM, AND CHOLESTEROL CONTENT OF COMMONLY USED FOODS

	PORTION	K CAL (CALORIES)	TOTAL FAT (gm.)	SATU-RATED FAT (gm.)	SODIUM (mg.)	CHOLES-TEROL (mg.)
Miscellaneous (cont.)						
Olives, canned:						
green	4 medium	15	2	0.2	312	0
ripe, pitted	2 large	15	2	0.3	68	0
Onion powder	1 tsp.	5	TR	TR	1	0
Oregano	1 tsp.	5	TR	TR	TR	0
Paprika	1 tsp.	5	TR	TR	1	0
Pickles, cucumber:	1 (3¾"					
dill	long)	5	TR	TR	928	0
sweet gherkin,	1 (2½"					
1 small whole	long)	20	TR	TR	107	0
Popcorn (see Grains & Grain Products)						
Relish, chopped sweet	1 tbsp.	20	TR	TR	107	0
Salt	1 tsp.	0	0	0	2,132	0
Soy products:						
Miso	1 cup	470	13	1.8	8,142	0
Tofu						
(1 2½" × 2¾" × 1")	1 piece	85	5	0.7	8	0
Tahini (sesame)	1 tbsp.	90	8	1.1	5	0
Vinegar, cider	1 tbsp.	TR	0	0	TR	0
Yeast:						
baker's, dry, active	1 package	20	TR	TR	4	0
brewer's, dry	1 tbsp.	25	TR	TR	10	0
Mixed Dishes and Fast Foods						
Beef & vegetable stew	1 cup	220	11	4.4	292	71
Beef pot pie, 9" diam.	⅓ pie	515	30	7.9	596	42
Chicken à la king	1 cup	470	34	12.9	760	221
Chicken & noodles	1 cup	365	18	5.1	600	103
Chicken chow mein:						
canned	1 cup	95	TR	0.11	725	8
home recipe	1 cup	255	10	4.1	473	75
Chicken pot pie, 9" diam.	⅓ pie	545	31	10.3	594	56
Chili con carne, canned with beans	1 cup	340	16	5.8	1,354	28

TR = nutrient present in trace amount
NA = not available

THE CALORIE, FAT, SODIUM, AND CHOLESTEROL CONTENT OF COMMONLY USED FOODS

	PORTION	K CAL (CALORIES)	TOTAL FAT (gm.)	SATU-RATED FAT (gm.)	SODIUM (mg.)	CHOLES-TEROL (mg.)
Chop suey, with beef & pork	1 cup	300	17	4.3	1,053	68
Macaroni & cheese:						
canned	1 cup	230	10	4.7	730	24
home recipe	1 cup	430	22	9.8	1,086	44
Quiche Lorraine, 8″ diam.	1 slice	600	48	23.2	653	285
Spaghetti and tomato sauce:						
with cheese, canned	1 cup	190	2	0.4	955	3
with meatballs:						
canned	1 cup	260	10	2.4	1,220	23
home recipe	1 cup	330	12	3.9	1,009	89
Fast food entrées:						
Cheeseburger, 4-oz. patty	1 sand.	525	31	15.1	1,224	104
Chicken, fried, with skin:						
½ breast (5.6 oz. with bones)	4.9 oz.	365	18	4.9	385	119
drumstick (3.4 oz. with bones)	2.5 oz.	195	11	3.0	194	62
Enchilada	1	235	16	7.7	1,332	19
English muffin with egg & cheese	1 sand.	360	18	8	832	213
Fish sandwich, large (fried)	1 sand.	470	27	6.3	621	91
Hamburger: regular	1 sand.	245	11	4.4	463	32
4-oz. patty	1 sand.	445	21	7.1	763	71
Pizza, cheese, 15″ diam.	1 slice (⅛ pie)	290	9	4.1	699	56
Roast beef sandwich	1 sand.	345	13	3.5	757	55
Taco	1 taco	195	11	4.1	456	21
Nuts and Seeds (See chart page 20)						
Poultry						
Chicken:						
Broilers/Fryers, light meat:						
with skin, fried	3½ oz.	246	12.1	3.3	77	87
without skin, fried	3½ oz.	192	5.5	1.5	81	90
with skin, roasted	3½ oz.	222	10.9	3.1	75	84
without skin, roasted	3½ oz.	173	4.5	1.3	77	85

THE CALORIE, FAT, SODIUM, AND CHOLESTEROL CONTENT OF COMMONLY USED FOODS

	PORTION	K CAL (CALORIES)	TOTAL FAT (gm.)	SATU-RATED FAT (gm.)	SODIUM (mg.)	CHOLES-TEROL (mg.)
Poultry (cont.)						
with skin, stewed	3½ oz.	201	10.0	2.8	63	74
without skin, stewed	3½ oz.	159	4.0	1.1	65	77
Broilers/Fryers, dark meat						
with skin, fried	3½ oz.	285	16.9	4.6	89	92
without skin, fried	3½ oz.	239	11.6	3.1	97	96
with skin, roasted	3½ oz.	253	15.8	4.4	87	91
without skin, roasted	3½ oz.	205	9.7	2.7	93	93
with skin, stewed	3½ oz.	233	14.7	4.1	70	82
without skin, stewed	3½ oz.	192	9.0	2.5	74	88
Broilers/Fryers, wings:						
with skin, fried	1 wing	103	7.1	1.9	25	26
with skin, roasted	1 wing	99	6.6	1.9	28	29
with skin, stewed	1 wing	100	6.7	1.9	27	28
Capon:						
with skin, roasted	3½ oz.	229	11.7	3.3	49	86
Duck:						
with skin, roasted	3½ oz.	337	28.4	9.7	59	84
without skin, roasted	3½ oz.	201	11.2	4.2	65	89
Turkey:						
Light meat, roasted:						
with skin	3½ oz.	197	8.3	2.3	63	76
without skin	3½ oz.	157	3.2	1.0	64	69
Dark meat, roasted:						
with skin	3½ oz.	221	11.5	3.5	76	89
without skin	3½ oz.	187	7.2	2.4	79	85
Breast, smoked, commercial	3½ oz.	120	4.0	0.6	959	31
Soups						
Canned, condensed:						
Asparagus, cream of,						
made with milk	1 cup	161	8.2	3.3	1,041	22
made with water	1 cup	87	4.1	1.0	981	5
Bean with bacon, made with water	1 cup	173	5.9	1.5	952	3
Beans with franks, made with water	1 cup	187	7.0	2.1	1,092	12
Bean, black, made with water	1 cup	116	1.5	0.4	1,198	0

TR = nutrient present in trace amount
NA = not available

THE CALORIE, FAT, SODIUM, AND CHOLESTEROL CONTENT OF COMMONLY USED FOODS

	PORTION	K CAL (CALORIES)	TOTAL FAT (gm.)	SATU-RATED FAT (gm.)	SODIUM (mg.)	CHOLES-TEROL (mg.)
Beef broth bouillon	1 cup	16	0.5	0.2	782	TR
Celery, cream of,						
made with milk	1 cup	165	9.7	4.0	1,010	32
made with water	1 cup	90	5.6	1.4	949	15
Cheese,						
made with milk	1 cup	230	14.6	9.1	1,020	48
made with water	1 cup	155	10.5	6.7	950	30
Chicken broth, made with water	1 cup	39	1.4	0.4	776	1
Chicken, cream of,						
made with milk	1 cup	191	11.5	4.6	1,046	27
made with water	1 cup	116	7.4	2.1	986	10
Chicken gumbo, made with water	1 cup	56	1.4	0.3	955	5
Chicken noodle, made with water	1 cup	75	2.5	0.7	1,107	7
Chicken noodle with meatballs	1 cup	99	3.6	1.1	1,039	10
Chicken rice, made with water	1 cup	60	1.9	0.5	814	7
Chicken vegetable, made with water	1 cup	74	2.8	0.9	944	10
Chili beef, made with water	1 cup	169	6.6	3.3	1,035	12
Clam chowder:						
Manhattan, chunky, ready to serve	1 cup	133	3.4	2.1	1,000	14
Manhattan, made with water	1 cup	78	2.3	0.4	1,808	2
New England, made with milk	1 cup	163	6.6	3.0	992	22
New England, made with water	1 cup	95	2.9	0.4	914	5
Consommé, with gelatin, made with water	1 cup	29	0	0	637	0
Minestrone, made with water	1 cup	83	2.5	0.5	911	
Mushroom, cream of,						
made with milk	1 cup	203	13.6	5.1	1,076	20
made with water	1 cup	129	9.0	2.4	1,031	2

THE CALORIE, FAT, SODIUM, AND CHOLESTEROL CONTENT OF COMMONLY USED FOODS

	PORTION	K CAL (CALORIES)	TOTAL FAT (gm.)	SATU-RATED FAT (gm.)	SODIUM (mg.)	CHOLES-TEROL (mg.)
Canned, condensed (cont.)						
Oyster stew,						
made with milk	1 cup	134	7.9	5.1	1,040	32
made with water	1 cup	59	3.8	2.5	980	14
Green pea,						
made with milk	1 cup	239	7.0	4.0	1,048	18
made with water	1 cup	164	2.9	1.4	987	0
Potato, cream of,						
made with milk	1 cup	148	6.5	3.8	1,060	22
made with water	1 cup	73	2.4	1.2	1,000	5
Shrimp, cream of,						
made with milk	1 cup	165	9.3	5.8	1,036	35
made with water	1 cup	90	5.2	3.2	976	17
Split pea with ham,						
ready to serve	1 cup	184	4	1.6	965	7
Tomato bisque,						
made with milk	1 cup	198	6.6	3.1	1,108	22
made with water	1 cup	123	2.5	0.5	1,048	4
Turkey noodle, made with water	1 cup	69	2.0	0.6	815	5
Turkey vegetable, made with water	1 cup	74	3.0	0.9	905	2
Vegetable, chunky, ready to serve	1 cup	122	3.7	0.6	1,010	0
Vegetable, vegetarian, made with water	1 cup	72	1.9	0.3	823	0
Vegetable with beef, made with water	1 cup	79	1.9	0.9	957	5
Dehydrated soups:						
Beef broth, cube	1 cube	6	0.1	0.1	864	TR
Chicken broth, cube	1 cube	9	0.2	0.1	1,152	1
Onion soup mix	1 packet	115	2.3	0.5	3,493	2
Cup of Soups, prepared with water:						
Chicken noodle	6 oz.	40	1.0	0.2	957	2
Onion	6 oz.	20	TR	0.1	635	0
Tomato vegetable	6 oz.	40	1.0	0.3	856	0
Reconstituted with water:						
Chicken noodle	1 cup	53	1.2	0.3	1,284	3

TR = nutrient present in trace amount
NA = not available

THE CALORIE, FAT, SODIUM, AND CHOLESTEROL CONTENT OF COMMONLY USED FOODS

	PORTION	K CAL (CALORIES)	TOTAL FAT (gm.)	SATU-RATED FAT (gm.)	SODIUM (mg.)	CHOLES-TEROL (mg.)
Celery, cream of	1 cup	63	1.6	0.2	839	1
Leek	1 cup	71	2.1	1.0	966	3
Onion	1 cup	28	0.6	0.1	848	0
Oxtail	1 cup	71	2.6	1.3	1,210	3
Pea, green/split	1 cup	133	1.6	0.4	1,220	3

Sugars and Sweets
Candy:

	PORTION	K CAL (CALORIES)	TOTAL FAT (gm.)	SATU-RATED FAT (gm.)	SODIUM (mg.)	CHOLES-TEROL (mg.)
Caramels, plain or chocolate	1 oz.	115	3	2.2	64	1
Chocolate:						
milk, plain	1 oz.	145	9	5.4	23	6
milk, with almonds,	1 oz.	150	10	4.8	23	6
milk, with peanuts	1 oz.	155	11	4.2	19	5
milk with rice cereal	1 oz.	140	7	4.4	46	6
semi-sweet, chips	6 oz. (or 1 cup)	860	61	36.2	24	0
sweet, dark	1 oz.	150	10	5.9	5	0
Fondant (uncoated mints, creme filling, etc.)	1 oz.	105	0	0	57	0
Fudge, chocolate, plain	1 oz.	115	3	2.1	57	0
Gumdrops	1 oz.	100	TR	TR	10	0
Hard candy	1 oz.	110	0	0	7	0
Jelly beans	1 oz.	105	TR	TR	7	0
Marshmallows	1 oz.	90	0	0	25	0
Custard, baked	1 cup	305	15	6.8	209	278
Gelatin dessert	½ cup	70	0	0	55	0
Honey	1 cup	1,030	0	0	17	0
	1 tbsp.	65	0	0	1	0
Jams & Preserves	1 tbsp.	55	TR	0	2	0
	1 packet	40	0	TR	2	0
Jelly	1 tbsp.	50	TR	TR	4	0
	1 packet	40	TR	TR	4	0
Popsicle	1 (3 oz.)	70	0	0	11	0
Puddings, canned:						
chocolate	5 oz. can	205	11	9.5	285	1
tapioca	5 oz. can	160	5	4.8	252	TR
vanilla	5 oz. can	220	10	9.5	305	1

THE CALORIE, FAT, SODIUM, AND CHOLESTEROL CONTENT
OF COMMONLY USED FOODS

	PORTION	K CAL (CALORIES)	TOTAL FAT (gm.)	SATU-RATED FAT (gm.)	SODIUM (mg.)	CHOLES-TEROL (mg.)
Sugars and Sweets (cont.)						
Puddings, dry mix, made with whole milk:						
Chocolate:						
instant	½ cup	155	4	2.3	440	14
cooked	½ cup	150	4	2.4	167	15
Tapioca	½ cup	145	4	2.3	152	15
Vanilla:						
instant	½ cup	150	4	2.2	375	15
cooked	½ cup	145	4	2.3	178	15
Sugars:						
Brown, packed	1 cup	820	0	0	97	0
White:						
granulated	1 cup	770	0	0	5	0
	1 tbsp.	45	0	0	TR	0
	1 packet	25	0	0	TR	0
powdered, sifted	1 cup	385	0	0	02	0
Syrups:						
Chocolate flavored syrup or topping:						
thin type	2 tbsp.	85	TR	0.2	36	0
fudge type	2 tbsp.	125	5	3.1	42	0
Molasses, blackstrap	2 tbsp.	85	0	0	38	0
Table syrup, corn or maple	2 tbsp.	122	0	0	19	0
Vegetables and Vegetable Products						
Alfalfa seeds, sprouted, raw	1 cup	10	TR	TR	2	0
Artichokes, globe or French, cooked & drained	1	55	TR	TR	79	0
Asparagus, green, cooked from raw:						
cuts and tips	1 cup	45	1	0.1	7	0
spears	4 spears (½″ diam)	15	TR	TR	2	0
Bamboo shoots, canned, drained	1 cup	25	1	0.1	9	0

TR = nutrient present in trace amount
NA = not available

THE CALORIE, FAT, SODIUM, AND CHOLESTEROL CONTENT OF COMMONLY USED FOODS

	PORTION	K CAL (CALORIES)	TOTAL FAT (gm.)	SATU-RATED FAT (gm.)	SODIUM (mg.)	CHOLES-TEROL (mg.)
Beans:						
Lima, frozen, cooked:						
Fordhook	1 cup	170	1	0.1	90	0
Baby limas	1 cup	190	1	0.1	52	0
Snap beans, cooked, drained:						
raw	1 cup	45	TR	0.1	4	0
frozen	1 cup	35	TR	TR	18	0
canned, drained	1 cup	25	TR	TR	339	0
Bean sprouts:						
raw	1 cup	30	TR	TR	6	0
cooked, drained	1 cup	25	TR	TR	12	0
Beets, cooked, diced or sliced	1 cup	55	TR	TR	83	0
whole beets, 2″ diam.	2 beets	30	TR	TR	49	0
canned, drained, diced or sliced	1 cup	55	TR	TR	466	0
Beet greens, leaves and stems, cooked	1 cup	40	TR	TR	347	0
Black-eyed peas, cooked and drained:						
from raw	1 cup	180	1	0.3	7	0
from frozen	1 cup	225	1	0.3	9	0
Broccoli, raw	1 spear	40	1	0.1	41	0
cooked, from raw	1 cup	45	TR	0.1	17	0
cooked, from frozen	1 piece	10	TR	TR	7	0
cooked, from frozen, chopped	1 cup	50	TR	TR	44	0
Brussels sprouts, cooked, drained	1 cup	60	1	0.2	33	0
Cabbage, raw,coarsely shredded	1 cup	15	TR	TR	13	0
cooked, drained	1 cup	30	TR	TR	29	0
Cabbage, Chinese:						
cooked, drained	1 cup	20	TR	TR	58	0
raw	1 cup	10	TR	TR	7	0
Cabbage, red, raw	1 cup	20	TR	TR	8	0
Cabbage, Savoy	1 cup	20	TR	TR	20	0

THE CALORIE, FAT, SODIUM, AND CHOLESTEROL CONTENT OF COMMONLY USED FOODS

	PORTION	K CAL (CALORIES)	TOTAL FAT (gm.)	SATU-RATED FAT (gm.)	SODIUM (mg.)	CHOLES-TEROL (mg.)
Vegetables (cont.)						
Carrots, raw:	1 carrot					
whole	7½″ × 1⅛″	30	TR	TR	25	0
grated	1 cup	45	TR	TR	39	0
Carrots, cooked:						
from raw	1 cup	70	TR	0.1	103	0
from frozen	1 cup	55	TR	TR	86	0
Carrots, canned	1 cup	35	TR	0.1	352	0
Cauliflower:						
raw	1 cup	25	TR	TR	15	0
cooked	1 cup	30	TR	TR	8	0
Celery, raw	1 stalk	5	TR	TR	35	0
	1 cup	20	TR	TR	106	0
Collards, cooked:						
from raw	1 cup	25	TR	0.1	36	0
from frozen	1 cup	60	1	0.1	85	0
Corn, sweet, cooked:						
from raw	1 ear	85	1	0.2	13	0
kernels, from frozen	1 cup	135	TR	TR	8	0
cream style	1 cup	185	1	0.2	730	0
whole kernel	1 cup	165	1	0.2	571	0
Cucumber with peel ⅛″ thick)	6 slices	5	TR	TR	1	0
Dandelion greens, cooked, drained	1 cup	35	1	0.1	46	0
Eggplant, cooked, steamed	1 cup	25	TR	TR	3	0
Endive, curly	1 cup	10	TR	TR	11	0
Ginger root, raw	3½ oz.	49	1	0	6	0
Hominy, canned, white	1 cup	140	0	0	710	0
Jerusalem artichoke, raw	1 cup	115	TR	0	6	0
Kale, cooked, drained	1 cup	40	1	0.1	30	0
Kohlrabi, cooked, drained	1 cup	50	TR	TR	35	0

TR = nutrient present in trace amount
NA = not available

THE CALORIE, FAT, SODIUM, AND CHOLESTEROL CONTENT OF COMMONLY USED FOODS

	PORTION	K CAL (CALORIES)	TOTAL FAT (gm.)	SATU-RATED FAT (gm.)	SODIUM (mg.)	CHOLES-TEROL (mg.)
Lettuce, raw:						
Butter or Boston	1 head	20	TR	TR	8	0
Iceberg	1 head	70	1	0.1	49	0
Loose Leaf (as romaine), shredded	1 cup	10	TR	TR	5	0
Mushrooms, raw, sliced	1 cup	20	TR	TR	3	0
cooked, drained	1 cup	40	1	0.1	3	0
canned, drained	1 cup	35	TR	0.1	663	0
Mustard greens, cooked	1 cup	20	TR	TR	22	0
Okra	8 pods	25	TR	TR	4	0
Onions, raw	1 cup	55	TR	0.1	3	0
chopped, sliced	1 cup	40	TR	0.1	2	0
cooked	1 cup	60	TR	0.1	17	0
Onions (scallions), white portion only	6	10	TR	TR	1	0
Onion rings, breaded, fried, from frozen	2 rings	80	5	1.7	75	0
Parsley, raw	10 sprigs	5	TR	TR	2	0
Parsnips, cooked	1 cup	125	TR	0.1	6	0
Peas, edible pod, cooked	1 cup	65	TR	0.1	6	0
Peas, green, raw	¾ cup	84	0.4	0	2	0
canned, drained	1 cup	115	1	0.1	372	0
frozen, cooked, drained	1 cup	125	TR	0.1	139	0
Peppers, bell, raw	1 (3 oz.)	20	TR	TR	2	0
Peppers, hot chili, raw	1 pepper	20	TR	TR	3	0
Potatoes:						
baked with skin	1 (8 oz.)	220	TR	0.1	16	0
baked pulp only	1 (8 oz.)	145	TR	TR	8	0
boiled	5½ oz. raw	120	TR	TR	5	0
Potatoes, french fried, frozen:						
oven heated	10 strips	110	4	2.1	16	0
fried in vegetable oil	10 strips	160	8	2.5	108	0
Potato products, prepared:						
Au gratin:						
dry mix	1 cup	230	10	6.3	1,076	12
home recipe	1 cup	325	19	11.6	1,061	56

THE CALORIE, FAT, SODIUM, AND CHOLESTEROL CONTENT
OF COMMONLY USED FOODS

	PORTION	K CAL (CALORIES)	TOTAL FAT (gm.)	SATU-RATED FAT (gm.)	SODIUM (mg.)	CHOLES-TEROL (mg.)
Potato products, prepared (cont.)						
Hash browns, from frozen	1 cup	340	18	7.0	53	0
Mashed, home recipe:						
milk added	1 cup	160	1	0.7	636	4
milk & margarine added	1 cup	225	9	2.2	620	4
from dehydrated flakes	1 cup	235	12	7.2	697	29
Potato salad, made with mayonnaise	1 cup	360	21	3.6	1,323	170
Scalloped potatoes, home recipe	1 cup	210	9	5.5	821	29
Potato chips	10 chips	105	7	1.8	94	0
Pumpkin, canned	1 cup	85	1	0.4	12	0
Radishes	4	5	TR	TR	4	0
Rutabaga, cooked	½ cup	35	0.1	0	4	0
Sauerkraut, canned	1 cup	45	TR	0.1	1,560	0
Seaweed (kelp), raw	1 oz.	10	TR	0.1	66	0
Spinach, raw, chopped	1 cup	10	TR	TR	43	0
cooked from raw, leaf	1 cup	40	TR	0.1	126	0
cooked from frozen, leaf	1 cup	55	TR	0.1	163	0
Spinach soufflé	1 cup	220	18	7.1	763	184
Squash, cooked:						
summer, sliced, cooked, drained	1 cup	35	1	0.1	2	TR
winter, baked	1 cup	80	1	0.3	2	0
Sweet potato, cooked:						
baked in skin, peeled	1 (6 oz.)	115	TR	TR	11	0
boiled without skin	1 (6 oz.)	160	TR	0.1	20	0
candied	3 oz.	145	3	1.4	74	8
Tomato, raw	1 (4 oz.)	25	TR	TR	10	0
canned, solids & liquid	1 cup	50	1	0.1	391	0
Tomato juice, canned	1 cup	40	TR	TR	881	0

TR = nutrient present in trace amount
NA = not available

THE CALORIE, FAT, SODIUM, AND CHOLESTEROL CONTENT OF COMMONLY USED FOODS

	PORTION	K CAL (CALORIES)	TOTAL FAT (gm.)	SATU-RATED FAT (gm.)	SODIUM (mg.)	CHOLES-TEROL (mg.)
Tomato products, canned:						
paste	1 cup	220	2	0.3	170	0
puree	1 cup	105	TR	TR	50	0
sauce	1 cup	75	TR	0.1	1,482	0
Turnips, cooked	1 cup	30	TR	TR	78	0
Turnip greens, cooked	1 cup	30	TR	0.1	42	0
Vegetable juice cocktail, canned	1 cup	45	TR	TR	883	0
Water chestnuts, canned	1 cup	70	TR	TR	11	0
Watercress	8 sprigs	3	0	0	1	0

Users of this table should keep in mind that the data are provisional at this time.

THE DIETARY FIBER CONTENT OF SELECTED FOODS

FOOD ITEM	TOTAL DIETARY FIBER
	gm. per 100 gm. *(about 3½ ounces)* *edible portion*
Baked Products	
Bagels, plain	2.1
Breads:	
Boston brown	4.7
Bran	8.5
Cornbread mix, baked	2.6
Cracked wheat	5.3
French	2.3
Hollywood-type, light	4.8
Italian	2.7
Mixed-grain	6.3
Oatmeal	3.9
Pita:	
White	1.6
Whole wheat	7.4
Pumpernickel	5.9
Reduced-calorie, high-fiber	
Wheat	11.3
White	7.9
Rye	6.2
Vienna	3.2
Wheat	3.5
Toasted	5.2
White	1.9
Toasted	2.5
Whole wheat	7.4
Toasted	8.9
Breadcrumbs, plain or seasoned	4.2
Bread stuffing, flavored, from dry mix	2.9
Cookies:	
Brownies	2.2
With nuts	2.6
Butter	2.4
Chocolate chip	2.7
Chocolate sandwich	2.9
Fig bars	4.6
Fortune	1.6

THE DIETARY FIBER CONTENT OF SELECTED FOODS

FOOD ITEM	TOTAL DIETARY FIBER
	gm. per 100 gm. *(about 3½ ounces)* *edible portion*
Oatmeal	2.9
Oatmeal, soft-type	2.7
Peanut butter	1.8
Shortbread with pecans	1.8
Crisp bread, rye	16.2
Graham	3.2
Honey	1.7
Matzo:	
Plain	2.9
Egg/onion	5.0
Whole wheat	11.8
Melba toast:	
Plain	6.3
Rye	7.9
Wheat	7.4
Rye	15.8
Saltines	2.6
Snack-type	1.2
Wheat	5.5
Whole wheat	10.4
English muffin, whole wheat	6.7
French toast, commercial, ready-to-eat	3.1
Muffins, commercial, oat bran	7.5
Pancake/waffle mix, regular, prepared	1.4
Buckwheat, dry	2.3
Taco shells	8.0
Tortillas:	
Corn	5.2
Flour, wheat	2.9
Waffles, commercial, frozen, ready-to-eat	2.4
Breakfast Cereals, Ready-to-Eat	
Bran, high fiber	35.3
Extra fiber	45.9
Bran flakes	18.8
Bran flakes with raisins	13.4
Corn flakes:	
Plain	2.0
Frosted or sugar-sparkled	2.2
Fiber cereal with fruit	14.8
Granola	10.5

THE DIETARY FIBER CONTENT OF SELECTED FOODS

FOOD ITEM	TOTAL DIETARY FIBER
	gm. per 100 gm. (about 3½ ounces) edible portion
Breakfast Cereals, Ready-to-Eat (cont.)	
Oat cereal	10.6
Oat flakes, fortified	3.0
Wheat and malted barley:	
Flakes	6.8
Nuggets	6.5
With raisins	6.0
Wheat flakes	9.0
Cereal Grains	
Amaranth	15.2
Amaranth flour, whole grain	10.2
Arrowroot flour	3.4
Barley	17.3
Barley, pearled, raw	15.6
Bulgur, dry	18.3
Corn bran, crude	84.6
Corn flour, whole grain	13.4
Cornmeal:	
Whole grain	11.0
Degermed	5.2
Farina:	
Dry	2.7
Cooked	1.4
Millet, hulled, raw	8.5
Oat bran, raw	15.9
Oat flour	9.6
Oats, rolled or oatmeal, dry	10.3
Rice, brown, long grain:	
Raw	3.5
Cooked	1.7
Rice, white:	
Long grain:	
Cooked	0.5
Precooked or instant:	
Dry	1.6
Cooked	0.8
Medium grain, raw	1.4
Rice flour:	
Brown	4.6
White	2.4

THE DIETARY FIBER CONTENT OF SELECTED FOODS

FOOD ITEM	TOTAL DIETARY FIBER
	gm. per 100 gm. *(about 3½ ounces)* *edible portion*
Rye flour, medium or light	14.6
Semolina	3.9
Tapioca, pearl, dry	1.1
Triticale	18.1
Triticale flour, whole grain	14.6
Wheat bran, crude	42.4
Wheat flour:	
White, all-purpose	2.7
Whole grain	12.6
Wheat germ:	
Crude	15.0
Toasted	12.9
Wild rice, raw	5.2
Fruits and Fruit Products	
Apples, raw:	
With skin	2.2
Without skin	1.9
Apple juice, unsweetened	0.1
Applesauce:	
Unsweetened	1.5
Apricots, dried	7.8
Apricot nectar	0.6
Bananas, raw	1.6
Blueberries, raw	2.3
Cantaloupe, raw	0.8
Figs, dried	9.3
Grapefruit, raw	0.6
Grapes, Thompson, seedless, raw	0.7
Kiwi fruit, raw	3.4
Nectarines, raw	1.6
Oranges, raw	2.4
Orange juice, frozen concentrate:	
Prepared	0.2
Peaches:	
Raw	1.6
Canned in juice, drained	1.0
Dried	8.2
Pears, raw	2.6
Pineapple:	
Raw	1.2

THE DIETARY FIBER CONTENT OF SELECTED FOODS

FOOD ITEM	TOTAL DIETARY FIBER
	gm. per 100 gm. (about 3½ ounces) edible portion
Fruits and Fruit Products (cont.)	
Canned in heavy syrup, chunks, drained	1.1
Prunes:	
Dried	7.2
Stewed	6.6
Prune juice	1.0
Raisins	5.3
Strawberries	2.6
Watermelon	0.4
Legumes, Nuts, and Seeds	
Almonds, oil-roasted	11.2
Baked beans, canned:	
Sweet or tomato sauce:	
Plain	7.7
Beans, Great Northern:	
Canned, drained	5.4
Chick-peas, canned, drained	5.8
Cowpeas (black-eyed peas):	
Cooked, drained	9.6
Hazelnuts, oil-roasted	6.4
Lima beans:	
Cooked, drained	7.2
Pecans, dried	6.5
Pistachio nuts	10.8
Tahini	9.3
Tofu	1.2
Walnuts, dried:	
Black	5.0
English	4.8
Pasta	
Macaroni (see Spaghetti)	
Macaroni, protein-fortified, dry	4.3
Macaroni, tricolor, dry	4.3
Noodles, Japanese, dry:	
Somen	4.3
Udon	5.4
Noodles, spinach, dry	6.8
Spaghetti and macaroni:	
Dry	2.4

THE DIETARY FIBER CONTENT OF SELECTED FOODS

FOOD ITEM	TOTAL DIETARY FIBER
	gm. per 100 gm. (about 3½ ounces) edible portion
Cooked	1.6
Spaghetti, dry:	
Spinach	10.6
Whole wheat	11.8
Popcorn:	
Air-popped	15.1
Vegetables and Vegetable Products	
Artichokes, raw	5.2
Beans, snap:	
Raw	1.8
Beets, canned:	
Drained solids, sliced	1.7
Broccoli:	
Raw	2.8
Cooked	2.6
Brussels sprouts, boiled	4.3
Cabbage, red:	
Raw	2.0
Cooked	2.0
Cabbage, white, raw	2.4
Carrots:	
Raw	3.2
Cauliflower:	
Raw	2.4
Cooked	2.2
Celery, raw	1.6
Cooked	3.7
Canned:	
Cream-style	1.2
Cucumbers, raw	1.0
Lettuce:	
Butterhead or iceberg	1.0
Romaine	1.7
Mushrooms:	
Raw	1.3
Boiled	2.2
Onions, raw	1.6
Onions, spring, raw	2.4
Parsley, raw	4.4

THE DIETARY FIBER CONTENT OF SELECTED FOODS

FOOD ITEM	TOTAL DIETARY FIBER
	gm. per 100 gm. *(about 3½ ounces)* *edible portion*
Vegetables and Vegetable Products (cont.)	
Peas, edible-podded:	
Cooked	2.8
Peppers, sweet, raw	1.6
Potatoes:	
Baked:	
Flesh	1.5
Skin	4.0
Boiled	1.5
Spinach:	
Raw	2.6
Squash:	
Summer:	
Raw	1.2
Cooked	1.4
Winter:	
Raw	1.8
Cooked	2.8
Sweet potatoes:	
Raw	3.0
Cooked	3.0
Tomatoes, raw	1.3
Sauce	1.5
Turnip greens:	
Boiled	3.1
Turnips:	
Raw	1.8
Boiled	2.0
Vegetables, mixed, frozen, cooked	3.8
Watercress	2.3

USDA: Human Nutrition Information Service, Nutrition Data Research Branch, September, 1988.

Bibliography

BOOKS

Bowes and Church's Food Values of Portions Commonly Used. J. B. Lippincott, 1983.

Cooper, Kenneth, *Controlling Cholesterol.* Evans, 1983.

Farquhar, John W., *The American Way of Life Need Not Be Hazardous to Your Health.* Norton, 1979.

Pritikin, Nathan, *The Pritikin Promise: 28 Days to a Longer, Healthier Life.* Simon & Schuster, 1983.

Roth, Harriet, *Deliciously Low.* New American Library, 1983.

Roth, Harriet, *Deliciously Simple.* New American Library, 1986.

BOOKLETS

Center for Science in the Public Interest: *Saturated Fat Attack Slide Charts: Eating Smart Fat Guide, Eating Smart Fast Food Guide, Eating Smart Addictive Guide.*
For information write to: Center for Science in the Public Interest, 1501 16th Street N.W., Washington, DC 20036.

National Cholesterol Education Program. National Heart, Lung, and Blood Institute. For information write to: National Institutes of Health, C-200, Bethesda, Md. 20892.
So You Have High Blood Cholesterol, 1987.
Eating to Lower Your High Blood Cholesterol, 1987.

National Heart, Lung and Blood Institute, *Exercise and Your Heart,* NIH Publication #81-1677, Bethesda, Md. 20205.

U.S. Department of Agriculture, *Composition of Foods: Beef Products,* Agricultural Handbook #8-13. Revised August, 1986.

U.S. Department of Agriculture, *Composition of Foods: Finfish and Shellfish,* Agricultural Handbook #8-15. Revised September, 1987.

U.S. Department of Agriculture, *Composition of Foods: Fruits and Fruit Juices*, Agricultural Handbook #8-9. Revised August, 1982.

U.S. Department of Agriculture, *Composition of Foods: Legumes and Legume Products*, Agricultural Handbook #8-16. Revised December, 1986.

U.S. Department of Agriculture, *Composition of Foods: Nuts and Seeds*, Agricultural Handbook #8-12. Revised September, 1984.

U.S. Department of Agriculture, *Composition of Foods: Vegetables and Vegetable Products*, Agricultural Handbook #8-11. Revised August, 1984.

U.S. Department of Agriculture, *Nutritive Value of Foods*, Home & Garden Bulletin #72. Revised 1981.

U.S. Department of Agriculture, *Provisional Table on the Dietary Fiber Content of Selected Foods*, September, 1988.

U.S. Department of Agriculture, *Sodium, Think About It*. U.S. Department of Health and Human Services Home and Garden Bulletin #237.

U.S. Surgeon General, *The Health Consequences of Smoking: Cardiovascular Disease*, A report of the Surgeon General, November, 1983. Available from Office of Smoking and Health, 5600 Fishers Lane, Rockville, Md. 20857.

PERIODICALS AND NEWSLETTERS

The Harvard Medical School Health Letter. For information write to: P.O. Box 10945, Des Moines, Iowa 50340.

Newsletter of Cholesterol Educational Program. Cholesterol and Coronary Disease: Reducing the Risk.

Nutrition Action. For information write to: Center for Science in the Public Interest, 1501 16th Street N.W., Washington, DC 20036.

Tufts University Diet and Nutrition Letter. Customer service: 1-800-247-5470.

University of California, Berkeley, Wellness Letter. For information write to: P.O. Box 10922, Des Moines, Iowa 50340.

ARTICLES

Report of the National Cholesterol Education Program Expert Panel on Detection, Evaluation, and Treatment of High Blood Cholesterol in Adults. *Archives of Internal Medicine*, Vol. 148, January, 1988.

Anderson, James W., and Bridges, Susan R., "Dietary Fiber Content of Selected Foods," *American Journal of Clinical Nutrition* 47:440–7, 1988.

Index

PLUME

Looking Good and Felling Good with PLUME

(0452)

☐ **DIET FOR A NEW AMERICA** *How Your Food Choices Affect Your Health, Happiness and the Future of Life on Earth* by **John Robbins.** An updated and revised edition of the book that changed people's lives by exploding popular food myths and heightening dietary awareness. (299782—$14.95)

☐ **DELICIOUSLY LOW: The Gourmet Guide to Low-Sodium, Low-Fat, Low-Cholesterol, Low-Sugar Cooking by Harriet Roth.** Delight your tastebuds while protecting your health—with this unique collection of spectacular "alternative" recipes from a noted pioneer in low-risk, high-quality cooking. Compard with their "traditional" counterparts, these recipes positively glow with lightness and flavor sensation. Every health-conscious food lover will be delighted with the results. (262666—$9.95)

☐ **CALORIES AND CARBOHYDRATES by Barbara Kraus.** Ninth revised edition. This most accurate and dependable calorie and carbohydrate guide gives counts of many brand-name and fast food products as of basic foods. Recommended by doctors for weight control. (265592—$9.95)

☐ **WALK IT OFF** *20 Minutes a Day to Health and Fitness* by **Dr. Suzanne Levine and Ronni Sandroff.** An easy and proven system for toning up and trimming down, from America's favorite podiatrist. (265355—$8.95)

All prices higher in Canada.

Buy them at your local bookstore or use this convenient coupon for ordering.

NEW AMERICAN LIBRARY
P.O. Box 999, Bergenfield, New Jersey 07621

Please send me the PLUME BOOKS I have checked above. I am enclosing $_____ (please add $1.50 to this order to cover postage and handling). Send check or money order—no cash or C.O.D.'s. Prices and numbers are subject to change without notice.

Name _____

Address _____

City _____ State _____ Zip Code _____

Allow 4-6 weeks for delivery.
This offer is subject to withdrawal without notice.